American Pulp

American Pulp

HOW PAPERBACKS BROUGHT MODERNISM
TO MAIN STREET

Paula Rabinowitz

PRINCETON UNIVERSITY PRESS

PRINCETON AND OXFORD

Copyright © 2014 by Princeton University Press

Published by Princeton University Press, 41 William Street, Princeton, New Jersey 08540

In the United Kingdom: Princeton University Press, 6 Oxford Street, Woodstock, Oxfordshire OX20 1TW

press.princeton.edu

Cover art: Guy Pène Du Bois, *Portia in a Pink Blouse,* 1942. Indianapolis Museum of Art, gift of Mrs. Booth Tarkington, 62.3. Estate of Guy Pène Du Bois, courtesy of GRAHAM, James Graham & Sons, New York.

Use of Richard Wright's photograph and notes: Copyright © 1941 by Richard Wright; Copyright © 2014 by The Estate of Richard Wright. Reprinted by permission of John Hawkins & Associates, Inc., and the Estate of Richard Wright.

All Rights Reserved

ISBN 978–0-691–15060–4

Library of Congress Control Number: 2014935810

British Library Cataloging-in-Publication Data is available

This book has been composed in Garamond Premier Pro and Van Dijk

Printed on acid-free paper ∞

Printed in the United States of America

10 9 8 7 6 5 4 3 2 1

For my father and the memory of my mother, whose
bookshelves were full of pulp.

Focus on the tragic melancholy of the bright stare
Into nowhere, a hole like the black holes in space.
'In bra and panties she sidles to the window:
Zip! Up with the blind. A fragile street scene offers itself,
With wafer-thin pedestrians who know where they are going.
The blind comes down slowly, the slats are slowly tilted up.

Why must it always end this way?
A dais with woman reading, with the ruckus of her hair
And all that is unsaid about her pulling us back to her, with her
Into the silence that night alone can't explain.
Silence of the library, of the telephone with its pad

—John Ashbery, "Forties Flick"

Contents

Preface

....

It's hard to pin down the exact date when print is supposed to have died. Perhaps the summer of 2010, when Amazon announced it had sold more e-books than hardback books and journalist Rob Walker, creator of the "Consumed" column for the *New York Times*, saw a future for books "as useful raw material for conversion into an impressive variety of artworks." He even located "an online tutorial for using the pages of 'cheap paperback books at the thrift store' to make what amounted to wallpaper."[1] Or perhaps it was the year before, when Peter Campbell, reviewing two new volumes for the *London Review of Books* on book-cover design, described the "new titles on the table in the bookshop, [as] a cast of hundreds, gather[ing] for a curtain call. Like the chorus girl who breaks rhythm on the night a talent scout is in the audience, they will try any trick to catch your eye" because there are too many publishers vying for customers' attention. When competition for readers' attention is fierce, "the product and the advertisement are bound up together," as Richard Hollis and other Penguin graphic designers knew.[2]

But, of course, it has been more than a decade since 2004, when Google began digitizing whole library collections and independent bookstores fell to Barnes and Noble and Borders; then a few years later, Borders disappeared too.[3] In 2007, a professor of Victorian literature showed me her new Kindle. For a scholar of Thackeray, the device was a miracle, allowing her to transport his entire opus in one thin package—and fully searchable too! Those fat Penguin editions could not hold a candle. Books were surely dead. In early 2013, Amazon announced that it "had a patent to resell e-books." The expectation was that even e-book sales would now plummet "because an e-book, unlike a paper book, suffers no wear with each reading," so conceivably could be digitally recirculated forever.[4] Yet each year more and more print books are published, even as we hear that fewer and fewer hours are spent reading them; eyes glued instead to various screens. The book, printed on paper, lives on still: "Paper is the star" of the 2014 Whitney Museum Biennial, declares Carol Vogel.[5]

"The Doorway," AMC's April 2013 season-opening episode of the television series *Mad Men*, began with Don Draper and his young wife, Megan, tanning on Waikiki Beach, the peak of Diamond Head looming in the background. He is reading John Ciardi's translation of Dante's *Inferno* in the 1954 Mentor Classic edition from New American Library. It seems in our electronic age, we must return to that moment in the middle of the last century when bikinis occupied the same blanket as the paperback. "Midway in our life's journey, I went astray," reads Ciardi's Dante in a voice-over by Jon Hamm. The series *Mad Men* tracked the shift from advertising focused on print—in magazines, newspapers, and billboards—to another visual media: television. Its explorations of post–Korean War social changes in race relations, sexual mores, and family dynamics are mirrored in the advertising world's confusion about new technologies available to American consumers—air travel, television sets, stereo headphones. The Drapers have taken a plane to the Hawaii Hilton in pursuit of new advertising clients and new modes of marketing pleasure, but Don clings to the past. He's in the middle of his life and he strays.

This conundrum about paper, its recurring disappearance and the attendant anxiety this seems to provoke, is at the heart of *Amer-*

ican Pulp. How is it that at the very moment when Americans were first entering the age of television, millions and millions of books were being sold—and read—across the country? What did these objects offer their postwar readers? And why have these objects maintained such a fascination for scholars and artists, modern effigies of Giovanni Battista Piranesi's ruins, but better because as bearers of dust on one's own shelves they can be handled and manipulated, traded and tossed aside. In "A Tour of the Monuments of Passaic, New Jersey (1967)," earthworks artist Robert Smithson begins his journey into entropy with print: "On Saturday, September 30th 1967, I went to the Port Authority Building on 41st Street and 8th Avenue. I bought a copy of the *New York Times* and a Signet paperback called *Earthworks* by Brian W. Aldiss. Next I went to ticket booth 21 and purchased a one-way ticket to Passaic." After perusing the newspaper, he

> read the blurb and skimmed through *Earthworks.* The first sentence read: "The dead man drifted along in the breeze." It seemed the book was about soil shortage, and the *Earthworks* referred to the manufacture of artificial soil. The sky over Rutherford was a clear cobalt blue, a perfect Indian summer day, but the sky in *Earthworks* was "a great black and brown shield on which moisture gleamed."[6]

A paperback book about decay, a desiccation that turns dirt to dust, travels across the Hudson, west to New Jersey, toward the further promise of America, spelling out an alternative vision of a landscape glimpsed from a bus window for an artist whose work will transform the land.

American Pulp is about the kind of paperback books that sat on my mother's nightstand all through my childhood. Books with slightly risqué covers. Books like Harrison E. Salisbury's *The Shook-Up Generation,* which featured a picture of New York City juvenile delinquents on its cover, or Boris Pasternak's *Dr. Zhivago*. Or any of the many hundreds of books reprinted by the New American Library of World Literature that sold for a quarter or thirty-five cents during the 1950s and early 1960s. Pasternak's novel was the first long book I read the summer after sixth grade. I'd lie in the grass in the backyard of our suburban New Jersey house with the paperback I had taken from her nightstand, pretending I understood it, and thus, to some extent, my mother, but all the while paging frequently to the back where the catalog of proper names and diminutives was listed to remember who was who. That book has disappeared, yet I am still fascinated by those evocative tokens of my girlhood, a girlhood spent wishing I were a grown-up like the ones on the books' covers. I've spent a lifetime collecting these disintegrating books, first by lifting them from my parents' shelves, then by shuffling through piles of junk at used bookstores, Salvation Army shops, or yard sales, and now by searching on AbeBooks.com.

I was supposed to finish *American Pulp* in 2012, the year my mother died, but I couldn't. The books, which appealed to me once as cheap icons of maturity (as both literary works and smutty objects), with their brittle, mossy pages, now feel like corpses. They were, of course, meant to pass away: the paper of poor quality, the bindings barely holding the pages, the covers prone to puckers, rips, and tears. They speak to me of my mother's death, of the deaths of all those like her: smart women who made it out of the Depression and into the bright world of 1950s suburbia, who had high intellectual pretensions but little money, whose habits of reading were forged in the public library, and who were now stuck at home with young children and confined by domestic life. In his brief history of the New American Library, Richard J. Crohn quotes from a letter he received from a midwestern housewife: "If you knew how bored I get looking after two small children, doing housework, and seeing the same old neighbors day after day, you'd understand what a godsend your inexpensive books have been. I never knew that books could be so interesting, and I'm proud of the library of your books that I'm building—for the first time in my life."[7] These paperbacks, like any book, offered escapes to worlds far from the tedium of housework—but they offered something more. They were theirs, to be owned, collected, accumulating on shelves waiting to be dusted.

My research for *American Pulp* has taken me to archives across the country. Very few archives are devoted exclusively to pulp, and most of these consist of fairly random collections of paperbacks, usually pulp fiction, bequeathed by donors. One exception is the New American Library collection at the Fales Library at New York University. Its holdings include not only the books themselves (located off-site somewhere in New Jersey) but the New American Library company papers—editorial reports, royalty statements, and letters from consumers. A more typical archive is the Jean-Nickolaus Tretter Collection at the University of Minnesota. Named for its donor and first curator, it includes Tretter's own collection of GLBT books, which remain an important source for queer studies. The collection's new curator, Lisa Vecoli, has been an avid collector of lesbian pulp since she was a girl and is expanding holdings in that area. Housed in the vast limestone caves carved out of the banks of the Mississippi River, the books sit in a climate-controlled storage facility, laying claim to the same authority as antique maps, government documents, and the records of early computing in Charles Babbage's papers. To access these books, first available wrapped in brown paper only through the mail, one must follow the usual protocols governing archives; once the visitor has signed in and been assigned a desk, they arrive on rolling trays boxed in gray archival cartons. Then you sit at your table, often alone in a quiet and chilly room, select one from a large box, and read tales of fist-fucking and sailors and rent boys.

I also spent days at the Donald and Katharine Foley Collection of British Penguins at Berkeley's Bancroft Library. Here, each book is carefully placed in an individual archival folder inside an archival box, isolated from the rest. Thus the power of the collection amassed on a shelf, as it would be in a bookstore or one's library of orange and cream covers (for literature; other colors—purple, blue, yellow, and red—indicate biography, nonfiction, puzzles, mystery, etc.), is dispersed, as each book becomes separated into a discrete unit, losing connection to its tribe. For literary critic James Wood, and many others, these books lined up together had offered "the cover of canonicity, whereby authors . . . given authority as a Penguin Modern Classic (I remember my brother saying solemnly to me, as we loitered by his bookshelves, 'If I publish a book, I would want it to be done by Penguin'), turned out to be blasphemous, radical, raucous, erotic . . . [T]hese paperbacks glowing, irradiated by the energy of their compressed content, seething like porn . . . ," as he carried them home from the bookshop to his bedroom, were swelled by their thrilling content and by their sheer numbers.[8] The Bancroft Library's archival practice might save the books but wrecks their raucous force.

And then there is the George Kelley Paperback and Pulp Fiction Collection at the university library at Buffalo, perhaps the strangest and most moving I worked in. The books—25,000 of them, ranging from the late 1930s but mostly printed between the 1960s and the 1980s, a period of little interest to my scholarly self but replete with personal meaning for their owner—sat for years, cluttering the donor's house. When his wife insisted that either they go or she would, he donated these thousands of titles to this local academic library, his alma mater.[9] Buffalo took them, which is highly unusual for a library, as preserving these quasi-ephemeral items is difficult and costly.

The library keeps the Kelley Collection books in a locked cage on an underground floor in the center of an area open to library users with tables and chairs available for reading. Each one is stored in a plastic bag, which I assume has some official archival purpose. They are arranged with spines facing out in archival boxes cut open for easy viewing and stacked and shelved, more or less chronologically, in double and triple rows. I was locked in the cage among them and given complete access to wander amid all of the material. If I wanted to get out—to go the bathroom or sit and read—I needed to ring a bell and a librarian would come to release me from the cage. It was a book cell, and I was now an inmate. I spent all day there and came back the next looking through this storehouse, searching for the few interesting titles lurking within the stock. The garish, pink and forest green covers from the 1970s, with shiny, bold, sometimes embossed lettering and almost no illustrations, dominated the collection. Still, I found some gems, as one always does in archives or used bookstores, photographed them, read some, and copied relevant passages on my yellow legal pads.

On my last day, I talked at length to the archivist in charge of the collection. She hinted that the library wanted to sell the collection because it was expensive to maintain. I thought the University of Minnesota might be interested, as there were many hard- and soft-core sex books, some with gay and lesbian themes. The librarians wanted to keep the collection intact, but realized that selling off parts might at least lead to some funding for its maintenance, so they gave me all the relevant information. In the end, I could not interest anyone at Minnesota in salvaging these mostly dreadful books that had sat in someone's basement, perhaps read once, and that were now locked in an underground cage outside of Buffalo, New York. Their upkeep just isn't worth it. Nonetheless, the library at University of Buffalo cannot dispose of them now: They have been collected and cataloged. They are ... there.

Midway in our life's journey ... the books stay.

American Pulp

....

CHAPTER 1

Pulp: Biography of an American Object

> There is real hope for a culture that makes it as easy to buy a
> book as it does a pack of cigarettes.
>
> —Eduard C. Lindeman, New American Library
> advertisement flyer (1951)

> The growth of paper-bound books has been, in simple fact, a
> giant stride forward in the democratic process.
>
> —Freeman Lewis, president of
> the National Conference of Social Welfare

Scenes of Reading

During my research at the archives of the New American Library at
New York University, I found a letter from a grateful reader describing how he'd stopped by the neighborhood candy store on the way
home from choir practice to pick up a pack of cigarettes, grabbed
a book along with the newspaper, and discovered, hours later, that
he had spent the entire afternoon immersed in reading. Many other
readers wrote in with similar stories. They wanted to let the publishers and authors know how much readily available cheap books

meant to lonely readers in the middle of the last century, and they wanted more of them.

In another archive, at the Winston Churchill Library in Cambridge, England, I found the remnants of a journal kept by an escaped prisoner of war, or perhaps he was a deserter from the French Foreign Legion, jailed in Casablanca. The journal, entitled "Diaries of Fedor Minorsky (alias Theodor Harris [son of noted Orientalist Vladimir Minorsky])," details the escaped prisoner's long trek across North Africa, including the reading matter he somehow managed to find while making his away across the barren Rif and Atlas Mountains. With loving detail, he retells the stories found in a pulpy American magazine and one book, Christopher Morley's 1925 novel, *Thunder on the Left*, which he picked up somewhere. His writing veers into a sort of purple prose, on one hand, and modernist stream of consciousness, on the other, depending on which of the two texts this British officer was reading and rereading during his trek.[1] His accounts recorded in his journal might be seen as an inversion of James Thurber's 1939 *New Yorker* story, "The Secret Life of Walter Mitty" (made into a movie in 1947 starring Danny Kaye and remade in 2013 with Ben Stiller in the lead), where the henpecked, suburbanite editor of paperback adventure tales imaginatively inserts himself into the books' plots and vicariously lives the life of swashbuckling adventurer. This officer actually was living dangerously.[2] Elsewhere, in another archive at Boston University housing Meyer Levin's papers, I found letters from Levin's wife, the recently deceased writer Tereska Torrès, whose scandalous autobiographical novel, *Women's Barracks*, precipitated a congressional hearing. These letters recounted the various suits and countersuits provoked by Levin's novel *Compulsion*, about the notorious "crime of the century"—the murder of a teenage boy by University of Chicago students Nathan Leopold and Richard Loeb—and his dispute with Otto Frank over Levin's dramatic adaptation of *The Diary of Anne Frank*.

Books are intimate objects, and reading verges on the illicit, even as it is encouraged by parents and schools. The paperback revolution sparked a certain form of reading—what I call demotic reading—as it lured readers with provocative covers at an affordable price into a new relationship with the private lives of books and so with themselves. In the creation myth of the founding of modern paperbacks, Penguin Books by Allen Lane, recounted on the back of the lined notebook with a reproduction of the Penguin cover of Emily Brontë's *Wuthering Heights*, which I bought at an independent bookstore in Berkeley to use while doing archival research, we learn that wanting something to read triggered this new commodity, a revival of a nineteenth-century form fallen out of fashion. Written in the flip and confidential prose of Penguin back-cover biographies, the tale goes as follows:

He just wanted a decent book to read . . . Not too much to ask, is it? It was in 1935 that Allen Lane, Managing Director of Bodley Head Publishers, stood on a platform at Exeter railway station looking for something good to read on his journey back to London. His choice was limited to popular magazines and poor-quality paperbacks—the same choice faced every day by the vast majority of readers, few of whom could afford hardbacks. Lane's disappointment and subsequent anger at the range of books generally available led him to found a company—and change the world. . . . The quality paperback had arrived—and not just in bookshops. Lane was adamant that his Penguins should appear in chain stores and tobacconists and should cost no more than a packet of cigarettes.[3]

Lane's experience as a reader was essential to the origins of the quality paperback, which, under his tutelage, was conceived as an alternative to the "poor-quality paperbacks" then on sale. His signature look—"dignified but flippant"—combined the sober tripartite two-toned cover with the playful penguin sketched from life at the London zoo.

The concept and the brand migrated to the United States after war broke out in Europe. In fact, paperbacks were stolen, some say, by Ian Ballantine and Robert de Graff, both of whom had worked at Penguin in the 1930s and carried the idea across the pond. Other stories assert that they were brought by Allen Lane to Kurt Enoch and Victor Weybright to become New American Library (NAL), because in the United States vast resources of paper meant books could still be widely printed during wartime. In America, the books remained for sale in train stations, newsstands, and candy stores, but the covers were transformed. They often imitated the sensational covers displayed on movie and true detective and romance magazines, but occasionally also hinted at the new art movements percolating in the wake of Europe's mass destruction, as did Robert Jonas's cover for the 1947 Penguin edition of Henry James's *Daisy Miller* (plate 1). And the logo was subtly altered: birds were forbidden (Penguin had a lock), so the clever founders of NAL hit on Signet as a sly allusion to that ugly duckling.[4] This being America, after all.

A lowly yet somehow revered object, the paperback book exemplifies a modernist form of multimedia in which text, image, and material come together as spectacle to attract and enthrall a recipient, its audience, its reader. This medium was designed for maximum portability and could move seamlessly from private to public spaces. Guy Pène du Bois, a midcentury modernist art critic and painter derivative of Edward Hopper's style, like many of his contemporaries—especially photographers John Vachon, Walker Evans, Jack Delano, Russell Lee, and Esther Bubley—was fascinated by the act of public reading and by the materials and circumstances that enticed readers (figures 1.1, 1.2, 1.3, 1.4, and 1.5). The image of the woman reading in private had long been a subgenre of portraiture in Western art, but these modern artists captured a moment when silent, solitary reading entered public spaces. These artists noticed the flood of magazine covers displayed in public newsstands that brought an array of images and type styles into view, fleetingly glimpsed while passing by; but sometimes—as when Allen Lane needed something to read on his train—capturing the eye, arresting the step, and landing in someone's hands when the buyer found a seat, to completely absorb her. Reading in public offers an uncanny experience as one slips into the private world of the book while also remaining vigilant, for example, if one is on the train so as not to miss one's stop or have one's purse picked. The public reader is always at once immersed and on guard (plate 5).

Often Pène du Bois's paintings depict scenes of reading where two or more women are seated together, strangers on a train most

Figure 1.1 John Vachon, Newsstand, Omaha, Nebraska, November 1938. Library of Congress, Prints & Photographs Division, Farm Security Administration/Office of War Information (FSA/OWI) Collection [LC-USF34-008939-D]. Note that the stands are full of magazines but no paperbacks.

Figure 1.2 Arthur Rothstein, Magazines at newsstand, Saint Louis, Missouri, January 1939. Library of Congress, Prints & Photographs Division, FSA/OWI Collection [LC-USF334–0o30s5-M462571-D].

Figure 1.3 (*facing page top*) Photographer unknown, Newsstand with foreign language newspapers, Fall 1941. Library of Congress, Prints & Photographs Division, FSA/OWI Collection [LC-USF346–001359-Q-C].

Figure 1.4 (*facing page bottom*) Jack Delano, Chicago, Illinois. Newsstand in Union Station train concourse, January 1943. Library of Congress, Prints & Photographs Division, FSA/OWI Collection [LC-USW3–015452-E]. By this time, the kiosk prominently displays a selection of paperbacks.

Figure 1.5 Esther Bubley, Pittsburgh, Pennsylvania, Passengers in the waiting room of the Greyhound bus terminal, September 1943. Library of Congress, Prints & Photographs Division, FSA/OWI Collection [LC-USW3–037110-E]. Note the paperbacks hanging above the women's heads.

likely, each absorbed in her own book, isolated within its world, yet linked by the shared act of reading. But one of Pène du Bois's paintings, *Portia in a Pink Blouse*, now hanging in the Indianapolis Museum of Art, merits special mention (plate 6, *top*). Since the sixteenth century, in both Europe and Asia, the relationship of woman and book has been so widely depicted as to be almost a genre of painting, perhaps simply because it gave models something to do during long hours of sitting. In *Portia in a Pink Blouse*, however, this iconic relationship is altered. A woman sits at a café table, capped by a black hat with a mesh veil covering her face, staring into space away from a bouquet of pink and blue flowers that dominates the frame. Although she is not reading, a book is at the center of this portrait; she is saving her place with her finger as she looks off, out of the picture frame, to her left. The book is a paperback, an NAL paperback to be exact, judging by the layout of the cover with its title and author clearly legible: Portia wrote this book, which means she is at once a somewhat upscale writer (NAL only published reprints) and a popular one at that (NAL usually produced runs of a single title in the hundreds of thousands). She is on display along with her wares.

The painting is intriguing for any number of reasons: its pink color scheme; its evocation of the film noir femme fatale obscured by a black veil; and its tableau still life of flowers, table, and book with text, a nod to Henri de Toulouse-Lautrec, Edgar Degas, Pablo Picasso, and the entire corpus of café images by them and others. The table looks Parisian, and Pène du Bois—born in Brooklyn to natives of New Orleans and having traveled to Paris in 1905 and again in the 1920s—has positioned Portia amid emblems of modernism: a woman alone in public, seated at a table that might have once been used by Édouard Manet's *Absinthe Drinker* or any of the dissolute women seated beside him. (A few years after creating this portrait, Pène du Bois returned to New Orleans to paint women at an absinthe house.) But most important, she is the *author* of a paperback, which dates the image—to the 1940s. War is on, but her preoccupations are elsewhere; she is Portia LeBrun, the poet, author of the book entitled *All Is Crass* or maybe *All Is Grass*, it is hard to tell. The painting was completed in 1942, the year Orson Welles was filming *The Magnificent Ambersons*, based on Booth Tarkington's novel, and was given to the museum by the author's wife: Mrs. Booth Tarkington. But, as a review in the *New York Times* indicates, she had commissioned a portrait in 1939—the year Penguin came to America—so perhaps it was the first painting of this modern object, the pocket-size paperback.[5] In fact, Portia's been pulped. Pène du Bois *had* already painted a portrait of Portia in 1939. In this painting, she sits properly upright in a chair, facing directly out from a canvas dominated by dull oranges, browns, and burnt sienna, primly dressed in a rust-colored, man-tailored suit. By 1942, Portia has become a louche woman, no longer seated inside a domestic space but on the prowl in her garish pink and black—colors that would dominate the covers of pulp during the next decade. Her right hand is hidden within the open pages of the book, which is propped up by her left hand. It is as if she is fingering its pages, much as Sigmund Freud saw Dora doing with her *Schmuckkasten*; Portia's masturbating in full view. Pène du Bois was known for his derivative paintings of high-society patrons; thus he was hardly the populist Edward Hopper was (see his 1943 painting *Hotel Lobby* [plate 6, *bottom*], also in the Indianapolis Museum of Art, where a lone woman sits in an armchair, legs stretched before her shod in elegant pumps with ankle straps, reading a magazine across from an elderly couple, and watched by the clerk, who lurks in the shadows). Its architecture focuses on the erotics of the woman reading in public, her legs, sheathed in silk stockings, claiming attention. Hopper's public space is actually far more claustrophobic than the private hotel room where another woman sits reading in 1934 Chicago (J. Theodore Johnson, *Chicago Interior*, plate 7, *top*), but both hint at interiority and loneliness. So this 1942 portrait, commissioned by a friend, of a woman writer seated with her paperback, impatiently searching for someone, is more than a paean to the idle rich, which was the painter's hallmark; it is a hymn to modern life—where a woman alone can sit in public on display, like a pulp cover beckoning from a rack, and read a book, her book, an advertisement for herself.[6]

Of course, women were not the only public readers; it was widely assumed that pulp fiction's target readership was male.[7] But this easy transit between public and private, where the portable book, the pocket book, as the earliest American brand was called, could move from inside the home to inside the pocket or pocketbook and then be pulled out at any free moment, seems especially emblematic of modern femininity. In fact, Hopper's original conception of *Hotel Lobby* foregrounded a man reading, but as the work came to fruition, he refigured the lone reader as a young woman, a more fitting avatar of the modern urban subject.

The distinctions between what could be read in private or in public were not obvious. Moreover, pulps' global invasion was not a simultaneous occurrence; their incursion into readers' homes varied across nations. As Pritham K. Chakravarthy recalls from her 1960s childhood in Chennai, Tamil Nadu, the serialized fiction that was read at her proper home—with stories yanked out and hardbound for summer reading—were not the racy fare she and her friends imbibed on the school bus from other more sensational magazines read by the driver: "I remember when this story [*En Peyar Kamala* by Pushpa Thangadurai] was being serialized in the mid-seventies. The journal was kept hidden in my mother's cupboard. The subject matter was deemed too dangerous for us young girls. Since I was not allowed to read it at home, naturally, I read it on the school bus. Thanks to Natraj [the driver]."[8] This true crime tale of a kidnapped Tamil girl working in a Delhi brothel (where another native Hindi-speaking prostitute spent her free time reading Hindi pulps) was enormously popular, running for weeks. Since at least the 1930s, when pulp achieved massive success in India thanks to increased literacy, available printing, and the influence of the "British penny dreadful" and "American dime novel," a female readership of popular fiction predominated.[9] Women's reading of fiction has long elicited various social anxieties—about female idleness and the commercialization of literature. By 1933, Sudhandhira Sangu was dispensing "The Secret of Commercial Novel Writing":

1. The title of the book should carry a woman's name—and it should be a sexy one, like "Miss Leela Mohini" or "Mosdhar Vallibai."
2. Don't worry about the storyline. All you have to do is creatively adapt the stories of [British penny dreadful author C.W.M.] Reynolds and the rest. Yet your story absolutely must include a minimum of half a dozen lovers and prostitutes, preferably ten dozen murders, and a few sundry thieves and detectives.
3. The story should begin with a murder. Sprinkle in a few thefts. Some arson will also help. These are the necessary ingredients of a modern novel.
4. You can make money only if you are able to titillate. If you try to bring in any social message, like Madhaviah's *The Story of Padhmavathi* or Rajam Iyer's *The Story of Kamalabal*, forget it. Beware! You are not going to lure women readers.[10]

These directions for crime fiction in Tamil differ from those offered by George Scullin to aspiring American true crime authors in 1937. In "Crime Pays," published in *Writer's Digest*, Scullin explains that visuals were essential for selling a story to a true crime magazine. With most magazine covers featuring women—as victims or perpetrators—and with the new emphasis on the photographic essay within the slicks (*Life* magazine began in 1936), "[p]hotographs to illustrate fact-detective stories are of vital importance."

Because "copy" is not enough in the face of movie culture, photographs (not the painted illustrations from early 1930s magazine cover art) were central to engaging readers. What editors needed to accompany the facts were images, and images designed to narrate—"first . . . The victim, the murderer, the officer . . . Then comes scene stuff. The house in which the murder took place, the field in which the body was discovered, the bridge from which the killer leaped in making his escape, the car he wrecked in his flight, the clues which led to his capture . . ."[11] Will Straw argues that with the emergence of cinema and mass-circulated magazines (and I would argue paperback book covers) "crime [like religion or nature] has generated full-blown approaches to visuality, large-scale systems for aesthetically rendering the world as a whole." These, of course, reference "guns and bodies," but, as he maintains, "Crime is suggested . . . when . . . streets or parks are shown as empty . . . or when darkness is cut by beams of electric illumination."[12] In short, the iconography of danger, especially for the female, is essential to conveying urban space as a zone of criminality and to selling it as a visual form as recognizable as a pastoral landscape or the beatific virgin. All this, of course, had already occurred in "Paris, Capital of the Nineteenth Century," according to Walter Benjamin's reading of Charles Baudelaire's poems and Eugène Atget's photographs. As historian Vanessa Schwartz elaborates, "The visual representation of reality as spectacle in late nineteenth-century Paris created a common culture and a sense of shared experiences through which people might begin to imagine themselves as participating in a metropolitan culture because they had visual evidence that such a shared world, of which they were a part, existed."[13] Producing and consuming the world of spectacle was an essential part of modern life. Americans may not have gotten to it first, but when they arrived, *Pow!*

It would seem we are a far cry from Paris or my mother's bedside nightstand or Portia LeBrun's portrait, but reading the paperback book—even *Dr. Zhivago* in a suburban backyard in the early 1960s—was part of a process that included mass-circulating popular magazines and movies featuring crime fiction and true crime stories, whose combination of "cyanide and sex," to use Will Straw's term, appealed to women as much as to men. The exposé covers Straw collects, with titles such as "The Strange Case of the Ravaged Housekeeper" or "Murder Tryst of the Minnesota Beauty" or "My Mommy is Shot," as much as "I Was a Stooge for the Commies" and "Sex, Schoolbooks and Switchblades," depict domestic space as a zone of mayhem—as dangerous as "Sniper on 42nd Street" and as alluring as "Paris' Sidewalk Salesgirls." They show how the startled look of the woman, either interrupted in her crime or frozen as its victim ("Woman at Bay"), is part of the iconography that both enabled and was enabled by modern woman's mobility and her ability to carry not only the snub-nosed pistol in her purse but the Pocket Book in her pocketbook as well.

Objects on the Shelf

The Hare with Amber Eyes tells the story of Edmund de Waal's netsuke collection inherited from his great uncle and the saga of how his uncle came to possess these objects, first owned by *his* great uncle or second cousin Charles Ephrussi, a Parisian art critic and scion of one of Europe's wealthiest Jewish families, fabulously rich grain dealers from Odessa. Edmund de Waal says of his ancestor that the trip he took to Italy in the mid-nineteenth century, a vagabonding Grand Tour, turned Charles Ephrussi "into a collector. Or perhaps . . . it allow[ed] him to collect, to turn looking into having and having into knowing."[14] Looking, having, and knowing form a progression of possession as the object of desire moves from outside inward, first into the home (the vitrines holding the netsukes) and then into the mind as a source to be studied, analyzed, handled, and described. Knowing means narrating, as what had been seen and held becomes storied. All collecting then tends to death, decay, ruin, and the eventual collapse of the collection, and of the collector as the materials disintegrate, get lost, and as the set breaks apart. For miraculous reasons, Charles Ephrussi's netsuke collection remained intact, even as the family it belonged to was destroyed. These tiny objects, any and all of which might have been lost, held together across continents, wars, and mass murders, merit the amazing book by de Waal. They tell us how objects held together hold history.

"For a collector," writes critic Walter Benjamin in "Unpacking My Library," "ownership is the most intimate relationship that one can have to things."[15] Collectors need collections. That seems obvious; but how and when does the presence of random objects coalesce into a collection? When are collections personal and private obsessions lining one's walls and when are they part of a nationalizing project that seeks to create a body of work in the name of collective identity?[16] At what point does mere possession develop into that more "intimate relationship" of ownership, when the sheer numbers of the things—things that are at once the same yet different; discrete yet part of a series, reproducible yet unique—become a collection, visible, with a life of its own?[17] When are you transformed from someone just looking to one who must have, who becomes what is known in the collecting world as a "completest," one who knows it all?[18]

I cannot remember when I began amassing pulp. They were the books my parents owned, bought to be read because they were cheap. I took some of them with me when I left home as a teenager. Something about their size, their covers, and their smell attracted me—mementos of my childhood hauled from apartment to apartment. Then I began to consciously seek out some of these pulp books—though not any one would do. Don't ask me why, but I was interested only in the pulp versions of "great literature." I have no idea how this began—looking for the pulp Faulkner, the pulp Freud, the pulp anthropology book, the pulp physics text. Pulp meant to be pulp, true trash, never intrigued me—or not at first. I wanted the special thrill that came from seeing Nathaniel Hawthorne's name on a cheesy cover, the pleasure of seeing the most revered writers brought low, sitting right next to John O'Hara or worse, covers with cellophane peeling, pages yellowing just the same. Without knowing it, New American Library was my brand.

At some point, the collector becomes conscious (shifts from looking to having and then knowing), acknowledges the power of the collection, and searches for additions to it in order to refine its dimensions, then builds a separate case for it, catalogs and analyzes it, who is the person who sorts by size or color or some other system. The books acquire value, a secret value, not for "their usefulness," as Benjamin notes, but "as the scene, the stage, of their fate," which is to evaporate. A collection is always disappearing, even as it grows. It recedes into its owner's past, and foretells her passing. Its very density cannot hold off decay; it's already a memory in the making, holding a perverse appeal akin to that recounted by Henry James in *The Aspern Papers*. In addition to the leftovers from my parents' bedside tables, my collection includes the cheapest edition of this or that novel, those traded while hitchhiking across Europe or Brazil, and, more recently, my scholarly study of censorship and women's pulp fiction. It was forged in the fortuitous first apartment just steps from Moe's Bookstore on Telegraph Avenue in Berkeley and from countless other used book stores around the world, from library book sales and garage sales, from trash bins, and now from the comfort of my office as I peruse AbeBooks.com—that's where I recently acquired the three different versions, from the 1940s, 1950s, and 1960s, of Ann Petry's 1946 novel *The Street*, each with a different cover modeled on Billie Holiday or Lena Horne (in her role in *Stormy Weather*), then Dorothy Dandridge, and finally Lena Horne as she looked a generation later (plate 14 [*top*], [*bottom left*], and [*bottom right*], respectively). Marrying my husband, an avid sci-fi reader during the 1950s, netted me a wonderful cache of racy Ace double-sided visions of atomic and robotic apocalypse. Their flyleaves explain that with the advent of nuclear weaponry, these works of fantasy actually offer keen sociological insights.

After a while, people know your taste and pick up little finds for you—as a friend of a friend did when he snagged a copy of Don Kingery's novel *Paula* for me at a book fair. Some books are disintegrating, held together by rubber bands or paper clips, stuffed in Baggies. I love some for their garish colors, their nods to modernist art styles, and their abstractions. I love some for the contrast between the cover art, with its lurid femme fatale, and the demure picture of the woman author on the back. I love some for their back-cover blurbs: "A sort of female Hemingway," declares one about the author of *Louisville Saturday*, Margaret Long. I love some for their prudishness. On the copyright page of Fletcher Flora's risqué novel *Leave Her to Hell!*, we are informed, "A professional model posed for the cover art of this book," a sultry blond whose slip strap has fallen off her shoulder. I've not read them all. Try to and they fall apart. Besides, that's not the point of book collecting—anyone can read a book, probably has read this very book, at least once. The collection is for keeps—a spectacle for when there is nothing to read; insurance against the disaster of *Fahrenheit 451* (a thirty-five-cent Joe Mugnaini illustrated Ballantine Books paperback original, 1953); meant to be stashed away, rarely revealed as it exposes too much; an oracle of one's death, the boxes sprung open by one's survivors and the tawdry stuff cherished. Here I am: an open book.

In 2009, Chinese artist Song Dong's installation on the floor of the Museum of Modern Art's atrium, entitled *Waste Not*, laid out the objects kept by his mother in her tiny *hutang*—hundreds of shoes, plastic ice cream containers, the shiny and colorful shopping bags one acquires from shopping in China's quality shops, dried and compressed slivers of laundry soap, combs, dozens of chairs and pots and broken umbrellas—everything a life might collect and store, in this case, stuffed within the tiny footprint of a home dwarfed by the expansive space of the museum. The melancholic tribute to the smells and stains that cling to old things, stuff that in its place would be invisible and should have been tossed out long before, but once exposed to view became emblems of time and loss, evoking embarrassment in the outsider who looks upon this life of stuff with an ache of recognition, a whiff of distaste for the abjection and poverty expressed. And, of course, an anxiety about one's own accumulating archive—and what kind of spectacle it might be

if one's son were to unpack it in public. "Yet," as Olivia Judson remarks in a meditation on the objects, including many books, left
behind in a rambling house after her parents both died, "when
someone is dead and belongings are all that is left, dispersing those
belongings feels like an erasing of that person's physical presence on
the earth."[19]

I recently reread Henry Roth's great Depression novel, *Call It
Sleep*. It's a ninety-five-cent Avon paperback with classy rounded
corners, the 1964 first paperback edition, one of those owned by
my parents and taken by me from their house when the novel was
assigned in a class I took as an undergraduate. I read it then in
awe—perhaps this reading experience was behind my decision to
specialize in 1930s literature. It gave me some inkling of my parents' lives as children, though the novel is set in the Lower East Side
in the first decades of the twentieth century, and my parents, far
poorer than David Shearl's parents, were both in the Old Country and in the new, lived in Williamsburg and Bedford-Stuyvesant
when the novel was being written. (It was first published in 1934,
with a second printing in 1935; then the publisher, Robert Ballou,
went bust.) The protagonist Davy's secret world of love, fear, guilt,
and visionary seeking gripped me and still does. This is a terrifying
novel, resurrected the year after Maurice Sendak's *Where the Wild
Things Are*, a book I did not read as a child but discovered as a par-
ent. Sendak had modeled Max's monsters on his uncles and aunts,
figures that come straight out of Davy's world and the Old World
remnants of mine too—not the American-born aunts and uncles
but their parents and the other old Jews one encountered occasionally on visits to apartments in Brooklyn.

I have *Call It Sleep*, along with dozens of others salvaged in
one way or another from my mother's apartment over the years,
especially when I moved her out of it and into an assisted-living
apartment near me. Culling her shelves of the self-help and pop psychology (she had been a psych major at Brooklyn College, studying

with Abraham Maslow) she had poured over as she contemplated and initiated her divorce from my father, I decided I was only keeping paperbacks published before the 1970s, only those with the distinctive stained edges of the early years of paperback publication, only those with the gold borders of Signet or Mentor books, only those of value—to me. The rest I loaded into a large black plastic garbage bag that I hauled across the street where trash cans were arrayed along the curb, as it seemed to be garbage day on that side. But the haul weighed a ton, and as I bumped the bag down the long flight of stairs from her Westbeth loft to the street below, the plastic tore as it scraped across the sidewalk, so when I reached the street, the entire bag had shredded. I pushed the books back toward her curb and hurried back into her place. I had much work to do in the few hours before the movers showed up. As I worked, sorting and arranging her paintings and clothes and art books and journals and sketchpads, I'd occasionally glance out the window to see passersby sifting through the books and picking up one or two from the pile, this being Greenwich Village and the strollers—mostly early-morning dog walkers—book-collecting types (how else had my mother amassed her vast store of these but at sidewalk sales, used bookstores, rummage sales, the stash in her building's laundry room, or found in the trash on walks through her neighborhood?). By the time I went out to meet the moving truck, the pile had disappeared, and with it my guilt, as I had never in my life thrown a book away, perhaps the only sin I recognize, destruction of words, even silly words compiled and bound into that sacred object, a book, promising a scene of reading. It seems I was reversing a trend that Harlequin Books—which my mother would never have read; her schlock remained at the slightly higher level of Belva Plain—had inaugurated in the 1980s of packing new Harlequin novels in boxes of Hefty garbage bags.[20]

This is the conundrum of the archive—richly theorized over the decades since Michel Foucault outlined it in *The Archaeology of Knowledge.* What remains, what is saved, cataloged, and taxonomized, "the order of things," is as seemingly arbitrary as "a certain Chinese encyclopedia" found in Jorge Luis Borges's "Analytical Language of John Wilkins" that had provoked Foucault's laughter and generated his inquiry into the deep systems of modern thought and information.[21] The tension Foucault limns between utopias, "a fantastic, untroubled region," "a place of residence," like the archive or even the bookshelf, and heterotopias, which shatter the myriad "sites so very different from one another," haunts my story of why these books that hold such deep fascination for me (at least those from the immediate postwar decades) and for the many others who develop websites devoted to their covers and contents. They are really little more than junk to be hauled across a street and tossed or, in the case of the Kelley Collection, preserved in a kind of book jail to the dismay of those charged with keeping them.[22]

Utterly fascinating and alluring in their cheap form, yet a nuisance, like any trash littering public and private spaces, these used books, remnants of others' reading, cheap and available and essentially the same, yet "so very different from one another," offer an expression of democracy unlike many others. They are keys to demotic reading, an experience of literature that traverses many social distinctions. Robert Scholes and Clifford Wulfman speak of "the hole in the archive" because the remains of the many modernist little magazines founded a century ago have been lost, or if retained have been denuded of their form, stripped of advertisements so central to the modernist aesthetic that links text and image; but this is also a problem for paperback books produced in the more recent past, despite the fact that in 1950 hundreds of thousands of paperback books were bought by public libraries, such as Brooklyn's and Cleveland's, for their "Put 'N' Take" plan.[23] Libraries lack space, like all of us. So books end up on the streets, sold, like the millions of *xiao ren shu* (little people's books) produced during and after the Cultural Revolution in China and now cluttering the stalls of street merchants all over China's bustling cities, tokens of childhood trips to local lending libraries where stories of valiant heroes fighting imperialist Japanese, or of Lenin or Mao, or of Chinese opera heroines struggling to survive taught a generation to read. Or they get pulped—tossed out, as did hundreds of thousands of paperbacks during periods of economic squeeze, like that following the Korean War in 1953, or more recently, when Penguin India pulped, that is, destroyed all remaining copies of theologian Wendy Doniger's 2006 book, *The Hindus: An Alternative History*, after a successful four-year lawsuit found it in violation of the Indian Penal Code.

The monotony of the paperback—its uniform dimensions and the ways in which it blurs the lines between high and low, fiction and nonfiction, text and image—allows for readers to embrace them for various reasons, often having nothing to do with reading, including how the spectacle of paperback attracts one to purchase it (as the reader who wrote to NAL did one afternoon in a candy store in the Bronx) or being attracted to something on its cover (as Charlotte Nekola was after her older sister Jane pulled the paperback edition of *Jane Eyre* off her shelf to show her dreamy younger sister how both of their names were inscribed there, sending Charlotte on a mission to read it and eventually become an English professor). One reads these books for the dirty parts—as does Paul Newman's nephew in the film *Hud*—or for a summertime beach read; or for a sense of sophistication, as I had, sprawling in my backyard, a sixth grader reading *Dr. Zhivago*; or for "company," which is what a *Pocket Book of Verse*, "one of the first paperback anthologies ever published," provided William Styron for the two years he was in the naval hospital at Parris Island during World War II (the same book, "found on the jo-house seat," had sustained Ezra Pound during his postwar imprisonment in Pisa);[24] or because of an intense interest in math and science, coupled with teenaged alienation, that led him to empathize with the bizarre and otherworldly, as did my husband, an avid sci-fi reader in the 1950s; or to pass the time on "the troopship,

U.S.S. *Maui*, leaning against the stack reading *The Robe*" in an Armed Services Edition on V-J Day, as had Pierson Davis;[25] or "while living in a tent for two years . . . totally bored" on the armistice line in Korea in 1955, as had architect Peter Eisenman, who recalls: "It was the first year of the Vintage paperbacks. There were Alain-Fournier, Albert Camus, Jean-Paul Sartre, and André Gide, which my brother [at Cornell] kept sending to me as they came out. I had the collection from one to thirty or whatever."[26] Long before Vintage paperbacks, John Updike "remember[ed] as a boy the dramatic arrival, in the town variety store, of a rack of Pocket Books, mostly mysteries, whose discreetly lurid covers were covered by a thin sheet of cellophane that tended to curl at the corners and could be peeled entirely off by persistent little fingers. They cost a quarter, compared with a dime for a comic book, and had much more text, as well as sexier covers."[27]

Paperbacks propel demotic, even democratic, reading; one reads above or below one's "level," grabbing whatever is at hand. Or, finding nothing to read in them, one keeps them because books, a library of paper garishly colored, produce a spectacle, taking up shelf space, and accumulate weight when placed alongside others, their heft accruing meaning for the owner, "a dam against the springtide of memory," for "the collector's passion borders on the chaos of memories."[28] The shelves threaten collapse.

Bringing Modernism to Main Street

What is pulp? Steamy fiction? Sleazy magazines? Cheap paper? Or might it be a technology, a vehicle that once brought desire—for sex, for violence—into the open in cheap, accessible form? Or, and this is the question that motivates this book, might it be part of a larger process by which modernism itself, as high literature and art but also as a mass consumer practice, spread across America?

This is a story of paper, or rather of paperback books, produced in massive numbers between the late 1930s and early 1960s. These throwaway items hold within their covers a rich history of literary tastes; they point to, even reflect, a democratizing literacy and the new forms of identity and community that emerged in mid-twentieth-century America. The covers themselves present new visions of the American landscape and its inhabitants. In contrast to the tabloids and sensational crime and romance magazines that created what Simon Bessie called in 1938 "jazz journalism," these mass-market, or as they were called "pocket-size books," fostered a more intimate realm of feeling even as they participated in a vast industrial empire of pulp cultural forms.[29] The mechanisms of pulping a work entailed a process of redistribution or, more precisely, remediation: writings often created for an educated and elite audience took on new lives by being repackaged as cheap paperbacks. For example, in 1952, Signet reissued an NAL edition (No. 950) of stories by Thomas Wolfe with the provocative title *Only the Dead Know Brooklyn*; the stories, from the 1930s, had first appeared in hardcover from Scribner's, as well as in pulp and slick magazines. But they had already been gathered into a collection in 1947 as an NAL edition with the far less enticing title *Short Stories* (reissued in 1949), NAL No. 644. Where the first paperback edition featured the signature abstract cover of modernist illustrator Robert Jonas, with a cascade of a broken column, a marble bust of a man, and a stylized Brooklyn Bridge flowing from a dark navy background into a lighter shade of blue, the retitled volume presented a high-baroque, steamy cover by Rudy Nappi. Noted for his illustrations of such titles as *Girl-Hungry, Backwoods Hussy, Gang Moll*, and *Reefer Girl*, Nappi also illustrated many of the nurse pulps flooding the market in the 1950s, such as *Woman's Doctor* and *Private Nurse*. In the 1952 edition, a woman dressed in a tight pink sheath leans alluringly against the front stoop; poised behind two trash cans, a boy in a leather jacket leers over her shoulder, while deep in the background looms the Brooklyn Bridge. Why would Thomas Wolfe ever look homeward when he could wander the "wilds of Brooklyn," as the back-cover blurb proclaimed? These new (and old) paperbacks traveled far beyond their intended circle of readers into the hands of anyone with a quarter to spare. In this way, Tess Durbeyfield, Daisy Miller, Connie Chatterley, and Holden Caulfield, not to mention Mike Hammer and Sam Spade, were among the thousands who made it onto Main Street.[30]

The story of modernism's pulping is a reclamation project that might begin, as one must when rummaging for the secondhand, in any number of places. Picture, for instance, a married soldier from Brooklyn, who lies in a ditch to survive days of a firefight in Normandy during World War II, reading Lytton Strachey's *Queen Victoria* in an Armed Services Edition paperback. Or consider the young James Agee, poised to begin writing his rhapsodic examination of three tenant farmers, *Let Us Now Praise Famous Men*, buying a copy of the true crime magazine *Actual Detective* and scribbling about it across pages and pages of his journal one lonely night in Atlantic City. Or think of Richard Wright, still an aspiring novelist in Chicago, collecting hoards of crime stories from pulps and tabloids, then drawing on these to write *Native Son* and *12 Million Black Voices*.

Or focus on the cover art, perhaps with a look at the sleazy naturalism of James Avati (known as "the Rembrandt of Pulp"), who immortalized the residents of his small New Jersey town as models for the dramatic scenes that peopled his steamy covers, displayed in racks found in drugstores, candy stores, and bus and train stations across America. Turn over a copy of a Dell mystery, with its Gerald Gregg cover of detached body parts floating in space, to look at the maps hand-drawn by Ruth Belew, one of the few women doing cover (admittedly back-cover) art (plate 2). Or peek into the Union Square studio, near that of painter Arshile Gorky, shared by Willem De Kooning, Maxfield Vogel, Bart van der Shilling, and

Robert Jonas in the mid-1930s. Pay special attention to Jonas, who, with de Kooning, worked as a window dresser at A. S. Beck's department store, and helped organize the left-wing Artists' Union before becoming a staff cover artist for Penguin and New American Library, where his cubist-inspired covers pared down the lurid expressionism of most paperbacks into clean lines and bold primary colors. Indeed, one might discover in the files of the New American Library—with its motto "Good Reading for the Millions," where Robert Jonas served as art director—how millions of editions of books by black and gay writers were sold to a nation still living under a slowly cracking Jim Crow and solidly homophobic society, so that the decadent Sally Bowles spread across James Avati's cover of Christopher Isherwood's *Goodbye to Berlin* could seem part of the national landscape (figure 1.6).

The story of how pulp brought a secondhand modernism to midcentury America ironically could also be told after the fact, as the paperback revolution was ending, mainstreaming into higher-priced trade paperbacks used in college courses, by attending to the weeklong December 1952 congressional hearings on "Current Pornographic Materials" held by Ezekiel Gathings's (D-AR) committee. These hearings put paperbacks under scrutiny for their alluring covers, exemplified by Tereska Torrès's *Women's Barracks*, an account of her time in the women's Free French Army, with a cover that signaled the lesbian content within. This story might also track the long history of various censorship trials, including the efforts to suppress *Fanny Hill* (first banned in Massachusetts in 1821), which ultimately led to the 1963 Supreme Court ruling in *A Book Named John Cleland's Memoirs of a Woman of Pleasure v. Massachusetts, 383 U.S. 413 (1966),* which had the curious distinction of having an object—in this case a paperback book published by G. P. Putnam—bring suit against a state. Or one might peruse an earlier Supreme Court decision: the landmark 1948 ruling on obscenity delivered through the complex appeals upholding the censorship

937

(SIGNET) **Bohemian Life in a Wicked City**

Goodbye to Berlin

CHRISTOPHER
ISHERWOOD

A SIGNET BOOK
Complete and Unabridged

Figure 1.6 Christopher Isherwood, *Goodbye to Berlin* (Signet/NAL, 1952). Cover by James Avati.

in New York of Edmund Wilson's *Memoirs of Hecate County*. Ultimately, the scandal surrounding this book became a marketing tool for the 1961 paperback edition, which was emblazoned with the words "Not for Sale in the State of New York" across its front cover. By then, paperbacks favored text over image on their covers. Censorship trials and government surveillance, university courses and increased college attendance, and the steep economic downturn following the Korean War all contributed to the shift in cover styles. The heyday of "the great American paperback," as collector Richard Lupoff calls it, lasted a mere generation. In recent years, archivists have had to grapple with the as yet unanswerable question of how to maintain authors' manuscripts in the digital age, since each new generation of computers makes the retrieval of early drafts nearly impossible.[31] The book, even in its shoddy pulp form, would seem to be a stable relic of past technologies. Yet paperbacks, like tabloids, were rarely collected by libraries or archives; they are almost as immaterial as digital bits. If these archives exist, the holdings are haphazard and incomplete, which, as Nancy M. West and V. Penelope Pelizzon, the authors of *Tabloid, Inc.: Crimes, Newspapers, Narratives* explain, curtails our understanding of narrative mobility and its readership during the twentieth century. Now, think about the contemporary sculptures of artist Long-Bin Chen, who carves discarded New York City telephone books into Buddha's heads and builds installations out of abandoned and deaccessioned library books, reminding us of the tension between ephemera and memory, disappearance and continuity that clings to materials. Or consider how pulp lives on as a postmodern form to be sampled by artists and authors such as Gertrude Stein (postmodern avant la lettre), Charles Bukowski, Robert Coover, Richard Prince, or Joseph Kosuth. In effect, the story of American pulp is the story of American modernism. Pulping is the process by which Americans became modern.

In this tale, pulp traverses theaters of war, the Congress and courts, writers' notebooks and journals, artists' studios, and the ordinary people who bought, traded, and read these books everywhere. The pulping of almost everything suggests that the kinds of mash-ups of politics, popular culture, and high art we think of as hallmarks of our contemporary postmodern culture—the culture of YouTube clips, 'zines, sampling, web blogs, tweets, and so forth—actually has an antecedent in the supposedly outmoded technology known as "the book" and the seemingly passé activity of reading printed paper. For, despite the arrival of radios and televisions in the home during the period of paperbacks' mass appeal, despite the power of Hollywood during these decades, paper—and the books printed on flimsy sheaves—continued to entrance consumers throughout the twentieth century. The motto on the back of early Pocket Books explains the lure of the paperback: "Kind to your pocket and your pocketbook." The many books on paperbacks—from coffee table editions featuring lush illustrations (like Richard A. Lupoff's *Great American Paperback* [2001]) to paperback histories of paperback publishers (like Clarence Petersen's *The Bantam Story: Twenty-Five Years of Paperback Publishing* [1970]) or catalogs (like William H. Lyles, *Dell Paperbacks, 1942–Mid-1962: A Catalog-Index* [1983]) to memoirs by pulp writers (like Frank Gruber's *Pulp Jungle* [1967]) to scholarly studies (like Kenneth C. Davis's *Two-Bit Culture: The Paperbacking of America* [1984]) and, more recently, David M. Earle's *Re-covering Modernism: Pulps, Paperbacks, and the Prejudice of Form* [2009])—speak to their ongoing seduction and fascination, a process that seems to be revived for each generation. In 1899, Henry James almost predicted the paperback revolution when he noted in his essay "The Future of the Novel" that "prolonged prose fables," as he referred to novels, "will stretch anywhere . . . will take in absolutely anything . . . as cheaply as possible" (figure 1.7). The book, he presciently pointed out, "is almost everywhere . . . directly aided by mere mass and bulk." *American Pulp* is, in other words, a history of a degraded form or "a biography of an object." This book tells the story of how pulp paperbacks transmitted the ideas, images, and sensations of modern life, indeed of modernism itself, across a restless nation, a nation still riven by class antagonisms, racial divisions, gender biases, and sexual angst. Yet, at the same time, as mass culture spread, it formed intricate webs among various sectors of the population. Americans saw themselves becoming more homo-

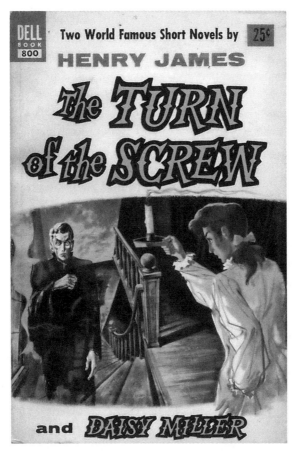

Figure 1.7 Henry James, *The Turn of the Screw and Daisy Miller* (Dell, 1954). Cover by Walter Brooks.

geneous, even as they were expressing new identities—as youth, as African Americans, as gays. These differences were forged in part through the common consumption of the debased but valued objects of mass circulation. In their quotidian nature, their everyday use, cheap paperbacks delivered art, eroticism, philosophy, literature, adventure, history, and science to vast numbers of people, and thus made an impact on American political and social life in unexpected ways. Oscillating between the canon and kitsch, high and low, the secondhand modernism that was America's offered its citizenry an environment meshing commercial mass culture with avantgarde aesthetics and new political formations.

American Pulp's investigations of the effects of the paperback revolution on constructions of American racial, class, sexual, and gender relations stand at the crossroads of two major and as yet essentially distinct avenues of research and scholarship: New Modernist studies and the history of the book. A recent explosion of work links together popular and vernacular forms with canonical and avant-gardist modes.[32] This work has coincided, but often not communicated, with studies that pursue intensively archival research into national printing and publication histories, contributing to a sociology of reading and productive literary practices, which, until recently, largely focused on the pre-1900s.[33] Bringing insights and methodologies gleaned from the New Modernist studies to bear on the history of the book and vice versa, *American Pulp* gestures toward a significant contradiction within American literary modernism. As a movement that arrived in North America after the fact, modernism was always distilled through the obsolescent energies of modern life coursing across the continent.

An evanescent form, cheap paperback books and pulp magazines before them fostered the spread of America's pulp modernism. From Jorge Luis Borges's first US publication in *Ellery Queen's Mystery Magazine* to 1940s GIs' battlefront letters disputing the version of "La Belle Dame sans Merci" included in an Armed Services Editions poetry collection, throwaway reading matter set the stage for an explosion of new forms of literacy and identity among an increasingly mobile postwar population. Circulating paperbacks, through their lurid covers and daring subject matter, made visible to wide audiences lesbian and gay experiences of emerging desire and homophobic encounters, African American perceptions of white racism and black cultural expression, modernist experimental prose, or scientific inquiry. Science, sociology, art, and history—an entire liberal arts education—became available to working people through such imprints as New American Library's Mentor Books, setting the stage for the postwar expansion of higher education. These ubiquitous books were distributed outside traditional book publishing venues and their circulation precipitated new forms of reading communities. As a scandalous and demotic form, however, paperbacks were the target of censorship.

Strolling by advertising billboards and the other trashy emblems of modern urban culture along the "one-way streets" in late 1920s Berlin, Walter Benjamin found the secret to the "insoluble antinomies" of contemporary life in "The Newspaper," among many other ephemera. In Benjamin's readings of the incidental, the cast-off matter of bourgeois culture, a recognition of another modernism, a vernacular modernism of the streets, experienced as shock on the visceral levels of sound and image, evokes, in his description of Eugène Atget's photographs, "the scene of a crime."[34] Contemporary studies of modernisms, the multiple means through which modernity found its expression, have extended the range of what literary history traditionally calls modernism. In "The Waste Land," T. S. Eliot, riffing on Baudelaire and Dante, disparaged the "unreal city" full of immigrants, workers, and prostitutes leading tawdry lives, speaking "demotic French." His characterization of the streets influenced subsequent literary criticism, which cast high-modernist texts in an agonistic struggle to reclaim cultural authority from the unwashed masses. Reams of paper have been filled detailing how a virile literary modernism represented a break with feminized consumer culture. But there is another version of this story of modernism, one that finds writers and artists pushing the limits of form within conventional genres—or rather finding within mass media and genres the means to a modernist expressivity. Gertrude Stein was keenly attuned to detective fiction, penning her own murder mystery, *Blood on the Dining-Room Floor*, in 1948. This view of modernism foregrounds literary investigations into scenes of crime, as content and context, but also notes the ways literature itself becomes criminalized through censorship.

The arena of the law, and paradoxically battles over obscenity, became central to modernism's mainstreaming. When a book was "Banned in Boston," the epithet might ensure large sales. When the "Exiles Returned," from their Bohemian years in Paris or Berlin carrying home their hidden copies of *Ulysses* from Europe after the 1929 Crash, they circulated a new mode of literary expression. Later, in Eastern Europe, the clandestine circulation of samizdat writing had a political impact on repressive regimes. Even the repression of marginalized subjects and deviant desires destabilizes social hierarchies when scandalous trials make visible new forms of identity and sexuality. All these encounters with the state and the law open new aesthetic possibilities. To help understand the place of paperbacks in this complex exchange, *American Pulp* considers them as a form of secondhand modernism that through their sheer excess—the flashy covers, the millions of copies—and even through their criminalization, allowed readers access to the modern.

Kin to the penny dreadfuls and dime novels of the nineteenth century, pulp fiction became popular in the 1920s and 1930s mass-marketed magazines devoted to crime, passion, and science: *True Love, Amazing Stories, Black Mask*. By the mid-1920s, pulp had entered slang as a term for nonsense and excess—over-the-top sentimentality. The first successful pulp paperback line in the United States was published in 1939 by Pocket Books. Wartime rationing and the Armed Services Editions made them patriotic; they fueled the postwar explosions in higher education. The paperback revolution propelled mass literacy, opening a landscape of pulp novels that ranged from bohemian enclaves and artists' colonies in Greenwich Village to gothic mansions in Greenwich, Connecticut. It included the steamy bayous of Louisiana, the divorce ranches of

Reno, Nevada, Los Angeles bungalows, and Viennese cafés. These cheap twenty-five-cent books found in bus and train stations, soda fountains and candy stores, drugstores and newspaper kiosks called out to a mobile population of workingmen and women commuting on trolleys and subways to work in midsize cities, or crisscrossing the country as traveling salesmen or leisured vacationers. Their lurid, colorful covers telegraphed stories of sex and violence that traversed class and racial boundaries. Small enough to be tucked into a breast pocket or handbag and read at a lunch counter or on the streetcar, the more risqué and daring books could be hidden and read late into the night. They are portable tokens of the public and mass experience of the movie theater but meant to be savored alone. These are novels of escape, escapist literature, where rebellious daughters attend art school or sing in nightclubs, running from their conventional middle-class homes only to discover that their dreary stay-at-home mothers also harbor secret knowledge and secret desires for escape. They are incantations of a private world of fantasy found behind *The Blank Wall*, as Elisabeth Sanxay Holding named it in 1947.

The many subgenres of pulp fiction echo crises in twentieth-century history: in the 1930s novels, Nazi spies must be tracked down and working-class solidarity celebrated. In the 1940s, war-wounded men spread violence across the home front, and sensible workingwomen must understand them; in the 1950s, the scene shifts to Eastern Europe, where communist plots are thwarted by perky American wives. In the 1960s, the "system," with its vast computer networks and military budgets, traps freewheeling, artistic men and women. And there's more: stories about waitresses, jungle explorers, schoolteachers, artists, chanteuses, secretaries, divorcees, movie extras—any woman anywhere could become a femme fatale. Pulp fiction offered writers a living and a means to imagine the exotic in everyday life. Dangerous men, even men with Princeton or Harvard degrees and combat medals, menace placid suburbs.

College dormitories might be brothels. An apartment complex houses unseen threats; housewives hide dead bodies. Simple household objects, like a hammer, become deadly weapons. But, through its reprints, pulp also domesticated the unusual, transforming the foreign or the arcane and scientific into a conventional American middle-class narrative: On the back cover of the Pocket Book edition of Eve Curie's biography of her mother, Marie Curie becomes more than a brilliant scientist—she is also "the young Polish girl, poor, beautiful . . . whom Pierre Curie found . . . strangely sweet."

The hundreds of pulp novels, biographies, and travelogues comprise an archive of American tastes and habits, as popular culture increasingly became privatized, capturing a moment before TV antennas cluttered the suburban landscape. Yet when families sat isolated before their new sets mesmerized, pulp still circulated inside and outside the home. Pulp's sensational reception, including censorship, on the one hand, and celebrity, on the other, enables a view into the diverse ways men and women of all ages were exposed to and experienced modern popular literary expression. This medium can be seen in part as an effort to bring high modernism to Main Street by importing the icons of seedy American alleys—neon-lit bars, empty diners, smoky hotel lobbies—into modernist narrative form, a form that could be digested by a largely working-class readership. Leopold Bloom had traversed the Dublin streets one June night at the beginning of the century; the geography of desire leading a returning vet to contemplate murdering his two-timing wife (Ann Petry's *Country Place*) or a young woman to pick up a forlorn traveling salesmen for a night of lousy sex and too much liquor on a cross-country train (Mary McCarthy's *Company She Keeps*) is at once vaster and more restricted in midcentury America.

The language of pulp speaks of pent-up desire or keyed-up anger: its simple, suggestive prose bursts from the cheap bindings of the Avon, Fawcett, Dell, Ace, Medallion, Gold Medal, Bantam, Cardinal, Penguin, Lion, and Signet paperbacks. But there is more to it. Virtually anything could be pulped: Nobel Prize winner William Faulkner's *The Wild Palms* became "a haunting story of lovers confronted by the relentless pressures of a morality which no one can defy without disaster." French classics, like Honoré de Balzac's *Droll Stories*, reveal "wit and wickedness in the 16th century," as its cover proclaims. And, of course, soft-core paperback "originals" brought readers to *The Lusting Drive* by Ovid Demaris. Even the "dream and sex theories" of Sigmund Freud, Margaret Mead's ethnographic "study of adolescence and sex in primitive society," and George Gamow's physics text, *The Birth and Death of the Sun*, were transformed into pulp packages. In America, modernism cannot be separated from kitsch, mass culture, vernacular, and other popular forms. Pulp, lower grade than newsprint, is a paper stock destined to disappear, and modernism was supposed to be an artistic movement finished off by World War II. Made from the leftovers of paper production, pulp paperbacks were meant for the trash can, not the museum or library. Although these books were recycled throughout popular culture in comic strips, radio shows, movies, and television, they should not have survived. Yet they endure and provide a window onto the ways in which modernism cruised Main Street.

For example, adapting pulp fictions' codes, in the wake of Allied forces vanquishing fascism, black writers might investigate the racism of white characters through attention to their perversities, as had William Gardner Smith in *Last of the Conquerors*, with its tagline "Love Among the Ruins," a tale of interracial/international love set in postwar Germany. Young lesbians might be attracted to the covers of March Hastings's *Three Women* or Claire Morgan's (pen name of Patricia Highsmith) *The Price of Salt*, as much for their depictions of lesbian attire—white button-down blouse and dark skirt or skimpy white silk slip under prim sheath—as for the erotic connections offered by their plots. A newly visible gay male desire and community, sparked by the mobilizations of wartime, meant readers could gaze at Truman Capote stretched out on a divan on the back cover of his novel *Other Voices, Other Rooms*, and understand that its front cover illustration by Robert Jonas—of a broken window framing a blurry couple in the distance—signified on Manet's *Dejuener sur l'herbe* as it opened the closet, what Henry James had noted as a "smashed . . . window all this time most superstitiously closed." And, too, the photograph on the back cover nodded to the convention of gay male authors' self-display dating from Walt Whitman's open top button on the flyleaf of *Leaves of Grass* as far back as 1855. By 1951, New American Library was using this cover to help market Capote's short story collection, *A Tree of Night*. Editors noted in their internal memoranda:

> This book should be tied in as closely as possible with OTHER VOICES, OTHER ROOMS and with this spectacular young author himself. His "high vixibility," [*sic*] not only because he is an exotic, as well as an outstanding young writer, but also because of his widely reproduced picture, will amount to a good many newsstand sales. Newsstand-wise, these stories should be sold as by American's most sensational young author.[35]

From its inception, New American Library took pride not only in its discerning literary taste but also its progressive attitude toward sexual and racial minorities. In an assessment of a mystery novel, *A Bullet in the Ballet*, described "lyrically" as "a really charming murder story" by newspapers in New York and London, editor Arabel Porter commented to publisher Victor Weybright that she "found the book absurd, and in very poor taste" because of the "chortling and sniggering about the male dancers who are fairies." Calling it "sneering," she concludes, "I didn't like the book; don't think it up to our standard. Further, I think the attitude toward the ballet portrayed in the book is not only cheap, but also dated."[36]

This, then, is *not*, or not only, a study of the B genres—Westerns, spy novels, bodice-rippers, romances, police procedurals—usually associated with pulp fiction. Paperback books opened worlds for readers and writers alike—providing access to literature thought to be beyond the capacities of most readers, on the one hand, and enabling audiences larger than most writers expected, on the other. Thus, William Faulkner's works appeared as yet another series of "swamp-book" tales about *Tobacco Road*, Erskine Caldwell's wildly popular novel that established a whole terrain of low-down Southern gothic sex tales. As readers and authors, modernists moved into and through the avenues of pulp—found in pockets, on magazine racks, bookshelves, and eventually the courts and Congress—blurring the lines among kitsch and canon and modernism and postmodernism. And this was a curiously American function, beginning in the nineteenth century, when words, Gertrude Stein argues, "began to detach themselves from the solidity of anything, began to excitedly feel themselves as if they were anywhere or anything, think about American writing from Emerson, Hawthorne Walt Whitman Mark Twain Henry James myself Sherwood Anderson Thornton Wilder and Dashiell Hammitt [*sic*] . . . as well as in advertising and in road signs."[37] She makes clear, as she abandons punctuation, that this propulsion accelerated in the twentieth century.

Paperbacks circulated sensation—not only in the form of sexuality and violence (though certainly this was crucial)—but also by developing new sensibilities aware of racial, gendered, and queer expressions. For example, the story of Ann Petry's second novel *Country Place* reveals how African American writers were courted and introduced to a broad readership through publisher's pulping, on the one hand, and via their creation of narratives about white characters, on the other. From William Gardner Smith to James Baldwin, from Richard Wright to Chester Himes, from Ann Petry to Ethel Waters, and on to Frank Yerby, paperbacks brought the voices of black writers into white (and black) bedrooms, often by inserting criticism of racism into stories with white protagonists. As the magazine *Color* declared in 1949, "America's Top Negro Authors" were amassing huge recognition: "Ten Million People Have Read These Books," the headline insisted, listing Wright's *Black Boy*, Yerby's *The Foxes of Harrow, Golden Hawk*, and *The Vixens*, Petry's *The Street*, Walter White's *A Man Called White*, Roi Ottley's *Black Odyssey*, and Willard Motley's *Knock on Any Door*.[38]

The pulping of Faulkner—or Truman Capote, Richard Wright, Carlos Bulosan, or any twentieth-century American detective novelist from Cornell Woolrich to Vera Caspary, not to mention Sigmund Freud, Honoré de Balzac, Margaret Mead, George Gamow, or even William Shakespeare—instantiates an important contradiction within American modernism: its secondhand nature, its repetition of what has already been. Books by foreigners sometimes written centuries before were repackaged into modern American fare, even as new works delving into the long history of American racism swept into millions of households. America, the epitome of a modern nation—founded on the principles of Enlightenment modernity—was late to the ball of modernism. Modern before others, it received modernism belatedly, as an import, a modernism already in use, a used modernism that found its emblem in pulp. As Gertrude Stein explained it during her University of Chicago lectures in 1935:

> But here in America because the language was made so late in the day that is at a time when everybody began to read and to write all the time and to read what was written all the time it was impossible that the language would be made as languages used to be made to say what the nation which was coming to be was going to say . . . but they will tell this story they tell this story using the exactly same words that were made to tell an entirely different story and the way it is being done the pressure being put upon the same words to make them move in an entirely different way is most exciting, it excites the words it excites us who use them.[39]

In America, modernism could never be simply an aesthetic movement; it was always tied to finance, industry, technology, immigration, and consumption across a landscape that was unevenly acclimated to modern life. The vast space and spectacle of the United States meant that the millions of paperback books flooding the markets would find their way into all sorts of pockets. As Stein noted, "all through the history of American literature you will see how the pressure of the non daily life living of the American nation has forced the words to have a different feeling of moving . . . it is in its last expression in the road signs which are a further concentration of the thing they did to the words in advertising."[40]

American Pulp ultimately examines these very personal and intimate forms and materials of modern life found in the homes, purses (also called pocketbooks), and hip pockets of teenagers, workers, housewives, and almost everyone else with a bit of spare time and spare change. A story of quotidian objects, widely available and yet also somehow secreted or forgotten, this book meanders across law, art, government, war, literary forms, race relations, sexuality, crime, and popular media, which all intersect within the economics of publishing. It's a many-hydra-headed beast, opening to scrutiny a history of reading in modernist America. Communities of readers developed literally out of the pockets and pocketbooks of Americans. Pulp's materials and institutions helped determine the trajectory of modern life for the rest of the American Century and on into our postmodernist moment of the ostensibly paperless office and e-book.

CHAPTER 2

....

Pulp as Interface

> Imagine an aesthetic (if the word has not become too depreci-
> ated) based entirely (completely, radically, in every sense of the
> word) on the *pleasure of the consumer*, whoever he may be, to
> whatever class, whatever group he may belong, without respect
> to cultures or languages: the consequences would be huge,
> perhaps even harrowing...
> —Roland Barthes, *The Pleasure of the Text* (1975)

> The medium is the massage. Any understanding of social and
> cultural change is impossible without a knowledge of the way
> media work as environments.
> —McLuhan and Fiore, *The Medium is the Massage*
> (1967)

Collecting is a passion, and we know from pulp fiction that passion is deadly. One hoards to stave off death—one's own, obviously,
but also of the object, the thing kept, kept among other things just
like it. Books are supposedly among those items falling into disappearance as e-books replace paper and for various reasons become
objects ripe for salvage.[1] Repositories of what has gone before them,
collections are memento mori, reminders of the past. But at one

time—the period I am investigating in this book, the late 1930s to the early 1960s, the era of the American Century—paperbacks were dynamic media, akin to our digital world of interactive electronics. Their pervasiveness achieved a kind of blanketing of culture that brought the words of thinkers and writers of every stripe into a vibrant relationship, through intense visual and linguistic stimulation, with an enormous mass of people. Paperbacks linked objects and ideas to bodies, brought intimate longing and fear into public view, and circulated social experiences into the privacy of one's home and one's head. Pulps were precursors, imagining their own demise; they were also, paradoxically, bulwarks against it.

Reading does this, and mass-marketed paperback books served their consumers pleasure. *The Pleasure of the Text*, limned by Roland Barthes, outlined what Richard Howard, riffing on Susan Sontag's call for "an erotics of art" to replace hermeneutics, declared "an *erotics of reading*."[2] Barthes's evocative textual pleasure was primarily a private one, but pulp operated across wide public spaces; it was a medium that massaged. Sheer numbers meant these books democratized reading, allowing even poor and young people access to book ownership. This demotics of reading occurred by way of a handy object—packaged for portability, designed to allure, priced to sell—establishing pulp as an interface among the masses, the author, and the thing itself. It was Marshall McLuhan who first used the nineteenth-century scientific term "interface" (as a noun) for "the surface lying between two portions of matter or space," as a figuration for "means or place of interaction between two systems . . . a meeting point" in his 1962 book, *The Gutenberg Galaxy*.[3] By 1967, "interface" had also become a verb in *The Medium is the Massage*, where McLuhan notes "[a] strange bond often exists among anti-social types . . . This need to interface, to confront environments with a certain antisocial power, is manifest in the famous story 'The Emperor's New Clothes.'"[4] McLuhan understood media—technologies as extensions—as vehicles for increasing communication among those both within and outside grids of power. The paperback book, like earlier and subsequent innovations, expanded what could be seen and touched by individuals en masse as they collectively brushed against one another through and within the privacy of reading. As Geoffrey O'Brien notes, "The paperback—insignificant by definition—serves as a talisman that guides us unharmed through the real world of violence and death," and, I would add, sexuality and desire.[5]

Pulp worked at the borders of several overlapping fields or systems. As this book argues throughout, pulp linked high modernism to the vernacular, moved social concerns into bedrooms—and reversed this move at the same time—and crossed the multiplying media appearing in the twentieth century: tabloids, magazines, radio, film, television. It was transmedial; that is, it crossed forms of representation both within itself (cover and content) and across sign systems and various media, seemingly before its time. Moreover, pulp recognized this, often quite self-consciously.[6] For instance, in the books and stories that skirt the edges of mainstream literature and trash, one finds myriad scenes of reading and movie watching that foreground this transmedial process. Crucial to establishing the links between the pretensions of a writer to establish his or her literary credentials and those of the reader, whose taste is placated by frequent allusions to works beyond the scope of crime, perversity, desire, and sensation operating within the work, these scenes of characters engrossed in books rivet the nexus of consumption. Reading pulp, in the form of the eroticized paperback objects of postwar America, meant entering the frontier, the contact zone, in Mary Louise Pratt's formulation of colonial encounters, between high and low, secrecy and disclosure, forging a collective intimacy at once mass mediated and private.[7]

Joan Schenkar describes the mid-twentieth-century New York publishing world as "rampant" with "cross-propagation, conflation, and confusion of 'low' and 'high' literary genres and categories . . .

especially because pulp publishers often printed the kind of writing that the more respectable publishers turned down. *Weird Tales* . . . gave America's greatest playwright, Tennessee Williams, his first public exposure . . . in 1928."[8] As David Madden pointedly asked in 1968, "Instead of poring over manuscripts in rare book rooms in Buffalo, Boston, New Haven, Los Angeles, and Austin, why not raid the dark, smelly secondhand bookstores in the same cities for dusty, greasy paperbacks?"[9] In them one would find source material on what "affect[s] the nerve centers of mass experience" (xxii). Finding references to many of Shakespeare's heroines in William Rollins Jr.'s 1932 *Mark Mask* story "Chicago Confetti," as the detective tries to recount the goings-on of the Vassar-educated moll named Desdemona Kelly (sometimes passing as Ophelia or Rosalind), is a joke that might never be noticed or one that allows its reader to participate as an insider.[10] According to Madden, "Faulkner's art in *Sanctuary* stands between his raw material and the reader of true detective magazines (made immediate with photographs) who undergoes similar experiences in one official report after another. To him, Faulkner is unknown, [James M.] Cain is real," because Cain taps into what he called "the logos of the American countryside" (xxiii, xx). In Madden's view, both the story of crime—often allegorically moving from family, small business, rackets, and insurance to American capitalism and the government collusion in it—and its mode of narration, by tough-guy writers like Cain or Cornell Woolrich churning out hard-boiled prose, tapped a peculiarly modern American sensibility.

Cain was working off the tabloid pages of the 1920s in crafting his tales of adultery, murder, and their end results. The notorious Ruth Synder case served as the basis for two of his most chilling novels—*The Postman Always Rings Twice* and *Double Indemnity*—but even before this sensational crime story, where a young Queens housewife induced her dimwitted, corset salesman lover to murder her husband and stage it as a robbery, another "True Story of

Crime and Celebrity in 1920s New York," the saga of the Bobbed Haired Bandit, had overwhelmed the pages of *True Detective* and the tabloids.[11] The working-class reading public was immersed in the language of crime reporting, as laundress-turned-bandit Celia Cooney explained in her "Own Story." But the story of bobbed hair and criminality also infiltrated the slicks, including the slickest of them all, the *New Yorker*. Two days before Snyder and partner-in-crime Judd Gray, who was found hiding out in Syracuse, were convicted and sentenced to die in the electric chair, the magazine featured a spoof of the numerous authors covering the trial, which included various three-named female writers, such as Peggy Hopkins Joyce, Mary Roberts Rinehart, and Aimee Semple McPherson, but also D. W. Griffith and Will Durant, among many others. The column, entitled "More Authors Cover the Snyder Trial," features paragraphs by "Gertrude Stein," "James Joyce," and "Ty Cobb." Stein's contribution begins simply: "This is a trial." It continues: "I can tell you have told you will tell you how it is. There is a man. There is a woman. There is not a man. There would have been a man. There was a man. There were two men. There is one man. There is a woman where is a woman is a man. He says he did. He says he did not. She says she did. She says she did not. She says he did. He says she did. She says they did." For Joyce, "Trial regen by trialholden Queenscountycourthouse with tumpetty taptap mid socksocking with sashweights by jackals . . ." While Ty Cobb gives the play-by-play: "It's not like the Cry Baby bandits—four bawls and a walk to Sing Sing. Synder merely hit into a double play and was out a mile, Syracuse to New York to Syracuse."[12] At every turn, readers of tabloids, newspapers, pulp, and slick magazines were immersed in a rich and playful linguistic field that served to bring crime home but also smudged the edges dividing high modernism (Stein) from popular culture (Cobb). Kenneth Fearing's great postwar noir novel, *The Big Clock*—set in the world of a New York magazine publishing house with titles at once suggesting both slicks and pulps—demonstrates how pervasive this mash-up became by the 1940s. At one point editor George Stroud, who runs one of Janoth Enterprises middle-brow magazines, sits in Gil's Tavern perusing his copy of "*The Creative Review*. There was a promising revaluation of Henry James" in it. But he's too busy solving, or rather stalling, a murder case for which he is prime suspect. "And that meant, to begin with, wrecking Georgette, Georgia [his wife and daughter], my home, my life."[13]

Interfaces

Vera Caspary's *Laura* offers a case study in pulp as interface among these threads (plate 9). In it, the eponymous heroine, ostensibly a murder victim turned suspect, reveals her prejudices about detectives to Mark McPherson by alerting him to all she knows about them—gleaned from watching movies and reading detective stories. He in turn needs to revise his understanding of "dames" when he peruses her bookshelf, pulling titles he himself has admitted reading while laid up in a hospital after a shoot-out with a notorious gangster in the past. The duplicitous murderer and newspaper gossip columnist Waldo Lydecker reveals to the investigating officer Sergeant Schultz that he has no alibi as he "had eaten a lonely dinner, reviling the woman for her desertion, and read Gibbon in a tepid bath."[14] To which Detective McPherson replies, "I've read Gibbon myself, the whole set, and Prescott and Motley and Josephus' *History of the Jews*" (8). As the plot unravels while McPherson pursues Laura's killer, Lydecker remembers how he chastised Laura for trying to get him to endorse the "cheap fountain pen," called the Byron, that she is marketing: "And how dared you take the sacred name of Byron? Who gave you the right?" (12). In a novel written in multiply narrated sections complete with footnotes to the works of Lydecker, including a mention of his essay "Of Sound and Fury"

(Shakespeare and Faulkner get a shout-out here) "in the volume *Time, You Thief,* by Waldo Lydecker, 1938" (16) but which gestures to John Dos Passos's and Kenneth Fearing's use of all capitalized sensational headlines: "SEEK ROMEO IN EAST SIDE LOVE-KILLING" (28), one cannot escape the many scenes of reading. Moreover, this admixture of high and low owes much to the *New Yorker*'s spoof of sensational crimes: Laura keeps a worn copy of *Gulliver's Travels* and an autographed baseball signed by Cookie Lavagetto of the 1938 Dodgers on her desk directly below her portrait, fetishized by the detective in Otto Preminger's 1944 film version of the novel, which was painted by Stuart Jacoby, "one of the imitators of Eugene Speicher" (34), an artist whose portraits convey the "hazy idealism of an old Breck shampoo ad."[15] Thus the novel, which is filled with insider tips—from the police procedures offered in McPherson's narrative, to Waldo's gossipy tale, to Laura's private diary, to the deposition of her fiancé Shelby Carpenter—opens up various borders of sexual, class, and ethnic crossroads available to city dwellers and those who read about them.

Laura Hunt turns up alive; she might be one of the undead. The actual murder victim was a model who "used to work in a mill in Jersey" and was named Jennie Swoboda but passed as Diane Redfern: "It's like a bad novel," remarks Waldo (113). An antique dealer, Claudius, who inadvertently helps uncover the murder weapon, is named "Cohen" but "was more like a Yankee than a Jew" (115). A bad artist becomes a celebrity when his subject is murdered: "the public . . . know him as they know Mickey Rooney . . . he is reproduced in *Life, Vogue, Town and Country* . . ." (50). A detective is molded by his early reading of Robert Ingersoll; the presumed murder victim and then presumptive murderer, Laura Hunt, notes he is "not so hardboiled" (78) after they spend an evening together, while he reveals his "life story . . . like a combination of Frank Merriwell and Superman in ninety-nine volumes" (77). "I'm the Arabian Nights," he declares after she discloses her dislike for detectives

(78): "In detective stories there are two kinds, the hardboiled ones who are always drunk and talk out of the corners of their mouths and do it all by instinct; and the cold, dry, scientific kind who split hairs under a microscope" (77–78). But McPherson fits neither stereotype.

Accounts of the murder are revealed by all the main characters in a cascade of competing stories. Caspary's novel is a playful and knowing nod to the "contradictions" of Laura, the woman and the novel—and the genre of the police procedural as well. It is emblematic of pulp as interface. Serialized shortly after the 1942 Ginger Rogers film *Roxie Hart*, in which the up-and-coming vaudeville dancer insists she is a murderer to keep her name in the Chicago newspapers, *Laura* understands the uncanny ways that crime, like baseball and jazz, is an all-American pastime, and pulp is the vehicle to cash in on it: "Her one great had been Bach, whom she learned to cherish, believe it or not, by listening to a Benny Goodman record" (58). It's as if Caspary set out, as the United States entered World War II, to write a novel designed to make Theodor Adorno's hair stand on end. A novel that recycles culture into a hash slung at a diner and nods to middle-brow taste: "Coney Island moved to the Platinum Belt," as Waldo noted (29). A novel that revels in class passing, as McPherson's "proletarian prudery" is at war with his high-brow knowledge gleaned as an autodidact; and of gender passing, as modern career women, B girls, and effete collectors commingle. A novel where the detective worries that he "sounded like a detective in a detective story" while talking to Shelby (121), whose face and body resembled "the young men who drove Packards and wore Arrow shirts and smoked Chesterfields" in advertisements (119). A novel revealing various modes of queer passing as successive characters—Waldo, Mark, Laura, Diane, and Shelby come out, so to speak, in the text.[16]

Shelby, Laura's kept man and smooth Southern gentleman, had been having an affair with Diane Redfern, whose downtown room was strewn with "stacks of movie magazines . . . some of those confession magazines" but who modeled in "Fifth Avenue furs" in her portfolio photographs hung on her grimy walls (118). She moves into Laura's apartment and buys a bottle of cheap bourbon for her lover, then slips into Laura's nightdress, which she is wearing when she answers the door on her fateful night. If she becomes a sort of body double for Laura ("Laura is Diane and Diane was Laura" [113]), Waldo's campy persona—a "fat, fussy, and useless male of middle age and doubtful charm" (18)—is attracted to Mark but sees him as a rival who may be "hero, but not the interpreter" (18) of his "heroine, Laura, my greatest creation" (159); he wants Mark to understand that his "love" for Laura is "Jovian" (14). He queries Mark once Diane's identity becomes known: "Do you know the secrets of her gay life in Greenwich Village?" (105). Then he "put on a show and nothing could stop him. He got up with the champagne glass in his hand and gave an imitation of Laura as hostess to a lot of cocktail-drinkers. He did not merely speak in a falsetto voice and swing his hips the way most men do when they imitate women. He had a real talent for acting" (106).[17] They first meet at Waldo's apartment, where his "collection of glass and porcelain, [his] Biedermeier and [his] surface of lusters" repels Mark (17), yet Mark consents to dine with him a few times at the intimate Italian restaurant where Waldo usually ate with Laura, even ordering the exact dishes they shared. The rather coy way in which Caspary signals Waldo's gay sensibility was exaggerated by Preminger in the film version, which begins with the amazing scene of an emaciated Clifton Webb as Waldo bathing in a marble tub fitted with a typewriter and inviting Mark to retrieve his robe for him as he stands up.[18]

By the time Laura's voice is heard, it becomes clear that another form of passing is also going on—Laura herself is passing as the femme fatale, a natural role for the modern, urban, single, beautiful woman. She describes herself in that role perfectly: "He will find me like a slut in a pink slip with a pink strap falling over my shoulder, my hair unfastened. Like a doll, like a dame . . ." (175), and he does: "She looked as guilty as Ruth Snyder" (179);[19] but it is Waldo who really fits the bill.[20] "Waldo was hiding something," comments Mark in his concluding detail of the case (177). But Mark had already pegged him as a corpse, whose "prose style was knocked right out of him" (69): "He was like a caricature . . . The Van Dyke beard, the stick crooked over his arm, the well-cut suit, the flower in his buttonhole, were like decorations on the dead" (100). At their first dinner, Waldo recounts to Mark the plot of his story of necrophilia, about a young Amish man who helps an injured Philadelphia woman and then spends his life in her pursuit. When he sees her again, he is working as an undertaker's apprentice—and she is in a coffin, dressed in white satin slippers and a lavender shroud. " 'Conrad of Lebanon' in the volume *February, Which, Alone* by Waldo Lydecker, 1936," records footnote two of the Caspary novel (65), revealing Waldo knows the detective will fall in love with the beautiful corpse he is investigating. Laura's diary, which begins by noting the incongruity of the situation and of its narration ("It was unreal; it was a scene from a Victorian novel" [159]), later quotes Waldo verbatim, and mimics precisely the aspects Caspary zeroes in on: the ways her novel is at once a mockery of pulp and its form of modernism—Eliot's unreal city meets "Lizzie Borden"—and a clever version of it.

> Consider the mutations of this murder case, the fascinating facets of this contradictory crime. A murder victim arises from the grave and becomes the murderer! Every large daily will send its ace reporters, all the syndicates will fill the courtroom with lady novelists and psychic analysts. Radio networks will fight for the right to establish broadcast studios within the court building. War will be relegated to Page Two. Here, my little dears, is what the public wants, twopenny lust, Sunday supplement passion,

sin in the Park Avenue sector. Hour by hour, minute by minute, a nation will wait for the dollar-a-word coverage on the trial of the decade. (169–70)

Even in 1942, only three years after paperbacks were getting re-established in the United States, Caspary knows her readers know what a pulp fiction cover will look like—with a slut in a pink slip with a pink strap falling off her shoulder and disheveled hair falling around it—and what its blurb will say: "A murder victim arises from the grave and becomes the murderer!" Right down to the exclamation point. Every reader has already read this book, heard this radio serial, seen this movie, bought the true crime magazine— and many more too—so references to Cassius, Sade, Shylock, Darwin, Sibelius, Sir Walter Scott, Gulliver, Frank Meriwell, and even Alice Duer Miller (one of those three-named lady authors so reviled by the cynical newsmen in Nathanael West's *Miss Lonelyhearts*),[21] whose novel had become a Fred Astaire/Ginger Rogers musical with music by "Jerry Kern," only add frisson (60–61). And they have already read tabloids, police blotters, and true romances with hackneyed clichés like "My heart beat like a drum in a Harlem dance band" (80) or "Thunder crashed again. Then I saw her" (71). They have seen enough movies and advertisements to recognize a smile "like the King of England in a newsreel showing Their Majesties' visit to coal miners' huts" (94), not to mention to understand, despite Preminger insisting that it would pass by moviegoers, the "Freudian" symbolism of the walking stick. Caspary's novel stages the scene of the borders of pulp—a cliché in itself—where, like the contact zones and interfaces between cultures, demotic reading can occur.

Caspary herself inhabited something of a border zone, a Communist Party member who, during the heyday of pulp from the 1930s to 1950s, wrote novels, screenplays, and plays, as well as short stories, and later, an autobiography. Her first novel, *The White Girl*

(1929), recasts the trauma of racial passing by absorbing her own sense of alienation—as the daughter of Sephardic Jews assimilating into middle-class American culture—into a memory of a light-skinned black girl she knew from high school. It relies on the tragic mulatto theme, much as had Nella Larsen's 1929 novel, *Passing*, but in this case the heroine's suicide follows upon her fiancé's discovery of her race after inadvertently meeting her brother.[22] *Laura* both thematizes crossing, here across class, sexual, and ethnic and regional borders, as well as the ways in which this mobility calls forth intermediality. Radios, particularly a broken one that keeps Laura from learning she is assumed murdered while she is in Connecticut, newspapers (both tabloids and serious dailies), pulp magazines, advertisements, and movies all figure in the plot. *Laura* itself was multiply mediated. According to Caspary, it began around 1940 as a play, morphed into a 1942 *Collier's Magazine* serial, "Ring Twice for Laura," was published as a complete novel first in hardcover then as a pulp, rewritten again as a play, and then sold to Twentieth Century Fox producer Otto Preminger in 1943, where it got reworked as a screenplay to become the 1944 film. The serialized novel's title already nods to Cain's 1934 novel about the Ruth Snyder case, *The Postman Always Rings Twice*, setting up its readers to view Laura as a femme fatale in the mode of Cora. *Laura* is only one of any number of examples of American pulp as an effect of and vehicle for transmediation that inserts these paperbacks into a landscape in which the reader is also situated and one that brings to focus the changing status of women and workers.

Further evidence, in this case of the role of pulp in revealing America's racism: Bob Jones, Chester B. Himes's antihero in *If He Hollers Let Him Go*, speeds across wartime Los Angeles highways in his 1942 Buick Roadmaster, playing the dozens with his coworkers at the Atlas shipyard, and finds himself in debates about contemporary black literature with a variety of characters— his fiancée Alice's mother urges him to read an article by Eleanor

Roosevelt in *Negro Digest* (52); the Greek waiter at the fancy hotel where he dines with Alice slips him a note from the manager telling him not to return but apologizes by asserting that he's going to quit and write an exposé in the *People's World*; Alice's father reports on a story about "our fighters" in the *Pittsburgh Courier* (77); and a few of Alice's middle-class social worker friends ask him about his thoughts on Lillian Smith's *Strange Fruit* and Richard Wright's *Native Son* (83–84).[23] Bob Jones is a college-educated black man from Ohio inundated daily with the racism of fellow workers, casual acquaintances, the zoot suit riots against Mexican American youth, the sight of his Japanese American pal, "Little Riki Oyana singing 'God Bless America' and going to Santa Rita with his parents the next day" (7). In fact, "the whole structure of American thought" is aimed at diminishing him and other racial minorities through violence and expropriation (176).

He confronts this racism as he attempts to escape it through popular culture: he "stopped a moment to look at the rows of white faces on the magazine stand." The movies offer no solace either: "There was nothing that interested [him] at the Paramount—just a lot of white faces on the marquee billboards—nothing at Warners" (75). When he does slip into Loew's to avoid the sneers of white pedestrians, he "never found out the name of the picture or what it was about. After about five minutes a big fat black Hollywood mammy came on the screen saying, 'Yassum' and 'Noam,' and grinning at her young white missy; and [he] got up and walked out" (76). The only escape comes from music—the jukebox in a bar, the records stacked on a Philco combination player spinning Harry James's "Cherry" and "All for You" by Nat King Cole (64), and the car radio, where "One of Erskine Hawkins' old platters, 'I'm in a Lowdown Groove' was playing" (98). These references to consumer products (and there are many more to various items of clothing and dress as Bob Jones changes from his work overalls and tin hard hat to his downtown zoot suit finery) and popular songs and newspapers are part of the mediated space of American pulp during and immediately after World War II. They are designed to engage the reader in a familiar yet bizarre world—a world of murder and rape; a world of dreams that invade waking and make it impossible to differentiate reality from fantasy—for the characters in the books and their readers. Like Caspary's Laura, Himes's Bob Jones, with his everyday name, moves in and out of various classed and sexualized urban spaces—but in this case, within Los Angeles not Manhattan, and because he is black, these locations are exposed also as racially charged. Like Caspary, Himes himself moved across many social landscapes—from prison to Paris as an expatriate writer, from college student to criminal to machinist, from communist to detective novelist.

The cover of the 1949 New American Library (NAL) Signet edition (No. 756) of Himes's 1946 novel (figure 2.1, *left*) features a scene from the end of the novel by artist James Avati. Avati, known as the Rembrandt of Pulp, was noted as an illustrator who read every word of every book in order to extract a key scene—usually with a little sex, as the studio head in Preston Sturges's *Sullivan's Travels* demanded—to illuminate the content, often melding features from his friends, family, and neighbors living in his New Jersey town into distinctive types used for his models; working at the typical high-speed rate of pulp, he produced two to three covers a month. In this case, the cover features a tall blond woman clasping her unbuttoned shirt together with one hand and pointing accusingly with the other to a black man dressed entirely in white seated below her. Behind her, peering through an open door, are three white men in T-shirts—one holding a hammer—poised to rush in. Above the title, written on a bright orange band, is the tagline: "As Powerful as 'The Street' and 'Last of the Conquerors,'" which featured Avati's first NAL cover.

Victor Weybright was a leader among American paperback publishers, bringing black authors to a wide, that is, white, audience; Ann Petry's *The Street*, abridged in 1949 as

756 As Powerful as "The Street" and "Last of the Conquerors"

SIGNET BOOKS

If He Hollers Let Him Go

CHESTER B. HIMES

SIGNET BOOKS

Figure 2.1 Covers of Chester Himes, *If He Hollers Let Him Go* (Signet/NAL, 1949), cover by James Avati (*left*); and Silver Studios (Berkley, 1958) (*right*).

NAL No. 710, presented a view of Harlem life that revealed its racist political economy, as white gangsters controlled black gangsters who controlled everyone else; it culminated in a brutal attempted rape escaped only when the victim murders her rapist. *Last of the Conquerors*, also 1949 (NAL No. 706), one of a number of postwar novels NAL brought out, explores the experiences of black GIs

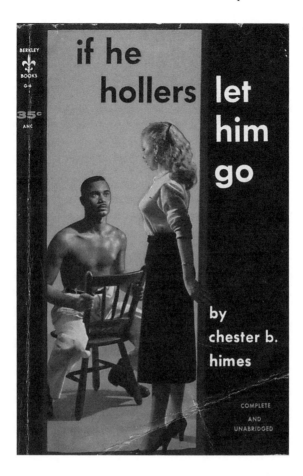

in occupied Germany—and the interracial sex available as German girls bartered themselves for money and cigarettes. Avati's covers always stage complex scenes in deep focus, with foreground and background action narrating a suspense-filled situation fraught with the potential for sex and violence.[24] They are deeply realistic and more detailed than most covers, even ones that superficially look similar (as, say, that of Mickey Spillane's novel *Kiss Me Deadly* [NAL No. 1000]) yet somehow convey a heightened dreamlike sensation. The

novel features a series of explicit dream sequences, each full of sur-
realistic emblems hinting at deep-seated fears and desires for sex,
violence, and revenge. Himes's vivid descriptions of dreams and fantasies, found in other examples of American pulp, helped popular-
ize Freudianism during this period.[25]

Whether actually name-dropping particular titles or considering the place of reading (or moviegoing or listening to music) in
the lives of the detectives, criminals, molls, and others populating
pulp, scenes of reading and media consumption place the paperback within literary history and within the field of various forms
of popular media. They also bring the reader into the scene so that
reading paperbacks opens out from the private encounter with
the book onto other, larger spheres of the culture industry: books,
magazines, films, and songs. The paperback and the popular novels
first appearing in hardback that serve as source material inscribe the
demotic reading these books produced. Martha Gellhorn's 1944
novel of interracial marriage in the French Caribbean, *Liana* (plate
11, *top*), was "the only one of [her] books which fetched up on the
New York Times Best Seller List." As she recalled in 1986:

> The book went into paperback, a piece of information that
> somehow escaped me until—passing through New York—I
> saw a copy in a drugstore. The cover was a picture of a beautiful
> light black girl, scantily clad: luscious. I wondered who on earth
> would buy this book in drugstores; the thought, sadly, maybe all
> the girls of Harlem, hoping to meet themselves. It sold 150,000
> paperback copies, as I remember. Not memory but fact, because
> I discovered the contract during a recent clean-out of files: my
> royalty was one penny, one U.S. cent, per copy, half of which
> reverted as usual to the hardback publisher. How to become
> rich and famous.[26]

The novel "grew from a wonderful lunatic journey through the Caribbean" that she took in 1942 and was written while she remained

home (for a "spot of domesticity" with her husband Ernest Heming-way, who felt lonely when she traveled) rather than "reporting in the Western Desert."[27] Gellhorn's tale of being pulped encapsulates the strange border zone of paperback sales: they occurred beyond the locations of booksellers and were meant to move, to be sold—surefire hits (her only book to make the "Best Seller List") that would appeal broadly (150,000 was the minimum run for a paper reprint) and be available in drugstores to "all the girls in Harlem," among many others. This system is part of what turned pulps into an interface, in this case, connecting previously distinct modes of production and distribution with imagined readers.

If books could move out of bookstores and libraries into drug-stores, they could be viewed as at once ubiquitous items necessary for daily life—like newspapers, toothpaste, candy bars, or cigarettes (at least as they were viewed in the 1940s and 1950s)—and thus part of the vast array of consumer products flowing across America, and as private tokens acquired in the very shops where personal items and medical prescriptions necessary for particular purchasers could be found. Ann Petry's pulpy novel of postwar veterans' return to small-town life, *Country Place*, revolves around the town's drug-store (Petry's father, and other family members, including herself, were pharmacists in Old Saybrook, Connecticut), where the em-barrassing secrets of romance (candy boxes [or condoms?]) and dis-ease (insulin) might be discreetly observed. The books themselves became other drugs for sale.[28]

Mash-Ups, High and Low

Gellhorn had little idea of what her novel would look like once it found its way into paperback as a Popular Library title; her complex investigation of racial, sexual, and class propriety looked no differ-ent from any other trashy exploration of interracial sex in the early

1950s. It fit into a visual lexicon emerging as the civil rights movement was gathering steam with the Montgomery Bus Boycott and the fight over integrating the nation's schools and universities was garnering national attention.[29] But it was not uncommon to find an unusual mélange of authors contributing to pulp magazines. For example, the thirtieth anniversary edition of the "world's leading science-fiction magazine," *Amazing Stories*, contains, not surprisingly, "an anthology of . . . classics covering three decades," including a story by Isaac Asimov and "predictions for 2001 A.D." by Robert Heinlein, as well as contributions by far less well-known authors Bradner Buckner and B. W. Sandefur. There are also predictions by Sid Caesar, Salvador Dalí, William Steig, and Robert Lindner, whose book *The Fifty-Minute Hour*, a popular account of his psychiatric practice, was read in the homes of intellectuals who might never purchase a copy of *Amazing Stories* in 1956. Philip Wylie, whose screed *Generation of Vipers* inaugurated the popular mom bashing of the postwar years, left his contribution blank, inserting a matrix of dots instead. Salvador Dalí predicted a merger of art and science, but Dr. N. Gonzalez, director of research at Eagle Pencil Company, claimed that while many new inventions would transform work and leisure in the future, all these designs would be drawn by hand, using graphite-filled, wood-cased pencils. William Steig looked forward to the end of "cartooning," as ridicule would be replaced by honest laughter, and Sid Caesar foresaw "the pocket TV set" (236–46). Amazing.

The saga of Caspary's *Laura* shows how fluid the movement from one genre or venue to another was; borders are meant to be crossed. This freedom to migrate across audiences could be seen in other genres as well: in 1944 William Faulkner published "The Hound" in *Ellery Queen's Mystery Magazine* (*EQMM*) (and lost its prize in the 1946 contest to Manly Wade Wellman), and the first English-language publication by Jorge Luis Borges (which won its annual prize) appeared in a 1948 *EQMM*.[30] Madden noticed that "tough-guy" writers could morph into "proletarian" authors and back again during the 1930s.[31] He extrapolates from Alfred Kazin's 1942 view, "The violence of left-wing writing all through the thirties, its need of demonstrative terror and brutality, relates that writing to the hard-boiled novel . . . of writers like John O'Hara, James M. Cain . . . and many others."[32] As R. V. Cassill argues of Jim Thompson's gruesome *The Killer Inside Me*, "the mode of the paperback original, husks and all, turns out to be excellently suited to the objectives of the novel of ideas. (See Balzac on Stendhal for definition theorof)."[33] This admixture of high and low was visualized on the paperback covers that appeared in racks across the country on the 1940s and 1950s, a process David Earle called "re-covering modernism," erasing distinctions between Faulkner's novels and smut. For instance, the reprint of George Orwell's 1934 *Burmese Days* (plate 11, *bottom*) screams it as "A Saga of Jungle Hate and Lust" on the 1952 Popular Library cover connecting it to Helga Moray's 1934 novel *Tisa*, which declares "She Was his Captive but He Was her Slave" on its 1953 Popular Giant reprint.

In her memoir of the 1920s, "A Year of Disgrace," Josephine Herbst, author of a major work of radical literature—the three-volume Trexler trilogy consisting of *Pity Is Not Enough*, *The Executioner Waits*, and *Rope of Gold*—described her work as a reader for the "pulp mill" Dell Publishing Company in 1927, the same year Sacco and Vanzetti were executed. She makes clear that this admixture of high and low was built into the industry, which hired "bright boys out of Yale and Princeton." She recalls:

There were a dozen magazines going full blast, a dozen editors, a dozen desks, a dozen bottles of bootleg gin concealed in a lower drawer. You had to have the stuff to wade through the day. Our publisher . . . held up Dreiser and other "big names" who had made a start in similar enterprises. . . . Cooped up in a small office with a meek woman in black who read true-confession

magazine, I might mix up her monologue with the manuscript
I was trying to read ... her voice was the voice of an endless soap
opera that now and then disengaged itself from a recount of her
love life with a Japanese "poet" to sing the virtues of Katherine
Mansfield.[34]

Hope Hale Davis, another 1930s Communist Party member, describes how in early 1931, while still in the hospital after giving birth
to her daughter, she was putting together an issue of a magazine she
developed to be sold in department stores, where pulps would later
appear. *Love Mirror*'s

> quick success ... was due to designing both the fiction and ar-
> ticles to help out readers solve their problems, and in the de-
> pression problems were desperately tangled. "Since my husband
> lost his business," a woman might write to our Beatrice Fairfax,
> "he won't come to bed till after he thinks I'm asleep." Then one
> of my fiction writers who understood how male pride affects
> virility would create a story in which the wife helps her husband
> build a confidence based on more than a weekly paycheck.[35]

The "success" led to a job offer from Delacorte, in 1933, to create a
new "pulp," *Cupid's Diary*, which "was no worse than *Love Mirror*,
a name forced on [her] magazine as companion to *Movie Mirror*"
(6). At the time, while Davis was "thinking up the Young Love plots
that editors wanted" (12), she was married to Irish journalist Claud
Cockburn, reading Leon Trotsky's *History of the Russian Revolution*
during her lying in, and receiving a "mint copy of *Miss Lonelyhearts*
... from Pep Weinstein." It "touched [her] closely, too closely ... He
had transmuted what he had laughed at in the letters readers had
written to [her] magazine into a pathos [she] found almost unen-
durable" (13).

While she worked the pulps, Herbst and her husband, John
Hermann, had been living in Greenwich Village, hanging out with

Katherine Anne Porter, Allen Tate, and Ezra Pound, and reading *transition*. They drank at speakeasies where someone might notice your copy of *Three Lives* and remark, "I see you are carrying Gertie with you."[36] The worlds of bohemia, the avant-garde, communism, and pulp overlapped so thoroughly during the 1920s and 1930s— "Pep Weinstein," already publishing as Nathanael West, was soon off to Hollywood, along with Faulkner, Hemingway, Fitzgerald, and Huxley, all enjoying "some time in the sun"[37]—that it is hardly surprising to discover this cross-genre, multimedia exuberance in American pulp. American writing in the 1930s, according to Kazin, "embodied the discovery of Hollywood as well as the docks and the logging camps, the tabloid murder along with the sharecroppers" (290). And this concoction contributed to its total effect; pulp served as the glue, the matrix, the interface, the emblem of this dangerous, energetic, and incommensurable amalgam.

Intermedia

Madden's argument for the genre of tough-guy writing inherently crosses media and genres: "novels are written out of other novels . . . Movies come out of novels, but movies also inspire novels" (xxii). He reiterates Kazin's chain linking novels, Hollywood, tabloids, sharecroppers, and the docks to point to an essential facet of American pulp—it was a total package, available for a quarter, with "complete and unabridged" text, lists of other books that might be of interest to the reader, and very often a juicy cover image that referred to or became the basis for the movie version of the book. By the mid-1950s, after the Gathings Committee hearings were held in Congress, this convergence of book and film had become a staple of Hollywood musicals. If *Singin' in the Rain* (1952) returned to the dawn of talkies to take on its newest media rival—television— other postwar films, such as *The Secret Life of Walter Mitty* (1947) with Danny Kaye as the nebbishy pulp editor, *Artists and Models* (1955) with Jerry Lewis as the comic-book obsessed writer, and *The Band Wagon* (1953) with a fading Fred Astaire reasserting his dancing presence in the tour de force number based on a Mickey Spillane story and its cover, spoofed the pulps by producing lavish set pieces and numbers around their plots and hard-boiled prose (figure 2.2).

While Cold War investigations into communism and pornography were going on, Hollywood was returning to American paranoia—the first time it surfaces as film noir tragedy, the second time as farce. *Artists and Models* includes a segment on the 1952 Gathings hearings, as well as on various congressional investigations of communist spies, as Jerry Lewis ends up on a television talk show discussing the pernicious effects of comics on America's youth and both US and USSR spies wonder how a secret formula for rockets could be transmitted through a comic book. Danny Kaye lives out the fantasies of pulp in his daydreams to escape the doldrums of suburban life, and a few years later Tom Ewell not only succumbs to *The Seven Year Itch* one summer because Marilyn Monroe has sublet the apartment above his while his wife and son are away in Maine, but finds that his job as an editor—of pulpy books—has their lurid prose leaking into his unconscious. He imagines his wife in the arms of a friend, with all the adverbial allure of a trashy book.

Hollywood films, like all media, according to McLuhan, are notorious for assimilating one medium into another, beginning with vaudeville and melodrama and running through novel adaptations, radio plays, Broadway theater, and so forth. But often the anxieties of the industry's status—regarding threats of censorship and anti-monopoly litigation—were displaced onto other forms of mass media, so while there are many films set in Hollywood, there are countless more set in newspaper offices, or relying on radio, publishing, or backstage theatricals as backdrops. In the 1951 thriller, *Tomorrow Is Another Day*, coscripted (and based on a story) by left-wing

Figure 2.2 Backdrop for Fred Astaire in the opening to the number "Girl Hunt" in *The Band Wagon* (d. Vincente Minnelli, 1953).

pulp novelist and Hollywood front for blacklisted Dalton Trumbo, Guy Endore, the protagonist—Bill Clark/Mike Lewis—is on the lam after his girl, Cay, kills her lover, a cop. He has only recently been released from prison after decades of serving time for killing his abusive father when he was thirteen. The two end up picking lettuce in the San Joaquin Valley. He is recognized by the son of another migrant picker, who sees his picture in *True Crime Stories*, a pulp magazine featuring "murderers still at large" and listing a one-thousand-dollar reward for their capture. The boy's mother at first resists turning him in, but when her husband has an accident and she needs money for his care, she calls the cops. The cops let both Bill and Cay go, as they know (from his convenient offscreen deathbed confession) she has shot her lover in self-defense, and they berate the press, especially the pulps and tabloids, for pushing them to parade the faces of criminals, even when unwanted. In the midst of the House Un-American Committee (HUAC) hearings and Hays Code's sway, Hollywood deflected onto the true crime magazine pulp any hint of sensationalism and scandal.

Pockets, Inside Out

Roland Barthes declared the age of photography the era of the "publicity of the private," and what this hints at is that this period, modernity, emphatically ushers in privacy itself. The emergence of a medium keyed to the intimacy of the moment enmeshed the privacy of the public and of publicity in a process that frayed the borders of propriety: "the private is consumed as such, publicly (the incessant aggressions of the Press against the privacy of stars . . . testify to this movement)."[38] In the face of publicity's onslaught, Barthes seeks to retrieve interiority or intimacy in part through possession of the single photograph he will "linger over . . . scrutinize" (99). Hardly the totemic object of desire enshrined in the image of his dead mother in the Winter Garden, which catapults his "Reflections on Photography"; still, the paperback achieves some of its talismanic qualities, especially the ways a vehicle designed for public exposure can be brought into one's own recesses. The Pocket Book, readily available yet easily hidden, might serve for its owner as another such emblem, beyond the snapshot Barthes examines, of this crucially modern experience of unveiling interiority through a cheap paper object—destined for "refuse: either the drawer or the wastebasket . . . it flourishes a moment then ages . . . Attacked by light, by humidity, it fades, weakens, vanishes; there is nothing left to do but throw it away" (93). These works on paper resist decay by their very possession, even as they fade and crack and rip apart.

Supposedly one can still dig up discarded books along the banks of the Erie Canal near Buffalo, New York, which are lined with tossed-out paperbacks pulped, that is, remaindered with their front covers ripped off, and dumped when they had not sold during the recession of 1953.[39] Paper, despite Barthes's necrotic image of it, is slow to disintegrate, and legend has it that one can still unearth these moldy books by digging around the waterway; the milieu of the paperback is one of decay, as Madden writes, "dark, smelly secondhand bookstores," whether or not they are literally moldering along the Erie Canal (xxi). Madden's elegiac inquiry into the works and world of Hammett, Chandler, and Cain resonates with Barthes's meditation on the photograph: "Is History not simply that time when we were not born?" (64). "Removed in time, these novels appear to project a kind of expressionistic image or metaphor of the decade that was. These tough novels," Madden continues,

are epiphanized in our common consciousness into poetic images: as on an electronic-age urn, the gang leader stands forever in the nightclub doorway, his henchmen behind him. The face may change from Muni's to Robinson's to Cagney's to Bogart's, but the stance is unaltered. And scholars explicating Joyce are no less affected than the janitor sweeping out the offices of university presses all over the American dreamscape. (xxix)

The death mask of these works investigating America moves us into the private spaces of those who hold onto their images—and that is virtually everyone from scholars to janitors—to be occasionally resurrected and installed in individual and collective memory.

That's why Phillip Marlowe sweats through his encounter with the orchid-growing General Sternwood in his hothouse, which begins *The Big Sleep*: "The old man didn't move or speak, or even nod. He just looked at me lifelessly."[40] Surrounded by the fleshy, sweet-smelling "nasty things . . . The old man licked his lips watching me . . . with funereal absorption, like an undertaker dry-washing his hands."[41] Again, the novel thematizes a crucial element of pulp, its intimate association with death, making it essential that it appear in a pocket edition meant to be carried in the pocket or pocketbook of its reader as a totem. In fact, the first paperback edition of the novel published by Avon in 1943—just four years after its hardcover edition by Knopf, with a dust jacket devoid of representational images, the three-word title floating across a sea of blue and red clouds dotted with specks of contrasting colors—informs its readers on the back cover, under the reproduction of Shakespeare's portrait and the logo "Good Books—Great Authors," that "Because the New Avon Books are easy to open, light to hold, thrilling to read, and compact to carry or store in clothing or bags, they are ideal as gifts to the Armed Forces." The front cover, with its blond cadaver surrounded by pink orchids, inscribes the big sleep within—and maybe awaiting its overseas reader (plate 12).

The intimacy of the hothouse where Marlowe meets General Sternwood, though private and removed from public scrutiny, literalizes the bars and speakeasies, the settings which are so essential to pulpy writing, as well as the drugstores with soda fountains and magazine racks where they could be purchased. These are hothouse environments where the casual drink or cup of coffee while perusing the newspaper or reading a paperback can lead to explosive encounters, even death. Edgar Ulmer's B-movie film noir, *Detour*, begins with a fateful cup of coffee at some nameless diner. Hemingway used it in "The Killers," and the bars and speakeasies dotting the pulp landscape are simply too numerous to follow. Guy Pène du Bois, a painter friendly with Edward Speicher (and mentor to Laura's portraitist), etched this oddly deathlike aspect of the paperback in his *Portia in a Pink Blouse*. Such seedy but public venues meant the paperback book became the object of various obscenity trials in the United States and Britain, which brought the state into close proximity to the privacy of the scene of reading—whether bedroom or subway—and reinforced the confusions between private and public spaces.

Demotic Reading

Pulps confused who got to read what and where this would occur; these broken borders point to why demotic reading was scandalous reading. D. H. Lawrence's notorious novel *Lady Chatterley's Lover*, published for the first time in the United Kingdom in a 1960 paperback by Penguin in its unexpurgated version on the thirtieth anniversary of his death, with a print run of two hundred thousand, was prosecuted under the British 1959 Obscene Publications Act. When it was finally deemed fit to appear in the popular form of a paperback, which as a Penguin under Allen Lane's insistence meant it would have the simple orange and cream bands of color across its cover (but this being an anniversary number of a series, it also sported a firebird above the title and an introduction by Richard Hoggart), word got out that it was to be immediately confiscated, thus forcing booksellers into the fray (figure 2.3, *right*). Penguin decided to save their outlets the legal expense and "handed . . . a dozen free copies of the book" to the police.[42] The entire print run had sold out within hours of its release and was then exonerated after a six-day trial in which Dame Rebecca West and E. M. Forster, among thirty-three others, testified on its behalf.[43] "Lady Chatterley was indeed on trial," as the prosecution turned from the book's "tendency" to deprave its readers, to whether she was "having adulterous sexual intercourse."[44] The novel and its variations had already appeared in numerous paperback editions in the United States. *The First Lady Chatterley* was published in 1944 by Dial Press and in 1950 appeared in paperback. NAL issued *Lady Chatterley's Lover* in 1946 as "The Great Novel that Shocked the World," so the traveling of a pulp from one form to another even

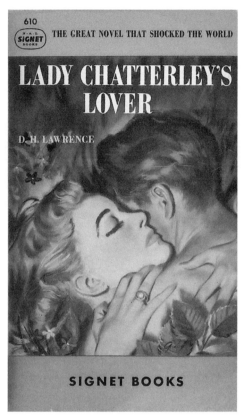

Figure 2.3 D. H. Lawrence, *Lady Chatterley's Lover* (Signet, 1950). Cover artist, George Gross; *above. The First Lady Chatterley* (Avon, 1950). Cover artist unknown; *facing page.*

entailed going from one paperback company to another, one version to another, as it moved up or down the paperback hierarchy (figure 2.3, *left*).

So Himes's *If He Hollers Let Him Go* traveled from the relatively upscale NAL in the 1940s to the much less savory Berkley Books in 1955 with a new cover from Silver Studios, which specialized in racy and realistic covers (figure 2.1, *right*). This one removed the

interracial encounter from the shipyard to an unmarked space of
solid red background. Madge is standing and rather than wearing
the work clothes of a shipbuilder is dressed in heels and white shirt-
waist and black skirt, a secretary's outfit. Bob sits backward astride
a wooden chair with slats, shirtless and in white pants (these and
Madge's blond hair all that remain from the Avati painting). Moreover, this cover is not drawn but is a rendering of a photograph be-
speaking its realism.

Not only were images transferred and rearranged and revised from one generation of paperback to another but titles as well. In 1936, Random House first published *No Letters for the Dead*, a lyrical novel about a woman who becomes a prostitute to support herself, by Gale Wilhelm, one of the few lesbian authors writing positively of women's sexuality, left-wing politics, and working-class concerns during the 1930s. It appeared in a lovely understated hardcover edition by the legendary book designer and graphic artist Ernst Reichl, who had designed *Ulysses* for Bennett Cerf. Pulped in 1951 under the same title with a cover baring two sets of shoulders—hers in the foreground and his behind—by Lion Books (figure 2.4), it became *Paula* (a frequent code name for lesbians in many pulps) in the 1956 Lion Books edition (plate 13, *top left*)—usually a paperback original publisher that specialized in lesbian pulps.[45] The cover, showing a nude woman staring into a mirror as she sits before an open jewelry box, offers an image of a female Narcissus, again featuring a signal of this novel's potential lesbian content, even where none was found. The title and the tagline "She sold herself—for her lover's sake" are framed in hand-sketched uneven black lines. In case this was too subtle and missed by readers, the blurb by Carl Sandburg on the first page, preceding the title page, declares, "In her chosen area, Gale Wilhelm is as completely unafraid as Walt Whitman the American, Oscar Wilde the Englishman, [and] Baudelaire the Frenchman."[46] By the end of the decade, it had transformed again—another publisher, Pyramid, brought it out as *No Nice Girl* (plate 13, *bottom*). Here the cover offers a documentary feel with its photograph tinted a deep blue and black, reminiscent of Blue Note or Impulse jazz album covers, and a sinister urban street with a tough girl walking it.

This novel about how a woman resorts to prostitution during the Depression when she cannot find work as either a pianist or a typist—the two skills she possesses—is also a novel about the New York and San Francisco music and art scenes and unemployment, unwed motherhood, and prison, written in a quasi-epistle form. The setup is beyond bizarre: Paula, a piano accompanist for dance rehearsals and recitals, loses her son, who dies of pneumonia; her married lover is accused of murdering his wife after she commits suicide. At first Paula gets work as a typist and writes letters to San Quentin: "I'm sitting at the window, writing on *The Seven Pillars of Wisdom* . . . which I haven't opened" and later, while playing accompaniment for a ballet school class, remembers "a Hungarian film" she and her lover Koni had seen in the past (28). But this is in New York. She takes off cross-country for San Francisco to be nearer to Koni, who is waiting out his sentence, drifts into prostitution when she cannot find a job, and finally is taken up as a rich man's mistress. Through all this she continues writing love letters describing her rooms and workplaces—inventing fictions about both until her man gets out. The paperback editions of the novel span the 1950s and, despite its original publication date in the 1930s, figure as a barometer of deep anxieties about women's sexuality and women's labor, and the connections between them and women's writing during the immediate postwar years.

In 1959, the same year *No Nice Girl* appeared, Dell published a paperback original also entitled *Paula* by Don Kingery, author of *Good Time Girl* and *Swamp Fire*, billed as another *Tobacco Road* or *God's Little Acre*, signifying its sensationalism, as the Erskine Caldwell "swamp fever" novels had been on trial for obscenity.[47] Its cover painting by Mitchell Hooks displays a woman's back posed nude, holding a drape that falls off her body, her high heels kicked askew. She stands before an ornately framed mirror that reflects a portion of her naked body in reds and oranges (plate 13, *top right*).[48] These 1950s covers refer to the many impressionist paintings of women dressing or undoing their hair while seated or standing before a mirror, and thus give an art-historical veneer to the titillating view of female nudity. The novel, like so much pulp, is a first-person narrative. It follows Joe, a carny turned oil rigger who ends up working for wealthy, impotent Sam Forsythe, who is married to a much younger woman, Paula. Forsythe likes surrounding himself with football players, so the narrator goes after Paula, who ends up pregnant. Of course, the old man ends up dead in a car wreck. "I knew I was going to kill him."[49]

Joe Carter, twenty-nine, lives in an apartment above their Houston garage, which is filled with books—Stendhal's *The Red and the Black*, *Gulliver's Travels*, a little of Freud, *War and Peace*, and something called *Common-Sense Economics*, which he reads in a desultory manner, mentioning that he misses, but somehow still zeroes in on, the point of each: *The Red and the Black* ("it seemed like a lot of trouble to get somebody killed" [28]); *Gulliver's Travels* ("It wasn't until I read the back of the wrapper that I found out it was satire" [41]); Freud, "where everything you did, no matter what, seemed just another try at crawling back into the womb." Reading Tolstoy, he "lost track of all the relatives and finally skipped everything but the battles" (30). His literary criticism might be understood as a librarian's catalog of good books to read. But the novel is also a primer on extramarital affairs: "I found out something else, though. It's toughest on the third party. The odd man takes the punishment. It isn't the wayward wife who suffers most, or the betrayed husband. It's the poor bastard outside in the cold, wondering what's going on inside, wondering if *he* knows, or if *she's* ready to break down and confess, if the whole thing's about to blow up and everybody will know it before him" (49–50; italics in original).

As Joe bides his time plotting Forsythe's murder, he continues to read: "I got through part of *Huckleberry Finn* and *20,000 Leagues Under the Sea*. I tried part of *Moby Dick*. I couldn't keep my mind on any of them" (77). This double education provided by pulps is an invitation to readers to roam across America—as Joe moves from place to place—and across diverse narratives, from tawdry sex and the simple art of murder to the curriculum of an English major. In fact, after Paula inherits a million dollars, "We made love in the bedroom on the pink satin sheets . . . I brought a book of Keats from the apartment and tried to read some of it to her, but couldn't carry it off " (97). He has also reconnected with his brother, who earns his living as "Jumbo—The World's Fattest Human." He also needs something to read: "I think I'll try some philosophy or something. Whatever happened to Tom Swift, anyhow? . . . Tom Swift. Tom Swift and his flying machine. Tom Swift and his underwater warship . . . Bring me Scott's *Diary*. I want to read it again" (99).

In a switch ending indebted to Cain's *Postman* and *Double Indemnity*, Paula is sent away for ten years for the murder of Joe's brother, the fat man who Joe knows committed suicide, and is implicated in her husband's death, but Joe is let off for his crime. The insurance company fails to pay Paula off because Sam Forsythe's brother, Nathan, inherited his estate. The woman "might look sweet and innocent but she's pretty damned smart . . . *too* smart. She knew you managed to kill her husband. She also knew she couldn't file a claim for payment because it would bring the bloodhounds down on both of you. What she didn't realize was that when she didn't file, the insurance boys *really* smelled something," Joe's lawyer tells him, echoing Walter Huff in *Double Indemnity*, as he argues for copping a plea (154). A woman's sexual transgressions will be punished in 1959 as surely as in the 1930s; her "search for fulfillment" means disaster for her. Let that be a lesson.

Joe's illicit sexual affair with Paula is intimately tied up with his reading; both afford him access to a kind of indecipherable knowledge not without precedent in either the realms of literary or pulp adultery. D. H. Lawrence's Mrs. Bolton "was sure Connie had a lover," and the fact seems confirmed by an act of reading: Clifford asks Connie, " 'shall I read to you, or what shall it be?' and her reply, 'Read Racine'[which he does] in the real French grand manner" and upon finishing declaims, "one gets all one wants out of Racine. Emotions that are ordered and given shape are more important than disorderly emotions."[50] This pedagogical impulse within

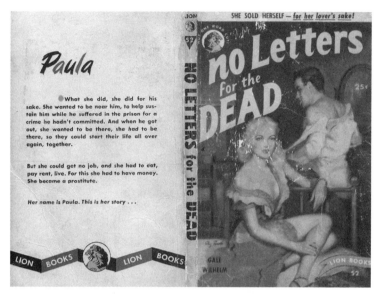

Figure 2.4 Gale Wilhelm, *No Letters for the Dead* (Lion Books, 1951). Cover by Ray Pease. The paperback editions drop Wilhelm's dedication to her mother and father as if this presentation by a dutiful daughter would mar the risqué elements of the book.

reading matter and at the scene of reading has been the subject of the novel and of criticism about it for centuries. In her 1982 study, *Becoming a Heroine*, Rachel Brownstein recalls her 1950s adolescence spent, in part, "[b]ehind the locked bathroom door, sitting on the terry-cloth covered toilet seat" reading Henry James's *Wings of the Dove* but also *Forever Amber* and *Gone with the Wind*.[51] She goes on to note that "[t]here are many heroines of novels who read, with intensity about heroines," citing Rachel Vinacre of Virginia Woolf's first novel *The Voyage Out*, who is given a copy of Jane Austen's *Persuasion* by a certain Mrs. Dalloway and Gibbon by a young man interested in her.[52] George Eliot, the Brontës, Austen, Woolf, James—their novels all feature scenes of reading, at once private "miracles" and often acts of defiance that insert the reader into a larger political discourse.

So, too, it seems from Don Kingery's *Paula,* where the likes of carnival sideshow acts and oil riggers also devote stolen moments to reading. This world of nonmonogamous sex and its link to nonheterosexual relations through reading is part of the interface of pulp, which produced new forms and new forums for gay or nonmonogamous sexualities and artistic or bohemian identities. In surveying various art and physical culture magazines (so-called gay beefcake), David K. Johnson has found numerous examples of "lifestyle" pages including pictures of men reading magazines and books (by gay authors) mixed in with the rest of the men posing in the baths.[53] Those imagined "Harlem girls" grabbing a copy of Martha Gellhorn's *Liana* off the swivel rack of a corner drugstore, in fact the druggist himself, as in Martin Ritt's film *Hud* or Ann Petry's *Country Place,* are engaged in a form of consumption that is more intimate and less uniform than the acts of "citizenship" Liza-beth Cohen describes as emerging within the "Consumers' Republic" of postwar America. These proliferating books, so cheap that anyone could afford them, offered a different type of escape from the tedium of Cold War suburbia than those acquired during "one of history's great shopping sprees," which brought consumer goods into middle-class homes.[54] The demotics of reading that American pulp helped foster and made visible through its form—the total package of a pocket-size, paperbound, shiny covered book on sale for a quarter—enabled other kinds of belonging.

Journalist and screenwriter Ben Hecht's 1954 memoir, *A Child of the Century,* which came out as a Signet paperback the following year, explains why, in the immediate postwar years, reading had lost its power for him. His discourse on all things criminal and trashy, which he witnessed on the city beat in Chicago—"I once wore all the windows of Chicago and all its doorways on a key ring. Saloons, mansions, alleys, courtrooms, depots, factories, hotels, police cells,

the lake front, the roof tops and the sidewalks were my haberdashery" (142)—is followed by "Some Bookish Thoughts."[55] Why read
when Chicago is full of stories?

> a dentist arrested for raping a patient during office hours whose
> crime was immortalized (for one edition) by the headline,
> "Dentist Fills Wrong Cavity" . . . A fire gutted the Stockyards
> and seven firemen died trying to shoo the bellowing cattle out
> of the flames . . . A man stood naked in front of the Congress
> Hotel screaming the world was coming to an end, and he bore
> out his contention, in part, by dropping dead when the police
> laid hands on him . . . Investigators revealed the new county
> hospital had pillars stuffed with straw instead of cement . . . and
> the assistant keeper of the morgue died of poison from eating
> the leg of one of the corpses in his custody . . . the yellow cabs
> fought the checkered cabs, and passengers were tossed into
> the gutter . . . A janitor ravished a child behind a coal pile in a
> Halstead Street basement, and Theodore Dreiser wrote a play
> about it called *The Hand of the Potter* . . . (142–44)

And the beat goes on for eight more pages. Of course he couldn't
read anymore! After this, "novels are unable either to surprise or
inform" him.

> Organs lust, plots twist, characters writhe, psychology comes
> up with sea bottoms in its teeth, good and bad battle it out on
> a mat of phrases . . . The modern novelist, rid of asterisks, has
> lifted biology from under the counter where Fanny Hill and
> Justine blushed in secret. His heroines are nude as eels. Their
> legs fly open like compasses. (153)

New fiction has "substituted gynecology for romance," and between
the clinical, experimental, and traumatic modes of expression,

nothing compares to the wild Chicago streets or the used books that filled his shelves:

> It was once different. I worked in Chicago, but I lived, a little madly, between book covers . . . I read constantly. I read on my way to cover stories, while waiting for cardinals to die, murderers to hang, embezzlers to confess, fires to ebb, celebrities to speak. Rashkolnikov, Lord Jim and Thaïs went with me into the police stations. Stavrogin, Des Esseintes and Salammbô; Zarathrustra, Sanine, Prince Bezukhov, Père Goriot, Candide, Julien Sorel and Oblomov; Tess, Maggie, Odette . . . were ever at my elbow. (154)

What Hecht found so objectionable in the 1950s was part of what had made Chicago his own. When the zones separating "all the windows of Chicago and all its doorways" began to collapse into Hecht's life, "lived madly between book covers," he gave up on books and the world they revealed to him because these objects now let everyone wear this "key ring." Reading across or between, within or below, aside or above what one knew from life or the movies or radio or literature was made possible and accessible for "the millions" by this handy technology.

The demotics of reading spurred on by pulp had appalled Donald Davidson, one of the Twelve Southerners who contributed to *I'll Take My Stand*, the 1930 volume promoting "The South and the Agrarian Tradition," even before the 1939 introduction of Pocket Books. Like Lyle Lanier, another contributor to the anthology, who sees "the Philosophy of Progress" epitomized by industrialization and the consequent masses—of production practices and of social relations—as a vision of a "corporate age" in which "more people [are] doing the same thing in the same way and perhaps at the same time," Davidson shudders at "the shop girl [who] can get a ten-cent print of Corot to hang above her dressing-table, or buy her dollar edition of Shakespeare, with an introduction by Carl Van

Doren."[56] This is because "the shop girl does not recite Shakespeare before breakfast," even having consumed this cheap edition she possesses; instead, "she reads the comic strip with her bowl of patent cereal and puts on a jazz record while she rouges her lips. She reads the confession magazines and goes to the movies" (35). Lanier's vision of mass consumption is astute. He explains that the "fact that along with ten million other persons a man eats potato chips made in Detroit" does not ensure a sense of community among them, because the "two thousand patrons of a modern movie palace engage in no real communication or interaction" (145). What the masses do—together or alone, in public or in private—cannot overcome the anomie of modern urban American life for these poet-critics. This disdain for mass forms of entertainment, including reading cheap books, by the Southern Agrarians, however, did not interfere twenty years later with the publication of Robert Penn Warren's 1939 book *Night Rider*—which appeared in a Signet NAL abridged edition, complete with a James Avati cover to go with the scene of adultery and vigilantism culled from within—nor with it being reprinted by Berkley some years later (plate 10).[57]

The crude and crass literary marketplace had been decried by authors long before the Southern Agrarians deplored shopgirl reading habits. In her 1908 story "Expiation," Edith Wharton savages literary commerce in New York as genres are carved up: natural history and bird life (*Nests Ajar*) over here: "there's a fairly steady demand for pseudo-science and colloquial ornithology"; uplifting tales of Christian sacrifice over there; risqué exposés of modern marriage mores in yet a third corner, not to mention the crossovers, like *How the Birds Keep Christmas*. [58] These genres, each written by a different member of a decent but declining society family, capture distinct audiences and garner requisite reviews, ensuring small but steady sales. Only a scandal might push a book into the heights of popularity, as occurs when the bishop (who writes Christian homilies, such as *Through a Glass Brightly*, to raise money for his church) publicly denounces his niece Paula Fetherel's bland account of modern marriage, to which she gave the provocative title *Fast and Loose*, causing its sales to soar, assuring her notoriety as onlookers stop her to admire her work, and actually reaping enough royalties to pay for the renovations to her uncle's cathedral chantry.

Wharton has a wonderful time skewering these arrivistes who are following on the heels of her friend and mentor Henry James's intuition a few years before in 1899—a moment when America had not yet claimed its ownership of the coming century, but James knew it was only a matter of time as it was already jostling for position— that an explosion of books and their readers would remake the literary world. When James mused about "The Future of the Novel," he declared the "prolonged prose fable" to be the most supple, malleable, capacious vehicle for conveying "impressions," thus offering "an image in the mirror" of America.[59] Anticipating the arguments of Russian formalist critic Mikhail Bakhtin, James claimed for the novel a preeminent place of "all pictures [as] the most comprehensive and the most elastic. It will stretch anywhere—it will take in absolutely anything. All it needs is a subject and a painter. But for its subject, magnificently, it has the whole human consciousness" (338).

James also understood that the novel had its physical manifestation in the book, a technology that "is almost everywhere, and it is in the form of the voluminous prose fable that we see it penetrate easiest and farthest. Penetration appears really to be directly aided by mere mass and bulk" (336). He saw how the "flare of railway bookstalls . . . the shop-fronts of most booksellers . . . the advertisements of the weekly newspapers and . . . fifty places besides" would spread the book, as its most "elastic" form, the novel, ensured a new social compact among readers because the mass production and consumption of books opened into view areas previously closeted off from public scrutiny. With new readers—particularly young people and women of all ages—came the new writers Wharton would catalog: "so," concludes James, "we may very well yet see the female elbow itself, kept in increasing activity by the play of the pen, smash with final resonance the window all this time most superstitiously closed" (343).

In his brief polemic, written at one century's end, James anticipated the shape of the twentieth-century novel; he also outlined the forms of its manufacture, attending to ways in which "the future of fiction is intimately bound up with the future of the society that produces and consumes it" (341). When he noticed that the future of fiction could be glimpsed in the shards of the smashed windows separating women from all that the novel might encompass—that is, life—as they elbowed their way into public view, he might already have been picturing his brother William's brilliant student, Gertrude Stein. In gesturing toward a new readership of young people, he implied that others confined by class, race, or ethnicity would also break into prose to produce their images in the mirror of fiction, and they would do so, in part, because of their intimate access to books.

More than sixty years later, reviewing J. D. Salinger's *Frannie and Zooey* for *Partisan Review*, critic Leslie Fiedler confirmed James's prediction.

> We have been . . . living through a revolution in taste, a radical transformation of the widest American literary audience from one in which women predominate to one in which adolescents make up the majority . . . And the mode demands, in lieu of teen-age novelists who somehow refuse to appear, Teen-age Impersonators . . . among whom one might list, say, Norman Mailer, Jack Kerouac, even William Burroughs—certainly the Salinger who wrote *The Catcher in the Rye* and invented Holden Caulfield, a figure emulated by the young themselves.[60]

These teenage impersonators—black, working-class, and women writers—joined the avant-garde modernists on the shelves and nightstands of the nation, crafting its distinctive twentieth-century vernacular: a slangy interface, a demotics of reading, a borderland of pulp. In the decades between when Wharton's Paula Fetherel elbowed her way into New York literary fame and other Paulas—lesbians, artists, even murderers—wandered the streets of Greenwich Village, San Francisco, and Houston, the "mass and bulk" of racy paperbacks, at least, if judged by their covers, spread a vision of the American century as a paperback nation.[61] Moreover, the history of the spread of paperbacks as a recursive process was repeated in the historiography of the books themselves as successive generations of scholars and enthusiasts rediscovered these pervasive objects and recounted their saga.

The potato chip eaters, moviegoers, paperback book and confession magazine readers, and jazz record listeners, women like Laura, might stay up late one night finishing off *Paula* to discover that the heroine of the 1959 version landed in jail for murder and that the 1956 version remained a kept woman when her lover died attempting to escape San Quentin weeks before his release. Pulp's interfaces, "the fifty places besides" where James indicated books might be found during the twentieth century, when education exploded—by 1950, three of five eighteen-year-old Americans had graduated from high school and the girl's name Paula reached its height of popularity at number forty-six—brought a secret thrill, along with political paranoia, in the form of a cheap, portable talisman.

CHAPTER 3

Richard Wright's Savage Holiday: True Crime and *12 Million Black Voices*

> Even the True Story magazines were revolutionary documents when they fell into the hands of the folk Southern Negroes. They instilled restlessness, a capacity for credulity, and an eagerness to move forward to new experiences.
>
> —Richard Wright

> For the corpse is not dead! It still lives! It has made itself a home in the wild forest of our great cities, amid the rank and choking vegetation of slums! It has forgotten our language!
>
> —Richard Wright, *Native Son*

> The revolution that calls itself the Investigation had its rise in the theaters of communication, and now regularly parades its images across them, reiterates its gospel from them, daily and hourly marches through the corridors of every office, files into the living-room of every home. These avenues of communication are television, radio, picture magazines, motion pictures, magazines of news interpretation, digests of news digests, newspaper chains, syndicated features, the house journals of chain industries.
>
> —Kenneth Fearing, "Reading, Writing, and the Rackets"

"Americans don't like being lied to by their leaders," declared Frank Rich in a *New York Times* op-ed column, referring to the brouhaha over then president George W. Bush's press secretary, Scott McClellan's, 2008 memoir about the run-up to the Iraq War, "especially if there are casualties involved and especially if there's no accountability. We view it as *a crime story*, and we won't be satisfied until there's a resolution."[1] Frank Rich, who began his career at the *Times* as a theater critic, taps into a pervasive tendency within modern(ist) American culture: an enduring fascination with sensational crimes and melodramatic endings. As D. H. Lawrence recognized at the beginning of the twentieth century, "America hurts . . . America is tense with latent violence and resistance."[2] Crime, no matter how pervasive, in this way of thinking, is always a singular event perpetrated against an innocent victim by a corrupt or deranged individual, a grotesque figure who often appears as normal as one's next-door neighbor, and who, once identified, is subject to justice carried out through methodical detective work. Despite the systemic nature of criminality—both as an enterprise involving corporate or state structures and within a justice system targeting certain populations and not others—crime is narrativized in America as local and unique. It scintillates because of its very discreetness, yet it is capable of endless resuscitation as a coded language for the deeper violence and criminality it both mimics and shrouds. "True crime," writes Mark Seltzer, "is one of the popular genres of the pathological public sphere." It tracks "the abnormal normality of the world."[3] So, like Louis, the French inspector played by Claude Rains in *Casablanca*, we are always "Shocked! Shocked!" to discover gambling, or anything else illegal, is going on in Rick's American café.

I have titled this chapter after Richard Wright's 1954 novel, *Savage Holiday*, a study in just the kind of one-off criminality Rich is talking about: one day, a seemingly normal guy—one who works, incidentally, or did so until the day before, in a business concerned with crime, insurance—inadvertently causes a death that leads him to commit a venal murder that ends up headlining the news. While a youth in Mississippi, Wright was fascinated by crime, from observing the "bad black boys," as he calls them, who went down to white supremacist violence in a flame of glory, to his use of the Robert Nixon case as the basis for *Native Son*, to his investigations of Cross Damon's Nietzschean reasoning for murder in *The Outsider*. Crime narratives offer a means—as they have in Western culture at least since Oedipus or Cain and Abel—to understand violence, rage, mortality, family, nation, you name it.

Counterintuitively, reading "True Story magazines," those bastions of excess and incredulity, opened "a capacity for credulity," according to Wright, which I take to mean an incisive, and, in Jim Crow America, seemingly improbable, idea that black people could pursue their dreams and desires, could believe in themselves—not America's lies—and "move forward to new experiences." Wright's comment reflects a deeper understanding of the role of the word *True* in the title of these pulpy magazines than Theodor W. Adorno had when he read *True Astrology* magazines a few decades later: "They fall in line with the pattern of modern mass culture which protest the more fanatically about the tenets of individualism and the freedom of the will, the more actual freedom of action vanishes."[4] Wright's insight is mirrored in the findings of E. Franklin Frazier, who believed that young black girls were reading true romance magazines and other pulp melodrama to forge identities that contrasted with their parents' message of racial uplift.[5] Like Kenneth Fearing, whose entire opus of poems reads like the text of a true crime magazine, and who himself wrote a number of important works of pulp fiction, Wright sensed that true story magazines could be read against the grain and as such uncover American lies.[6] In this, Wright understood the particular mode of American modernist thinking that wedged critique into popular forms, as these keenly debased genres and the media of their dispersion "instilled restlessness."

In modern America, as Frank Rich suggests, the crime story holds a particular sway for both its pervasiveness—we live in a nation founded over and over again on violence and war, on the one hand, and it invades daily life through popular media, on the other—and for its undercover nature. Foundational violence gets forgotten; even as murder, or at least its narration and depiction, fills leisure time. In this form, it is also a commodity circulating within an economy that trades on desire and exhaustion. It also serves, in Nicholas Abraham and Maria Torok's terms, as a crypt—a repository, at once ever-present yet inaccessible, of that which fundamentally determines subjectivity. [7] A forgotten, untranslatable, encysted language, its presence within a substratum of identity exudes ongoing and intense pressures—restlessness, if you will—shaping consciousness that cannot be named or even felt directly; its access is circuitous, found in traces of materials gleaned elsewhere.

Wright plumbed America's history of crime as a crypt; he understood its use for containing and also conveying—telescoping ideas about class, money, sex, love, race—social forces. [8] A close reader of trash, from his earliest exposure to pulp magazines, he deployed what he had learned in his novels and essays: "I read tattered, second-hand copies of *Flynn's Detective Weekly* or the *Argosy All-Story Magazine* or dreamed, weaving fantasies about cities I had never seen." [9] Crime, as a narrative device, enabled, as it had for two of his inspirations, Theodore Dreiser and Fyodor Dostoevsky, his explorations of psychological and economic forces, showing how the two collide in an individual. But it did more for Wright—or rather he did more with it—and this is the subject of this chapter: how Richard Wright's and Edwin Rosskam's phototextual book, *12 Million Black Voices*, supplements the crime narrative, or, better, inverts it, to make clear that *the* crime, that which the American people (or at least white Americans) had been lied to and been lying to themselves about, was the crime of slavery and its attendant Jim Crow laws and culture of racism. This was *the true crime story* that Wright was exploding/exposing—America's crypt encrypted, thoroughly evident yet utterly unrecognized, its corpse not dead but haunting us still.

Using the format of the true story magazine—its typography and layout an iconography of documentary noir that sensationalizes facts through clipped prose and embedded photographs and diagrams, inherited from Jacob Riis's 1890 *How the Other Half Lives*—and a plot partially indebted to the police procedural, as each chapter amasses evidence of America's criminal past, Wright and Rosskam pried open America's uncanny crypt to listen to its voices.[10] Jeffrey Allred argues for the "pedagogical stance" of the text, whose collective "we" does not encompass everyone but "figures readers as pupils . . . and divides groups along lines of class, race, and region" (though it does not demonstrate an equally attentiveness to sex and gender, I might add) in order to instruct them.[11] In this, *12 Million Black Voices* fulfills the basic requirements of the ideological novel as a genre according to Susan Rubin Suleiman: to entertain and to instruct.[12] True story magazines were consummately novelistic as well, ensuring that lessons were learned as excitement was sensed. Moreover, by accessing that which cannot be readily seen—Riis's mercury flashes or, later, Weegee's midnight perp walks, come to mind, as does Freud's interpretations of dreams—true story magazines popularized the "case" and its study. Wright mined the magazine culture of the mid-twentieth century and put its residue to use, as did Edwin Rosskam, whose career took him to Paris in the 1920s as an expatriate painter where he ended up working on a surrealist magazine. Then, after traveling to French Polynesia as a photographer for the government, he returned to the United States in the 1930s and got a job on a new tabloid Philadelphia paper, a Democratic rival to the *Inquirer*, where he became what he characterized as, forgetting Riis's work in New York, the first photographer/journalist, both making pictures and writing stories. From there, he did a stint at Henry Luce's picture magazine, *Life*, before being hired by Roy Stryker to supervise the distribution of the Farm Security Administration (FSA) photographs.

In their collaboration and in their attention to popular magazine culture, Wright and Rosskam were not necessarily unique. James Agee and Walker Evans, who worked, respectively, for Luce's *Fortune* and Stryker's FSA during the 1930s, conceived of a plan to start a magazine and book series that would challenge Time Inc.'s magazine empire by using photography and journalism to explore the perverse nature of modern America. This series, according to Agee's journals, would include "General content: some text, some pictures. Records, symbols, science, analysis, discussion & criticism . . . Characteristics: absolute absence of ingratiation; excellence of reproductions; plainness; the utmost cheapness wherever possible: a steady correction of every fashion."[13] One volume might be dedicated to "A sampling of news clips . . . poems: composed of advertisements, news photographs, and photographs, and photographs personally made. . . . An analysis of misinterpretation (or worse) of crime and of excellence, as found in newspapers, magazines, courts & speeches."[14] It never got off the ground, though Evans's postcard collection and his scrapbooks of juxtaposed images provide a glimpse of how it might have been laid out.[15] Remnants of their project remain in their 1941 phototextual extravaganza *Let Us Now Praise Famous Men*.[16] But *12 Million Black Voices* features a closer resemblance to the tabloid aesthetics so formative for Wright and Rosskam. The two Depression volumes, published within months of each other (April and November 1941), coming too late, after the fact, as world war was shifting the focus of writers and photographers, and for very different reasons, speak across various divides—white/black, textual/visual, poetic/factual, middle-class readers/impoverished subjects.[17] As many contemporary reviewers noted, they spoke to each other and to "mass" culture and its politics as well.[18]

Agee, born to an upper-middle-class family in Tennessee a year after Wright was born in Mississippi, undertook his project to record three Southern white tenant farmers under many of the same conditions as Wright's project on "folk Southern Negroes"—a deep understanding of American popular cultures of North and South, a love of photography, a skepticism about literature, and a love of movies. When Agee was taking a break from the three weeks he and Walker Evans spent sleeping on the porch and front room of the Burroughs' house in Hale County, Alabama, in July 1936, he skipped out of Mills Hill into town, found a prostitute and a drink, and let us know about it. Two years later, as he began working on "the book," as he referred to *Let Us Now Praise Famous Men* to Father James Flye, he picked up some magazines as a diversion while in Atlantic City.[19] Ten or so pages of detailed description follow the layout of the pages, creating a mini-screenplay for a film noir detective story in his intimate journal.

Monday 10. [January 1938]

Friday afternoon-evening-night. Saturday morning frustration

Atlantic City. Sunday night. Picture Detective.

Two magazines: Picture Detective and another. They have revived the old gangster pamphlet ideas of police photographs and taken it into more general crime. The other devotes itself to women in crime. I brought this instead (lacking money for both) for the picture on the cover. As Walker says they must be thoroughly aware of the pathological public they feed + count on. From circulation it might be possible to intimate sadistic population but not really: big [buy?] enough stores [stares?] of it so that a huge number — one issue in these [three?]. Part of my own interest in that. I'm not made sick by work of these

as Via is. It is of greatest good for the sets and properties surrounding the murders and crimes—and for various faces. The
lunch room street scene dominated by Indian Simmons; and
inside . . . The bathroom linoleum and sink where the cop dies.
The desk, radiator and shirt. Even the dark paint around the
latch and handle of the door . . . the 2 cars. The lunchroom mirror the corpse, and dawn outside. The bare hallway to Weir's
room and the carpet on it. The room where all that DESPER-
ATE, CRAMPED AND LONELY FEELING [FUCKING?]
TOOK PLACE. The wallpaper. The Kentucky road. All the
Kentuckian faces. The Armstrong Hotel. . . . The cover picture
disembodied from any context is one of the most frightening I
know. The completely savage world. The hard flash does a great
deal. 2 kinds of idiot cruel laughter. None of them look like
cops. They look like special appointees of a Kafka but American
second world disguised as cops. . . . I like the reversed 5 ¢ and
the 5 across the street, the neon hamburger, to ogle and again
the 2 faces looking at the camera. Unposed faces looking at a
camera have a special human expression nearly unprecedented
(Not quite; some paintings show these faces). Of this in its vari-
eties + of its uses there must be investigation analysis and study.

Rain in all these pictures . . . (figure 3.1)

He goes on for pages until "I wrote till 3. a new start on the Alabama book."[20] That "the Alabama book," *Let Us Now Praise Famous
Men*, one of the signal works of American modernism, was mid-
wifed through Agee's close encounter with tabloid prose and imagery alters its appearance. Along with *Picture Detective*, which might
be read in an Atlantic City hotel room or on board the bus pulling
out of the Port Authority bound for the seaside, it too "marches
through the corridors of every office, files into the living-room of
every home," appearing as a pulpy artifact—intimate and brainy,
perhaps, but clearly pulp.

At the same time as Agee was deconstructing the pages of *Actual Detective*, Wright was jotting notes to himself that would become the source materials for *12 Million Black Voices*. Despite Rosskam's protest to the contrary (and it is true that the first typed, complete draft of the text is dated January 1941), Wright had been preparing for this study at least since 1938 when he began collecting documentary materials on Chicago housing and notes on African American history and folk culture; in fact, if one does a close comparison of *12 Million Black Voices* and *Lawd Today*, his material for the photo-text dates from 1934. Wright's notes include a thirteen-point outline that moves from "1 Breaking away from Home" through "4 Traveling about nation" to "5 Leaping over the barrier of soil" then "of nation" to "10 Scottsboro & Herndon" and "12 The triumph of mass idea," which creates "13 The new surge of confidence."[21] Essentially, this trajectory in thirteen steps traces the path of *12 Million Black Voices* but might also be said to outline the distribution routes of pulp magazines and paperbacks. And while it is clear that the "mass idea" comes out of "11 mass racial movements and white labor"—that is, through the Popular Front of the Communist Party of the United States of America (CPUSA), it is imperative to remember, as Michael Denning has demonstrated, that the political "mass" of the "Cultural Front" was deeply attached to popular or mass culture, too.

True story magazines, with names like *True Crime*, *Detective Annals*, *Actual Detective*, *Picture Detective*, and so on, were ubiquitous during the 1930s and 1940s at newsstands, bus depots, train stations, drugstores, and kiosks across small-town and big-city America. Magazines, as a collective form, were everywhere, and everywhere they were, they invited readers into their crypt of sex and death. If sensational crimes of passion dominated the US magazine culture, Spanish Loyalist culture was permeated by the phototextual layout revealing the crimes of fascists against the people, for instance.[22] Violence—whether personal or political—found its mass expression through this medium. FSA photographers John Vachon and Russell Lee, especially, were drawn to the newsstands of America as locations that drew readers to peruse the hidden recesses of desire—criminal, erotic, economic, and mobile—locked within the pages of *True Romance*, *Better Homes and Gardens*, and *Popular Locomotion*. Some were more wholesome (economy and mobility); others more lurid (murder and sex). It was at the newsstand in a Memphis bank lobby where Wright first encountered H. L. Mencken's name as he was skimming the papers: "One morning I arrived early at work and went into the bank lobby where the Negro porter was mopping, I stood at a counter and picked up the Memphis *Commercial Appeal* and began my free reading of the press."[23]

Even more than newspapers on display, magazines beckoned: "the cover picture disembodied from any context is one of the most frightening I know," wrote Agee in a notebook he kept for *Let Us Now Praise Famous Men* of the December 1938 issue of *Actual Detective*. "The completely savage world. The hard flash does a great deal . . . for the sets and properties surrounding the murders and crimes—and for various faces." He bought the magazine "for the picture on the cover."[24] This "savage world" encapsulated by this "frightening" picture stirred Agee, as it did many others, to buy the magazine, as he himself lolled in a hotel in Atlantic City, reading and masturbating and thinking about how to proceed with his new love and his new work—on a Savage Holiday of sorts from his job at *Fortune*. The cover of *Actual Detective*, like dozens of others, was meant to attract buyers, not merely readers. Wright had not purchased the Memphis newspaper with Mencken's column; having no money, he had read it and replaced it. Rosskam noted this same problem with Archibald MacLeish's phototextual book *Land of the Free*, which he argued could be browsed at the bookstore and left back on the shelf unsold because it lacked enough words to hold attention. Instead, the magazines that sold well combined image with enough text to draw in the customer—who needed time, much more time than was available at a street-corner kiosk, even if browsing was encouraged—to thoroughly absorb the desire and depravity without being caught.[25] The covers served as "dark mirrors" into contemporary culture; they relentlessly pointed into the crypt (figures 3.1 and 3.2).

The text of *12 Million Black Voices* begins in misrecognition—"and we are not what we seem," starting with the book's first image by Dorothea Lange of a sharecropper's hands, whose racial identity cannot easily be determined, cradling a hoe. [26] It plays with (white) readers' interpretative abilities to see and understand images and language, ending thirty thousand words later with the insistence, "Look at us and know us and you will know yourselves, for *we* are *you*, looking back at you from the dark mirror of our lives!" (146; emphasis in original). Seeing in the "dark mirror," one peers into the crypt, a mise en abyme without reflection, a black hole.[27] Wright's prose, unlike MacLeish's "shooting script," needed to be read in one long sitting—but it also could be extracted into captions that would link image to image. Acutely attuned to film and to pulp as serialized narrative modes, writer Wright and photo-director Rosskam knew how to draw in and keep the audience.

Agee bought *Actual Detective* and studied it as a "document," in Walter Benjamin's sense of the term. Mining the one-way streets of 1920s Berlin, Benjamin analyzed the imperatives, handbills, leaflets, and other "primitive" writing he passed while perambulating the decadent city, accumulating them in "Post No Bills": "The document serves to instruct. With documents, a public is educated. All documents communicate through their subject matter . . . The fertility of the document demands: analysis. A document overpowers only through surprise."[28] The "savage" covers of *Actual Detective* represented the more popular forms (and surrealist versions) Benjamin referred to as "documents" that "serve to instruct . . . through . . .

their subject matter . . . the outcome of dreams." Their more respectable modes he linked to the "New Objectivity," referencing its
many forms prevalent in Weimar Germany, which "fashionabl[y]
appeal[led] to facts—hostile to fictions removed from reality . . .
it attacks theory."[29] For Benjamin, their "political significance was
exhausted by the transposition of revolutionary reflexes (insofar as
they arose in the bourgeoisie) into objects of distraction, of amuse-
ment, which can be supplied for consumption."[30] "Its stock in trade
was reportage," he later explained. Both its photographic and literary forms "owe the extraordinary increase in their popularity to the
technology of publication: radio and illustrated press."[31] The New
Objectivity, Benjamin further complained, "has made the *struggle
against poverty* an object of consumption" (776; emphasis in original). Precisely as Agee would rail against those who read his book
and felt pity, outrage, or aesthetic transport. Truth had become a
commodity to be pulped.

This consumerist sentimentality could only be overcome, according to Benjamin, "when we—the writers—take up photography."
In so doing, the photograph would be augmented with "a caption
that wrenches it from modish commerce and gives it a revolutionary use value" (775). Wright would surely agree.[32] His own photography and his intimate participation in the February 1941 South
Side shoot with Rosskam and Russell Lee, from which most of the
images for parts 3 and 4 of *12 Million Black Voices* derived, connects Wright's work to another "sensational modernist," in Joseph
Entin's phrase. Like Bertolt Brecht, who was the hero of Benjamin's
1934 address to the Institute for the Study of Fascism in Paris, "The
Author as Producer," Wright was taking advantage of every "trick
of the [epic] trade"—foremost among them what Benjamin saw as
montage, in which "the superimposed element disrupts the context
in which it is inserted." By bringing together songs, sermons, sociology, case study, biography, fiction, and poetry with photography,

Figure 3.1 Cover, *Actual Detective Stories of Women in Crime* (December 1938). This is the issue that James Agee purchased and mentions in his diary.

Figure 3.2 Cover, *Actual Detective Stories of Women in Crime* (December 1940).

the "principle of interruption" (778) forced audiences to see the underworld of "folk history," as Wright had originally subtitled his book. There are no black criminals sensationalized in true story magazines, which depicts crimes across class boundaries, from shady suburban lawns to sleazy city dives, within white America; instead, black criminals appeared in the pages of daily tabloid newspapers that Wright clipped for his records as he compiled an archive on the Robert Nixon case. His extensive tear sheets also included details about a black nurse who bludgeoned a white nurse to death in Tennessee and other sordid descriptions of black-on-white crime. In addition to *Hollywood Crime* (figure 3.3), Wright's newspaper morgue archives the serialized 1938 exposé of slum housing—many of the photographs (which are unattributed) perhaps coming from the FSA—entitled "Misery." Like Jacob Riis's earlier newspaper exposés of New York tenements, which became the images for the first phototextual volume, *How the Other Half Lives* (1890), these pictures traded on scandal and bordered on stereotype, as did the emerging form of the case study, to which this series, like Riis's reports, nod (after all, it is Chicago, with its school of sociology).[33] The page layout indicates how easily assimilated the medium of urban squalor exposé, the case study, is with such dubiously newsworthy items as Dorothy Lamour's divorce and Shirley Temple's tenth birthday (figure 3.4). As Benjamin described it in 1934, "The scene of this literary confusion is the newspaper; its content, 'subject matter' that denies itself any other form of organization than that imposed on it by the reader's impatience."[34]

Despite potential drawbacks that resulted from a formulaic mode of description and unconscious use of stereotypes, the case study was a central device for Wright, borrowed from sociologists Robert Parks, Louis Wirth, and Horace Cayton, and from his reading of Freud and Dostoevsky.[35] Like almost every other modern(ist) author, Wright discerned in the case study a literary form capable

The Crime
HOLLYWOOD

BILL SMITH, special investigator for the Owl Drug Company in the Los Angeles district, stood facing the big steel vault in the basement of the firm's Hollywood-Cahuenga Boulevards branch store in the heart of the movie colony, a puzzled expression on his face.

Chester Graham, assistant manager at the store, had placed $1100 of the firm's money in that safe the previous evening. Then he had carefully locked the safe, locked the doors of the building, and gone home.

When A. B. Humphries, the manager,

came in to open up for business the following morning, he found the safe still locked—but the $1100 was missing. There were but three men who knew the combination that would open the safe—Humphries, Graham, and the company's district supervisor.

Immediately the manager discovered the robbery, he telephoned his assistant, rousing him from sleep to bring him hurrying down to the store. Then he called his head office, who dispatched Bill Smith to make an investigation.

And Smith, faced with a crime so fantastic that it did not seem possible ex-

cept for the fact that the money had vanished, got on the phone and talked to our chief, Captain Tom Carmen, head of the robbery detail. Carmen summoned Detective Lieutenant Leon D. Egan and me, and gave us the details as he had them.

"The way Smith tells it," he said, "it's an inside job. No sign of forcible entry. Safe door not damaged. If the money went into that safe last night, then it must have been taken by somebody who had access to the store, and knew the safe combination."

We found Bill Smith and Manager

42   TRUE DETECTIVE

Figure 3.3 Page layout from *Hollywood Crime* (August 1941) from Wright's personal archive.

of charging the document with the energy of the dream, as Benjamin noted, and, of course, as Freud recorded. The entire premise of the case study rests on unpeeling the onion, but to what? Abraham and Torok describe this space that cannot be plumbed as an emptiness, a recess emanating effects seemingly without cause. In notes for *12 Million Black Voices*, entitled "We Want What You Want,"

Figure 3.4 Page layout of *Chicago Sunday Times* (1938) from Wright's personal archive.

Wright lists a bizarre series of demons and desires compelling him: "1. War, 2. Mulatto, 3. Mix Marriage—history 4. Negro women 5. Oppression has made Americans los(v)e[?] masks. 6. Author should speak collectively—- 7. Method & process of slavery is a principle working in forms [or focuses or forums] today, 8. Positive approach * 9 [blank]."[36] *12 Million Black Voices* unearths the crypt of America, the "method and process of slavery" and racism, not because it was hidden—it was an open sore, "a principle working in forms today"—but because this very availability was deferred, located in the sensational journalism crowding street corners. America's True Crime Story is the crypt holding the corpse and haunting the recesses of every space of America. Like the Wolf Man's magic word analyzed by Abraham and Torok, it needed an adept caseworker, one attuned to voices, to (un)cover it, one who could speak as "we" to "you." Wright first depicts it in Bigger but has Max read him, or speak him, for us; then, a year later, "we" shows and tells "you"—like a how-to manual—in *12 Million Black Voices* exactly as the detectives uncovering true crime reenact the scene, lurid yet matter-of-fact; collective crime demands a plural narrator.

Wright's attention to the media showed that he recognized its power as a force of coercion and liberation for black Americans: "to paint the picture [of how] we live on the cotton, corn, cane, rice, and tobacco plantations is to compete against mighty artists—the movies, radio, magazines, newspapers and even the church. For they have painted one picture, charming, idyllic, romantic. But we live another, full of fear."[37] However, as the epigraph I begin this chapter with indicates, he sensed how much the mobilization of desire through religion, advertisements, Hollywood movies, radio broadcasts, and screaming tabloid headlines describing the "Python Killer" who "killed six men . . . drugged 'em and then smothered 'em to death with pillows when they was sleeping" or "Tiger Woman," or "the Cat Killer," or "the Canary Girl, the one who had the sweet voice and killed all her babies" served to forge urbanity. These dangerous women, like the "thrill guys, Loeb and Leopold," offered a violent vision of betrayal and defiance, perverse though it may be, to norms of behavior by pretty women, sweet-voiced mothers, or well-heeled college students.[38] The cascade of stories were steps on the road (or pathway, as Wright says in his 1938 notes) linking folk culture to popular culture, the popular to the political. If all of these assorted middle-class white people could go berserk, certainly it was possible, even logical, that impoverished black men and women might too.

This was precisely the lesson the reviewer for *Harper's* took from *12 Million Black Voices*: "After reading and looking at this short history of the Negro race in America, in prose and remarkable photographs, one does not wonder that there are occasional crimes committed in Harlem. One wonders why there aren't more, in the face of the crimes which our society has committed against the black man."[39] But if sensational criminality—and its vengeful assault on black women—is ever-present in Wright's fiction, it is not evident in *12 Million Black Voices*, which offers a dialogue with its white readers as it expressly ignores the "talented tenth" in favor of a story of a segment, "a debased feudal folk," only recently become visible because of "urbanization," in part through tabloids, in part through the FSA (xx) (figure 3.5).

This book, conceived as a "shooting script," reads like a novel in which the reader/viewer—"you"—becomes a participant in the underlying crime, the one that is unremarkable because ubiquitous. For Ann Petry, "the novel as social criticism" was a necessity in the United States because "the arguments used to justify slavery still influence American attitudes toward the Negro. If I use the words intermarriage, mixed marriage, miscegenation," she explains, "there are few Americans who would not react to those words emotionally. Part of that emotion can be traced directly to the days of slavery. And if emotion is aroused merely by the use of certain words, and the emotion is violent, apoplectic, then it seems fairly logical that novels which deal with race relations should reflect some of this violence."[40] "You" don't just "see their faces," as Erskine Caldwell and Margaret Bourke-White would have it in their phototextual reportage; instead "you" are indicted by and inducted into the narrative precisely for *not* seeing, *not* hearing, *not* knowing this story, these faces, these kitchenettes, this (folk) history. "This is the black

Figure 3.5 Russell Lee, Five children of Pomp Hall, Negro tenant farmer, studying their lessons by lamplight, Creek County, Oklahoma, 1940. Library of Congress, Prints & Photographs Division, FSA/OWI Collection [LC-USF34–035231-D].

'J'Accuse,' " notes Richard F. Crandell, critic for the *Herald Tribune* (in his 23 November 1941 review entitled "Dark Thoughts on Dark Citizens").

Contemporary reviewers, black and white, read the text to *12 Million Black Voices* as at once a "cartoon," a "novel," an "autobiography," a "stereotype," and "pamphleteering." For those writing in the black press, the volume performs "the cardinal literary sin: oversimplification." "Biased and depressing," its content presents "a betrayal of facts," in its "resort to melodrama." As a polemic, its novelistic traits seemed to undercut its sociological purpose. Most saw the pictures differently. The anonymous (and presumably white) reviewer for *US Week: A National Journal of News and Opinion* declared the photographs "clinch the argument. They are magnificent.

Apparently there never was a Negro who was not (to use a hackneyed word) photogenic. Culled chiefly from the files of the Farm Security Administration, U.S. Department of Agriculture, these pictures are unforgettable—black bodies caught in postures of resignation, despair or joy, hands eloquent of toil, eyes searching, questioning in a way that we cannot evade."[41] These reviewers recognized the interplay between voice/text and vision/photograph as a dynamic and dialogic one even if they sometimes found the words lacking.

It is obvious from the typed manuscript that Wright wrote the original fifty thousand words comprising the text in practically one sitting. This was material intimately known to him, as life story, as research, through observation and analysis, and from his earlier fiction, from his journalism about Harlem, his clipping collection on housing in the South Side, and on media hysteria about black criminality.[42] He's telling his story to be sure—but he's telling 12 million stories too, a figure Max also cites in *Native Son*, and it is not necessarily a tale of uplift but of collectivity (333). Likewise, Rosskam, the "photo-director," as Viking called him, gathered together images produced under government aegis (and in two cases news media and in one case Richard Wright's own camera work) by many different artists, and freely cropped the pictures to put them into dialogue with one another and with Wright's prose, culling captions from the text to dramatize image and choosing photographs to reinforce text (figure 3.6). John M. Reilly calls the book a "simulated sermon" indebted to the "oral utterance derived from the spontaneous arts that shape the orations of the preacher; it is a secularization of the sacred moral voice of the folk." Wright becomes a "vernacular orator"—and as such, through his incorporation of the "shared 12 million subjects"—he achieves "a uniquely modern personality."[43] Because, I would add, of the uniquely modern form of the book— its attention to mass media, as well as to collectivity.

heard tall tales about us, about how "bad" we are, they react emotionally
as though we had the plague when we move into their neighborhoods. Is it
any wonder, then, that their homes are suddenly and drastically reduced
in value? They hastily abandon them, sacrificing them to the Bosses of the
Buildings, the men who instigate all this for whatever profit they can get
in real-estate sales. And in the end we are the "fall guys." When the white
folks move, the Bosses of the Buildings let the property to us at rentals
higher than those the whites paid.

And the Bosses of the Buildings take these old houses and convert them
into "kitchenettes," and then rent them to us at rates so high that they
make fabulous fortunes before the houses are too old for habitation. What
they do is this: they take, say, a seven-room apartment, which rents for
$50 a month to whites, and cut it up into seven small apartments, of one
room each; they install one small gas stove and one small sink in each
room. The Bosses of the Buildings rent these kitchenettes to us at the rate
of, say, $6 a week. Hence, the same apartment for which white people—who
can get jobs anywhere and who receive higher wages than we—pay $50 a
month is rented to us for $42 a week! And because there are not enough

Figure 3.6 Page layout from first edition of *12 Million Black Voices*, photograph by
Richard Wright (November 1941). Archie Givens Collection of African American
Literature, Special Collections and Rare Books, University of Minnesota Libraries.

Claiming that the book reflects Rosskam's signature style of layout, typography, and captioning, Maren Stange argues for his "invoking in its arty informality the medium's expressive and symbolic possibilities," and recognizes its modernism. The full-page bleeds and closely cropped images contribute, she goes on to suggest, a sense of the complicated dialectic between "placelessness and boundedness posited in the text."[44] Rosskam's design advances Wright's textual argument, even, or especially, when it is out of sync with it. But Wright himself clearly understood the "double-voiced," polyphonic conversation between text and photos as a modernist novel format coming directly from *True Crime* and other popular publications. As Rosskam recalled, "Dick Wright really knew that stuff cold; he knew where everybody was, and he knew everybody in the Negro world of Chicago. And I don't know if many white men had the opportunity to see it the way we saw it. Man, that was an experience. We did everything from the undertaker to the gangster ... I was not on the staff then, I went out with Russell Lee to finish the coverage, was in Chicago and that was used later on in The Voices, Twelve Million Black Voices, because he couldn't do migration without showing, finally where migration went to. Migration went to the city."[45]

Again, like contemporary critics Walter Benjamin and Mikhail Bakhtin, Wright understood from the novelists he loved, the three "Ds"—Dostoevsky, Dreiser, and Dos Passos—that tabloids, newspapers, billboards, and the ephemera of the city provided key elements of modern consciousness and that the novel offered a venue for its vocalization, "migration went to the city" and spoke in many dialects. In *Lawd Today*, Wright recounts verbatim, complete with all diacritical marks, the entire text of a religious flyer sent in the mail by "St. Paul." Side 1 asked:

"WHICH RAILROAD WILL YOU TAKE??????????????????
ALL HOURS OF THE DAY AND NIGHT SPECIAL

TRAINS ARE RUNNING FROM: Thomas Paine Avenue, Dime Novel Park, Theatre Lane, Dopedel, Blasphemers' Hall, Smokers' Furnace, Masturbation Alley, Prostitution Boulevard, Dancehall Station, Highball Lagoon, Adultery Depot, Greed Mountain, Gambling Pause, Ingersoll Canyon, Evolution Grounds, and Communist Junction." Signed by Prince Lucifer, President!!!!!!!!!!!!,##############, ********************—
—————— -. . . . . "'''''''''''''''''''''''''????????????????] (*LT*, 140–41)

The flip side revealed salvation.

He knew from his attention to the "way we saw it," that the novel must become a visual form. An accomplished amateur photographer who studied how-to manuals, Wright understood the importance of a visual text, one that mimicked the onslaught of words and images found everywhere as instilling "restlessness" within "the modern personality." His photograph of the sign in the Brooklyn apartment used in the first edition of *12 Million Black Voices* recalls others by FSA photographers attentive to signage—Walker Evans, Dorothea Lange, and Esther Bubley (whose 1943 photograph *Colored Dining Room in Rear* of a bus stop hash house replaces his of a sign in a Brooklyn window advertising an apartment for rent, *No Colored*, in later editions), in particular. Rosskam, too, learned "an understanding of the use of photographs as a language. From there it was only a short step to photographs with captions as a language, and then only another short step further to photographs with text so combined, that they complimented [*sic*] each other at all times."[46] It was a lesson Wright had imbibed through his early reading and his sensational experiences as a city dweller. America's cities, with their open crypts, were an urban modernist's dreamscape. Wright viscerally embraced his status as "a city boy," in Robert Sklar's words for the ethnic gangsters of 1930s Hollywood; and in doing so, he understood text as texture, lived experience.

Seeing and knowing ("when you see us . . . and think you know us . . . we are not what we seem" [10]), the spectral crypt of "our strange history" requires attending to that which appears invisible, but it also means reading every visible sign as if it were a clue destined to solve a ghastly crime. Karla F. C. Holloway explains that for African American writers, and particularly Wright, both the "place of reading" (attics and bedrooms) and the "act of subterfuge" needed to acquire books from libraries in the segregated South, but also the "booklist," with the names of authors repeated "awakens his 'impulse to dream,'" setting the stage for a "hunger . . . for books, new ways of looking and seeing" as he recalled in *Black Boy*.[47] Recreating the feel of detection, tracing signs, symbols, and clues, was part of Wright's project as a mythologizing, that is to say, modernist, realist. *Lawd Today* maps out the bridge hands the four postal workers play as a newspaper bridge column would, substituting north, south, east, and west with their names. *12 Million Black Voices* is laid out like the city pages of a metro paper. Anticipating Adorno, who would find precursors to the Authoritarian Personality in popular astrology columns,[48] Wright details how pictures were read as vehicles to establish psychological evidence central to true story magazines:

> "Her eyes is close together, meaning she's mean."
> "And her bottom lip pokes out, meaning she's deceitful. She fooled folks."
> "And that thick neck? What it say about it?"
> "That means," read Al: "Uncontrollable passions, masculine feelings." (*LT*, 118)

Wright claimed that "The huge mountains of fact piled up by the Department of Sociology at the University of Chicago gave me my first concrete vision of forces that molded the urban Negro's body and soul," and through them became able to "tell my story. But I did not know what my story was, and it was not until I stumbled upon science that I discovered some of the meanings of the environment that battered and taunted me."[49] Sociology and Marxism offered insights, but the pulps, tabloids, and true crime magazines also became, in their own degraded way, "documents," "science," and "meanings." This multiply constructed "modern personality," as Reilly calls it—at once individuated and collective—is akin to the invention of the dialogic characters/narrators in Dostoevsky's novels, according to Bakhtin. In fact, the double-voicing and the polyphonic qualities of novels, here augmented by multifaceted images—taken for purposes not precisely aligned with Wright's narrative—make this book into an example of a modern novel, according to Bakhtin's definitions, especially when one thinks of the reader as the second term (which for Bakhtin happened through the author/narrator dyad) between collective narrator "we" and the addressee "you."

The novel: a "double-voiced" form, Bakhtin echoing W.E.B. Du Bois's term, "a twoness" that can both observe and participate. Thus Carla Cappetti's insistence that modernism be understood as an ethnographic project; and in Benjamin's terms, a visual one, while for Bakhtin, a vocal one. Much of Wright's work slides among case study, autobiography, choral poetry, and fiction; this text does it explicitly in an effort to invent his new mode of decryption. He had absorbed Dostoevsky's method, reveling in his subject matter. Bakhtin, writing of "Discourse in the Novel" and often citing Dostoevsky as a prime example, notes that "the novel is the realm in which biography, consciousness and social convention come into immediate dialogic field of vision." They do so through the incorporation and interpolation of texts extraneous to narration—poems, songs, newspaper headlines, and so on. This is a visual process but an aural one as well. The novel's true subject is the "speaking voice," which becomes multiply polyphonic and double-voiced as authors', narrators', and characters' voices intermingle, contradict, and come into "contact zones" with one another across "thresholds" to meet the reader.[50] That contact zone encompassed the "dusty land" and the "hard pavement," "we" and "you," where true story magazines, themselves novels of America and soon to be packaged between the bright but savage covers of paperbacks, crossed the thresholds from newsstands to bedrooms—bringing public and private into contact with the corpses buried but still speaking through the 12 million and more black voices. Within a few years, they would be heard by millions of readers, not as sounds but as words on the pages of pulp written by black and white authors and circulated far beyond Chicago's South Side.

....

CHAPTER 4

Isak Dinesen Gets Drafted: Pulp, the Armed Services Editions, and GI Reading

During the Second World War more than sixteen million American men and women served in the nation's armed forces. This large array of citizens represented a panoply of America—first-generation immigrants from Brooklyn ghettos, farmers from midwestern states, sharecroppers from the South, and out-of-work factory hands from the industrial heartland among them. Many had grown up in poverty as the Depression raged across their childhoods, often with little more than a meager education. In addition to mobilizing and training this enormously diverse population for warfare, the United States government saw an opportunity—extending the social service projects, such as the Works Progress Administration (WPA) and Civilian Conservation Corps (CCC) of Franklin Delano Roosevelt's New Deal—in order to develop the kinds of citizenry necessary for postwar American hegemony. This enormous project of social engineering included health campaigns to inoculate the population against various diseases, but for some it meant training in hygiene as the army teamed up with Cannon towels to instruct servicemen in bathing techniques (plate 4, *bottom*).[1] It also provided a significant opening for education deemed essential to soldiers and sailors operating efficiently in sophisticated battlefield conditions.

The war offered corporations and manufacturers varied sources of income as merchants and companies retooled for war production. Among the hardest hit industries during the 1930s Depression years was the book business. While public libraries reported record levels of use during the decade, publishers were constrained by costs—often offering books in runs as small as three hundred volumes for emerging authors—with little expectation that financially strapped libraries or book-buyers could afford them. Like Cannon towels (not to mention Ford trucks), booksellers and publishers recognized that the war opened new markets; teaming up with librarians and others interested in reading, literacy, and books, these foresighted devotees of book culture sought to take advantage of the new concentrations of potential readers stationed around the world by providing/presenting reading materials to millions of servicemen and women. The Council on Books in Wartime organized to promote books as essential tools of a democratic nation through a variety of programs.[2] The lightweight books they invented, printed on catalog and pulp magazine rotogravure presses, formed the basis of both the paperback industry's postwar explosion and the government's ongoing efforts to improve the health, training, and literacy of draftees and enlistees, many of whom entered the services malnourished, poorly educated, and unemployed, escaping destroyed farms and cities devastated by the Depression.

This was not the first time a war contributed to government-sponsored cultural expenditures meant to uplift its citizens deployed for war. The federal government's interest in theater predates the Depression-era Federal Theater extending back to the Liberty Theaters dotting World War I army bases. These twentieth-century American forays into state-sponsored and thus political performance set the stage, so to speak, for the spread of books to service members during World War II. With its association to burlesque, vaudeville, and minstrel, theater in America has always held a certain risqué and populist sensibility—often at odds with civic campaigns. Yet it was precisely this legacy that brought theater to several military bases in 1917. Designed to provide a "constructive" alternative to honky-tonks, Liberty Theaters were devised by the education section of the US Army through the War Department's Commission on Training Camp Activities, under the leadership of Raymond Fosdick, as tools to "uplift" morale and morals among bored troops soon to be mobilized overseas. Weldon Durham details how Progressive Era concerns over the commercialization of theater, which limited the possibility of community plays by turning the public into consumers rather than participants, were hastened by the advent of motion pictures. These fears fed plans to control draftees after Woodrow Wilson entered the war.

With a captive audience of hundreds of thousands of working-class men, drafted from farms and cities and far less educated than expected, the Training Camp Activities were designed "to police the camps and supply recreation programs" by ensuring that wholesome recreation would keep draftees busy during leisure time.[3] Almost fifty Liberty Theaters were constructed on bases across the country, bringing musicals, melodramas, and domestic comedies by Broadway professionals, touring shows, and stock companies; these joined impersonators, soldiers' talent shows, Chautauqua tent lectures by the Red Cross, and D. W. Griffith's *Intolerance* to provide wholesome entertainment. Theaters would be more playgrounds than cabarets.

The War Department tried and ultimately failed to emulate the settlement house movement's use of pageant and community plays to instill a sense of citizenship among urban immigrants for its enlistees. However, because the needs of the armed services were often at odds with those of theater professionals—actors, stagehands, and producers—recruited to develop the Liberty Theaters, tensions over professionalism and amateur volunteers, commerce and community, and patriotism and subversion, as well as the speed of the war's end and the influenza epidemic, contributed to the demise of these federally funded theaters. This saga of good intensions and conflicting interests was played out again through the Armed Services Editions publications. Nevertheless, the legacy of government sponsorship of the arts as part of a concerted effort at social amelioration—either for audiences or practitioners—permeated the armed services, and ultimately contributed to the efforts of the Council on Books in Wartime a generation later.

The council worked with the Office of War Information (OWI) and the navy and army (the two branches of the service interested in this project) to develop posters devoted to promoting free expression—contrasting Nazi book burning to the openness of democracies. Its other activities in support of the war effort were radio broadcasts and the Overseas Editions—translations of books that "would give the people of Europe a picture of what Americans are like" into French, Italian, and German (with plans for some in Chinese and Japanese) for distribution throughout liberated Europe and Asia.[4] The OWI saw the Overseas Editions as a propaganda vehicle, part of the Psychological Warfare Branch, to spread reading materials into liberated areas immediately after their invasion. The "Imperative" book series was designed "to promote war-related books [but] proved a failure," noted Kenneth Davis, perhaps because its first book about "the story of the early Philippine campaign and General MacArthur's withdrawal . . . called . . . 'America's Little Dunkirk'" was entitled *They Were Expendable* by W. L. White.[5]

However, the council's most significant accomplishment was the development of the Armed Services Editions (ASEs)—cheaply produced and ingeniously designed books, almost all complete and unabridged—to be distributed free to troops around the globe (figure 4.1). Realizing that simultaneously providing entertainment for those spending long and boring hours aboard ships or even on various fronts, and offering a range of books geared to all levels of literacy, was crucial for morale, the navy and the army enthusiastically (the army more so than the navy, which was derelict paying its bills) embraced this project, which was a "boon" for soldiers and for book dealers and publishers.[6] The editions were ensured a captive readership that would hopefully develop a lifelong attachment to reading (this worked) and help develop readers from even those with limited education (this worked, too). As serviceman Jack Howard wrote the council on 17 October 1944, "Many servicemen, especially those overseas where there is little else to do during sparing [sic] time are acquiring a new habit, that of reading—a result of time on their hands and availability of reading material."[7] Looking ahead to the postwar period, the council worried about the surplus materiel (this would include books) to be dumped for sale and ensured that the books, which became the property of the armed services upon shipment, could not be resold after the war as surplus (unlike the canteens, fatigues, boots, etc., that made up my youthful wardrobe). Thus, as literally an army of readers was created through the millions of books distributed, publishers were assured future sales of the same books delivered free during wartime.

Paper was key to all of this: heavily rationed during wartime, the emergence of Penguin and Pocket Books paperbound books in the United States in 1939 provided the inspiration for this project.[8] The books were designed "to be printed on roll-fed, letterpress rotary presses" (used to print pulp magazines and newspaper inserts), stuffing between 1,400 and 2,500 characters per page in double columns, and in uniform numbers regardless of the title.[9] During and immediately after the Second World War, 1,180 books were made available as this consortium of publishers, librarians, and booksellers, recognizing the severe limitations placed on publishing by wartime paper rationing, desired to "achieve the widest possible use of books contributing to the war effort."[10] The ASEs provided cheap editions of hardcover and paperback originals to servicemen and

Figure 4.1 Unknown photographer, overstuffed crates of books for shipment overseas. Used by permission, Princeton University Library. From the Council on Books in Wartime Records, Public Policy Papers Division, Department of Rare Books and Special Collections, Princeton University Library.

women in compact form. Designed to fit neatly into the breast or hip pockets of GI fatigues or navy blues, the books were offered free to the armed services on the condition that they not be dumped on the market as postwar surplus; authors received the usual one cent per book royalties for paperback reprints.

Among those selected were two of Karen Blixen's recently published story collections, unusual on two counts, as the author was female and not American, but a few years later, she would be noted by none other than ur-teenager Holden Caulfield as the author of one of his favorite books, *Out of Africa*.[11] Books selected for the series included such popular titles as John O'Hara's *Butterfield 8*, about a New York call girl; Westerns by Zane Grey; Charles Beard's *The Republic* (subject of the major censorship battle resulting from the 1944 Soldiers' Vote Act, in part for its inclusion of the Constitution and mention of the names of political parties and political offices); eventual blacklisted screenwriter Albert Maltz's complex novel about Germans and Nazism, *The Cross and the Arrow*; Nazi spy thriller *The Fallen Sparrow* by mystery writer Dorothy B. Hughes; and *Strange Fruit* by Lillian Smith (banned in Massachusetts); as well as numerous best sellers long since consigned to the dustbin of publication history (the two most requested titles being Betty Smith's *A Tree Grows in Brooklyn*, filmed from a screenplay by leftist Tess Slesinger in 1945, and Lloyd C. Douglas's *The Robe*, a popular biography of Jesus that became a Hollywood epic after the war,[12] followed a close third by the sexy romance *Forever Amber* by Kathleen Winsor, made into a film directed by Otto Preminger in 1947). The choices depended on wartime publishing trends, army and navy suggestions, servicemen's and women's requests, legal controls, censorship, and the editorial taste of the small book selection committee, which met at various members' New York apartments to hammer out monthly lists of thirty (later forty) titles meant to appeal to a diverse readership (figure 4.2). For instance, Bennett Cerf, editor of the Modern Library, was a significant participant, and although publishers were not supposed to advocate for their authors, it is clear that his presence influenced certain choices—perhaps including Blixen, though the timing of this selection and the fact that Denmark was one of the countries receiving Overseas Editions suggests this might have been a gesture toward the besieged nation.[13] Publishers and authors regularly lobbied the council on behalf of recently published (or as yet unpublished manuscripts, some by servicemen themselves), sending press releases and testimonials that were duly acknowledged by the council staff.

The success of the Armed Services Editions (123,535,305 volumes of 1,180 titles, 99 of which were reprints of earlier ASEs,

```
/Editions for the Armed Services, Inc.
ESTABLISHED BY THE COUNCIL ON BOOKS IN WARTIME
    40 EAST 49 STREET, NEW YORK 17                    *REPRINT
            Plaza 8-0500                     ** CONDENSED FOR WARTIME READING

                            "X" LIST

**X-1.   775   SOME LIKE THEM SHORT by William March
  X-2    776   COLLECTED POEMS OF RUPERT BROOKE
  X-3    777   CANARY by Gustav Eckstein
  X-4    778   A GENIUS IN THE FAMILY by Hiram Percy Maxim
  X-5    779   ON BORROWED TIME by Lawrence Edward Watkin
  X-6    780   HORSETHIEF CREEK by Bliss Lomax
 *X-7    781   LOU GEHRIG by Frank Graham
 *X-8    782   YOU KNOW ME, AL by Ring Lardner
 *X-9    783   THE PHANTOM FILLY by George Chamberlain
 *X-10   784   SHERIFF OF YAVISA by Charles H. Snow
  X-11   785   THE SO BLUE MARBLE by Dorothy B. Hughes
  X-12   786   BLIND MANIS BLUFF by Baynard Kendrick
  X-13   787   PATRICK HENRY AND THE FRIGATE'S KEEL by Howard Fast
  X-14   788   THE BRUISER by Edward L. McKenna
  X-15   789   PAYOFF FOR THE BANKER by Frances & Richard Lockridge
  X-16   790   THIS IS OUR WORLD by Paul B. Sears
  X-17   791   TRAIL SMOKE by Ernest Haycox
  X-18   792   APARTMENT IN ATHENS by Glenway Wescott
  X-19   793   THE BAREFOOT MAILMAN by Theodore Pratt
  X-20   794   THE LONG VALLEY by John Steinbeck
  X-21   795   KING SOLOMON'S MINES by H. Rider Haggard
  X-22   796   MR. TUTT FINDS A WAY by Arthur Train
  X-23   797   FORLORN RIVER by Zane Grey
  X-24   798   PATTERN FOR MURDER by Ione Sandberg Shriber
  X-25   799   BUTTERFIELD 8 by John O'Hara
  X-26   800   THE BISHOP'S WIFE AND TWO OTHER NOVELS by Robert Nathan
  X-27   801   WHEN WORLDS COLLIDE by Edwin Balmer and Philip Wylie
  X-28   802   WINTER'S TALES by Isak Dinesen
  X-29   803   FIVE WESTERN STORIES by Coburn, Foster, Ranger, McCulley and Wilson
  X-30   804   COMMODORE HORNBLOWER by C. S. Forester
  X-31   805   YANKEE WOMAN by Eric Baume
  X-32   806   THE HUDSON by Carl Carmer
  X-33   807   SUN IN THEIR EYES by Monte Barrett
  X-34   808   MEN AGAINST DEATH by Paul de Kruif
**X-35   809   MEN OF SCIENCE IN AMERICA by Bernard Jaffee
**X-36   810   GREAT STORIES FROM GREAT LIVES edited by Herbert V. Prochnow
 *X-37   811   MRS. PARKINGTON by Louis Bromfield
 *X-38   812   THE SEA HAWK by Rafael Sabatini
**X-39   813   AUTHOR'S CHOICE by MacKinlay Kantor
**X-40   814   RIDE WITH ME by Thomas B. Costain
```

Figure 4.2 "X" list, Armed Services Editions.

were delivered to the troops) spurred publishers to embark on series of their own in addition to the books shipped directly by them. This interaction between publishers and a branch of the US government—and between individuals consuming the books and the council—demonstrates the ways that reading as a practice cemented a complex social network comprised of service chaplains and orientation officers, who often maintained the unit's library; soldiers and sailors, who exchanged the volumes, lending them to British and Commonwealth Allied forces, whose much more constrained national economies could not afford the luxuries that the United States could provide its armed services (from Chesterfields to condoms); and commanders and hospital staff nurses who saw improved morale among those reading, as well as the mothers, wives, and friends of those overseas who had learned of the project and pleaded on behalf of their loved ones for specific titles or access to the books, which could only be obtained after a request by the commanding officer of a unit. The editions created a sense of commonality, even community, between readers and publishers that suggested an intimacy expressed across space via language, as indicated by a V-letter that Private G. W. McAdam sent on 23 September 1944: "Ever since I've been overseas I've had one of your Council books somewhere among my things . . . Selections of titles are outstanding, and I must admit I've been surprised to find such 'heavies' as Plato, Emerson, Lamb and Thackeray on the lists. There's certainly something there to please every taste and every level of mentality." He goes on to suggest adding "modern plays" and "some more poetry . . . Carl Sandburg, Stephen Vincent Benet, Vachel Lindsay, Sidney Lanier, George Santayana . . . might be especially good."[14] This reader prized the democratic range of texts available, and this wide array became central to postwar paperback production. But the books were also to possess "simple vocabulary and adult interest for the near-illiterates."[15]

Each letter was individually answered, most by form letter; however, every letter from a serviceman (and some servicewomen) containing a comment about an individual book—from complaints about the occasional abridged edition, to critiques of the selected Keats's poems for omitting stanzas from "La Belle Dame Sans Merci," which the reader knew from memory (Untermeyer wrote back to Sydney Norwick of his thrill that someone knew poetry so well, reminding him that indeed there were two versions of the poem), to analyses of the relevance of some titles, to shared experiences (Melville's *Typee* and *Omoo* arrived as troops were shipped to the Pacific theater and its many islands)—was personally answered with an acknowledgment or explanation addressing individual concerns.[16] Private Harry Bruton engaged in a long exchange with the council, outraged that it would reprint *North Africa*, a 1942 Oxford University Press book by Alan H. Brodrick that blatantly advocated imperialism and colonialism, and supported British racism: "the council was criminal" for publishing this book, he declared.[17] Letters to the council also contained suggestions for future titles, from Mencken to Eudora Welty's "A Curtain of Green," which Richard Wharton praised as "the finest group of short stories published since De Maupessant [*sic*] horrified the Victorian world with his absorbing tales."[18]

While the bulk of the letters thanked and praised the ASEs in rather conventional language limited by the space of a V-letter—PFC John V. Hagopian's comment on 26 October 1944 is typical: "They are a godsend to the G.I. bookworm overseas"—some chose to engage the council as equals; they were themselves authors, teachers, and editors in civilian life, after all.[19] Reading Shelley while being shelled turned the terror, but primarily the boredom, of war into an opportunity. Librarians, schoolteachers, and bibliophiles—whose somewhat stilted and pedantic commentary, often resulting in long exchanges over time (some with real effect, as suggestions became selections)—pointed out discrepancies among editions, bemoaned the inclusion of genre fiction, and despaired because classics in translation were rarely included: "Where was *War and Peace?*" one wondered. First Lt. Carl Helmetag Jr. decried

> your selection of books ... It is impossible to conceive of a worse selection and your policy of once in awhile slipping in a classic

to lend tone is to my way of thinking nothing short of bad taste and a poor showing of manners. This is no reflection on the classics such as *Jane Eyre* and *Wuthering Heights*, which I enjoyed reading again, but they are like the big tomatoes that the gyp dealers place on the top of the basket as a come on to get rid of a lot of inferior products. . . . Your know[ing] just because the soldier is far away and no longer exposed to the bright lights and the comforts of wartime America is not reason to believe that he will be satisfied with inferior products of literature.—I have about reached the point where I shall either have to give up literature completely or enlarge the policy I have of buying books directly from the publishers.[20]

Thomas Shaw (somewhere in the Philippines) engaged in a long correspondence with Philip Van Doren Stern, general manager of the council (who went on to be an editor at Pocket Books), offering analyses of soldier's literary tastes. His 2 February 1945 letter provides a cogent explanation of how a demotics of reading takes hold:

In my opinion, the reading of the men with whom I serve can be summed up in one word, "escape." When you have breakfast with a man and at supper time he has been buried—your relative values change. High cultural values seem silly to a jungle fighter. When he has a chance he reads *anything*—just so it blots out his immediate surroundings—he has no whiskey—no women—no night clubs—no change in scenery or faces—he is bored to extremity so he reads what he can get—I believe he prefers it exciting and action packed to the sexy.[21]

Some may have wanted to read Tolstoy, but lengthy nineteenth-century novels were impractical; the ASE books themselves limited pages—"there is always the fact to be considered that books have weight—and the G.I. does not carry an unnecessary ounce," reminded Shaw. Yet others recalled quite contrary images of the weight:

> It was on the Island of Saipan, the morning after a particularly trying night of heavy enemy mortar fire which had caused numerous casualties in our marine lines. I was walking along the road when I saw some of the dead being loaded gently into the backs of several trucks which had been drawn up to take their bodies to the division cemetery: I looked to see if I recognized any of the dead marines. There were half a dozen stretched out, some on their backs, and several face down. One of the latter was a young, fair-haired private which had only recently arrived as a replacement, full of exuberance at finally being a full-fledged marine on the battle front. As I looked down at him I saw something which I don't think I shall ever forget. Sticking from his back trouser pocket was a yellow pocket edition of a book he had evidently been reading in his spare moments. Only the title was visible—*Our Hearts Were Young and Gay*.[22]

Tales such as this one became part of the propaganda campaign of the council; letters were mined for apt quotes, almost like book blurbs, to publicize the project. An extract from a letter dated 23 December 1944 from Capt. Michael Chritzko, stationed in New Delhi, was marked for publicity purposes: "Life in India isn't too exciting and a good book goes a long way with most of us." He goes on: "'Spirits' help to [*sic*]! Years ago, I used to be quite discriminating in my choice of books. Maybe it was the good influence of C.C.N.Y. Now, I'll read anything I can get my hands on, including the 'who-dunits.'"[23] Low-level literacy among troops, combined with utter boredom and short time frames for reading, meant that light reading or shorter works were most desirable; even so, *Vanity Fair* and *Moby-Dick* were also ASE titles. Lillian Jonassen from Brooklyn excerpted parts of her husband's letter to her from "somewhere in England" in a letter to the council dated 22 September 1944 (also marked for use), clearly referring to D-Day:

> The day before the last battle started some supplies reached us, among them books and cigarettes. I got hold of a copy of Lytton Strachey's *Queen Victoria*, and managed to read a few chapters. We were pulled out suddenly, and the next time I became cognizant of it was some two days later. We had advanced through enemy artillery fire and had finally been pinned down in a field by that morter [*sic*] and machine gun fire. It appeared at first that there was no cover—no ditches around the field— but finally, after some close ones, I just dove head first into what appeared to be a solid growth of brambles and bushes. They broke under my weight, and I found myself in a rather deep ditch below the surface of the ground. Soon I became cramped and started to move; a lump in my pocket turned out to be *Queen Victoria*.
>
> It was pretty "hot" above; every once in a while a shell would burst and the wounded would go by to the rear. There was nothing I could do except wait. I started to read and found it a rather good substitute for just "sweating." There was a two way traffic above me, our shells going, theirs coming and bursting, and I kept reading of Victoria's "dear, dear, beautiful Albert," and his soft flowing mustache that she admired so much.[24]

If this soldier persevered through Victoria's reign, short stories were prized for quick but complete reads of a more literary sort; thus, collections and anthologies were popular, though the council did not want to create new collections.[25] Each month's list tried to contain a representative span of recently published fiction—genre and literary—a few volumes of poetry, plays, short stories, and nonfiction works appropriate to the war effort. Both *Seven Gothic Tales* and *Winter's Tales* appeared in 1945, toward the end of the second year of the program (and the war), which began publishing in September 1943; the two titles were examples of the contemporary literary fiction members of the council tried to encourage the army and navy to accept instead of the genre fiction the services often ordered.[26] Even so, the packaging offered up an author who seemed to step out of a dime novel. Because one of the criteria guiding the choices of titles was a "masculine" perspective, her biography stresses connections to both world literature and warfare.[27] Like her father, who lived among "Pawnee Indians in Minnesota" before turning to writing under a pseudonym, Baroness Blixen is described as a wild adventuress who hunted and worked the fields with Masai and Kikuyu in Kenya and dined with sheikhs in Somalia. Her dashing life story as a warrior princess becomes an essential element in her inclusion (not to mention her publisher Bennett Cerf). The construction of this tale about Isak Dinesen, less than a year after the Colonel Trautman memo was issued, quite bizarrely invokes elements that both accede to and contradict the edict to "Provide recent fiction, avoiding only the mediocre, trashy, mawkish and books with a decided feminine interest." Blixen is posed as "masculine," her work is "fiction of enduring value." Yet this biography of her—which stresses her "modernity" and her attraction to "men of various backgrounds"—is offered in a form that seems intended to be avoided: "the mediocre, subversive and trash" (figures 4.3 and 4.4).[28]

The Council on Books in Wartime appeared to be a thoroughly apolitical entity, an effort organized by the cultural and literary elite in New York, America's publishing center, to aid the war effort. Yet, because many of the recently published books were products of 1930s literary tastes—when proletarian and popular fiction leaked into each other—and because of various censorship battles, the council was often in the center of political skirmishes. Its widely circulated posters could be found in libraries, schools, and factories across the nation, reminding readers that "Books are Weapons in

Figure 4.3 Front cover, Isak Dinesen, *Winter's Tales*, Armed Services Edition.

WINTER'S TALES by Isak Dinesen

THE ELEVEN stories of this volume open a new world of enchantment and adventure. They include:

"The Young Man With the Carnation": Of a youth's adventure in Antwerp on a rainy night, and of how his invasion of a room he supposed his wife's led to a strange and reasonably comforting dialogue with God; "Sorrow-Acre": Of an old lord who essayed the role of a cruel god, and of how he was defeated by his victim and her son; "The Heroine": Of a group of prisoners taken as spies on the eve of 1870, and of how a lovely actress, who danced naked in Paris, saved them through her modesty; "The Sailor-Boy's Tale": Of a lad who killed a man, and of the yellow-eyed old Lapp woman who befriended him even as he had once befriended a trapped bird whose eyes also had been yellow; "The Pearls": Of a bride, and of the curious manner in which she made use of her necklace in order to teach her husband fear; "Alkmene": Of a girl, perverse and perhaps a little mad, who ran after the gypsies and found relief in witnessing a decapitation; "The Fish": Of King Erik, who ruled over Denmark six centuries ago, and of what befell when the sea returned to him a lady's ring; and "Peter and Rosa": Of a season when the Spring came late, and of two young dreamers, adrift on an ice-floe, who found a practical way of plucking ecstasy from death.

This special edition of WINTER'S TALES *by Isak Dinesen has been made available to the Armed Forces of the United States through an arrangement with the original publisher, Random House, Inc., New York.*

Editions for the Armed Services, Inc., a non-profit organization established by the Council on Books in Wartime

Figure 4.4 Back cover, Isak Dinesen, *Winter's Tales*, Armed Services Edition.

the War of Ideas" (figure 4.5). Its radio programs, produced for national broadcast, included NBC's book dramatizations "Words at War" and author interviews conducted by Bennett Cerf and others on "Fighting Words" for WMCA and WQXR's "Books are Bullets." Each series' scripts (dramatizations and interviews) prepared by the council veered into political critiques: this was a war against fascism.[29] Its list of "Imperative Books" was reprinted in *Publishers Weekly* and circulated to librarians throughout the nation; this included recommended "Books on the War" and "Woman's Power," as well as other titles deemed essential to an informed public. The Overseas Editions consisted of translated works from the United States and other Allied authors into the languages of nations occupied by German and Axis powers to be distributed to the populations through book drops and other clandestine means, and designed to spread democratic values both during and after the war. All this patriotic effort on behalf of the war resulted in the council's leadership organizing a major protest against the amendment by Robert Taft (R-OH) to the Soldiers' Vote Act of 1944, which limited texts referencing political parties (called Republicans and Democrats) from reaching overseas servicemen in an effort to cancel the enormous popularity of FDR. Three of the council's books were censored by navy liaison Isobel Du Bois—Charles Beard's *The Republic*, E. B. White's *One Man's Meat*, and *Yankee from Olympus* by Catherine Drinker Bowen, a memoir about Greece—because language contained within them suggested to censors an endorsement of a party or a reference to an elected office; the Greek demos or Plato's *Republic* surely were signals about how to vote, as were the words "democratic" and "republic," "president," "representative," or "senator."[30]

The council's stance on this legislation was confrontational and emerged first from the fact that Series Q, January 1945, immediately preceding the February issuance of Blixen's stories, included Lillian Smith's novel about interracial sex, *Strange Fruit*, which was

Figure 4.5 S. Broder, *Books are Weapons in the War of Ideas* (1942). Poster. US Government Printing Office. LC-USZC4–4267. Produced for public display in libraries by the Office of War Information and often distributed by the Council on Books in Wartime.

banned in Massachusetts, and which the US Postal Service had refused to send through the mail. Recognizing the contradiction of offering banners to bookstores and libraries that read "Books Like These Were Burned in the Slave Countries" with a list of titles, the council vigorously contested the bill; when it passed, in somewhat modified form, Stern wrote army brigadier general Joseph W. Byron that while the council would comply with the law, its members "strongly deprecate it as an abridgement of the freedom of the

Press."[31] The council recognized that its program had a wider reach than even the millions of service members reading these dainty yellow-covered books. As John Hench astutely notes, "Aided and underwritten by the government, these programs represent an economically minor but culturally significant aspect in the general expansion, even domination, of U.S. culture overseas in the second half of the twentieth century."[32]

Ultimately, the worst aspects of Ohio senator Taft's amendment were modified through negotiations, massive publicity campaigns, and threats to include this disclaimer in each book sent to the front: "This edition of _____ is complete except for textual changes necessitated by Title V of Public Law 277 from the Soldiers' Vote Act of 1944: 'Books of general circulation in the United States may be distributed to members of the Armed Forces, but any such book hereafter purchased by the Army shall not contain political argument or political propaganda designed or calculated to affect the result of any election for the federal offices mentioned above" (that is, president, vice president, presidential elector, member of the Senate, or member of the House of Representatives). The Taft amendment to the bill, originally designed to ensure that those fighting overseas could participate in the election, was being interpreted by the army quite literally, as the Trautman memo indicates. Others, including Senator Theodore Green (D-RI), crafted a counteramendment with softened language; council members met privately with Senator Taft and released a scathing press release on the topic. After two intensive months of negative publicity, the softened amendment passed and the army and navy backed down from its literalist interpretation of the statute.[33]

Still, after the passage of the Soldiers' Vote Act of 1944, every book had to be read before approval to avoid including any prohibited language, and Mrs. Stephen Vincent Benet and Louis Untermeyer were employed to read all selections once the army requested an expanded editorial staff to represent a broader array of viewpoints. (This was in part because of Rep. George Dondero's [R-MI] complaint of "Communistic propaganda" contained in Louis Adamic's *The Native's Return*, a charge that was inaccurate, since Adamic had already excised these passages after his break with the CPUSA.) Moreover, authors whose books were included in the ASE series wrote and complained that the council was not doing enough to counter wartime censorship. Two writers active during the 1930s in left-wing causes, James T. Farrell and Mari Sandoz, wrote open letters denouncing censorship by Allied governments.

Despite these controversies—and their own critiques— servicemen clearly felt an abiding connection to and gratitude for the council's work; they cherished the books, requesting copies for their own personal libraries and collections (not possible as the books were distributed in bulk to the army and navy for dispersal in common practice with that of any other ordnance) and traded them, forging links with one another through reading (figure 4.6). One writer described "A group of us, service men, both army and navy formed a discussion club. The topic for the evening generally centers around a book review. One of the members mentioned the 'Council on Books in Wartime' and the possibility of your council assisting us in reading materials."[34] This request could not be accommodated either. Still, readers continued to send in requests. The range of desired titles is astonishing and outlines the contours of demotic reading practices: Kahlil Gibran's *The Prophet*, John Steinbeck's *Tortilla Flats*, W. Somerset Maugham's *Of Human Bondage*, Irving Stone's *Lust for Life*, James M. Cain's *The Postman Always Rings Twice*, W. H. Hudson's *Green Mansions*, the ever-popular, humorous vignettes subtitled *My Life with Mother's Boarders* (which became a Hollywood movie after the war), and *Chicken Every Sunday* by Rosemary Taylor, part of a shipment to New Guinea and in constant demand.[35] So, too, were *Candide* and Farrell's Studs Lonigan trilogy, if less often than Lloyd C. Douglas's 1942 historical novel about the crucifixion or Betty Smith's poignant tale of Brooklyn. Cpl. M. Mednick wrote on 12 May 1944 to congratulate the council's choice to reprint *A Tree Grows in Brooklyn*: "While in the hospital convalescing her book has been a source of never-ending enjoyment to me. Not only because of its story alone, but of its startling realities that I myself had known in my childhood in Brooklyn. To me, it was living my life over again."[36] These individual requests and comments were echoed around the globe.

Those perceiving themselves to have higher tastes or other needs also asked for books on "psychological subjects," this from a psychotherapist working with GIs or for volumes with "spiritual" themes; yet, noted one writer, "Books of Poetry, Philosophy, Science and Theology have a very limited circulation among the forces." This comment from Leo Meltzer in a V-mail of 29 March 1945, who had asked for Thomas Wolfe's *Look Homeward, Angel* (much too long), was part of a long interchange with Stern that typologized the class (or at least taste) distinctions found among troops. Meltzer's quasi-scientific analysis of the reading practices of his compatriots is as follows: "By types the Most Popular Books are Mysteries, following it with a ratio of about 3:2 are Westerns, and a ratio of 3:1 to mysteries are adventure stories. Classed under adventure are travel books, certain biographies, Thorne Smith [a popular writer of the time] and James Furber [perhaps Thurber?] types of books."[37] His astute understanding of the troops' tastes and his own persistence as an epistolary pal of the council did have results; ultimately, Wolfe's tome became (albeit in abridged form) a title. One veteran who studied law after his service wrote the council wondering if the surplus books could be sent to jails and prisons, which, he noted, anticipating Erving Goffman, resembled the army as coercive institutions full of bored and often violent men.[38]

Like the Cannon towel ads, which entered and helped create postwar gay male culture as some of the first widely available popular beefcake, and codified an aspect of the emergence of gay identity,

Figure 4.6 Russell Lee, Magazines and reading matter of all kinds are definitely appreciated by the "Flying Sergeants." Lake Muroc, California, May 1942. Library of Congress, Prints & Photographs Division, FSA/OWI Collection [LC USW3–002919-D DLC].

the ASEs can be seen as part of the postwar drive to educate GIs that resulted in new forms of engagement with books and with the readers of books.[39] This effort to fund veterans' educations set in motion the enormous expansion of higher education institutions in the United States, whose curriculum was nurtured by the cheap and widespread circulation of paperback books. Reading throwaway books, often clandestinely, sanctioned by authorities—armies and universities, for instance—ultimately democratized taste as "trashy," "mawkish," "mediocre," and "subversive" books mingled promiscuously with those of "value" in PXs, engine compartments, foxholes, and later dormitories. Like her macabre and eerie tales that move in and out of fantasy and realism, past and present, Karen Blixen's pseudonym, which disguised her gender, and her ASE author's biography, which rejected a "decided feminine interest" and constructed her life from a "masculine viewpoint," exemplified the ways in which pulp—as a literal form used to transmit new sensibilities—brought modernist literature to the "near-illiterate" GI Joes, and eventually their Janes, of America. This wartime ephemera spread ideas and images that ultimately contributed to postwar countercultures.

Publishers' fears that free books would dampen book buying after the war were clearly unfounded. In the decade after troops came home, millions of twenty-five-cent paperbacks were scooped up and poured over by practically everyone. Just as war's end opened European film audiences to the dark cinema they dubbed "film noir," their textual counterparts circulated across continents. Japanese scholars of American literature often got their first exposure to the field by reading copies of ASEs their fathers or grandfathers had found and kept.[40] The variety of work made available by the Council on Books in Wartime spurred the sort of demotic reading made possible by pulp. The bursting crates of books thrown together and shipped overseas fed a sense that books were like all the other necessities in a soldier's kit—toothpaste, condoms, chocolates—the very items found on sale at drugstores and candy stores, along with magazines, tabloids, and pulps. The world of books, like the world itself, was pried open; it led to hunger for more.

CHAPTER 5

....

Pulping Ann Petry: The Case of *Country Place*

In 1947, Ann Petry's second novel, *Country Place*, appeared to generally scathing reviews. José Yglesias, writing in the Communist Party–affiliated journal *New Masses*, summed up responses by noting it was more suitable to "movies," "woman's magazine" or "lending library fare" so full of "formulas," "banalities," and "idiocy" that "even Ethel Barrymore could not quite come off" in the part of the rich old lady. In fact, he noted, "the one diversion the book offers" would be "to cast the book for the movies."[1] The *New York Times* noted, "Gossip, malice, calculation, infidelity, adultery, murder, sudden death, and a set of surprise bequests . . . are some of the dominant matters treated in *Country Place*."[2] Just the year before, Petry had been featured in the newly launched black mass slick *Ebony* (an African American version of *Life*) as a celebrity author, sharing cocktails with New York's literati following the fantastic success of her debut novel, *The Street*. (This spread, entitled "First Novel," opens with a full-page portrait of Petry as something of a stereotype out of 1940s movies—the prim but eager librarian poised at her typewriter, cigarette in one hand, ready to rip off her spectacles, loosen her bun, and pull a bottle of bourbon from her desk, as had Carole Douglas when Humphrey Bogart enters her used bookstore in *The Big Sleep*.)[3] Twenty years later, when

Country Place was mentioned at all, comments such as those by David Littlejohn in his book, *Black on White*, were typical. Despite her "intelligence" and "female wisdom," he finds that Petry writes "sordid plots," "Peyton-Place plots." He advises "reading the novel, skipping the plot."[4] This sounds paradoxical at best, damning at worst. But maybe he's on to something. Like the dozens of film noirs Hollywood was churning out while Ann Petry wrote her major works, her novels are best read as one views any example of B-movie genres: skipping the predictable plot and watching the film instead, noting the atmospheric lighting, catching the scraps of snappy dialogue, tracking the moody interiors. These go a long way toward providing a sense of why all three of her novels received such wide attention when they appeared in paperback editions during the late 1940s and early 1950s. She understood the pulp interface that connected story through media to readers.

For a writer who only produced three major adult novels—her best-selling (1.5 million copies and paperbacked three times) 1946 first novel, *The Street*, *Country Place*, and her sensational 1953 chronicle of an interracial adulterous love affair, *The Narrows*—it is curious how little attention the second novel has gleaned. This, despite it being paperbacked as one of the first New American Library Signet editions with a cover by the highly prized illustrator James Avati and chosen as a British Book-of-the-Month Club selection.[5] Even as Oxford University Press, Beacon Press, Houghton Mifflin (Petry's original publisher), Rutgers University Press, and Northeastern University Press, among others, have highlighted black women's literary history through extensive reprint series that include her first and third novel, *Country Place* remains hidden.[6] John O'Brien considers her, in part because of *Country Place*, "outside" the black literary tradition.[7] Until recently, if afforded attention, she is often dismissed.

Ann Petry's *Country Place* (set, like James Thurber's "Secret Life of Walter Mitty" [1941], in a small-sized town, hers on the Connecticut shore), limned the outlines of America's bucolic New England as a claustrophobic, dark, and sinister zone of social disarray—Grace Metalious's Peyton Place meets Nathaniel Hawthorne's Salem. Where social chaos appeared openly visible on the teeming city streets, rural America, with its drowsy small towns and its midsize cities built around a single industry—like *The Narrows's* powerful Treadway Munitions, based on Bridgeport's Remington Works— masked class, ethnic, and racial tensions within mostly impenetrable homes and isolated landscapes. It was not the sidewalks that seethed but the lone merchant or housewife trapped by four walls, which, in Petry's version, burst wide open with the returning veterans of midcentury's second world war.

Despite standard contract language prohibiting authors form publishing "scandalous" materials with New American Library, *Country Place* hints of scandal, even more melodramatic than what Petry's critics have noted is her penchant for plots with "scandalous doings"—"secret affairs, family skeletons revealed, brutal crimes, whispered evil adulterous intrigue"; or her "chewy" recourse to "melodrama" and "sordidness," a constant refrain in the reviews of all of her fiction.[8] And what she wallows or immerses her readers in is the outrage, the melodrama, the sordidness of racial cross-dressing, of passing, of refusing racial biography even as she announces its sociological effect.[9] "Some people in Connecticut," writes Rochelle Girson in the *Hartford Times* review of *The Narrows*, "thought grimly that the characters in her second novel, *Country Place*, were easily identifiable."[10] As a melodrama, *Country Place* relies on a set of stock characters—good and bad, rich and poor, insiders and outsiders—to stage its social critique. *Country Place*, lacking definite or even indefinite article, takes on the whole damned mess of the country, the nation; its manifest focus is white people— their relentlessly small-minded pursuits of base desires for sex and money. Paradoxically, its staginess, its seeming remove from the racial politics and social protest of her other works, masked Petry's intimate memories and experiences, her own autobiography. Unlike her other two novels, purposely based on her consideration of the novel as a form of sociology, this pulpy and largely forgotten work reveals traumas operating latently on an intimate level—written as they are through vast tropes of natural and human devastation in the wake of maelstroms and war. "In *The Street* I wanted to achieve a swift-moving, almost passionate style in order to heighten the story of Lutie Johnson and her small son, Bub . . . In *Country Place*, I tried to *under*write . . . I tried to get into the style something of the surface quiet of a small country town—a slowness of tempo . . . absorb[ed] almost unconsciously."[11] Julien D. McKee of Houghton Mifflin noted, in a letter to Petry accompanying the signed contract for the New American Library paperback, that its publisher Victor Weybright considered it "a good novel and perhaps a more mature novel than THE STREET . . . it lacks the sensationalism of THE STREET."[12]

Briefly, *Country Place* follows a few days in late summer hurricane season in a small town, Lennox, Connecticut, as returning World War II vet, Johnnie Roane, discovers his beautiful blond wife has been having an affair with the town grease monkey, Ed Barrell—fifty-five-year-old lecher, complete with hunting cabin (*the* country place), and wife stashed in a TB sanatorium. In addition, it compresses a subplot involving murder by chocolate overdose, interracial romance, and a struggle over a will into its slim binding. (New American Library books published during the 1940s were required to be less than 190 pages, so that the first paperback edition of *The Street* was an abridged edition, condensed by more than seventy thousand words.) Narrated by the town druggist "Doc," who begins his retrospective tale in typical hard-boiled fashion, with a first-person introduction of his own limitations—"a prejudice against women"—as a narrative frame, the plot moves through a series of revelations provided and sometimes provoked by the local cabbie, known as the Weasel.[13] As the Weasel picks up

and drops off customers, fills up his gas tank, and hovers around
the train station and Doc's soda fountain, various characters fill in
the gossip that substitutes for action. An interconnecting stream of
locals—Johnnie; his parents; his wife Gloria; Glory's mother Lil,
the gold-digging wife of Mearns Gramby, wealthy and cowed scion
of the town's upper crust Mrs. Gramby—are all regular riders, the
rich to and from their imposing house, which sits above the town;
the others from their modest bungalows. Even the Grambys' servants move in and out of narrative range via the taxi's rearview mirror and the drugstore's plate-glass window. Viewed in the Weasel's
mirror, the town is on reverse display, narrated after the fact, much
as Orson Welles, initiating this film noir convention, recounted
Citizen Kane. Whatever happens, the Weasel's been there first:
he utters Johnnie's thoughts "sticking his mouth into [Johnnie's]
mind" as he peruses Lennox after four years overseas (17). Similarly,
"I find you everywhere," remarks Mrs. Gramby to the Weasel. "Even
in my thoughts. You reach them before I do" (182). Doc's store-
front is not like those in the noir city featured in tough-guy fiction
of the 1930s and film noirs of the 1940s, "all wiggling neon lights
and cosmetic bars and aluminum cooking ware" beckoning passersby from the grimy pavement. His store, instead, faces the "town
green . . . where cows and sheep once grazed." Born in this village
"surrounded by water and . . . filled with the salt smell of the sea and
with the yammering sound of gulls," he possesses, as its sole druggist, an "intimate, detailed knowledge of its inhabitants." He knows
what medications they take, what books and magazines they buy,
which candy they prefer. Like the Weasel, who "speaks for Lennox"
(17), Doc's is the voice of a country place—insular, intimate. As the
Big Storm brews so too do the murderous rages of Johnnie and Lil,
the seething desires of Ed and Glory, the passionate interracial romance between the Grambys' servants, Neola and Portalucca, the
machinations of the Iago-like Weasel, and the storytelling panache
of Doc. In its wake, a new set of arrangements—domestic, environ-

mental, social, and economic—still cannot unsettle the "surface quiet" of this country place.

Based on Petry's experience of the devastating Hurricane of 1938—which left hundreds dead in Long Island and coastal Connecticut and Rhode Island, spurring floods as far inland as Hartford, destroying entire fishing fleets and railroad tracks in its path—the novel suggests Petry's effort to take T. S. Eliot's concept of the objective correlative and run wild with it. Marrying the environmental destruction of the weather to the social and psychological upheavals of World War II, Petry found the "perfect storm" to work through her training as a novelist, as she herself dealt with a husband home from the war. The actual events—hurricane and demobilization—separated by less than a decade, are temporally collapsed into a seething whirlwind of domestic rage. In her notebooks of the period, she constantly tallies the attributes of great fiction—its ability to take a bloody crime, for instance, as in *Passage to India* or *Native Son*—and push outward, or inward, from sensationalism to art. She used her immersion in small-town life and her work as a social worker and journalist during the war to explore the seamy side of an American pastoral, inadvertently finding a vehicle to express and explore some of her own ambivalences about marriage and art. Pulp about trashy white women provided a safe space to unveil, complain about, and analyze her own situation.

In *Country Place*, as the back-cover blurb of the 1950 Signet edition proclaims (figure 5.1), "Ann Petry has employed the same scalpel she used in *The Street*—to open the festering wound of Harlem—on a typical small town . . . Miss Petry shows the hidden sores and pollution which are masked by the cheerful façade of any County Place." "Johnny Comes Marching Home," declares the first boldfaced line of the blurb, and like an unreined stallion, Johnnie Roane's reentry into small-town USA sets the plot in motion.

Like so many works of popular culture during and immediately after World War II, *Country Place* ponders the "problem of the vet,"

Figure 5.1 Ann Petry, *Country Place* (Signet/NAL, 1950). Cover by James Avati.

which, along with the "disease hazards" of "sex delinquency" (as Elliot Ness pathologized interracial sex and unfaithful wives during wartime) was a growing concern among the military, law enforcement, journalists, social workers, and educators, not to mention pulp fiction writers and Hollywood B-moviemakers, during and immediately after the war.[14]

Vets were seen in the words of Glory, mimicking Richard Gunn, Horace Walpole's narrator in his 1931 novel, *Above the Dark Tumult*, as having "gone queer in the head" (149). She defiantly declares she "slept with Ed [because] he's a man and you're not" (142). By the mid-1930s, "queer" had come to mean both odd or crazy and homosexual or effeminate in American slang. Christopher Isherwood's 1945 *Goodbye to Berlin* (another NAL book with a James Avati cover posing a slutty young white women) put queerness into literary circulation. So Petry, like so many other pulp and noir writers, is linking the war to changes in masculinity and emerging sexualities: like so many postwar bohemians, Johnnie wants to move to New York and become a painter, while Ed runs a gas station. And even if the New York school will emerge as a hypermacho construct with Jackson Pollock and the rest drinking in the Cedar Bar, there is no mistaking that in America artists possess suspect sexuality; guys who work on cars do not. The 1947 film of Dorothy P. Hughes's 1946 novel, *Ride the Pink Horse,* refers to the antihero Lucky Gagin as "another one of those haywire vets."

In turn, the returned vet often finds his wife changed: Glory appears to Johnny as "a shadow of a woman," "a cheat" (142). Johnnie's dreams of escape can't compete with his wife's beauty— her blond hair—"a gleaming net," a "fetish" drawing him back to his old life (87). Glory likes her job as a cashier in the local grocery store, where she knows she's the best-looking woman in town and can flirt with her customers. She's not so sure she can compete on Fifth Avenue. She refuses sex with her husband upon his return; he rapes her, almost strangling her, and later pursues her to the cabin, where she and Ed tryst together, to kill them both. But he cannot bring himself to murder, running instead from the scene, feeling a "wreck," and only then can he declare himself "a veteran" (143). War was not enough; rather, the true vet experience comes after the war—with his wife's desertion. (It is quite possible that despite a long tour of duty, Johnnie never fired a rifle in combat, as the "kill ratio" during World War II was less than 25 percent and Johnnie's rank was as "Technical Sergeant," which meant he'd spent four years "grubbing around the insides of airplane engines" [25]).

Houghton Mifflin seems to have rushed *Country Place* into print following the 1946 Paramount film *The Blue Dahlia*, with an Oscar-winning screenplay by Raymond Chandler and starring Veronica Lake and Alan Ladd, who, as another Johnnie returned from "one bomber mission too many," discovers not only his wife's affair with a nightclub owner/gangster but his kid dead from a car smashup when she was drunk. When she turns up dead, he's pinned for her murder, although he insists on his innocence and must rely on his mentally and physically damaged war buddies to clear his name. Perhaps his amnesic war buddy did it, but Chandler's investigation into wartime guilt and violence was rewritten—laying the blame on a disgruntled night watchman—at the request of the US Navy.

But the theme of disturbed veterans' inability to return to civilian life had already entered popular culture while the war still raged in Europe and the Pacific. *Double Furlough*, a radio drama, aired Christmas 1943; its script by Charles Martin served as the basis for the spectacularly popular David O. Selznick–produced film *I'll Be Seeing You*, starring Ginger Rogers and Joseph Cotten, which opened a year later. The two meet on a train, both on secret furlough: she from prison for involuntary manslaughter; he from the service for psychological and physical wounds suffered in battle. They hide their stories from each other. When he learns where Rogers is disembarking, Cotten gets off the train, too, saying his sister lives in Pine Hill. He ends up in the local YMCA, obviously disturbed by the barracks-like room, and finally flips open the magazine he has purchased to read during his trip. The article is about the "neuropsychological" problems of soldiers, and Cotten must steady himself with an internal monologue before going to meet Rogers's family. It would seem that only a woman convicted of killing her boss when he tried to rape her (we later discover) can handle the burdens of the war-damaged man. This theme of soldiers' difficult reentry because of physical and psychological wounds, and the spunky yet devoted women needed to help them, would become the basis for the 1946 Academy-award winning film, *The Best Years of Our Lives*.[15]

Typically, in the postwar movie and fiction plot, the domestic front appears almost as violent and unstable as the combat zone. Elisabeth Sanxay Holding's novella, *The Blank Wall* (made into the film noir *The Reckless Moment* by Max Ophüls) suggests that because upstanding family men are away at war, criminals and gangsters have free access to middle-class women, who find their attentions strangely comforting, even as they involve naive housewives in murder, extortion, and blackmail.[16] This plot was not confined to the United States either. For instance, in Yasujiro Ozu's 1948 *Hen in the Wind*, the repatriated prisoner of war is immediately returned to work at Tokyo's Time/Life building, sliding back into his job in publishing, even though his city is a wreck, its streets in rubble, and its offices converted to dancehalls; but his homecoming is more troubled. He beats and rapes his wife after she admits she has prostituted herself to get money to pay for their son's hospitalization. This story of sexual betrayal was already circulating at home and abroad during the war. Novelist Josephine Herbst recounts her work in the Office of the Coordinator of Information (OCI) in DC as a propagandist using both her past experiences as a reader for pulps and a bohemian writer in Weimar Berlin, sending:

> paper bullets for the fighting men, who were to be twitched by their erotic roots and reminded that their home fire pullulated. Beware the horde of war prisoners and displaced persons— foreign types leaking in through crevices, who might be useful on the home front to spade the wife's garden, to plow, to feed the pigs, but many of whom were strong physical specimens. Could a woman's honor prevail over stark loneliness, dark winters, frost, the cries of the flesh? Did they want to come back from the gory front to find a stranger's chick hatched in their nest?[17]

Petry connects this grim vision of postwar marriage as a site of betrayal, violence, and greed to a dissection of small-town white America, equally steeped in horror. Each theme grows logically from *The Street*, though, as the outlines of the novel appear to suggest, parts of *Country Place* preceded her first novel. In *The Street*, which, like *The Narrows* (1953), also features many aspects of film noir's plots, Lutie Johnson the maid-turned-nightclub-singer murders her bandleader when he suggests she sleep with the white racketeer to get money to pay a lawyer to spring her son from a reformatory for stealing mail. She flees to Chicago on the train, revisiting the same station where she used to commute to her maid's job in Lyme, Connecticut. I have argued in *Black & White & Noir* that the figure of the white femme fatale (Camilo Sheffield in *The Narrows*, for instance) traffics across more than sexual borders; she moves through a dark city, a city populated by racial, sexual, and ethnic others who have access to a mirror world of corruption. This boundary crossing ties the femme fatale to her (often) black maid, who, like Lutie, travels from a chaotic urban zone to a seemingly benign suburbia. Petry astutely used these iconic venues. As a live-in maid at the Chandler's white-picket-fenced house, Lutie witnessed firsthand the corruption and deceit at the heart of white middle-class suburban marriage. Furthering an analysis that connects Petry's writing to film noir, Alan Wald discusses *The Narrows* as another example of the disturbances caused by the returning World War II veteran, whose participation in an unspoken violence opens new avenues for social critique, in this case about the contradictions black soldiers faced fighting Nazism.[18]

Shortly after *The Street* was published, Petry claimed in *Ebony* magazine that her next novel was also "about Negroes and other minorities as well."[19] In fact, she *had* been working on the sketches for characters that would populate *The Narrows* since 1944. Her notebooks are full of descriptions of Abbie Crunch and Mamie Prowther, as well as variations on the many plot twists—including rape, murder, pedophilia, bribery, gambling, and so forth—piling on details over the public outrage Paul Robeson's son's interracial marriage generated in photographs and reports in the local newspapers and radio broadcasts. "This is Enfield, Connecticut—a state which believes it is a modern state," she comments in her journals. However, this novel, like Richard Wright's 1953 *Outsider*, which also touches on an interracial affair situated within a bizarre noir plot, took almost a decade (also like Wright's) for Petry to complete.

In the meantime, likely begun before the war, *Country Place* responds in part to Petry's own feelings about her World War II vet husband's return. (While he was in the army, she lived on his stipend and the $2,400 Houghton Mifflin prize money, which allowed her to quit her job and write full-time.) In a notebook from 1949, while she was reworking *The Narrows* (Petry never followed notebooks chronologically and wrote over old pages, so dating them is difficult), after her daughter Elizabeth was born, Petry bemoans her loss of time for writing. This triggers a memory from the past: "I was writing *Country Place* when he came out of the army and he was annoyed on something, at least he was always complaining[,] that time it was about Brandford [*sic*], he was working on the docks, and before that at a hotel—then afterwards at the [*People's*] *Voice*—but never satisfied, never able to stick with anything, always irritable and fussing—some quality neurotic or infantile."[20] Clearly, Petry's own experiences as an eyewitness to the 1938 Hurricane and to her own returned vet husband "gone queer," fed what became her second novel. Despite her insistence that her next novel was to be about race relations, *Country Place* only touches on "Negroes and other minorities" tangentially, through the prejudices of many of the townspeople, who recoil at the Jewish lawyer and find the interracial romance of the Grambys' servant Neola (perhaps a play on the passing daughter, Peola, in Fannie Hurst's 1934 *Imitation of Life*) and their gardener, a Portegee, as he's called, an abomination.

It seems the novel's central focus on class *ressentiment* and combat-ruined vets required white characters: Petry had asked herself, in another notebook with materials for what would become *The Narrows,* with dates ranging from 1946–51 (that is, while she was finishing *Country Place*), "why is it not possible to do with Negroes in America—that endless fascinating many-faceted subject, what has been done with earlier phases of life by the French—and by Dickens[?]—You have a middle-class society represented by Mrs. Abigail Crunch and Miss Abigail Jackson which has felt the impact of wars, has seen vast changes inside its lifetime . . ."[21] Dissecting layers of bourgeois society could not occur in fictions of black Americans—they were not recognized as inhabiting it. Furthermore, for the most part, African American GIs did not face combat directly; they were proscribed from fighting and served in more auxiliary roles. Their return home was thus not staged as a betrayal by disloyal women. Instead, it was portrayed (in such novels as Gwendolyn Brooks's *Maud Martha* or Petry's *The Narrows* or Wright's *The Outsider,* all 1953, and before these by Chester Himes's *If He Hollers Let Him Go*) as a larger betrayal by white racist America; not the home but the country was the place of treachery after experiencing relative freedom overseas. *Maud Martha* closes with her reading the *Chicago Defender*'s report on lynchings in Georgia and Mississippi in a column side-by-side with one that covers a victory march of returning black vets through the South Side and "(on whose front pages beamed the usual representations of womanly Beauty, pale and pompadoured)."[22]

Like tabloids, film noir, and pulp fiction, *Country Place* required a convoluted plot of murder and greed that, had she not made her characters white, might have been deflected onto what she described as the "social criticism" novel of race and its pathologies.[23] Her two novels focusing on the black community—of Harlem or Monmouth, Connecticut—expressly link contemporary racial tensions to the long reach of slavery, war, and racism into Northern urban spaces. *Country Place,* by contrast, suggests another trajectory of outrage—the traditions of New England's pilgrims—which carries "a vein of violence running under the surface quiet" (7).

It is only one among many by black authors written during the 1940s and 1950s where whiteness codes black rage and alienation through ethnic or queer characters, or in which writers, stung by the sobriquet of "Negro writers" and trying to get out from under the shadow of Richard Wright—and many reviews of *The Street* called it "Black Girl" or "Native Daughter"—sought to broaden, which in publishing meant whiten, their perceived subject matter: Willard Motley's *Knock on Any Door*, James Baldwin's *Giovanni's Room*, and Zora Neale Hurston's *Seraph on the Suwanee*. Wright himself followed suit with *Savage Holiday*. At the same time, white and black novelists, such as Worth Tuttle Hedden (*The Other Room*), Lillian Smith (*Strange Fruit*), Chester Himes (*Pinktoes*), and William Gardner Smith (*Last of the Conquerors*), were anatomizing racism through explorations of interracial sex and its attendant violence; marketed as salacious with crossover potential, they became appropriate for pulp paperbacks, which assumed a minimum of 150,000 copies in sales.

Victor Weybright, publisher of New American Library, began his publishing career at *Survey Graphic*, which had published Alain Locke's "Harlem: Mecca of the New Negro," the germ of his groundbreaking 1925 anthology, *The New Negro*. As a contributor to the Urban League and NAACP, Weybright pushed for paperback distribution in African American neighborhoods to cultivate new audiences. His reprints of black authors, such as Alain Locke, as well as his commitment to publishing Farrell, Gore Vidal, and Norman Mailer, established NAL as a progressive press—interested in combating racial prejudice. As Weybright noted in his 1952 bid to Louis Armstrong for rights to his autobiography, *Satchmo*:

> We have one other unique asset . . . our outstanding position in the field of literature by Negroes and about the Negro in America. Five years ago, with the publication of James Weldon Johnson's *Autobiography of an Ex-colored Man*, we launched a

special effort to distribute our books, and especially those of
racial interest, in the Negro communities of American cities ...
We publish such books as *The Street*, books by Richard Wright,
Willard Motley, Chester Himes, and such books as *Strange
Fruit*, and encourage major wholesalers to add book specialists
to their staff for Harlem, South Chicago and the colored sections of scores of cities, North and South.[24]

Opening this work to new markets was not merely an altruistic
move; it was a financial one too. But the big moneymaking author
for NAL was Mickey Spillane, "a world celebrity ... tagged by Max
Lerner as the exponent of sex and sadism," whose popular quasi-
fascist lurid and misogynist detective stories supported the other
literary aspirations of the press. To combat this image, Weybright
"publicized the fact that Mickey Spillane was required reading at
William and Mary College in a course on existentialism."[25] Not
only were crime stories vehicles to unravel philosophy, because
crime plots enable violence to enter the narrative space of domestic
fiction, they reveal how social relations were altered in the immediate postwar era and further the paperback's demotics of reading.

By linking leftist and black authors to Spillane through stan-
dardized formats and similar cover art, NAL's works anticipate
a new postwar civil rights landscape, in some ways helping make
Brown v. Board of Education of Topeka, Kansas, the Montgomery
Bus Boycott, and their aftermath legible to a largely white working-
class readership through detailed chartings of cross-race intimacy.
They bring civil rights into popular cultural sites, much as film noir
coded changing racial and class relations through diabolical women
or, as Truman Capote's *Other Voices, Other Rooms* and Gore Vidal's
City and the Pillar popularized male homosexual desire, through
pulp. Always repressed within American popular forms, trauma is
deflected—from race to class and from both onto gender and sex.
Domesticity serves as the one sanctioned site in which political

tensions, renamed "private life," can be expressed and fought out—
often with murderous ends.

Furthermore, following the 1934 release by Bennett Cerf of
the first American edition of James Joyce's *Ulysses*, authors, such as
Petry, who listed Joyce as one of her three most-admired writers,
democratized the episodic, interiorized mode of narration, swerving from inside one character's stream of consciousness to another's
diary entries, for a mass audience. Making accessible a popular high
modernism through the mechanisms of pulp, these works further
shrink the already demotic Leopold Bloom to fit into American
pockets. Thus the crime and sex novels of pulp not only glimpsed
a political space where racial and class antagonisms could be expressed, they sought to do so as modernist literature—a pedagogic
project that was formal as well as thematic. As Raymond Chandler
put it, "All I wanted to do when I began writing was to play with a
fascinating new language, to see what it could do as a means of expression which might remain on the level of unintellectual thinking
and yet acquire the power to say things which are usually only said
with a literary air."[26]

As should be clear by now, pulp works to unravel realism
through the hyperreal immediacy of voices speaking vernacular.
Vera Caspary's *Laura* (1942) proceeds to uncover the heroine's
murder through chapters written in varying styles by a number of
characters—her patron Waldo Lydecker's columns and journals,
the investigating detective Mark McPherson's police report, Laura's
diaries, and her maid's recollections. In Kenneth Fearing's *The Big
Clock*, each chapter recounts a different character's point of view.
The fragmentary radio broadcasts, trial transcripts, and magazine
articles offer fragmentary memories of the many survivors of the
revolution in his earlier 1942 novel, *Clark Gifford's Body*. Edmund
Wilson's 1946 *Memoirs of Hecate County* and Mary McCarthy's
The Company She Keeps (1942) interlink stories from a single
consciousness: Wilson's "I" and McCarthy's "Margaret Sargent"

are both participants and observers of the many others with whom they drink, have sex, marry, argue, and divorce. These skillful moves from high to pulp modernism appeared more successful than Petry's efforts, however. One British reviewer of *The Narrows* found it "rather as though Dickens should try to write as Virginia Woolf."[27]

Like the shifting narrative technique of Michael Curtiz's *Mildred Pierce* (1945), or the multiple narrative and visual frames of classic film noirs like *Out of the Past* (1947), these popular works investigate desire and destruction through fragments and repetition, using corny devices such as reporters following stories, detectives filing reports, or cabbies picking up fares. In her notes for *The Narrows*, Petry plays with having Camilo study photography with photojournalist Jubine—who "believed that he could record the history of man in the 20th century just by taking pictures of the River Pye"—to explain why she too is covering the waterfront. Petry's reliance on a cabbie and a druggist—snoops (as she calls Jubine, the tabloid photojournalist of *The Narrows* modeled on *PM*'s in-house photographer Weegee),[28] ever-present in film noir as ciphers who can move through the city (taxi drivers and journalists) or dispense illegal substances—echo clichés from cinema: "While I stood there a car went by; its headlights made the black macadam road gleam . . . totally dark [except for the houselights] pinpricks obscured by driving rain" (74).

Like cinema, *Country Place* relies on the visual and narrative device of the frame: life viewed through mirrors and windowpanes. Doc frames himself as a "medium kind of man" (5)—he's middling in height, weight, age, intelligence—but he is also a medium: through him we learn the "truth," but, warning of "his prejudice against women," he reminds "truth has many sides" (7). Later he reframes "Weasel's words [which] had evoked a picture of raw hurt and pain and secret furtive love. Now he was putting a frame around it—a frame of laughter" (69). Following the obsessive return and replication of desires and crimes in film noir, framed so often through rain-soaked windshields, bevel-edged mirrors, and the slats of partially drawn Venetian blinds, and overheard or observed through optical and sonic recording devices, the Weasel watches his fares through his mirror, as Doc watches the town commons through his store window, each recounting others' words, thoughts, and deeds: watching and repetition—essential to the process of gossip—and to the labor of fiction writing. Critic Hilary Holladay notes that in *Country Place,* the "narrators and characters repeatedly encircle and encroach on each other's territory . . . telling and retelling . . . expanding circles of narrative" (66, 69).

Petry's Houghton Mifflin Literary Fellowship–winning novel, *The Street,* had elicited consternation among some African American critics, such as *The Crisis*'s James W. Ivey, for its brutal portrayal of Harlem's 116th Street, as a "seething cesspool of sluts, pimps, juvenile delinquents, and clucks . . . worthless as a picture of Harlem though interesting as a revelation of Mrs. Petry" (though one might note that Lyme, with its adultery, racism, suicide, and extortions hardly fares any better).[29] Almost a decade later, the reviewer for *The Sign* asks, "Why does she concentrate all of our attention on the sex life of the people?" Petry's ten years of experiences as a reporter for the *Amsterdam News,* and the *People's Voice* and *PM,* and as a social worker in the public school system, working in a school on the corner of 116th Street and Knickerbocker Avenue, led to her view of the constrictions of racism as spatialized: the modern lynch mob was the ghetto. Readers, especially black working-class women readers, grasped Petry's point (figure 5.2).

Married to a purported pulp mystery story writer, George D. Petry, her first publication (under the pseudonym Arnold Petri [and her clues send us to her pharmacy and chemistry classes]) was the mystery story "Marie of the Cabin Club," published in Baltimore's *Afro-American.*[30] An avid movie fan and admirer of Richard Wright, Theodore Dreiser, and James Joyce, the former pharmacist from Old Saybrook, daughter of the town druggist to whom the book was also dedicated ("He was 'Doc,'" an interviewer remarked, to which Petry replied, "Yes. Except that my father was black. 'Doc' of *Country Place* was white"), and fourth-generation New Englander, Petry's vision was shaped by her "definite progressive" politics, as she noted to *Ebony*, her work and the exposure to racial violence it provided, and her "planned reading in psychology and psychiatry."[31] Like Wright, she got the idea for her first novel from a newspaper clipping, "a brief item about a janitor in a Harlem tenement who had been arrested for teaching an eight-year-old boy to steal" and her third from an item about an elderly white woman killing a black man.[32] With her long-standing attention to tabloid news, a husband away in the army, and an acute knowledge of the discordance between the facade of American pastoralism and the brutality of its urban jungle, it isn't surprising that Petry chose to foreground the "faintly cheap horrors and contrivances" reminiscent of "the great Victorians or the tawdry moderns."[33]

The years 1946–47, after all, were the same years Hollywood produced such noirs as *The Big Sleep*, *Black Angel*, *The Blue Dahlia*, *Fallen Angel*, *The Killers* (1946), and *Born to Kill*, *Dead Reckoning*, *Fall Guy*, *Framed*, *Kiss of Death*, *Nightmare Alley*, and *Out of the Past* (1947). The exploding postwar publishing world brought out suspense novels, such as Elisabeth Sanxay Holding's *The Blank Wall*, Kenneth Fearing's *The Big Clock*, Dorothy B. Hughes's *In a Lonely Place*, and hundreds more. Bantam alone, one of dozens of paperback publishers churning out millions of books during the immediate postwar boom, which ended paper shortages, published eight titles a month in the mid-1940s. How could she not go for cheap and tawdry?

Initially imagining herself a short story writer, Petry wrote three "adult" novels during the heyday of film noir and paperbacks, Hollywood's B movies featuring the three Ds—death, depravity, and determinism—and pulp novels spreading the three Ss: sex, sin, and smoking guns. In many ways, her novels retranslated cinematic

Figure 5.2 Checking out *The Street*. Laundry Workers Union, undated. Photographer unknown, in Howard Gotlieb Archival Research Center at Boston University.

trash—already a translation of literary pulp—into narrative form. Like film noir, they encode an underworld geography of pulp modernism: they dwell on murder, violence, adultery, and prostitution, as the entire gamut of postwar anxieties about nuclear war, anticolonialism, holocaust, and racism get deflected mechanistically onto the streets of American cities and from there retreat into the bedrooms of the American home. Women on the move—WOW—trafficked back and forth across racial and class borders before settling into a testy motherhood (plate 3). But could these homebodies be trusted?

By the mid-1940s, the labor of pulp fiction writers, editors, and even readers was already a stock trope for the degradation of literature and triumph of the culture industry—and more broadly for the rise of "White Collar," the "Man in the Gray Flannel Suit," and other clichés of middle management. The pulp world was one of sex-crazed, frustrated women and nebbishy, emasculated men who, like James Thurber's Walter Mitty, suffered henpecked lives of dull repetitiveness, escaped only by recourse to fantasizing pulp adventure plots. Rollo (who in the film became Holly) Martins, in Graham Greene's screenplay for *The Third Man*, is a feminized writer of pulp Westerns. Asked to lecture on modern novels at the British Cultural Reeducation Section, he's interrogated about "the stream of consciousness" and what he thinks of James Joyce and *Ulysses*. (He replies that he doesn't read Greek and he's only influenced by Zane Grey.)[34] But pulp writers were also proud of their work ethic; they were producers who didn't write to order. Frank Gruber, a prolific contributor to *Black Mask* and other pulps from 1927 to 1967, criticized Joseph T. Shaw, editor of *Black Mask*, for trying to "Hammettize the magazine after the success of *The Maltese Falcon*." He expounds with great precision on the labor entailed in writing popular material:

I have in my writing lifetime published roughly four hundred stories. I have written fifty-three novels and I have turned out sixty-five feature motion picture screenplays . . . and perhaps a hundred television scripts.

I have written at least a hundred and fifty articles.

I have written western stories, mysteries, fantasy and science fiction, I have produced love stories and spicy stories. I have turned out reams of Sunday School stories . . . I have written perhaps as much as any living American writer.

This catalog indicates Gruber's generic versatility, and yet he takes pains to stress that "only the writer can write his story."[35]

Describing her job "reading for a pulp-magazine outfit," Herbst explained the links forging the new American modernism she sees already formed in 1927, "A Year of Disgrace," an industrial production line of "prim" writers, editors "reeking with gin," and a "soap opera"–voiced Katherine Mansfield wannabe who read manuscripts: "And as if to prove her claim that she could write, she might drift into a descriptive passage, filled with periods and semicolons, dashes and pauses, and in which she offered herself as a crucified relic of love with the flourish of Brutus extolling the death of Caesar."[36] This image of the pulp machine destroying men and art took comically sinister form in Kenneth Fearing's spoof *roman noir*—made into the classic Ray Milland film, *The Big Clock*. Based on his years of working at Time Inc., Fearing savaged the machinery of pulp as editor George, married to Georgette and father of Georgia, literally lives and works inside the Big Clock, Janoth Enterprises' repetitive mechanics of reproduction of time and life.[37]

> *Newsways, Commerce, Crimeways, Personalities, The Sexes, Fashions, Futureways*, the whole organization was full and overrunning with frustrated ex-artists, scientists, farmers, writers, explorers, poets, lawyers, doctors, musicians, all of whom spent their lives conforming, instead. And conforming to what? To a sort of overgrown, aimless, haphazard stenciling apparatus that kept them running to psychoanalysts, sent them to insane asylums, gave them high blood pressure, stomach ulcers, killed them off with cerebral hemorrhages and heart failure, sometimes suicide. Why should I pay still more tribute to this fatal machine? It would be easier and simpler to get squashed stripping its gears than to be crushed helping it along.[38]

In the films based on these novels and stories, Hollywood had used the expanding pulp industry to deride its own studio system, collapsing after television competed with both pulp fiction and the movies as popular mass entertainment.

Connecting pulp with suburban claustrophobia, these films find in pulps' architects a desire to escape the clock into a bohemian world of either avant-garde art (*Big Clock*), comic book superhero, space travel–induced stupor (*Artists and Models*), extramarital sex (*Seven Year Itch*) or a lost era of swashbuckling romance (*Walter Mitty*). But if pulp writers appear as exemplars of the clockwork regimentation of capitalist productivity, the clock stood for escape—from social work and other jobs—for Petry, who went on, in the late 1950s, to become "the first woman [by which I think is meant black woman] scriptwriter on the West Coast for Columbia Pictures," according to the *Baltimore Afro-American*.[39]

Petry wrote by the clock, recalling that while her husband was away at war, she survived modestly on his allotment and her prize money, thus she wanted to "maintain a more or less constant rate of production." With the "clock as a taskmaster, . . . the hands of the clock shamed me into writing," she remembered in her "Great Secret." The culture industry generating an industry of culture: if Fearing imagined the Big Clock superintending the spaces of routinized labor, Petry needed one to keep up her "rate of production"; having finished her first novel, she immediately set to work on the second one, *Country Place*, "like the shoemaker at work on his next pair of shoes."[40] With her meager allowance, she understood literary production as labor, as production—as a job—war work. Her accounts of expenses and earnings for a Friday in October 1942, for instance, read as follows:

Guild dues $1.75
New republic (3 mo) $1.00
Tin .15
Get well cards .20
Rent 18.00
Ink .10
Notebook .10
Picture frame .30
Apples .14
Melon .15

Celery .10

Shopping bag .02

Carfare .05

These coincide with her detailed notes drawn from a handbook on writing on trimming "half the ands" and gaining a "general increase in sensitiveness" by "reading aloud of noble prose and poetry" and "writing of verse," as well as her lists of books on economics, psychology, and culture to be studied, notes for characterizations, lists of titles, lyrics of racist nursery rhymes, lists of signs glimpsed in shop windows, a description of a cat fight observed on Riverside Drive, the smells of Central Park Zoo, and snippets of conversation overheard on the bus.[41]

This slippage between her intellectual investment in literary craft, gleaned from reading and studying Trollope, Dreiser, Wright, and Joyce, and her financial sense that fiction must be churned out by the clock on a deadline, links her work to so many other pulp paperback novels that sought to connect demotic reading across an array of authors. It is also part of the "scandalous" nature of her work—work she gave up, it appears, shortly after the birth of her only child in 1949 when she turned to writing children's and young adult books and returned to "a handsome white house with green shutters on the old Boston Post Road in Old Saybrook, Connecticut," where she was still working away like clockwork, it seems, but with less apparent rage: "She polishes words and she polishes silver: her collection of old silver is full of beautiful things, but they all require polishing!" says her biography at the end of *Harriet Tubman: Conductor on the Underground Railroad* (1955). These young adult biographies—on Tubman and *Tituba of Salem Village* (1964), strong, brave, rebellious, even scandalous, and, in mid-1950s and 1960s America, unknown black women—may have developed out of her frustration as a "novelist" and as the family breadwinner who must still do housework: "A thousand-page book wins a[n] MCM prize, B.O.M. [Book-of-the-Month Club] selection—and probably makes the author a half a million dollars—nothing happens to *Country Place*—in fact the boys let you off lightly with that one— would like beds made," she commented in her notebooks. Her children's biographies may be seen as a defiance of the celebration of the mid-1950s white woman embodied by platinum blond Marilyn Monroe, whose image infected even Petry's own books—or at least its covers (plate 15, *top*).[42]

Polishing that silver may have been just a ploy, just as Marie Curie became a shy Polish girl when her daughter's biography got pulped; Petry's is seething with righteous anger. Despite front-page coverage in Houghton Mifflin's 1947 catalog and wide reviews—some calling it a "razor sharp" slice of life about a GI and his faithless wife—she was still supposed to make the beds for the "infantile" guy. It's as if, now a suburban mother herself, she was embarrassed by her sympathy for the outrageous white and black women she creates in her novels. (In a journal entry from 1946, she writes herself notes on the difficulty of finding a place to breast-feed in the United States and wonders what would happen if a woman nursed a baby on the subway.)[43] She seems to be anticipating the "problem without a name" that Betty Friedan would announce almost a generation later.

While both Lil and Glory—the one frigid, the other hot, according to Ed—cheat on their husbands, looking for passion, escaping boredom, seeking money or a name, Petry does not really condemn them, nor does she condemn Lutie as a murderer, or for her escaping and abandoning her son to the authorities. Despite the dire consequences for black boys in the judicial system, her actions are perfectly logical within the sexual and racial codes of *The Street*. Even Camilo's slumming becomes a true passion; the narrative turns against her only after her sensational accusation of rape against Link and her exposure as a drunk driver through Jubine's tabloid photographs. Glory and Lil's stories, narrated by an avowed misogynist and his ferretlike sidekick, might be viewed differently had they been able to assert some narrative control as have Lutie or even Mamie Prowther in *The Narrows*. And this, of course, is part of Petry's strategy as a student of pulp conventions: blonds are dumb but devious. At least Glory might have had something to say for herself; she, who never gets the mother-love she deserves from Lil, "hard-boiled" Lil, only to be abandoned by her new husband when war breaks out, left living with in-laws (190). She—a "Lana Turner wasted in this town" (56)—is looking for love in all the wrong places. This sense of war's displacement of both men's and women's desires is the driving force in the 1946 film *The Best Years of Our Lives*, which finds echoes in *Country Place*.

Like Lutie, smitten by the lyrics of "Darlin'" and taken in by the smooth Boots, she might be excused for responding to Ed's sexual obsessions; he keeps nude pictures of her and her mother hidden in his wallet. She's been home with him watching "Ingrid Bergmann [*sic*] and Cary Grant in that last picture—or was it Jennifer Jones?" (59). This Gloria, and she's one of many—Gloria Grahame of the smashed face in too many 1940s and '50s film noirs, the damaged 1930s Glorias of *Butterfield 8* and *They Shoot Horses, Don't They?* Gloria—G-L-O-R-I-A!!! straight down to Patti Smith channeling a history of pissed-off Madonnas—is both siren and victim. Johnnie never challenges her gossiped reports of his wife beating; after all, he *had* raped her on his first night back. So he never discloses what he knows of her and Ed, preferring to slip away from her "net," drawn away from watching *his* Lana Turner in *this* country place to the art and action of city streets.

Reversing Johnnie's path to the noir city, Petry returned with her husband to her natal town, buying an eighteenth-century captain's house with a view of the Long Island Sound and a white picket fence to raise a daughter in a town in which she grew up feeling isolated. Cloaking her autobiography in the clichés of 1940s popular culture—haywire vets, small-town Lana Turners (who would play the uptight Constance MacKenzie in the film of *Peyton Place*), village gossips—Petry literally whitewashed her dark places. Fascinated by the reticence of New Englanders, especially middle-class New England blacks such as herself, Petry found she could reveal some of her own troubles with her country, her place, and her life as a black woman writing in the mid-twentieth century, through a far-fetched plot derived from various mass-media sources.

In 1970, exploitation film director Stephanie Rothman found that because her cheap B movies were "under the radar, yet widely popular" and spoke to an audience far more intelligent than big studios assumed, she could insert any content she liked as long as she included plenty of scenes of beautiful women (and men) taking off their clothes in the first reel.[44] From then on, she was relatively free to shape the story anyway she liked. B movies and pulp fiction, as popular forms floating under the radar, provide a covert opening for writers to broach socially taboo topics—interracial sex, homosexuality, abortion—often through unconventional narrative forms. Petry repeatedly claimed that "the weather" was the inspiration for *Country Place,* because shortly before decamping Connecticut for New York to marry George Petry, she observed the devastation the hurricane caused Old Saybrook. She cobbled her plots "from items in newspapers, from the weather, from conversations, from gossip."[45] Her list resonates with Gertrude Stein's 1936 inquiry into American writing: "And so we come to what is really what we write what we write is really a crime story." Stein distinguished between "human mind," which excites immigrants to America to write letters home full of "the weather and money," and "human nature," which is all about "sex and jealousy."[46] Like old newspapers full of yesterday's "events" and so passé the next day, nobody can write home about sex, jealousy, crime, or the news; that is the province of "writing." Petry's almost forgotten second novel melded "the weather" with "sex and jealousy"—human mind *and* human nature—allowing this "private person" a form.[47] Petry took a page from Stein and borrowed from "what is really what we write . . . a crime story," to write (about) home—the public space of her father's country pharmacy and the private place of her husband's unsettled return. She kept it well hidden, but like a purloined letter, in plain sight, like the mirror Doc left unsold on his counter "because the customers, male and female alike, enjoy admiring their faces in it" (190). Or so the story goes.

CHAPTER 6

Señor Borges Wins! Ellery Queen's Garden

Suburb of Gardens

> For years I believed I had grown up in a suburb of Buenos Aires, a suburb of dangerous streets and showy sunsets. The truth is that I grew up in a garden, behind a fence of iron palings, and in a library of endless English books.
>
> —Norman Thomas di Giovanni, *In Memory of Borges*

A well-known Argentine writer, whose first poems dwelled on his love of the violent backstreets of his native Palermo neighborhood of this port city, and whose passion included murder mysteries played out on the silver screen, was, in the words of one of his many editors, "a lifelong movie fan." A noted compiler of imaginary archival works, influenced greatly by the imaginary world of surfaces and planes of light and dark depicted by Josef von Sternberg in his early Hollywood explorations of desire and crime, Jorge Luis Borges was first published in English translation in the August 1948 issue of *Ellery Queen's Mystery Magazine* (*EQMM*). "Begun in 1941," the magazine was known "as a 'high-class' pulp venture."[1] Critic, detective story writer, and translator, Anthony Boucher urged Señor Borges, as he became known among detective fiction fans, to enter the magazine's Third Annual Detective Short Story Contest. He won, of course.[2] "The Garden of Forking Paths" joined works by Anton Chekhov, Ferenc Molnar, Karel Capek, and Gabriele D'Annunzio, not to mention the first English translation of a Georges Simenon story and a creepy tale by Cornell Woolrich, in the United Nations issue. The international scope of the submissions suggested to the editors of *EQMM* that, "while we have a long way to go politically, the planet Earth is truly One World detective-storywise."

In his many inventions of fake documents, reports, manuscripts, and memoirs, Borges contributed to pulp modernism, the demotic vernacular form of dark, antifascist surrealism emerging in the Americas during the 1930s and 1940s. First appearing in Spanish in the collection of the same name, "The Garden of Forking Paths" had three English-language translations, appearing in 1948 as a stand-alone story, in the 1962 *Ficciones* and in the 1998 edition of *Collected Fictions*. The history of this text connects Borges's theories and practices of spatial temporality, expressed through translation and documentation, to film noirs and pulp fictions by North American writers and film artists, and to the efforts by European theorists and artists to understand total war and mass death in the aftermath of World War II.

Pulp modernism and the demotic reading it engendered limned a future filled with the crush of frightening political and economic disruptions through familiar tales of seedy violence and tawdry sex found every day in the news. Translating political theory into domestic melodrama, pulp modernist works brought home the vast social chaos unleashed by the world wars and the Depression. Borges's prescient writings—gleaned by citing documentary artifacts too strange to be invented, which he observed on his daily walks around his noir city—refashioned geography and temporality into evidence in much the same way as had 1940s B movies based on the 1930s plot-driven, hard-boiled pulp fiction. These films and writings, often by left-wing émigrés and their offspring, also rely on a series of techniques indebted to labyrinthine fact-finding and recording (the police report, the journalist's notes, the case study, the diary, and the taped conversation) and baroque memory (the confession, the voice-over, and the Dictaphone).

Anticipating the role of mass media in creating rather than reporting events, Borges's soon-to-be-murdered victim became the source of the foreign spy's message. As the Sinologist Stephen Corbie/Albert (this character has different names in different versions of the story) observes just before his murder, silence and obfuscation—omission and periphrasis—also speak: a book (language) can be a labyrinth (space). "The Garden of Forking Paths" posits many possible futures, all coincident; it dubs space with time through narrative, so when an event becomes a news item and *read* about in the daily papers, where distance routinely collapses over one's morning coffee, the reader enters the plot. Its logic of the embellished anecdote, Borges's forte, overrides the extended characterization of the novel. As Borges reiterates, who needs to slog through the whole opus when his gestural summation will do nicely? In this statement, Borges was characteristically humble: knowing his own limitations, he disburdens the reader, ultimately putting into question any project such as this one, of interpretation.

The act of reading, of acute literary analysis, like that undertaken by Corbie/Albert, validates itself as a form of detection, a search for the gaps or the metaphors within and behind the story. The reader deciphers the riddle, the unspoken, the excised. Censorship in the form of too few or too many words is Freud's explanation for the unconscious process of repression. Additions or deletions, superscription and overwriting form an interlinked system that sustains neuroses.[3] What remains is revealing. But absence too is evidence. Fabricating a memory of dangerous streets and showy sunsets, a lurid scene of violence and excess, Borges charted a world of cardsharps and tango dancers, of knife fights staged on the theater of empty street corners. Instead, walled in within a garden by an iron fence, Borges spent a childhood immersed in another language, that of his grandmother, first reading Cervantes in English. A garden, a fence, a library: the enclosed garden of the labyrinth; the library and its endless books as textual maze, a living labyrinth. Detecting and elaborating this chiasmus would become Borges's lifetime project. Connecting space to time through narrative devices, all already noted, coded, and exploded in one of his earliest stories—the first to appear in his first reading language, English. In 1983, on the occasion of the first Borges lecture sponsored by the Anglo-Argentine Society of London, Borges sent out this thread to his British audience: a fenced garden and a library of endless English books—books without end, or an infinite library? In an enclosed landscape with a "mythical" city filled with a world of languages rendered into English, the sun never sets on the British Empire, even if in the Palermo neighborhood he lived in, filled with streets named Thames (pronounced Thomas), he gloried in its exuberant sunsets and "a bar, shelter of criminals." Elaborating, synecdochically, the part for the whole, he claimed: "My memory of the garden . . . your narrow spaces became a whole geography."[4]

Tale of Gardens

We must first of all decide what is meant by the ambiguous phrase "the end of an analysis."[5]

He believed in an infinite series of Time, in a waxing, dizzying web of times, divergent, convergent, and parallel.[6]

Hard to believe Buenos Aires had any beginning.
I feel it to be as eternal as air and water.[7]

The end of analysis—conclusion and goal—why get there? What's the solution to this riddle? Let's begin with the beginning of the tale: a reference to a reference book by a noted military historian, augmented with an editor's comments about the "unexpected light" thrown on this account by a fragmentary document—the confession of the criminal. On "page 242" of his history, Liddell Hart remarks about the inconsequential five-day delay of an Allied offensive because of torrential rains, notes the framing narrator of "Garden." Nobody writes anything in letters except about the weather, commented Gertrude Stein in *The Geographical History of America*, speaking of immigrant letters home, but apparently this was true in military communications as well. The documentary evidence consulted by social historians to divine the daily lives of everyday people offers little more than weather reports mimicking news in the local paper. Weather is constant yet, at least in some parts of the world—England among them—ever changing. But there is always more to the story than the weather, and the statement of a former English professor teaching in a German academy in the interior of China offers this supplement. Borges later noted that the "all-powerful malicious society, which before the war was China and now is the Gestapo or the international spies of the Third Reich," is part of a conventionalized Hollywood plot "that has surprised every spectator hundreds of times."[8] His story imbricates these two loci of pulp intrigue in the person of a Chinese English professor working as a German spy.

"A very interesting recent book is Liddell Hart's book on the real war, the First World War," Borges said about the writing of history in a lecture at the Royal Society of Arts, London, on 5 October 1983.[9] Surely he knew that for Londoners forty-three years after the Blitz commenced on September 7, the second war was also a "real war," perhaps *the* real war. Liddell Hart's 1930 book, *The Real War, 1914–18*, an enlarged edition published in 1934 as *A History of the World War, 1914–1918* (to which Borges refers in "The Garden of

Forking Paths") and reprinted in 1970 as *History of the First World War*, provides the conceit for Borges's 1941–42 story of espionage and coded messages delivered by means of murder, and its reporting of fantastic labyrinthine books and multilingual translators. Borges's lecture occurred on the heels of the 1982 Falklands War (Guerra de las Malvinas) between Great Britain and Argentina, which sundered forever whatever Anglophilia lurked among most of Argentina's populace. This slippage of time, "a very interesting recent book"—more than fifty years old and renamed twice to replace "real" with "world"—suggests the temporal mapping that is at the heart of the labyrinthine novel, *The Garden of Forking Paths*. Is this change an expansion or a contraction, from "real" to "world"? Which is the larger container, if size matters in graphing infinities? A real war, a world war—yes, the one that produced Borges's generation of surrealist writers and Freud's sufferers of shock; the one that, along with Spain's civil war, set so many artists and writers of the 1930s, from Pablo Picasso to Georges Bataille, from Diego Rivera to Man Ray, tracking the bull through his maze as they illustrated the surrealist journal *Minotaure*.

Considering that Borges thought Adolf Hitler was a buffoon who desired to lose the war that he had started, perhaps the "real" "world" war was actually the one still clinging to nineteenth-century—even eighteenth-century, the period of his favorite typeface—nationalist conceits, one for which a provincial colony could still conceivably mobilize, rather than become the refuge of war criminals and exiles. Or perhaps World War I was the real war because it was the war to shatter all those grand illusions, long since destroyed by the time the next one came around. In any case, Borges's conjunction of these three wars—the setting of "The Garden of Forking Paths" (1916 [World War I]), its first publication date (1941, or was it 1942? [World War II], both dates appear in literary histories), its first English publication date in the month of Borges's birth and the birth of the institution that supposedly would rid the world of war (1948 [United Nations]), and his reference to Hart's "recent" history in the wake of another minor and localized postcolonial war (1982 [Falklands/Malvinas])—curiously triangulates England, Germany, and Argentina (and China, which precedes Germany as a source of diabolic plots, and by way of its ending and the story's primary narrator, one nation named for a precious metal, silver; another, at least in the English language, for fine porcelain).

The labyrinthine novel by the Chinese provincial governor Ts'ui Pen, *The Garden of Forking Paths*, which gives Borges's story its title, written by an "illustrious ancestor" of the captured spy and deciphered by the scholarly man he endeavors to kill, serves as library, atlas, and maze. Here, truly, the garden and the library of endless books coalesce. Stephen Corbie/Albert, English barbarian, former missionary turned Sinologist, discovers a fragment of a letter in Ts'ui Pen's "renowned calligraphy" with the following bequeathal: *I leave to several futures (not to all) my garden of forking paths.* Much as the Aleph residing in the basement of Carlos Argentino Daneri's house on Calle Garay opens all space, the entire earth for view, enabling the descendant of Italian immigrant Daneri to compose his monumental poem, the narrative of *Garden* opens all futures. The Aleph renders multidimensional space—"the place where, without any possible confusion, all the places in the world are found, seen from every angle"—perceptible.[10] The *Garden* annihilates time. Resurrecting all temporalities by refusing to choose one plot over any other—neither cyclical nor circular, not an endless mirroring, nor a mise en abyme, but rather the transubstantiation of space and time, of language and structure, it is simply a novel: a form that can accommodate anything tossed into it, according to Mikhail Bakhtin, but that must always return to the search for lost time, because the eye moves across the page and the hand turns them over in sequence, and the reader is immersed in these actions. Like the knife, narrative is deadly and double-sided, at once blunt and sharp, twinned, as the dreamer's dream is redreamed by reading. All this, as Borges well knew, was the essence of pulp's demotic appeal.

Recent and real—several futures, not all—the times and places of war collapse, encompassing the entire twentieth-century world: the scope of Borges's life, born as he was in 1899, who lived and traveled throughout the West, conversing and reading its many languages despite residing "in the suburbs of the world. A remote spot/. . .either north or east or south." Borges's city, Buenos Aires, was a center on the periphery, eccentric, seemingly anywhere but the West. In his evocations of his boyhood, Buenos Aires became a place at once lost to and suffused with time. It pulsed with the sleepiness of an anxious distance, creating a place out of time. Behind the walls within this oxymoron—a decentered place, an atemporal moment—was his city full "of streets with names from the past," memory tracing a "crumbled path" ("The Cyclical Night," PA, 155). Its imagined leavings recur in the cycles of night and day. Disappearances become present; emptiness fills time and space as reading, dreaming and writing cannot be sundered. Everything figures into several futures. That's pulping—it makes use of waste, repurposes it.

Carlos Argentino's Aleph, located in the basement of a demolished house on a Buenos Aires street, became the source for his prizewinning volume of verse, *Argentino Extracts*, silver nuggets pilfered from around the earth, stored near a trunk in the basement of a house in the nation for which the fictional author was named, a madman, double and defeater of narrator Borges, whose own book—deliciously titled *The Cards of the Cardsharp*—gets not a single vote for the National Prize for Literature (1943). Of course, the nonfictional author Borges's own book, *The Garden of Forking Paths*, had lost the previous year, initiating the first journal issue dedicated to Jorge Luis Borges—Victoria Ocampo's *Sur*. Recent and real—to which we must add repeating.

Dubbed Poetry

> Summary and Recapitulation: "The part of this study which
> follows cannot be given to the public without extensive explana-
> tions and apologies. For it is nothing other than a faithful (and
> often word-for-word) repetition of the first part . . ."[11]

This is an account of dubbing, of the monstrous overlay of another's voice onto one body. "I, a Jew," declares Borges, knowing full well he cannot find the evidence to support his fantasy or refute the outrageous defamation invented by fascists in 1934. But even Moses was an Egyptian, or so that purveyor of the Jewish Science determined the same year.[12] And Borges himself, despite his many antifascist writings during the war, would, after the war, ventriloquize a soliloquy of "the Platonic idea of a Nazi" in "Deutsches Requiem" and then support the dictatorship that overthrew Juan Perón. That "ideal Nazi," "the Platonic idea of a Nazi," was a fantasy, a literary construct, because "no Nazi was ever like that, because they were full of self-pity."[13] Otto Dietrich zur Linde mimics the persona of the star—perhaps the blue angel—who is replaced by a body double, or whose voice is dubbed. For the postwar film noir about Nazi plots set in Argentina, the love goddess herself, whose singing was dubbed by Anita Ellis for her most notorious role as femme fatale Gilda, was refashioned from Spanish dancing chorine Rita Cansino into all-American icon Rita Hayworth, her pinup gracing the nose of an atom bomb–loaded B-29.[14]

The writer/editor/character Ellery Queen, invention of two cousins from Brooklyn, first put Borges into American print by publishing Anthony Boucher's translation of "The Garden of Forking Paths," in celebration of international peace and goodwill in the special United Nations issue of August 1948. As he listens to the story of his own brilliant and metaphysical kin, an "invisible, intangible pullulation" surrounds the spy Dr. Yu, who kills Stephen

Corbie (in one version; in other versions Stephen Albert), in the line of his dishonorable duty. It's dirty work, passing secrets by way of murder, leaving still more traces to be read later, but not as dirty as inspecting rabbits and poultry for the government of a dictator, as Perón would have liked Borges to do had he taken up his promotion from third assistant who cataloged books in some obscure suburban branch library when Perón took over Argentina in 1946. All wars come full circle—recent, real, repeating: "when Rome is dust, the Minotaur will groan / one more in the endless dark of its stinking palace" ("The Cyclical Night," *PA*, 155).

Why does the name of the victim—whose identity leads to destruction—change from one Anthony's translation (Boucher's) to another's translation (Kerrigan's) of it in *Ficciones*, that second one retained in the third version by Andrew Hurley, yet another "A," for author? What was Borges up to with this insignificant revision? Corbie is almost Corgie—a Welsh town—or perhaps a dog's pedigree? Not English enough, perhaps. Albert, the imperial queen Victoria's husband—so clearly English, or an homage to *Sur*'s editor, whom André Malraux called "the Empress of the Pampas,"[15] and to whom "The Garden of Forking Paths" is dedicated, or to the author/editor/detective Ellery Queen, who first brought this writer-from-the-pampas' prose to English? Was Albert closer to the Aleph than Corbie, who might almost be Edwin Arlington Robinson's "Richard Cory"? Or was this revision an oblique nod to the keeper of the labyrinth, publisher of *Minotaure*, Albert Skira? This authorial instability, which critic Jorge Hernández Martín suggests is typical within the detective genre—for authors whose many pseudonyms proliferate, and for characters whose identities are so often cloaked—apparently caused a stir when, in 1942, Borges teamed up with friend and fellow detective story maven Adolfo Bioy Casares to write as Honorio Bustos Domecq.[16] Translator and twin of Virginia Woolf's *Orlando*, whose giant estate is like a maze full of rooms impossible to enter, and of Franz Kafka, who wrote of

Chinese walls and left unfinished—like Prague's Golem—his long works, Borges dubbed time, space, and language, reducing each to "two or three scenes," not much more.

Gardening a Labyrinth

> . . . and the name of King Minos and of his palace, the Labyrinth. That is all, and beyond it nothing has remained but the traditions which were seized on by the poets.[17]

> Most likely the Greek fable of the Minotaur is a late and clumsy version of far older myths, the shadow of other dreams still more full of Horror.[18]

The labyrinth, home to the Minotaur—monstrous offspring of King Minos's wife's bestial desire for a beautiful white bull—is linked forever with the writings of Jorge Luis Borges. It is a place of endless folds, impossible to escape, except by way of retracing one's steps, aided by the ball of twine offered by Minos's daughter Ariadne. Borges was among the many writers and artists working in the mid-twentieth century fascinated by this myth. The devouring monster—half human, with the head of a horned bull—living within the inescapable maze constructed by Daedalus for his mother's husband, a king, and fed the flesh of seven virgins and seven young men sent every nine years from Athens to prevent Minos from razing the city. The inescapable garden, enclosing all who enter within its ever-expanding maze, its sole inhabitant a double being, half and half, a split subject: both fitting signs for the chaos and violence of war-torn and commodity-strewn wreckage of post–World War I culture. "In one of Chesterton's stories—'The Head of Caesar,' I think—the hero observes that nothing is so frightening as a labyrinth with no center." To Borges, Orson Welles's *Citizen*

Kane "is precisely that labyrinth" (*Cine*, 55). Of course, for Borges the labyrinth exceeded narrative—the world's literature, for instance, was "a living labyrinth," too (*Conv*, 16).

In the culture of the new, or the now, of the news, there is no escape from "the fearsome liberating still-life of crime," as Theodor Adorno calls it in "Late Extra."[19] The headless torso, "martyr to sex" in Baudelaire's poem "Une Martyre," in which the speaker gazes at a drawing by an unknown master, becomes the occasion for Adorno to rail against the "never-changing core," the "repetition" of the "archaic," which masquerades as the new,[20] that is the hallmark of Hitler's fascism ("a very clumsy idea," according to Borges [*Conv*, 21]), and beyond that the administered life of what Lizabeth Cohen would call "the consumers' republic," a world replete with the trashy repackaging of culture found in pulp. "The abstract horror of the news," "the craving for headlines" fetishize the sensational, screaming: "Extra, extra! Read all about it."[21] Crime, and its reporting, the devices by which its lurid coverage triggers further cravings for more headlines, another paperback, a cycle demanding another version, different yet recognizable, mazelike in its familiarity and involutions, is the essence of the detective form invented by Poe and brought to fruition in the midcentury Americas by Weegee's photography, Hollywood's film noirs, hard-boiled pulp fiction, and by Borges, who not only wrote them but edited a series that published English and American detective stories in Argentina as well.

Trapped in the overdetermined criminal world of monstrous double-dealing, the fantasy of danger outside the walls of the garden is replaced by the endless terror within—a dangerous suburb is subsumed by a garden and endless books or an endless book as labyrinthine garden. A system so closed and self-referential can only be understood by recourse to its own devices, its own logic. A murderer is left with "endless contrition, and my weariness" at his clever solution to his "problem": "how to report (over the deafening noise of the war) the name of the city named Albert." Like Oedipus, his

"Leader solved the riddle" and Germany bombed the city; he knows this because he "read about it in the same newspapers that posed to all of England the enigma of the murder of the eminent Sinologist Stephen Albert by a stranger, Yu Tsun."[22] Borges's concern with the labyrinth and endless books—with spaces, times, and objects that invert logic—echoed worldwide interest, intellectual and aesthetic (say, by Bakhtin, Benjamin, and surrealists) and sensational (say, by yellow journalism, Hollywood, crime and mystery writers, and their paperback-reading publics) in the ways totality might slip into totalitarianism.[23] The headline, the news item, the lurid crime story, hysterical responses to fascism, and its plague of mass violence: "the blitzkrieg, of London being on fire, of the country destroyed" excited Argentina's Nazis, Borges recalled (*Conv*, 21). Frida Kahlo's 1935 painting *A Few Little Nips* dramatizes the lyrics to a popular song celebrating the ruthless murder of a tough-guy's lover when he discovers her infidelity. These sordid incidents—the stuff of gangster films of von Sternberg, which Borges relished—could be found in his review of *Der Mörder Dimitri Karamasoff* : "The presentation of genuine, frank-hearted joy after a murder is one of its high points" (*Cine*, 23).

But what was it about this fragmentary myth of violence, love, and lost directions that sparked so much interest in artists during the mid-twentieth century? Picasso's series *Minotaur* was a private emblem of his sexuality, but it also referenced his outrage at the terror of the fascist's aerial bombing of Guernica. Frida Kahlo redeployed the monstrous chimera, as well as the erotic satyr, in her 1946 painting *The Little Deer,* which grafts her beautiful head and neck onto the body of a hind pierced by arrows, trailing blood in a wooded field. Labyrinths and Minotaurs, the stuff of myth and myths of Borges, were the domain of surrealists—among whom in his youth Borges counted himself. The *Minotaur* photograph by Man Ray (1933) transforms the shadowed torso of a young woman into the bull's head, emphasizing not only the cross-species transgression of the monster but the crossing of gender divides as well. *Minotaure,* published by Albert Skira between 1930 and 1939, was the foremost surrealist journal combining aesthetic and political essays. Mid-twentieth-century surrealism figured its critique of instrumentalized and militarized culture through this monster and his dizzying habitation. Like the Golem, a giant designed from esoteric knowledge and common clay, who wreaks vengeance on those who secretly formed it, this liminal creature and his inescapable home devours until it is destroyed.[24] Despite Borges's claims to the contrary, his fascination with the labyrinth—it's almost his trademark, and by the 1960s he acknowledged as much—points to a political project embedded within his dreamscapes. Like paperbacked pulp, Borges's infinitely forking garden grabs stock genres (crime and its detection) and stock myths (enigmatic narrators and murderous monsters) and puts them to work as private fantasies made public.

Forking Paths, Finally

> The Evening was intimate and infinite.
>
> —*Ellery Queen's Mystery Magazine* (105)

The Garden of Forking Paths was published in 1941–42 in Argentina, when Borges was noting the banality of the

> atrocious conspiracy by Germany to conquer and oppress all the countries of the atlas . . . It seems an invention of Maurice Leblanc, of Mr. Phillips Oppenheim, of Baldur von Schirach. Notoriously anachronistic, it has the unmistakable flavor of 1914. Symptomatic of poor imagination, grandiosity, and crass make-believe, this deplorable German fable counts on the complicity of the oblique Japanese and the docile, untrustworthy

Italians.... Unfortunately, reality lacks literary scruples. All liberties are permitted.... As versatile as it is monotonous, reality lacks nothing. (*SNF*, 206)[25]

It takes a Borges to discern this: the tacky literalness, as opposed to literariness of reality; the palimpsest of recurring times as 1914 folds onto, and so duplicates and inverts, 1941. (History repeats itself: the first time tragedy and the second as farce, so Karl Marx said; though we now know that in the twentieth century, tragedy returned as horror—and the Minotaur was Horror, for Borges.) When the story appeared in English, its context is ostensibly world peace, not world war. The cover of *Ellery Queen's Mystery Magazine*, August 1948, "All Nations Issue," celebrating the founding of the United Nations, features a cover by noted pulp fiction cover illustrator George Salter, in which a woman wearing only a long black glove—reminiscent of the one Rita Hayworth's Gilda slides off her arm in her "Put the Blame on Mame" striptease—is being threatened by another long-gloved arm (this one in chartreuse gloves) toting a gun from behind a striped blue, red, yellow green banner, comprising a universal flag of all nations, at once intimate and infinite (plate 4, *top*). Editor "Ellery Queen," the two-cousin Brooklyn writing team of Frederic Dannay and Manfred B. Lee (Danny and Manny?), which by this time, a few years after the magazine's founding by publisher Lawrence Spivak was really only one, as Dannay assumed editorial responsibilities, explains that the magazine would "raise the sights of mystery writers generally to a genuine literary form."[26]

Of course, as the editor goes on to note about Borges's appearance in this volume, this conjunction of Queen and the South American was overdetermined. Borges had noted in his fictional "Survey of the Works of Herbert Quain," published in the 1941–42 volume, including "Garden," that Quain's 1933 book, "yet another with this very title *The God of the Labyrinth*," had been published in November to be overshadowed the next month by the publication of Ellery Queen's novel, *The Siamese Twin Mystery*. The United Nations issue commences with a story by British mystery writer F. Tennyson Jesse (like Queen, Borges loved double names with double letters, see "Emma Zunz") about Siamese twin sisters working in a carnival. One sister, overcome with jealousy that the other is to be married, kills her other half (and thus herself) rather than suffer intrusion by a third. At the story's end, the editor queries the reader to divulge at what point was it clear the sisters were attached (answer: immediately, but then I know, as Borges did, Mark Twain's *Pudd'nhead Wilson*). Ellery Queen, pseudonymous amalgam of two Jewish cousins, "who is at the same time the author and the protagonist,"[27] must have appealed to Borges, who by the time of his English debut had been writing detective fiction with his friend Adolfo Bioy Casares as Honorio Bustos Domecq. Bioy Casares recalled later, "we used to talk alot about books and films (with a special bias for the plots: plots of novels, short stories, films, and even poems . . .). . . . Nevertheless, he once said to me: 'At the movies, we're all readers of Madame Delly.' "[28]

Borges may have disparaged the pair of authors called Delly and the pleasures their popular romances provided, but he was not immune to these plots and to their derivation from a two-headed author. After all, his first reading language was English (he translated Oscar Wilde's *Happy Prince* into Spanish at age nine); an avid fan of Edgar Allan Poe and Twain, his own explorations of plots of twinning and doubling were prodigious, continuing throughout his writing life, and could hardly have found a more comfortable venue for his first foray into American print. "Poe's tales," he tells us, "are divided into two categories which are sometimes intermingled: those of terror and those of intellect" (*AL*, 23). Of Kafka, whom he translated: "Two ideas—or more exactly, two obsessions rule Kafka's work: subordination and the infinite" (*SNF*, 502). And of Faulkner: "I know of two kinds of writers: those whose central preoccupation

Plate 1 Henry James, *Daisy Miller* (New York: Penguin, 1947). Cover by Robert Jonas.

Plate 2 Alice Tilton [pseudonym of Phoebe Atwood Taylor], *The Left Leg* (Dell, 1947). Cover by Gerald Gregg. Back cover map by Ruth Belew.

Plate 3 Adolph Treidler, *She's a WOW: Woman ordnance worker* (1942). Poster, 102 × 72 cm. US Government Printing Office-1942–0-498370. Poster promoting women's defense work during WWII with a note from the Ordnance Department of the US Army: "Keep 'em shooting." *Source*: Hennepin County Library Special Collections.

Plate 4 (*top*) *Ellery Queen Mystery Magazine*, August 1948. Cover by George Salter. Sherlock Holmes Collection. Special Collections and Rare Books. University of Minnesota Libraries. (*right*) Cannon towel advertisement. Tear sheet from *Life* (16 August 1943). The advertisement appears on the reverse of the front cover of the magazine, with a cover story asking, "How strong is Japan?" Jean-Nickolaus Tretter Collection in Gay, Lesbian, Bisexual and Transgender Studies, Special Collections and Rare Books, University of Minnesota Libraries.

Plate 5 Lily Furedi, *Subway*, 1934. Oil on canvas, 39 × 48¼ inches. Smithsonian American Art Museum, Washington, DC, transfer from US Department of Interior. National Parks Service. 1965.18.43.

Plate 6 (*top*) Guy Pène du Bois, *Portia in a Pink Blouse*, 1942. Oil on canvas, 32¼ × 30½ inches. © Indianapolis Museum of Art. Gift of Mrs. Booth Tarkington 62.3. (*bottom*) Edward Hopper, *Hotel Lobby*, 1943. Oil on canvas, 32¼ × 40¾ inches. © Indianapolis Museum of Art. William Ray Adams Memorial Collection. 47.3.

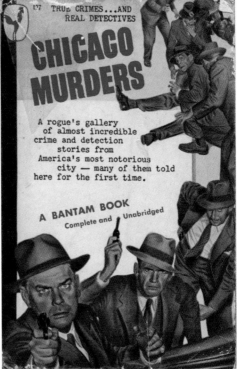

Plate 7 (*top*) J. Theodore Johnson. *Chicago Interior*, 1934, Oil on canvas, 28 × 34 inches. Smithsonian American Art Museum, Washington, DC, transfer from US Department of Labor, 1964.1.82. (*bottom*) Sewell Peaslee Wright, *Chicago Murders* (Bantam, 1947). Cover by Hy Rubin.

Plate 8 Richard Prince, *Washington Nurse* (2002). Ink jet print and acrylic on canvas, 182.9 × 114.3 × 4 cm / 72 × 45 × 1⅜ in. © Richard Prince. Photograph copyright the artist, courtesy Sadie Coles HQ, London.

Plate 9 Vera Caspary, *Laura* (Popular Library, 1950). Cover by Sam Cherry.

Plate 10 (*top*) Robert Penn Warren, *Night Rider,* abridged ed. (Signet/ NAL, 1950). Cover by James Avati (*right*); unabridged ed. (Berkley, 1956). Cover artist unknown.

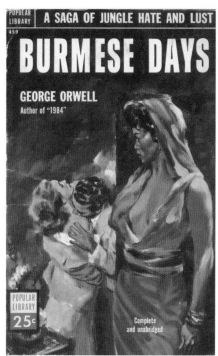

Plate 11 (*top*) Martha Gellhorn, *Liana* (Popular Library, 1953) and (*left*) George Orwell, *Burmese Days* (Popular Library, 1952). Cover artists unknown.

Plate 12 Raymond Chandler, *The Big Sleep* (Avon, 1943). Cover by Paul Stahr.

Plate 13 (*facing page top left*) Gale Wilhelm, *Paula* (Lion Books, 1956). Cover by Morgan Kane. (*facing page top right*) Don Kingery, *Paula* (Dell, 1959). Cover by Mitchell Hooks. (*facing page bottom*) Front and back of Gale Wilhelm, *No Nice Girl* (Pyramid, 1959). Cover by James Bentley. This is the third title of Wilhelm's 1936 novel *No Letters for the Dead* reprinted in the 1950s.

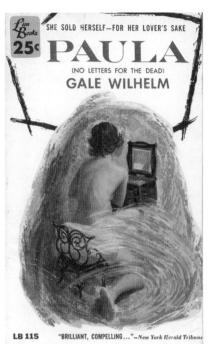

SHE SOLD HERSELF—FOR HER LOVER'S SAKE

Lion Books
25¢

PAULA

(NO LETTERS FOR THE DEAD)

GALE WILHELM

LB 115   "BRILLIANT, COMPELLING..."—*New York Herald Tribune*

DELL
FIRST
EDITION
B132

*A powerful novel about
a woman's search for fulfillment*

35¢

PAULA

By Don Kingery

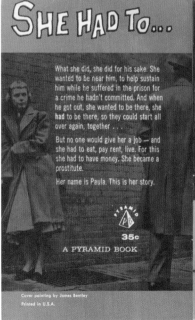

SHE HAD TO...

What she did, she did for his sake. She wanted to be near him, to help sustain him while he suffered in the prison for a crime he hadn't committed. And when he got out, she wanted to be there, she **had** to be there, so they could start all over again, together . . .

But no one would give her a job — and she had to eat, pay rent, live. For this she had to have money. She became a prostitute.

Her name is Paula. This is her story.

PYRAMID
35¢

A PYRAMID BOOK

Cover painting by James Bentley
Printed in U.S.A.

She sold herself—
for her lover's sake

PYRAMID
G440   35¢

NO NICE GIRL

Original Title:
No Letters for the Dead

GALE WILHELM

"Brilliant,
compelling..."
— N Y *Herald Tribune*

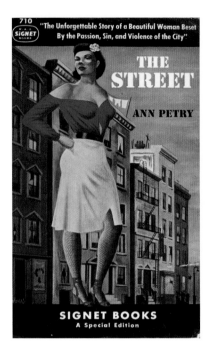

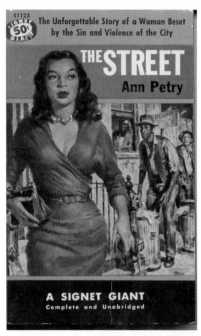

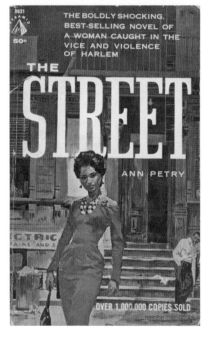

Plate 14 (*top left*) Ann Petry, *The Street* (Signet/NAL, abridged edition, 1949). Cover by Robert Jonas. Lutie as Billie Holiday or Lena Horne in *Stormy Weather*. (*top right*) Ann Petry, *The Street* (Signet/NAL, Giant unabridged edition, 1954). Cover by James Meese. Lutie as Dorothea Dandridge. (*bottom right*) Ann Petry, *The Street* (Pyramid Books, 1961). Cover by Dick Kohfield. Lutie as Lena Horne in the 1960s.

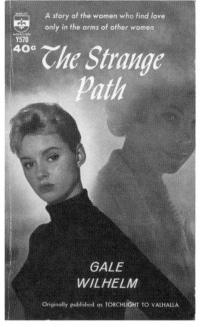

Plate 15 (*top left*) The white woman as Marilyn Monroe: Ann Petry, *The Narrows* (Signet/NAL Triple, 1955). Cover by Clark Hulings. (*bottom*) Two versions of Gale Wilhelm, *The Strange Path* (Lion Books, 1953) and (Berkley Medallion, 1961). Cover artists unknown. The novel was originally titled, *Torchlight to Valhalla* in 1936.

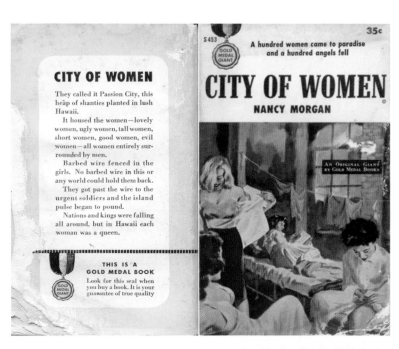

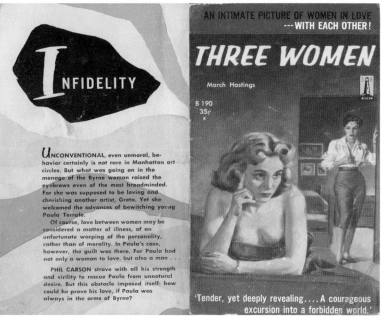

Plate 16 (*top*) Front and back cover of Nancy Morgan, *City of Women* (Gold Medal/Fawcett, 1954). Cover by Baryè Phillips. (*bottom*) Front and back cover of March Hastings, *Three Women* (Beacon Books, 1958). Cover artist unknown.

She went too far—too often

Leave Her to Hell!

A Dirty Rotten Trail To Murder!

It was a case that spelled trouble from the first come-on to the last bullet. I'm Percy Hand, not-so-private eye. You meet a lot of gals on the make in my business, but this case had too many dames.

It all started on the secluded patio of a blonde who liked nude sun-bathing. Before the case was over, one dame was dead, another missing, and The Mob was getting ready to write my epitaph in hot lead!

Printed in the U.S.A.

FLETCHER FLORA
An Avon Original

AVON
25¢

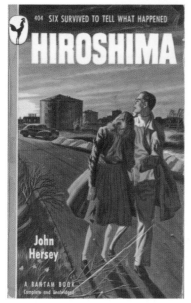

404 SIX SURVIVED TO TELL WHAT HAPPENED

HIROSHIMA

John Hersey

A BANTAM BOOK
Complete and Unabridged

A Novel Of America Under Atomic Attack

TOMORROW!

PHILIP WYLIE

35¢

Complete and Unabridged

A compelling new book by one of America's greatest novelists, author of "Generation of Vipers" and "Opus 21"

Plate 17 (*top*) Fletcher Flora, *Leave Her to Hell!* (Avon, 1958). Cover artist unknown, with disclaimer on copyright page: "A professional model was used for the illustration." (*bottom left*) John Hersey, *Hiroshima* (Bantam Books, 1948). Cover by Geoffrey Biggs. (*bottom right*) Philip Wylie, *Tomorrow!* (Popular Library, 1954). Cover artist unknown.

Plate 18 George Gamow, *The Birth and Death of the Sun* (New York: Pelican, 1945). Cover by Robert Jonas.

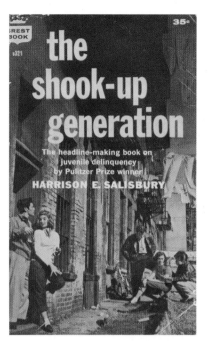

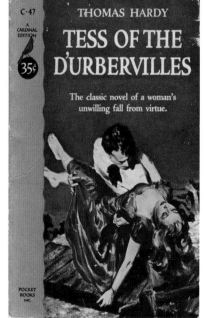

Plate 19 (*top left*) Harrison E. Salisbury, *The Shook-Up Generation* (Crest/Fawcett, 1959). Cover artist unknown. (*top right*) Meyer Levin, *Compulsion* (Cardinal Giant, 1957). Cover by Tom Dunn. (*bottom right*) Thomas Hardy, *Tess of the D'Urbervilles* (Cardinal, 1952). Cover by Baryè Phillips.

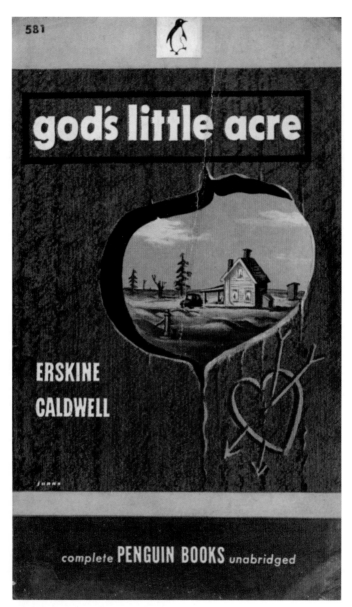

Plate 20 Erskine Caldwell, *God's Little Acre* (New York: Penguin, 1946). Cover by Robert Jonas.

Plate 21 Ralph Ellison, *Invisible Man* (Signet, 1953). Cover by James Avati.

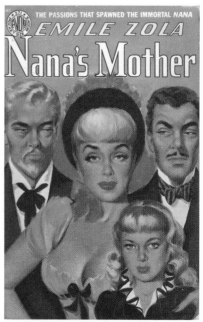

Plate 22 (*top left and right*) Émile Zola,
Nana (Pocket Books, 1941) and *Nana's
Mother* (Avon, 1950). Cover artists
unknown. (*bottom right*) Front cover
of Truman Capote, *Other Voices, Other
Rooms* (Signet/NAL, 1949). Cover by
Robert Jonas.

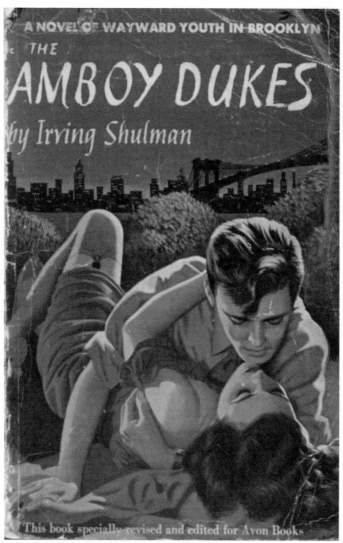

Plate 23 Irving Shulman, *The Amboy Dukes* (Avon 1948). Cover artist unknown.

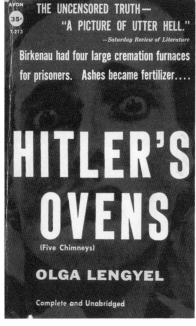

Plate 24 (*top*) Avon's *Double Indemnity* by James M. Cain, (1950). Cover by Tony Varaday. (*right*) Olga Lengyel, *I Survived Hitler's Ovens* (original title, *Five Chimneys*) (Avon, 1947). Underlying cover image from *This Must Not Happen Again!* by Clark Kinnaird (Pilot Press, 1945).

is verbal technique, and those for whom it is human acts and passions.... Faulkner likes to expound the novel through his characters" (*SNF*, 178). "The night was infinite and intimate" indeed: a double copula; a couple at once extensive and interior, like a dream. Borges intuitively understood W.E.B. Du Bois's sense that African Americans as modern subjects lived a "twoness," which, at the turn of the century, a few years after Freud's *Interpretation of Dreams*, he called "double consciousness." The double letters that so entranced Borges acted as visual markers of his own repetitions, signaling that the periphery of the Southern Cone could hold the keys to modernity.

"Garden," a tale within a tale within a tale, recounts the confession (only a fragment of which still exists), of a Chinese spy, Dr. Yu Tsun, professor of English at the Hochschule at Tsingtao, working for Germany—"such a barbarous country"—during World War I but written during World War II, whose mission brings him to one Stephen Corbie (in later translations, Albert), possessor of a book written, as it turns out, by the spy's ancestor. This book, product of thirteen years' labor, is actually a labyrinth, to which the ancient Chinese scholar devoted his life translating and decoding, the reverse of the procedure that both "inexplicably satisfied and, at the same time, disturbed" Borges in "The Wall and the Books," another Borges essay examining the will to power inherent in

> the man who ordered the building of the almost infinite Chinese Wall . . . the first Emperor, Shih Huang Ti, who also decreed the burning of all the books that had been written before his time . . . these two vast undertakings—five or six hundred leagues of stone against the barbarians, and the rigorous abolition of history, that is, of the past—were the work of the same person and were, in a sense, his attributes. (*SNF*, 344)

This double legacy of structural presence and memory's erasure slyly echoes Kafka, who imagined China and Amerika as vast spaces of unfinished plans. But *The Garden of Forking Paths* inverts the relationship between text and materials. An early precursor of hypertext, the novel, as labyrinthine space, consists of every possible narrative, refusing to foreclose any one possibility in the pursuit of its conclusion.[29] The text's utterly immersive quality, resurrecting aspects of its own past, is a fitting metaphor for the demotic, repetitive experience of reading pulp.

Escaping capture by the zealous Captain Richard Madden (an Irishman bent on besting his imperial masters by proving his own cleverness), Dr. Yu (who understands Madden's colonized mind because he is motivated to prove to his chief "that a yellow man could save his armies") boards a train at 8:50 on which are found these passengers: "a few working men, a woman in mourning, a young man absorbed in the Annals of Tacitus, a wounded and happy soldier." Noticing Madden's arrival at the platform just as the train pulls from the station, the spy assumes he will be caught but may still possess enough time to accomplish his deed as the next train does not depart for forty minutes.

Arriving in Ashgrove, Dr. Yu is asked by a group of children if he is going to Dr. Corbie's and is informed it is difficult to get to but can be found by following a long and winding path, if he keeps left at every fork. Pondering these familiar and inevitable directions amid the bucolic countryside, Dr. Yu realizes that they are used to escape a maze—something of which he is deeply familiar as the descendant of Ts'ui Pen, governor of Yunan, who spent thirteen years writing a novel and constructing a maze only to be murdered, leaving a nonsensical book and nothing else.

> Beneath English trees I meditated on this lost maze: I imagined it inviolate and perfect on the secret summit of some mountain; I imagined it erased by rice fields or sunk beneath water; I imagined it infinite, no longer constructed of octagonal kiosks and twisting paths, but of rivers and provinces and kingdoms. . . . I thought of a maze of mazes, a labyrinth of labyrinths, one

sinuous waxing labyrinth that should include the past and the future in some manner involve the stars. (*EQMM*, 105)

A maze of mazes, a labyrinth of labyrinths, inviolate and perfect, Dr. Yu's infinite regressions and repetitions envelop the earth and sky, the universe. "The chaos of the novel suggested to me that the book *itself* was the maze." This and the cryptic fragment of the letter in the Sinologist's possession, "*I leave to the various futures (and not to all) my garden of forking paths*" (*EQMM*, 107), provides him his eureka moment as a scholar and results in his senseless death.

But by 1916, Stephen Corbie/Albert should have already been pondering this fork in time as Robert Frost's "The Road Not Taken" ("Oh, I kept the first for another day! / Yet knowing how way leads on to way, / I doubted if I should ever come back") had appeared in the *Atlantic Monthly* in August 1915.[30]

> *The Garden of Forking Paths* is a vast riddle, or parable, whose meaning is Time; the *only* problem which does not figure in the pages of *The Garden.* . . . Always to omit a word, to seek refuge in inept metaphors or blatant periphrases, is perhaps the most emphatic method of stressing that word. It is the tortuous method preferred, in each meandering of his indefatigable novel. (*EQMM*, 109)

These last sentences, later translated as "inept phrases and obvious paraphrases, is perhaps the best way of drawing attention to it . . . in every meandering of his interminable novel" (*CF*, 100) and then as "awkward metaphors and obvious circumlocutions . . . at each and every one of the turnings of his inexhaustible novel" reveal the riddle or parable as also about text, about paper that holds ink and remains (*CF*, 126–27). Not only are the series of forking paths multiply available in this remarkable novel, but a series of translations form a dubbing, an overlay of one set of terms onto another, reflecting changing slang, subtler usages, greater elegance. Synonyms proliferate: in 1962, "periphrases" becomes "paraphrases"; would an American reader then or in 1998 recognize what a periphrasis is, or even what it means to paraphrase? Would an American reader of a pulp mystery magazine in 1948 be any more likely to know this rhetorical gesture? Apparently so—and this may be the result of the sort of promiscuous reading encouraged by paperbacks.

Erin Smith argues that the readers of pulp magazines were notoriously those who move their lips when they read, the ill-bred and ill-taught lower orders, but as I have been arguing all along, pulp encourages reading outside one's level in its demotic urge to get bought.[31] According to the *Oxford English Dictionary*, "dubbing," which does not appear to have a definition related to cinema among its meanings, refers to dressing (among other things) a fly-fishing hook or redoing old clothes, or picking a pocket, or conferring knighthood (often meant sarcastically). It's a system of costuming, of remaking one thing into another—a hook into a lure, old clothes into a more modish style, a crook into the possessor of another's property, an oaf into a knight—a hardcover into a paperback? "The possibilities for the art of combination are not infinite," notes Borges in "On Dubbing," "but they are apt to be frightening." Like

> the chimera, a monster with the head of a lion, the head of a dragon, and the head of a goat. . . . Hollywood adds a perverse artifice they call dubbing, they offer monsters that combine the well-known features of Greta Garbo with the voice of Aldonza Lorenzo. How can we fail to proclaim our admiration for this distressing prodigy, for these ingenious audio-visual anomalies? (*Cine*, 62)

But in another translation, we find: "a perverse artifice they call dubbing, they devise monsters that combine the famous face of Greta Garbo with the voice of Aldonza Lorenzo. How can we proclaim our admiration for this bleak magic, for these ingenious audio-visual deformations?" (*SNF*, 262). Written for *Sur* in 1945,

Borges's "Sobre el doblaje" registers that in Spanish the Americanized, shortened, and altered form of doubling, first used in *Variety* in 1930, according to *Webster's*, remained the unbastardized word with long philosophical and literary pedigree: two roads diverged, but both led to monsters.

Borges describes good writing as "sincere dreaming," a method of transforming the dreamers dream into another dream, believable by the reader—in fact, capable of being absorbed, even redreamed by the reader, an act of translation, even dubbing. Borges, thought of as a fabulist, a teller of elusive parables, is perhaps better considered as a shadow, a gumshoe, recording case studies. After all, on Calle Murillo in the city of Buenos Aires, one can find Alef Cueros, factory and outlet for leather goods of all sorts. The establishment is just down the block from the Doctor Max Nordau synagogue, which is across the street from an apartment building, number 666. The Buenos Aires of Borges's imagined youth—full of knifings and tangos, the Buenos Aires of Palermo: "The tango spawns a turbid / Unreal past in certain measure true: / An impossible recollection of having died / Fighting, on some corner of a suburb" ("The Tango," in *PA*, 158–60)—was revivified in part from memory and from dreams, but in part because nobody checked his facts. A sign of boredom, perhaps, "[e]asier than imagining it was to translate it into something else," he remarks of the later fables about chimera—but he could have been speaking of his own exhaustion with his staging of street-corner crimes (*BIB*, 63).

Borges is no realist but a documentarian nonetheless, achieving his version of the past through a kind of dubbing, which, unlike subtitles, re/moves traces of the prior text. It is he who both resided in and observed his place—the city, the garden, the library—and his time: of living and of reading. The twin, the double, "Borges and I: I like hourglasses, maps, eighteenth-century typography, etymologies, the taste of coffee, and Robert Louis Stevenson's prose; he shares these preferences" (*PA*, 200). The endlessly forking path, the mirror, the labyrinth, the aleph, the book, repeating story and image, gets "repeated and repeated." The knife, like the two-headed ax ("whose name," Borges reminds, "was *labrys*") with its double edge, its mirrored surface, its purpose, death, cuts through time, cuts down men who live on in song, in tales recounted and dreams dreamed along the perimeter.

Being eccentric, outside the center, resident of the exurbs of power in the global south, removed within "some subordinate position or other in an illegible library in the south side suburbs," as Carlos Argentino Daneri, the discoverer of the Aleph, is (*PA*, 139), allows entry into the "multitudes of America." This Whitmanesque sensation, uttered by a character named Borges, echoes Borges's own encounter with that other container of multitudes: Borges first read Whitman in German translation while a young man in Switzerland. The onetime subordinate in a forgotten library, who feels life and language pullulating (swarming, teeming like a mass of chickens), finds himself promoted by Juan Perón—the unmentioned one—to inspector of rabbits and poultry in the Córdoba municipal market. Resigning his government post until 1955 when he was appointed director of the National Library upon Perón's overthrow, Borges was offered a collection of eight hundred thousand volumes at the moment he loses—as had his grandfather and father before him—his eyesight. "There is no whole self," he repeats again and again in "The Nothingness of Personality" (*SNF*, 3–9).

In 1934, accused by the profascist journal *Crisol* of bearing "Jewish ancestry, maliciously hidden," Borges speculates upon why no one spends time tracking genealogies from "Phoenicians, Garamantes, Scythians, Babylonians, Persians, Egyptians, Huns, Vandals, Ostrogoths, Ethiopians, Illyrians, Paphlagonians, Sarmatians, Medes, Ottomans, Berbers, Britons, Libyans, Cyclopes, or Lapiths." He concludes, "The nights of Alexandria, of Babylon, of Carthage, of Memphis, never succeeded in engendering a single grandfather; it was only to the tribes of the bituminous Dead Sea that this gift was granted" (*SNF*, 110–11). Like hybrids, Jews proliferate in the anti-Semitic imagination, becoming a kind of monster, at once fascinating and abhorrent; they serve as liminal figures—like the Irish or the Argentines—at once within and outside of Western culture.

Borges was his own genre—no matter in what form he chose to write. It is this repetition, this impossibility of originality, that must be the final point of this disappointing adventure into the Garden. And it is clearly shabby, like the "disconcerting . . . feature[s] of our time . . . the enthusiasm generated across the entire planet by the Dionne sisters, for numerical and biological reasons" (*SNF*, 196). Replication, especially when it occurs in "the suburbs of the world," engenders cliché. That's the stuff of pulp. When Hollywood wanted to find a location exotic enough to stir fantasy, it looked south of the border, or occasionally to the Orient. The goal of most schemers in pulp fiction and film noir is to abscond with the money and the dame—or maybe it's really just the dame who absconds with the money—south, to Mexico, Rio, or Buenos Aires. In Billy Wilder's *Double Indemnity*, Walter Neff pleads with Barton Keyes to just give him a few hours before reporting his murders to give him a chance to cross the border, but in Cain's novel, Walter Huff and Phyllis Nirdlinger, escaping on a steamer to Mazatlán, slip together into the shark-infested sea to "meet [her] bridegroom."[32] Lizabeth Scott kills a slew of men and takes off south of the border with the cash that lands in her convertible one evening in *Too Late for Tears*; Kathleen Turner gets away with the money to spend her days lounging on a South American beach in *Body Heat*.

Sometimes the killers and the tough guys and their women find themselves already stranded there. Lauren Bacall meets Humphrey Bogart on a Caribbean island in the film *To Have and Have Not*; in *Gilda*, Johnny is saved, after stiffing angry sailors and longshoremen with his loaded dice on a Buenos Aires pier, by a gambling king, whose walking stick—"my friend," he calls it—conveniently sheathes a dagger. Ballin's illegal gambling casino fronts for a more sinister operation, trading tungsten with Nazis. Both men have been involved with Gilda—"two insane men in one lifetime"— who works as a singer first in Buenos Aires and then Montevideo, and whose tightly sheathed body and arms, and long, flowing hair, figure as the means of exchange between the men. Her hair and body: at once labyrinth and Ariadne's thread to escape it.

Hayworth herself had a past, and a future as the Lady from Shanghai. Daughter of the "Spanish" dancer Eduardo Cansino, her first incarnation in Hollywood "typed [her] as a Latin," despite the fact that she was born in Brooklyn.[33] "Men fell in love with 'Gilda' but they woke up with me," so her famous line goes, another in the saga of twins/doubles: two names, two careers, two national bodies. Spanish Rita Cansino, dancer with her father's name; American Rita Hayworth, star claiming her American mother's maiden name. Gilda's two dubbed songs—"Amado Mio" and "Put the Blame on Mame," one begging in Spanish for love, the other celebrating women's power in English—sung in the twin cities Montevideo and Buenos Aires, separated across the Rio Plata, display her duality: she's desiring love but not about to give up on a good time. Invariably, within pulp the double and desire become deadly or reappear as the couple, conventionally domesticated: finally reconciled, Johnny and Gilda will return as man and wife to a postwar US suburb; having taken various paths, they are headed home to a narrow backyard where they can forget the past. Not so Cain's Walter and Phyllis, who look "like what came aboard to shoot dice for souls in the Rime of the Ancient Mariner."[34]

Borges's remains, however, transfix the monsters produced by the double, by the unwieldy melding of species, of spaces, of times. His palimpsestic mapping of World War I over World War II, of China onto Argentina, of forking paths onto libraries leads across time and the Atlantic and keeps the memory of the Minotaur's demonology alive: "I felt again that pullulation I have mentioned. I sensed that the dew-drenched garden that surrounded the house was saturated, infinitely, with invisible persons. Those persons were Albert and myself—secret, busily at work, multiform—in other dimensions of time" (*CP*, 127). Like Ellery Queen, whose 1930's mysteries followed a predictable, if uncanny logic—"French Powder," "Dutch Shoe," "Chinese Orange,"—Albert and myself (Borges and I) puzzle their way through the maze together as one. The path leads inevitably to pulp.

CHAPTER 7

Slips of the Tongue: Uncovering Lesbian Pulp

> A woman should some day write the complete philosophy of clothes.
>
> —Theodore Dreiser, *Sister Carrie*

> [P]ieces of underclothing, which are so often chosen as a fetish, crystallize the moment of undressing, the last moment in which the woman could still be regarded as phallic.
>
> —Sigmund Freud, "Fetishism"

The department store, site of female consumer culture since the nineteenth century, demarcates a zone in which mostly middle-class women not only shop but in the process communally disrobe, sometimes literally together within a huge open space, occasionally under the supervising eye of the saleswoman, who monitors the cut and fit of the garments, more often alone before a full-length three-way mirror producing a solitary portrait. In another part of the modern cityscape, bohemia, female models shed their clothes and pose nude or draped in fabric for life drawing and painting classes in artists' studios. Each scene—commercial and aesthetic—depends on the discerning eye of the shopper, or of the artist, to note the details of curve, fold, cut, and color. These two modern gendered spaces—like the school dormitory or the locker room—offer institutionalized structures for public female nudity. Not surprisingly, they serve as the settings for depictions of female voyeurism and other same-sex forms of desire.[1]

Postwar American pulp fiction, one of the rare mass avenues open to depicting lesbian relationships during the 1950s, situated many plots within these two domains. The older woman, a professional working at the upscale department store, dressed with refinement and care, takes her younger protégé under her wing, training her and ultimately protecting and loving her (Valerie Taylor [pseudonym of Velma Young], *The Girls in 3-B*); the sophisticated bourgeois shopper signals to the working-class shopgirl her interest by commenting on her looks rather than her goods (Claire Morgan [pseudonym of Patricia Highsmith], *The Price of Salt*); the older bohemian artist instructs a young girl in sketching by disrobing and posing in her Greenwich Village apartment (March Hastings [pseudonym of Sally Singer], *Three Women*) (plate 16, *bottom*); and, in an earlier variation, in *We Too Are Drifting*, Gale Wilhelm had a lesbian artist modeling for her male mentor's woodcarving "Hermaphroditus."

These scenes from classic lesbian fiction borrow from set pieces strewn across twentieth-century American fiction that suggest a complicated interaction among narratives, female desire for material objects and displays of the female body more or less sanctioned as cross-class encounters in quasi-public spaces. They range from detailed scenes of shopping in Theodore Dreiser's *Sister Carrie* and *An American Tragedy* or Anzia Yezierska's *Salome of the Tenements* at the beginning of the century through midcentury pulp (all later made into movies), as in Raymond Chandler's *The Big Sleep* (here the art school is replaced by the antiquarian bookshop, both invariably fronts for pornography rings) or Cain's *Mildred Pierce* (where the department store is replaced by the restaurant as scene of a cross-class female workforce), to Elisabeth Sanxay Holding's *Blank Wall*, which became Max Ophüls's film *The Reckless Moment* (art school) and Vera Caspary's *Laura* (modeling agency) in the 1940s. Even during the 1950s with the emergence of lesbian pulp, the location of female encounters is quite circumscribed.

How to find other women, undress them, and describe them, and still retain an air of plausibility and discretion? Boarding school dormitories? Too European and upper class (though many classic lesbian novels do take place in the school or college dorm—Christa Winsloe's novel, *The Child Manuela,* which she turned into the screenplay for Leontine Sagan's 1931 film *Maedchen in Uniform*; Violette Leduc's 1960s novels, *La Bâtarde* and *Thérèse et Isabelle* [the latter became a film in 1968]; and the book that began the American flurry of lesbian paperbacks, Vin Packer's [pseudonym for Marijane Meaker] *Spring Fire*). The army? Possibly (Nancy Morgan, *City of Women*; Tereska Torrès, *Women's Barracks*; and Margaret Long, *Louisville Saturday*, all suggest that the armed services offer rich opportunities for same-sex romance); but, by custom and censorship, stories of sex and violence in the armed forces were curtailed during and immediately after World War II.[2] The bar? Too seedy (though that's where Ann Bannon's Beebo Brinker could be found on the prowl). All these erotic zones stray from middle-class, middle-American propriety; instead, two acts—shopping and art making—provide possibilities for almost any young woman to meet other women. The department store, where women worked, shopped, supped, and stripped together, and could congregate alone within the limits of legitimate middle-class and proper working-class behavior, and life-drawing class, where they could break out of these constraints at the bohemian edges of society by modeling or sketching in arty districts with studios, art schools, and secondhand bookstores and print shops: these became the site for the more "positive" representations of lesbian love. And, as Joan Schenkar notes of Patricia Highsmith's fascination with couture and models, "Fashion, after all, was the glamorous province of beautiful women."[3]

In a classic of the genre, for instance, Ann Bannon's (pseudonym for Ann Weldy) *I Am a Woman (in Love with a Woman—Must Society Reject Me)*, the prim lesbian finds herself drawn to her heterosexual roommate. Then, on a double date with her roommate and her boyfriend and his pal, descending the steps into a Greenwich Village gay bar, she finds a world of young short-haired girls dressed in open-collared white shirts and black trousers. At first repelled, she thrills to find a self-confident butch eyeing her in the bathroom. Try as she might to repress her desire, it springs forth uncontrollably until she can admit it and act. It has become a cliché to find lesbian pulp fiction described, in Joan Nestle's phrase, as "survival literature," a means through which 1950s middle-class heterosexual culture could be escaped, if briefly, and where a corresponding world of women's homoeroticism could be expressed and explored.[4] Gale Wilhelm's 1938 sensitive portrayal of a young woman's growing self-understanding and expression of her lesbian desire, *Torchlight to Valhalla*, became a Lion Book in 1953 with the new title *The Strange Path* and a wraparound cover depicting a brunette in a frilly dress brushing the hair of a blond in jeans and denim shirt, both smiling with full lipstick-red lips; in the corner, merging into the dark background, looms a stricken man sliding off the cover (plate 15, *bottom left*). By the 1960s, the cover features only a young woman with short hair in a black turtleneck—attire of a beatnik (plate 15, *bottom right*)—and the ghost of more feminine woman melting into the background.

Editor Katherine Forrest recalls how "[a] lesbian pulp fiction paperback first appeared before my disbelieving eyes in Detroit, Michigan, in 1957. I did not need to look at the title for clues; the cover leaped out at me from the drugstore rack: a young woman with sensuous intent on her face seated on a bed, leaning over a prone woman, her hands on the other woman's shoulders."[5] Others responded to this newly visible expressive culture with more ambivalence. Her "middle-class background" kept Gail Ellen Dunlap "frightened" of the "popular dyke literature" and "gay bars in New York." However, she recalls, as a student at Vassar, "the books I found! There was Djuna Barnes, Virginia Woolf, Jeannette Foster, Radclyffe Hall, Simone de Beauvoir, and Gertrude Stein."[6] Still, these high literary works barely contained the "desire so big" found in the cheesy paperbacks as the working-class daughter of a "mother who liked to fuck," Joan Nestle called it, bursting their cheap pages.[7]

Unlike the postwar growth of urban gay neighborhoods, fueled in part by demobilizing armed service members who decided not to return to Peoria—North Beach in San Francisco, Greenwich Village in New York, and the myriad cruising zones of John Rechy's *City of Night*—which became centers for gay male life and art, visible markers of lesbian spaces were far more difficult to discern.[8] In 1950s America, lesbians had, with the exception of a few bars or softball teams, no "subculture" legible through a history or navigable as a geography in the ways gay man had, recalls Lillian Faderman. She argues that lesbian pulp created what Benedict Anderson would call an "imagined community," which served to produce a virtual space for lesbian desire.[9] Lesbian pulp functioned as an interface weaving disparate readers together—not only by providing necessary stories but even if the books remained unread and merely glanced at by young women too shy to purchase them, the covers on display offered lessons in lesbian self-recognition and self-disclosure.

Ann Bannon described the "Golden Age" of lesbian writing during the 1950s when a group of writers "suddenly reached out and connected with women who were very isolated and sequestered, almost, in little towns across the country. . . . They [the paperback originals with lesbian themes] were widely distributed and they said this is how it is, this is who some of your sisters are."[10] Remarking on Barbara Grier's (writing as Gene Damon) reviews of lesbian pulp in *The Ladder*, as well as Marion Zimmer Bradley's compilation of lists and bibliographies for readers, Susan Stryker notes "the careful attention many mid-twentieth-century lesbian readers paid to lesbian-themed mass-market paperbacks, their hunger for affirming representations, their ability to tease out subtextual sympathies in books that were often overtly homophobic and misogynistic, and their loyal appreciation for authors who expressed carefully coded support for the kind of lives they led."[11] This ambivalence— enthusiasm (especially for positive images of lesbians) and detraction (because of the negative consequences often found at the novels' endings)—got repeated, as so often occurs in the remediation of pulp, a process that, as I have been arguing, includes its critical reception in more recent scholarship about lesbian pulp, according to Christopher Nealon.[12]

In addition to the "entertainment" and community value of these illicit novels—the legitimating expression of female erotic desire for another woman—noted by these historians, critics, and authors, they also served the other notorious function of the *roman à thèse* outlined by Susan Rubin Suleiman, of "instruction." Indeed, all domestic novels, according to Nancy Armstrong, are a form of the conduct book. In *Authoritarian Fictions*, her provocative study of French ideological novels written by both right- and left-wing authors during the interwar years, Suleiman identifies these two poles—entertainment and instruction—as keys to understanding what are essentially generic conventions of "the structure of apprenticeship" designed to nurture and encourage correct political behavior in the reader by a process of replication and homology as the reader undergoes a development parallel to that of the protagonist.[13] Of course, a novel must entertain—keep its reader reading until the end; this is especially important when the nature of the narrative presupposes some moral, political, or religious message derived from the tale, when instruction in proper ideas and behaviors of the reader was its primary purpose. While it might be counterintuitive to read a lesbian pulp novel as an example of an "ideological novel," the details accruing in these tales—details about the artifacts of clothing, down to bras and slips—did more than imagine new romantic and erotic possibilities; they also served as fashion manuals for young lesbians, especially those living far from gay centers like New York's Greenwich Village. Reading these novels (and studying their covers) nourished more than hidden pleasures; these books taught women how to shop, how to dress— right down to one's drawers—and how to check out other women and their attire for clues to their sexuality. In sum, they are how-to manuals, conduct books.[14]

In their groundbreaking work of lesbian ethnography, *Boots of Leather, Slippers of Gold* (note the significance of accessories), Elizabeth Lapovsky Kennedy and Madeleine Davis explore how working-class Buffalo lesbians shopped and dressed for bar and straight culture during the 1940s and 1950s. Lesbians knew which shops and tailors fashioned and sold men's clothing and shoes in sizes for women. However, "[s]ince 1940s lesbians did not actively introduce people to gay life, they did not instruct people in how to dress or carry themselves. Newcomers picked up what they wanted."[15] For example, they quote various white working-class butches' memories about the significance of wearing white T-shirts (in raunchy and daring tribute to James Dean and Marlon Brando) backward: "because we didn't wear a bra" . . . "you'd put them on backwards, so it would be higher up." "It covered you more . . . in the front." And so "camouflaged their bosoms," explained Sandy and Toni and Gerry. Those with larger breasts "would often modify the cups of their bras so their breasts wouldn't look so pointy."[16] But, according to Jackie, who lived in New Orleans in the 1950s, police "could arrest you for impersonating a man, so you had to be sure you were wearing three pieces of women's clothes." This meant, for butches, women's undergarments.[17] Donna Penn quotes a young woman's memories of learning how to identify (as) a lesbian: "I had been a closet gay before I got married, about 1948, which means I had a relationship with a woman, and I'd been in love with her but I thought I was the only person in the world. There was no others in the world. I had never read a gay book. I didn't even know the word 'gay' . . . I didn't know the word 'lesbian' . . . And I really believe that women used to dress mannish simply to get you to know who they were . . . In those days it was very important."[18] Clothing signified and paperbacks circulated. In fact, as historian Regina Kunzel notes in her study of unmarried mothers' "true confessions," these popular narratives "helped women find words to make such a confession, as well as the narrative templates with which to plot their stories."[19]

Complaining of the lurid covers that helped sell her Beebo Brinker series, Ann Bannon commented sardonically on the targeted heterosexual male audiences at which PBO (paperback original) covers were aimed:

> And speaking of clothes, where did all those pink tap pants come from? Those fluffy negligees? Those peach silk slips? In those days, real girls wore 100 percent cotton "lollipop" briefs, plain white. They provided coverage even our grandmothers could approve, from above the navel to below the buns. No need to wax the bikini line. None of those lacy pushup things, either. Bras were of sturdy cotton, circle-stitched so as to give our breasts no-nonsense conical points. Indeed, they appeared to be aimed fatally at anyone who got closer than three feet. As for outerwear, many of the covers exhibit young women in torn blouses, unbuttoned blouses, sheer blouses, and the occasional peignoir—standard issue, of course, for all self-respecting lesbians of the 1950s and 1960s.[20]

The gap between cover and content, between the outside and the inside, reverses the placement of the slip as undergarment, bringing it onto the surface, in fact, returning it to its original position on the outside rather than underneath one's clothing. Thus, it makes sense that it was the cover of Tereska Torrès's *Women's Barracks* (1950) that sparked the House Select Committee on Current

Pornographic Materials in 1952 to explore the problem of an exploding postwar American culture of salacious novels, films, and comics. There is little evidence that anyone in Congress had read this lively documentary account of life in the Free French Army, but they did look closely at its front cover, where in the foreground a woman in uniform, with short hair, smokes and watches various others in the process of getting dressed (figure 7.1). Curiously, regulation underwear includes pink brassieres and black panties in the "frank autobiography of a French girl soldier." The back-cover blurb notes the book tells "the story of what happens when scores of young girls live intimately together . . . with all of its revealment and tenderness."[21]

In a tidy example of Michel Foucault's hypothesis of the productivity of repression, it should be noted that in addition to spurring congressional hearings on pornography, the cover also suggested to one publisher (Fawcett Gold Medal) that lesbianism might sell; the result was Vin Packer's *Spring Fire* (1952).[22] Women's barracks and girls' dormitories, institutionalized zones of female intimacy, provided ready spaces for possible lesbian encounters. The effort to enforce conformity, especially through military uniforms, however, was undone once the girls disrobed. Even the brothel presented a form of collective female institution that suggested alternative sexualities, such as baronesses who worked as prostitutes to have sex with young men. The cover of the 1952 Pyramid edition of "the classic story of a Russian brothel," *Yama, The Hell-Hole,* by Alexandre Kuprin, a book that the *Nation* called "humane, graphic, very moral" (or so its cover declares) shows two women in partial undress. One is in a slip and the other wears a pink dress open to reveal her breast, which is covered by a white slip; they are playing cards on an unmade bed, behind them, outside the window, the clapboard houses of this railroad depot. Their (and their city of women sisters') undergarments reveal touches of individuality among the women, as each is positioned in a different stage of undress, which gives their bodies a kinetic and dynamic power. Even the army seemed to foster

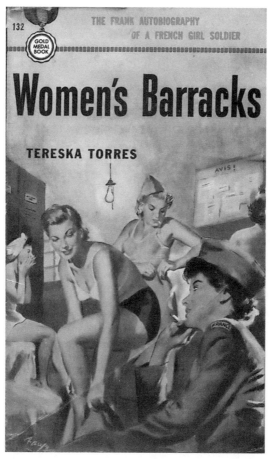

Figure 7.1 Tereska Torrès, *Women's Barracks* (Gold Medal/Fawcett, 1950). Cover by Baryè Phillips.

some freedom of movement and possibility of desire—it was the "Free" "French" Army comprising this *City of Women*. (plate 16, *top*).

All over the front covers, the slip is barely discernible within the body of the novel. Yet, according to the *Oxford English Dictionary*, the etymology of the noun "slip"—deriving from both "strip" (a narrow piece of fabric, a shoot, an offspring, the skin shed by a snake) and "slime" (the muck of mud potters use, the scum coating fish scales, fetid water)—followed this very course from exterior garment inside to become an "intermediate body."[23] First the name for the hole in a sacking cloth (like those in 1950s T-shirts), a child's dress, and a women's cloak, by the eighteenth century the slip had migrated from an outer covering of the dress inside to becoming a hidden covering for the body, worn deliberately close to the skin, its second.

In their ethnography, Kennedy and Davis track the traces of lived butch-fem lesbian culture in a minor American city during and immediately after the war years. The stories they recount detail how women learned to bind breasts or refashion bras to eliminate the pointiness of 1950s bras, shop for men's shoes, acquire short haircuts, tailor trousers with pockets, and so forth. But literature encroached on lives not yet actually lived, ones merely imagined; novels helped make lesbian lives possible, if only in fantasy, for those unable or unwilling to go to a bar, move to a big city, find a lover. Just as the British novel of the late eighteenth and early nineteenth centuries served to indoctrinate and make legible the new bourgeois women and her household, by stressing, like a conduct book, what kinds of clothing she should wear and what type of furniture and home accessories she should use to decorate her house, these pulp novels aided young, rebellious, and working-class women to find a way to dress the part, and acquire lesbian or bohemian identities.[24]

In March Hastings's novel, *Three Women* (1958), becoming an artist and becoming a lesbian entail the same process. Paula Temple, a girl from a working-class family who occasionally paints, is drawn to her fiancé's aunt Byrne, a Greenwich Village artist; she finds herself returning to Byrne's apartment alone, supposedly seeking instruction from the older artist in painting the female form. Paula begins "obediently" by sketching a coffee percolator. But almost immediately "[w]ithout embarrassment, as though it were the most everyday thing in the world, she [Byrne] unbuttoned her shirt and dropped it to the floor. Paula watched, speechless, as she unhooked her bra and tossed it aside. . . . 'All right, draw.' "[25] This scene of Byrne undressing for Paula as model is repeated across the narrative, until eventually the pretense of the artist's sitting gets dropped. "All right, draw," the declaration of the gunman in classic Westerns—those complicated scenes of repressed male homosociality—is now redirected into a command between two urban women artists not quite willing for their "lips to speak together" of mutual desire.[26] Still, each scene emphasizes in detail all the items of clothing Byrne wears—beige skirt, high heels, sweater, white garter belt, stockings, bra, panties, but not a slip (the slip on the cover slips out of the narrative)—which serve as guides for Paula's new wardrobe, too.[27] Preparing for her first visit to Bryne's apartment, Paula dresses carefully in black trousers and a white man-tailored shirt, as if she already knows the neutral attire of a discreet lesbian displayed on the book's cover.

Even if slip-wearing is not tied to a woman's desire for women, its extravagant display of sexuality marks her as a sister rebel. Margaret Sargent, Mary McCarthy's jaded "Bohemian Girl . . . a Vassar girl," the antiheroine of *The Company She Keeps* (1942), picks up and has sex with "the man in the Brooks Brothers shirt" aboard the Empire Builder, going west through Reno, lurid site of female independence and decadence—as a gesture of kindness to the pathetic businessman and as an ironic embrace of the American heartland, of the West (figure 7.2).[28] Despite a night of tawdry sex and the loss of her garter belt amid the sheets, she manages to retain some shred of her self-worth by fastening the brass safety pin holding her crepe de chine panties (known in French as a slip) together. This sign of a woman who obviously does not *plan* her conquests (107,117) leads her to be appalled when he later sends her several gifts of "glamour-girl underwear" (131). What femme fatale, after all, would wear torn undergarments? Like Bryne, Margaret Sanger was an artistic woman with a Greenwich Village apartment and thus with access to various sexual underworlds, such as the homosexual drag shows she boldly describes to her Brooks Brothers' shirt man. McCarthy charted connections among the sexual underworld, sexualized underwear, and lower Manhattan that extend beyond lesbian pulp to many early paperbacks.

In a sort of linguistic, homological poem (Downtown: Underground: Underwear: Down there) metonymically reversing part for (w)hole, the city becomes the female body and downtown her vagina. For instance, Gloria Wandrous, played by Elizabeth Taylor in the 1960 film of John O'Hara's 1935 novel (pulped in 1955) *Butterfield 8,* bursts into her Greenwich Village writer friend's apartment, revealing her disarray after absconding with her last-night lover's wife's fur coat to conceal her disheveled slip. Waking in her one-night stand's empty apartment, she is furious to discover her ruined dress and the crisp bills (two hundreds and a fifty) he left her for services rendered and to buy another dress. She takes off with his wife's goods; after all, she needs something to cover her slip.

Luce Irigaray has suggested that not only do women acquire commodities in the exchanges between men known as heterosexuality, they themselves are commodities whose value accrues through this exchange. When the goods get together, she argues, it is possible to imagine "these 'commodities' [who] refused to go to 'market'" and thus undo the decorative vision of the female body: "Exchanges without identifiable terms, without accounts, without end . . . Without additions and accumulations, one plus one, woman after woman . . . Without sequence or number."[29] In the return to the icon of the two women together, these covers convey at once the "commodities" on the market—they scream out sex to customers, both male and female—and their refusal, "one plus one, woman after woman." Slips—one lip surrounded by two sibilants,

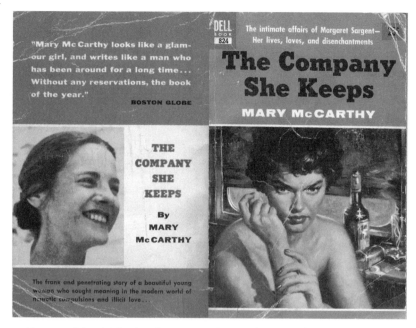

Figure 7.2 Mary McCarthy, *The Company She Keeps* (Dell, 1955). Cover by Robert Maguire.

slip, lips—lace on top and below, then, are already embedded in an alternative economy, an economy that typically defers display, but, in the case of these covers, uncovers the hidden value beneath the surface. Slips, in short, especially when offered on one of two or more women, are lesbian. "When our lips speak together" (205)— "that contact of *at least two* (lips), which keeps woman in touch with herself, but without any possibility of distinguishing what is touching from what is touched" (26), "closed and open, neither ever excluding the other, they say they both love each other. Together" (208)—they whisper desire. The slip on the cover, a cover full of women—even if it never appears in the contents—signals another love, another mode of the erotic; the two lips together both love each other. Women together, in slips baring shoulders, may be a come-on for men, but the come-on is complicated. The slip, like the lips, its inverse, is queer.

Referencing John Singer Sargent's scandalous 1884 *Portrait of Madame X,* which he later retouched to eliminate the fallen strap and thus restore Madame Gautreau's fallen honor (and claim his commission after her mother refused to pay), the image of the woman in the slip, strap falling off her shoulder, is a staple on the covers of 1950s pulp paperback books. The "professional model" posing for the cover of Fletcher Flora's cheesy novel *Leave Her to Hell!* signals her innate sluttiness because her strap hangs all the way off her shoulder (plate 17, *top*). She seems to be directed at the masculine gaze, but the author's name with its double Fs (echoing Tereska Torrès's double Ts), stamps this too as a lesbian fantasy. The hanging strap, sign of a slovenly woman provocatively in the middle of dressing or undressing or simply (though clearly not in Sargent's diamond-studded case) wearing a slip with straps too big for her white shoulders, invites scrutiny and incites desire, but it also points to the need of a better fit, provoking a maternal response, a saleswoman's response, to trim up the migrating strap with a tug and a pin. Slips, panties, and bras clothe the private regions of the body—"intimate apparel," they are called in American department store directories—hidden from view. But they are ever present: slips hanging too far below a hem; bra straps sneaking out from a low-cut shirt. Not only might they sneak into view, slips, especially cheap ones, made noise; nylon and other wartime manmade fabrics were "stiff." They could be heard crinkling and crunching under sweater and skirt or sheathe.[30]

Styles periodically brought the slip out of the closet, so to speak: the 1920s chemise dress mimicked lingerie. Novelist Katharine Brush (*Red-Headed Woman,* [1931]) precisely described these 1929 vintages as "tight and thin . . . knee-length," and Jean Harlow famously slithered around in it. The slip as dress has reappeared throughout the decades.[31] Until Madonna strutted around in her bodices and Jean Paul Gaultier reconstructed corsets and foundations into couture, undergarments were not to be seen through the clothing of good girls, though they could be admired, as Sister Carrie does at the corset counter of the Fair, "paus[ing] in rich reverie as she noted the dainty concoctions of color and lace there displayed."[32] As Farid Chenoune notes, by the 1920s, movies, fashion magazines, department stores, and their catalogs brought undergarments to the surface.

> In 1924, the Bon Marché store in Paris was offering cami-petticoats in cotton crepon for 9.75 francs, in brushed white finette (a cotton serge) for 18.50, in pure-wool jersey for 31, in crepe de chine for 49 and, the finest of the finest, in "openwork and eyelet lace, piece-dyed blue, pink, and black" at 79 francs. People were entering, as Louis-Ferdinand Céline put it, "a new period of democratically available fine underwear."[33]

This democratization of the slip, and its availability in the dynamic space of the department store, allowed even working-class women access to the secret attributes of decadent femininity. In the opening montage of *Red-Headed Woman*—the 1932 MGM film of Brush's novel with a screenplay by Anita Loos—which made Jean Harlow a star, we first see her at the beauty parlor, being transformed into a redhead; she then appears, tugging at her sheer bias-cut chemise, and asks her maid, "Can you see through this?" "I'm afraid so, miss." "Good," she replies. Finally, she slides a man's picture into a locket on her garter: "The boss's picture. It will do more good here than on his desk." In this movement from towel to silky dress, sheer as a slip revealing nothing underneath, to lacy thigh-high garter supporting her stockings, Lil Andrews has inventoried her arsenal of seduction necessary to get what she wants from rich men. This pre-Hays Code evocation of the role of the petticoat (or its lack) and garter in male seduction fires stories of the vamp, gold digger, and harlot throughout the 1920s and 1930s. The slip, with one strap hanging dangerously off the shoulder, is not only a signifier of rebellion against conformity but it exaggerates femininity as well, serving to snare a wealthy man.

The place of lingerie in lesbian pulp, while certainly designed to excite, also provided guidelines for how to achieve the "[s]lim and tailored, and not so damn sexy" look of Miss Ilene Gordon. Sales manager in a major Chicago department store, Miss Gordon is first seen by new salesgirl Barby wearing "suits and simple blouses, with one good bit of costume jewelry . . . all of a piece."[34] Soon after a few lunches with her supervisor, Barby, who has recently moved to the city with her two small-town friends, leaves apartment 3-B and moves into Ilene's Northshore Chicago apartment. She is deliriously happy watching Ilene in "her favorite lounging pajamas, blue and gold." Barby's older boss trains her, loves her, and supports the young woman damaged by rape, incest, and the pettiness of pinched provincial life. She also instructs her to "rumple your bed a little. This is the cleaning woman's day."[35] Knowing how to dress also means Ilene knows how to handle buyers and customers, as well as smoothly knowing how to live a closeted life: leave separately, hide your copies of lesbian pulp fiction, make her lover look like her roommate, and charm her younger lover's possessive father. Considered one of the earliest "pro-lesbian" pulps, *The Girls in 3-B* offered a picture of Beats and business, and of normalcy: lesbians who "acted human, who had problems and families, and allergies, and jobs, and so on."[36]

In another early lesbian novel, published first as a rare hardcover and then one of the first to be reissued as pulp, Claire Morgan's (Patricia Highsmith) *The Price of Salt*, the department store also serves as primal scene for an initial erotic encounter between a young employee and an older, sophisticated woman. When nineteen-year-old Therese, a budding set designer who works in the toy department of a large New York department store, first meets Mrs. H. F. Aird shopping for a valise for doll clothes, she notes her eyes, "gray, color-less, yet dominant as light or fire," but fixes on her voice, "like her [fur] coat, rich, supple and somehow full of secrets."[37] Therese's boy-friend is an artist in Greenwich Village who is struggling with his life-drawing class; she, having graduated from a convent school and the baleful blue eyes of Sister Alicia, works at Frankenberg's during Christmas rush. Highsmith triangulates Greenwich Village, artists' studios, and shopping within the first few pages, and the connec-tions between art making and shopping occur through clothing. (The French edition of the novel is entitled *Les Eaux dérobées*.) Like Dreiser's Sister Carrie, Therese, a designer, is acutely aware of dress. It becomes a vehicle of characterization. Dreiser might be said to have invented a realism that eschews interiority, substituting care-ful descriptions of surface details of clothing and accessories, for depth—that's his philosophy of clothes. Carrie notes, at her first meal with Drouet, "As he cut the meat his rings almost spoke. His new suit creaked as he stretched to reach the plates, break the bread, and pour the coffee."[38] We recognize, long before he enters the nar-rative, that Hurstwood will be significant because of the attention paid to his impeccable haberdashery. Therese reads apparel with Carrie's sharp eye.[39]

In the awkward prelude to Therese's first encounter with Carol, she visits the apartment of the hunchbacked Mrs. Robichek from "fifth floor—sweaters." Mrs. Robichek, a former dressmaker, pushes Therese to try on one of her now-outmoded creations (called the Caterina). After she briefly admires herself in a garnet red one, Therese finds herself swooning in her slip in the overheated room. Collapsing on a chair, she is covered with a blanket by Mrs. Ro-bichek who then *disrobes* to her corset, revealing her back brace, before she slides into bed. Therese lets herself out, thinking she has escaped, yet "she was not really escaping at all." This encounter—the young woman fed and clothed by the older, experienced woman—begins much lesbian fiction of the early period (1950–66). In this case, Mrs. Robichek, the grotesque hunchback, whose name suggests her state of possible undress, Robe in Check, appears perverse, predatory; she literally is a crippled woman, whom Therese imagines as the wicked witch entrapping her. Yet she has actually offered Therese a sort of haven from which "she didn't want to move" (16).

When she visits Carol's luxury suburban New Jersey house a few weeks later, Therese finds herself "reminded suddenly of Mrs. Robichek" as Carol tells her to "*slip* her shoes off," lie down, and then covers her with a blanket and gives her a glass of warm milk (59, emphasis added). Within minutes, Therese is detailing the secrets of her life to Carol, who is caressing her when the phone rings, shrilly interrupting their interlude together. Therese rises and puts her skirt and shoes on. Again, Therese has dozed on the bed of an older woman in her slip—not the lacy big corset and prosthetic brace of Mrs. Robichek or the green smoky silk she imagines clinging to Carol, but presumably her simple, workaday white nylon slip required of all 1950s proper young women.[40]

Accessories focus their interaction; they are a means of exchange: Therese buys a small black leather pocketbook for Carol that "looked like Carol," beautiful and expensive; Carol, in turn, purchases an expensive leather suitcase for Therese, a prelude to their monthlong cross-country road trip West. Carol's suburban New Jersey house, her car, and the handbag holding the incriminating letter replace Therese's bohemian apartment and bar, the art school, and the little theater as the zone of gay life. Initially crossing paths at the heart of bourgeois commerce, the two women exchange tokens of desire purchased in small specialty shops. But it is the department store, where women of differing classes meet and interact, linking downtown to midtown and beyond, that enables this relationship. These cross-generational stories of lesbian desire are thus inevitably cross-class tales as well. As such they owe much to the literary practices of 1930s proletarian writers, who, primarily middle class themselves, staged scenarios designed to foster interactions across class lines, for instance, Gale Wilhelm's 1935 novel, about artists, bohemians, and lesbians all working marginal jobs, set during the San Francisco general strike, *We Too Are Drifting.*

In Edmund Wilson's satirical novella about the 1930s, "The Princess with the Golden Hair," included in *Memoirs of Hecate County,* the art historian narrator maintains two cross-class affairs: between himself and his skinny but sexy Fourteenth Street dancehall lover from Brooklyn, supporting her child and helping out her husband, and with the upper-class married ice queen from suburban Hecate County whose body remains frozen even as she makes love to him until she masturbates to orgasm. Notorious for the New York State obscenity trial and subsequent Supreme Court case, *Memoirs of Hecate County,* consisting of interlocking stories, was banned in New York. "The Princess with the Golden Hair," the book's central tale, recounts the art historian's amorous involvements with these two women, who span a geography of New York class and ethnicity.

The narrator's two-year pursuit of wealthy Imogen finally pays off; watching her undress, he learns she wears an orthopedic brace beneath her expensive silk slip to correct a spinal problem caused by a childhood accident. Helping her fasten it after an evening of heavy kissing, he finds himself fantasizing about making love to her perfect body (her breasts round and firm compared to his emaciated proletarian lover's figure) with her brace on. She insists that he tighten the brace across her shoulders and chest, producing deep indentations in her flesh. Later on, while researching a painting in the New York Public Library, perhaps John Singer Sargent's *Portrait of Madame X,* which hangs in the Metropolitan Museum where the nameless narrator works, he comes across a book from the 1880s entitled *The Hysterical Element in Orthopaedic Surgery* that describes Imogen's symptoms, right down to the desire to wear the brace "so tight as to produce excoriations."[41] The conflation of illicit sex, art, and medical discourse that swirl around the princess is contrasted to the healthy eroticism of the ethnic girl getting by Downtown.

Describing Georgia O'Keeffe's still-life paintings exhibited in 1925 at Alfred Stieglitz's Andersen Gallery, Wilson, who was at that time art critic for the *New Republic*, made the extraordinary claim that female artists were incapable of objectification. Like formfitting underwear, they were simply too close to their materials. Objects represented did not reveal subjectivity but, instead, like one's most intimate apparel, women's paintings became so enmeshed in the psychic structures of femininity that they conformed to, even entered into, a woman's figure, leaving traces, like Imogen's brace, on the skin: "women seem to charge the objects they represent with so immediate a personal emotion that they absorb the subject into themselves instead of incorporating themselves into the subject . . . women artists have a way of appearing to wear their most brilliant productions—however objective in form—like those other artistic expressions, their clothes."[42] Wilson's comments as an art critic reveal sources for his 1946 novella. So, too, perhaps, was Frida Kahlo's 1944 painting, *The Broken Column*.[43]

For much of her life Frida Kahlo wore a plaster-cast brace, or one made of metal and straps, which she decorated with her own miniature frescos and which appeared in some of her paintings. The site of her prosthesis became a work of art—she painted her corsets and painted herself in them as Wilson theorized a woman artist would. Unlike Imogen's, Kahlo's back injuries were not hysterical symptoms. Kahlo's numerous operations on her injured and paralyzed spine; her many abortions and miscarriages; her addiction; her gangrene and leg amputation; her confinement to a back brace, wheelchair, and bed; and her wounds and poorly healed scars, some of which may have been self-inflicted through unnecessary surgery, were the basis for her own endless self-inspection and self-revelation. In the early 1940s, she underwent a series of spinal operations that left her severely scarred and unable to sit except with support from steel, leather, and plaster corsets. *The Broken Column*, from 1944, presents her lovely torso ripped apart, revealing an ionic column pieced together in broken sections. A brace fastens her body together; it is littered with nails partially driven into her flesh. She does not bleed but her eyes leak milk for tears. As Rafael Vazquez Bayad describes the painting, it is "a kind of homage to all those who suffer from spinal injuries . . . her torso split in two by a wide gap inside of which is a broken Ionic column. The architectural element is the artist's way of glorifying her infirmity, conferring on her fractures a certain art and beauty. An orthopedic corset like the ones she often had to wear wraps around the fragmented torso; it has the leather straps and metal buckles common to such contraptions. The beauty of the breasts, which Frida painted with utmost perfection, contrasts with the rest of the composition."[44] Undergarments here have become part of the construction of Kahlo's persona as damaged woman, revelatory artist; artifacts of injury, art, and science, she called them "punishment."[45] Like Imogen's rigid corset, Kahlo's enters her body, leaving marks upon it, constricting and constructing her identity, one that, like Imogen's self-arousal, moves decidedly away from conventional heterosexuality.

Meant to conceal and to be concealed, undergarments should remain invisible, only to become overcharged, revealing something of the inner sexual truth when they can be seen. Foundations, they were once called, designed to contour and reshape the female figure. A slip is at once there and not there, swerving between the workaday and demure and the erotic and decadent; all over the covers, barely legible inside the books. Like the cotton underwear that Aline Weinman sells at Diamond's Department Store in Leane Zugsmith's 1936 proletarian novel about the Orbach's strike, *A Time to Remember*,[46] or the backward white men's T-shirts sported by Buffalo butches in the 1950s, recounted by Kennedy and Davis, it might signify a connection to working-class identities and labor. Or as finery, excessive, like the sheer silk and lace items fingered by Sister Carrie at The Fair in Dreiser's Chicago, it hints at a realm of pleasure and wealth far above its lowly place covering breasts, buttocks, and pubis. As a medical device, the undergarment allows the invalid to endure pain at work; its macabre quality as a form of entombment that straps one into oneself, however, excites a certain sexual fetishism as well.

And so, of course straps hang off the shoulders on the covers of these pulpy books: bra straps, slip straps, gown straps. The movement from control to disarray: a motion from reined-in sexuality to its overt expression as the strap falls off the shoulder. Tight straps constrict, confine, remold the figure; loose ones undo constraints, offer full décolletage from shoulder to shoulder. Their location conveys an entire narrative: "A beginning of the work of condensation," Freud defines slips of the tongue.[47] Slips fall off the shoulder, fall off the tongue, record sales; slippers dangle off the foot; one slips one's shoes off. They are all-purpose fetish items running from head to toe, bridging private and public spaces, crossing class boundaries and borders of discretion. Slip, verb, transitive; intransitive; noun: escape, a narrow slit, a thin person, a slight thing, a lapse, and on and on. There are seven pages of definitions in the *Oxford English Dictionary* for slip, slipper, slippery, as adjective. From function to fetish to fashion, secrets of identity pass across social barriers through imitation, reading, and looking. The covers of many pulp novels function to telescope desire; often forums for fashion and movie tie-ins, they were part of the explosion of popular culture across various media occurring in postwar America.

The slips could never be too white, the fabric too sheer, the breasts too pointy, the hips too round, the stomach too flat, the cleavage too deep, the lace too intricate, the skin too smooth. With Jean Harlow falling out of her kimono into Clark Gable's arms in the jungles of Saigon in *Red Dust*, the slip haunts erotic imagination. It suggests private, self-contained pleasure; the slip and the body it sheathes outline the sex that is not one. For all the male eyes it is supposed to entrance, the slip is meant for women. In the 1950s: There was Joanne Woodward finally stripping down to a slip to survive that long, hot Mississippi summer. There was Marilyn casually chatting to her girlfriends Josephine and Daphne in the sleeper car because some do like it hot. There was diaphanous Blanche and gritty Stella inhabiting their desire so differently before Stanley's ripped T-shirt. And, most luminous of all, there was Liz, sizzling like a cat on a hot tin roof, surrounded by the no-neck monsters on Big Daddy's plantation. In the 1960s: Elizabeth Taylor running out of her john's apartment in her lace slip and his wife's mink coat in *Butterfield 8*; there was the zoom into Janet Leigh dressing herself after her tryst with her lover in *Psycho*, an echo of the keyhole view of Leigh undressing herself in her motel room in *Touch of Evil*. These iconic images rescript the formfitting, ruffled corsets of bar girls from Dallas to Vienna to Frenchy in countless Westerns, the slinky lingerie of Theda Bara and Mae West and all the gold diggers of 1930s musicals, melodramas, and screwball comedies.

Young female readers in midcentury America, like Sister Carrie before them, were quick studies; they observed and picked up traces of fashion advice—down to slips, socks and drawers—from the available sources. These included a newly popular genre, aimed primarily at straight men, but also hidden in the sock and underwear drawers of some young women—lesbian and bohemian pulp fiction. There but not there, like a slinky slip, the clothing in the lesbian and bohemian pulp novels splashed all over the covers could barely be found within. Still, this debased literature taught a generation of women how to dress down and undress together. In the slippage between cover and content, between visibility and disappearance, lie some hints of both Dreiser's quest for a philosophy of clothes and Freud's fantasies of the phallic woman. Like a new garment once consumed, the pulp lesbian and her bohemian sister become fodder for secondhand trade. Yet these cheap books, revealing women's secrets, did more than titillate; they taught.

CHAPTER 8

Sci-Unfi: Bombs, Ovens, Delinquents, and More

Pulps were essentially products of the Second World War. Allen Lane had launched Penguin in 1935 and then, in 1939, Ian Ballantine brought Penguin to the United States for its American branch. But it was also "stolen," as E. L. Doctorow recounted, by Robert de Graff and turned into an American product, reviving the paperbound book in the United States with Pocket Books and its kangaroo logo. During the war, the Council on Books in Wartime had joined with the army and navy to develop and deliver more than one hundred forty million paperback books to overseas servicemen and women, chosen relevant books for promotion, and inaugurated a program to distribute translations of American books to occupied nations. While the original impetus for the pocket book was as a cheap and pervasive reprint format for works of fiction, nonfiction quickly became part of publishers' lines. (Penguin differentiated genres by the color of the cover.) Nonfiction became important during World War II as citizens followed battle reports—and so needed an education in geography, political history, and technologies of warfare. With the advent of the Cold War and the nuclear age after the defeat of Germany and Japan, the interest in the global scope of threats meant a market for science writing, biography, and history, as well as the newer social sciences of economics, psychology, and sociology. Thus, World War II literally facilitated the spread of pulp, but the aftereffects of war's horrors—extermination camps, atomic bombings, and the Cold War—globalized terror in surprising ways. Pulp crystallized these sites of anxiety, paradoxically domesticating them as homegrown disturbances. Truth also got pulped.

Cloaking is essential to pulp, even though the aim of pulp paperbacks was to spread knowledge—good reading for the millions—by being seen. These books were made to seem as if they held secrets about women's sexuality, nuclear war, interracial sex, and the Holocaust that could be discerned as much by scrutinizing the covers as by reading between them. Take the 1948 first US paperback edition of John Hersey's report on Hiroshima. First published in the *New Yorker* to sensational acclaim, Alfred Knopf brought *Hiroshima* out in hardback while Penguin issued it in the United Kingdom almost immediately, each with a discreet, subdued cover mirroring the clipped, straightforward prose Hersey devised to relay the story of six survivors. However, in the United States, it was paperbacked as pulpy Bantam Book No. 404 with a cover depicting an average American couple fleeing an urban holocaust as an explosion appears, blotting the horizon—an image revived by Donald Siegel in his film *Invasion of the Body Snatchers* (1956) but found already on the 1955 Jack Finney novel, *The Body Snatchers*, as a Dell paperback with a cover by Jack McDermott. Thus, the story of America's destruction of a Japanese city, told in restrained prose through the accounts of six survivors and eyewitnesses, had transmogrified into a garish nightmare of American annihilation—presumably, given the title, by the Japanese. Inside, before the copyright page, is a note about the cover and its author.

When Geoffrey Biggs, a master of shadow and light technique in art, brought in his startling illustration for the cover of *Hiroshima*, everybody wanted to know: "Where'd you get those people . . . why *those* two?"

Biggs said he thought back to that August morning in a certain big industrial city and he imagined how *universally* terrifying that situation was, how it could strike fear into *anybody's* bones. "And I just drew two perfectly ordinary people—like you or me—and had them portray alarm, anxiety, and yet wild hope for survival as they run from man-made disaster in a big city—a city like yours or mine."

Ordinary? Anybody? Universal? Those people are white people, young Americans, the guy wearing the same kind of trench coat that Holden Caulfield wore in the notorious James Avati cover for the NAL paperback edition of *Catcher in the Rye*, the woman in her loafers and gathered skirt, which in 1948, was the height of New Look fashion. These two were a wholesome couple who could never be mistaken for the "Wayward Youth in Brooklyn" found on the cover of the 1948 Avon edition of the notorious pulp *The Amboy Dukes*, which features a boy and a girl lying on a rumpled trench coat with the Brooklyn Bridge and a large industrial city in the background. He has black hair cut in a DA (duck's ass or duck-tail), she has a tight red dress on; it's been hiked up as the two embrace to reveal the garter clasp holding her stockings. She's wearing red high heels (plate 23).

Both these books might have been found on the same racks in the hundred thousand newsstands and drugstores where paperbacks were available, especially in the years after World War II when concern about juvenile delinquency, precisely what sparked congressional hearings, produced a rash of books about teenage menace. *The Amboy Dukes* caused a sensation when it was discovered that a gang of boys in Brooklyn had relied on it as a how-to manual for serial sex with an older prostitute who they refused to pay after they picked her up and raped her. Social workers, judges, and clerics noted that the youths even knew which page (p. 26) would yield the information on the procedure, as the boys, smoking a reefer, scheme to rape the woman and steal back their money while each awaits "his turn." On the cover of *Hiroshima*, the woman's face is obscured by her hair as she looks down at her feet and the long shadow cast by the bright light behind the frantic couple. Her coat and skirt are ripped; perhaps she too has been raped, or escaped from some alien invasion. The tagline reads "Six survived to tell what happened," so that this image might be illustrating a science-fiction tale (figure 8.1). This was the case on the 1955 Dell cover for *The Body Snatchers* or later, in 1958, on the Popular Library cover of Philip Wylie's "novel of America under atomic attack," *Tomorrow!*, which links the fiery nuclear conflagration behind a madly fleeing woman to visions of her explosive sexuality as she holds her tattered dress across her shredded slip and runs away barefoot (plate 17, *bottom right*). The cover of *Hiroshima* set up the image of America under attack (plate 17, *bottom left*), although presumably, a reader in 1948 would recognize the meaning of the title; yet the cover was controversial enough that subsequent editions radically altered the artwork; but the image of cities in ruins and citizens on the run persisted elsewhere.

These covers were part of the visual landscape of the postwar era in which the boundaries of fiction and nonfiction bled across one another. They contributed visual and verbal elements to what George Lipsitz described as a "new working-class public culture during World War II."[1] Dell mysteries—and many other genres— included an illustrated map by Ruth Belew that provided a key to the locations of events inside the covers (plate 2). As Richard Lupoff notes,

> The map might show anything from a sector of the Pacific Ocean (*Queen of the Flat-Tops* by Stanley Johnston), a diagram of an apartment building (*Death in Five Boxes* by John Dickson Carr writing as Carter Dixon), the surface of the moon (*First*

Men in the Moon by H. G. Wells), Hopalong Cassidy's ranch (*Bar-20 Days* by Clarence E. Mulford), the Caribbean Sea (*Men Under the Sea* by Frank Meier), or the city of San Francisco (*Dead Yellow Woman* by Dashiell Hammett).[2]

Avon's back cover boasted that "Because every Avon title is selected primarily for maximum reading pleasure, Avon Books [with the Shakespeare Head imprint on the title page] have attained a wide popularity among the great American reading public. In these days of continual rising prices in almost every sphere of purchasing, Avon Pocket-Size Books remain at their pre-war price of 25c." With the war's end and a postwar inflationary market, Avon and other paperback publishers were still committed to their mass audience and its pocketbook. This was precisely what drove the censorship efforts of the courts and Congress, as did the covers, which, as I have been arguing, opened these books to promiscuous reading, a demotics of reading and category confusion.[3]

Within a few years—by the third printing in 1951—the *Hiroshima* cover had morphed again into an abstraction of an explosion: a white, jagged cloud splashed across a blue field with a brown stake running through it, forming one pole of the letter H. In eliminating any reference to people to emphasize the atomic action at work, this cover aligned with the erasure of social realism in force in 1950s abstract expressionism and New Criticism. By this time, the atomic bomb had been superseded by the vastly more powerful hydrogen bomb, which would be exploded in an aboveground test by the United States in November 1952, and the Soviet Union had developed its own nuclear weapons arsenal. *Life* magazine had immortalized Jackson Pollock's drip paintings, sending abstract expressionism into millions of living rooms. The cover's abstraction seems to universalize and aestheticize but again represses the victims of the bomb who are the subjects of Hersey's reportage. It is this process of simultaneously foregrounding terror and sensation

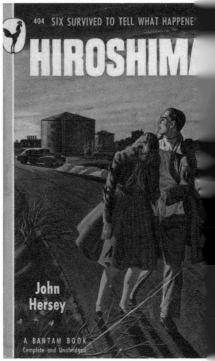

Figure 8.1 Variations on John Hersey, *Hiroshima* (London: Penguin, 1946); (New York: Bantam, 1948), cover by Geoffrey Biggs; *opposite page* (Bantam, fifth printing, 1956), cover photograph, Wide-World Photos.

while sending it home in the pockets and pocketbooks that is essential to pulp—a pathological nation's literary form. However, within a few years, Bantam was using an official photograph of a mushroom cloud on the cover; yet its first use still seemed to require a stylized effect to remove its import from documentary reality. In this mid-1950s version, an illustration—a dotted line and a cartoonlike outline of a miniature plane—hampers the full effect of the photograph. Thereafter, only the photograph of the bomb blast appeared on the cover; no reference to aerial destruction (and where it had occurred) can be seen (figure 8.1).

In 1947, Avon released one of the first paperback volumes of
what we now call Holocaust studies, Olga Lengyel's *Hitler's Ovens*,
unleashing the flood of memoirs that would follow upon the enormous popularity of Anne Frank's diary, published in Amsterdam
in 1947 and translated in a Pocket Books edition in 1952 as *Anne
Frank: The Diary of a Young Girl*. But before this "deeply moving
story of adolescence . . . ha[d] become a classic of our time," as my
edition says on its cover (with a photograph of Millie Perkins, the
actress who portrayed Anne in the 1959 film version), various publishers were dramatizing the horrors of Nazi extermination in paperback. Eugen Kogon's memoir and history, originally published in
1945 as *Der SS-Staat: Das System der deutscher Konzentrationslager*,

the story of this Christian anti-Nazi resister who survived internment in Buchenwald, appeared in 1955 as an American paperback edition with the compelling title *The Theory and Practice of Hell* from Berkley, one of the lesser pocket-size book publishers, known for its science-fiction list. This was a decade after the study was published in English in cloth but almost immediately after the publishing house opened. With its stark yellow cover featuring Nazi SS guards marching with their swastika flags before Hitler, it became one in the midst of "the voluminous concentration-camp literature of the past twelve years," and among the first works of Holocaust pulp to appear for the mass market to tell "what a German concentration camp was really like."[4] Moreover, the title's transformation shifted it from a rather straightforward report and history to become an entry point into hell, and the back-cover description stressed its "full and unexpurgated account of the activities of Hitler's dreaded SS—the masters of the most vicious system of sadistic cruelty in the history of the world." With the icons of Nazism emblazoned in red—the swastika and the double jagged SS—on the yellow cover, suggesting the yellow star Nazis mandated Jews wear and the sexually charged language of sadism, as well as the code for explicit language, "unexpurgated," the book transmitted "an unsparing account of the fiendish system that tortured and killed millions."

Similarly, *Five Chimneys*, a memoir by Hungarian/Romanian author Olga Lengyel about surviving Auschwitz-Birkenau as an assistant in the infirmary became the sensationally titled *I Survived Hitler's Ovens* in the 1947 Avon paperback. It also used photographs culled from newspapers to enhance its documentary effect and its title screamed of sadism. Yet its cover with a cadaver-like face in red and black also evoked horror genres. Decades later the book served as one of the sources for William Styron's controversial novel, *Sophie's Choice*.[5] Again, the evocative title *Five Chimneys*, originally used by Lengyel to convey how the landscape of memory was controlled by the monumentality of death and ashes, was literalized into the metonym of the oven, which even by the late 1940s had become one of the defining symbols of the Holocaust, but also creepily turned Hitler into Betty Crocker. The tagline reads "Birkenau had four large cremation furnaces for prisoners. Ashes became fertilizer." Moreover, the cover also nodded to the salacious aspect of the entire paperback process, as often books were abridged in order to fit into the rigid page limitations or occasionally to pass local censorship boards and so might note on the title page that the work was abridged or condensed, but the cover blurb prominently declared the book to be "complete and unabridged." It was "the uncensored truth—'a picture of utter hell,'" according to the *Saturday Review of Literature.* The bright yellow back cover was even more explicit in its production of this Holocaust pulp as porn, enticing readers into its "picture of hell": Two phrases: "DEATH CAMP . . . THIS BOOK CAN SHOCK YOU" dominate in red letters. The blurb explains, "It is the intimate, day-by-day record of a beautiful woman . . . It is the true, documented chronicle of organized sadism, systematic brutality, incredible personal humiliation, monstrous promiscuity and (continued on page one)" thus sending readers directly into the book's interior (plate 24, *right*).

All this marketing hype aside, these are serious books of nonfiction usually written for a fairly sophisticated readership, and it is precisely the hysterical prose, meant to grab the attention of readers, that put these books into the hands of those who might never have otherwise read them. They were meant to be taken up by wide audiences aware of current events and scientific discoveries, but they also might land in a less-suspecting reader's hand. As the refashioned titles of the two Holocaust pulps by Lengyel and Kogon suggest, history is at once terrifying and homey. It can be quite personal, "I survived" or "The Diary," but also can extend into a wide field as a scientific theory would. Science and its historical ramifications were always close to home and thus pervasive. The "Complete & Unabridged" biography of Marie Curie, by her daughter

Eve, published in an early Pocket Book edition in 1946 (figure 8.2), which actually lists each volume by number, had been printed in the hundreds of thousands when it first appeared. My copy is No. 147,460,279, its Perma Gloss cover peeling away. As the discoverer of radium, and as an Eastern European émigré, not to mention a wife and mother, Curie linked warfare and the home. One learns of Marie Curie's first encounter with her precious "treasure." "Full of curiosity and impatience, she wanted to open one of the sacks and contemplate her treasure without further waiting. She cut the strings, undid the coarse sackcloth and plunged her two hands into the dull brown ore, still mixed with pine needles from Bohemia. There was where radium was hidden."[6] Marie Curie's exuberant boldness, grabbing her sacks of Bohemian ore to feel the radium locked within, her name almost a homonym for her curiosity, is a fitting metaphor for the pull these sci-unfi pulps exerted on readers.

Julia Mickenberg traces a similar effort to entice readers by postwar children's literature publishers during the Cold War, one that paradoxically opened areas for left-wing writers because "science books could serve a Marxist agenda [show 'the dynamics of dialectical materialism' as 'really exciting to kids,' according to Betty Bacon of Young World Books] without having any explicit political content."[7] The fears that the United States lacked a rigorous curriculum in science became even more pressing after the war. "Between the nuclear fallout that followed World War II and the launch of Sputnik in 1957, science assumed a special place in the already politicized educational discourse . . . Scientific and technological achievement became an obsession for Americans, and the way to get there was clearly via the public school system."[8] Moreover, science could be used to challenge racial and gender stereotypes by exploring anthropology, biology, and the history of science. Paperbacks, by entering the world of nonfiction, were contributing to national renewal.

Figure 8.2 Eve Curie, *Madame Curie* (Pocket Books, 1946). Cover artist unknown. Cover from the 1939 Doubleday edition. Reprinted with the permission of Simon & Schuster, Inc. from *Madame Curie* by Eve Curie. Translated by Vincent Sheean. Copyright © Pocket Books, 1946. All rights reserved.

So, too, history, biography, and folklore served up counternarratives to the grand story of the nation. Left-wing author Meridel Le Sueur (who published the 1954 children's biography *River Road: A Story of Abraham Lincoln*) had used the pulps during the 1930s to provide an outline for her female proletarian novel, *The Girl*. Similarly, Ann Petry's pulpy 1940s and 1950s novels (all brought out in paperback) gave way in the late 1950s to her children's books, including the biographies *Tituba of Salem Village* (1964) and *Harriet Tubman: Conductor on the Underground Railroad* (1955). Bantam Books brought out *A Treasury of Folk Songs* in 1948, collected by Sylvia and John Kolb and dedicated, much like John Dos Passos's 1930s *U.S.A.* trilogy, "to the voice of the American people—who sang these songs as they built a continent of United States, dedicated to freedom, and who, today, believe in, and are beginning to sing of, a world of united nations, dedicated to peace." A few years later, in 1950, Pocket Books brought out an abridged edition of B. A. Botkin's *Pocket Treasury of American Folklore*, based on the Crown Publisher hardcover edition, which was a compendium of tales collected during the 1930s under the auspices of the Federal Writers' Project of the WPA. Mickenberg explains that children's books offered pictures of young people as "brave, independent thinkers" and adults with "the responsibility, along with the power, to make the world better."[9] They use the past to draw parallels to the contemporary moment in order to vivify and critique current events.

This pedagogical impulse on the part of left-wing writers and publishers in children's literature resonated with efforts among mass-marketed paperback publishers to democratically appeal to all Americans, as many came from similar political and publishing backgrounds. Their sensationalist yet sentimental efforts to garner readers depended in part on a sense that reading *this* book was urgent for understanding a frightening world and for making sense of one's domestic realm. The horrors of World War II brought home the need to know—about brainwashing (in the post–Korean War books), atomic weapons, Nazism and fascism, economics. And new modes of affective relations between men and women, and parents and children, meant that works of psychology, philosophy, and anthropology had special relevance. George Soule's *Introduction to Economic Science* (a 1951 Mentor Book from NAL) reveals how macroeconomics ("Government Power to Increase and Decrease Bank Credit," for instance) is tied to more private concerns ("How Money Appears and Disappears"). Its back cover proclaims simply, "This Book Tells You How to Understand Today's Economic Problems."

Some variation on "this book" can be found on the covers of many pulps. It is a phrase that allows readers to be assured that what they are purchasing has authenticity, yet will pack a punch. In the case of nonfiction pulps, especially those dealing with the immediate past of World War II, such as Tereska Torrès's *Women's Barracks*, billed as her autobiography, it provides a justification that contrasts with its juicy cover by Baryè Phillips of a women's dormitory where five women are arrayed in various states of dress, but that foregrounds the woman in full uniform, red lipstick, and nail polish, smoking and staring at another, who stares back at her while still in bra and panties as she pulls her skirt. The exchange of looks, the cigarettes, the sign in French, "Avis!," even the naked lightbulb hanging from the author's name, open another world—"frank," says the tagline; "France," says the badge on the uniform. "This is the story of what happens when scores of young girls live intimately together in a French military barracks. . . . So this book, with all of its revealment and tenderness, is an important book because it tells a story that had never been truly told—the story of women in war." The phrase "this is the story," returns to the early Pocket Books covers that were framed with the tag: "This is a GENUINE Pocket Book" and so assert a connection to the sources of the paperback revolution in the United States—among them the effects of World War II, which severed Allen Lane, who was an important connection for Ian Ballantine (founder of Bantam), Robert de Graff (founder of Pocket Books), Victor Weybright (NAL), and Kurt Enoch (also NAL) from wartime production of Penguin in the United Kingdom.

The Pocket History of the Second World War appeared in December 1945, just weeks after the hardcover edition appeared, and offered a collation of firsthand reports from British and American news sources of battle sites from Poland to Nagasaki. It was a mass-market retrospective of the war, providing, as its back cover claimed, "A New Kind of History," focused on eyewitness accounts of those on the ground as soldiers or reporters. It followed the 1943 Penguin Books Infantry Journal, *A History of the War: In Maps, In Pictographs, In Words*, by Rudolf Modley, issued in the format of the ASEs as part of an orientation course designed for servicemen and women, but expanded for public consumption in 1944 as "A Fighting Forces—Penguin Special" (figure 8.3). But there were hundreds of books appearing on the war, during and after, and the back pages of Eugen Kogon's *Theory and Practice of Hell* list many titles of interest to readers.

The paperback as an object and a phenomenon was intimately tied to the war, as American paperback publishers scurried to fill voids opened when shipping books from England ceased after war was declared on Germany in 1939, so it is not surprising how many books of "holocaust pulp" or "history pulp," especially about the war, appeared almost immediately after V-J Day. Kogon describes how the print shops of Buchenwald "prepared all manner of luxury books, greeting cards, artistic tablets and inscriptions, and the illustrated magazine, *The Pelican*" (this last somewhat uncanny, as Pelican was among the original Penguin imprint lines, mostly for nonfiction, launched in 1937 by Allen Lane; it eventually morphed into NAL Mentor Books). All featured high workmanship, so that a "beautifully bound report to Berlin" was said to be known for its "Typical concentration-camp work!"[10] Pelican Books, often with stunning covers by Robert Jonas, were crucial for popularizing arcane ideas from physics and mathematics, usually by physicist George Gamow, a professor at George Washington University. His 1940 book, *The Birth and Death of the Sun*, appeared as a Pelican edition in September 1945, explaining on its flyleaf: "This is the atomic age. We are on the brink of a future that may be terrifying

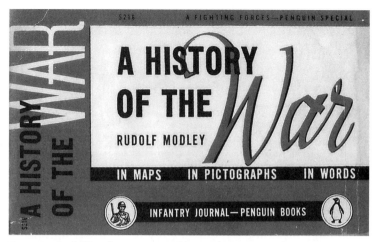

Figure 8.3 Rudolf Modley, *A History of the War* (Penguin, 1944).

or enthralling" (plate 18). It explicates how nuclear chain reactions occur in stars and have been made possible through atom-smashers and cyclotrons on Earth, and its appendix, written weeks after the bombs were dropped on Hiroshima and Nagasaki, acknowledges, "with all due respect to the effect of the atomic bomb on World War II, and its terrible significance in the wars of the future, a much more interesting speculation lies in the possibility of utilizing liberated subatomic energy for peaceful purposes."[11] A year later, as editors at NAL were considering reprinting the scathing 1929 antiwar novel by World War I veteran and imagist poet Richard Aldington, *Death of a Hero*, it was seen, in a reader's report, as possessing "an excellent chance of becoming a popular reprint. It has all the necessary elements—war and fireworks, sex, learning (pagan classics), cleverness, nobility, heaven-storming, revelation, disillusionment painfully come by, revolt and tragedy." More important, its nod to another era, another war, another devastation, and its "fluent and flamboyant discussion of society, amrriage [sic] and love, Christianity, birth control and other topics nowadays overshadowed by talk about atoms [and] the United Nations" made its backward glance to "those older subjects" a welcome relief to the very subjects paperback publishers were churning out.[12] In Preston Sturges's *Sullivan's Travels*, the producers tell director Sullivan that he can make his next film relevant to the Depression—"but with a little sex"—in order to keep its audience's attention. In a similar way, paperback publishers were aware of the problem of oversaturation, especially with depressing topics such as nuclear war. Thus, George Gamow felt compelled to see a bright side to splitting atoms, one that would permeate the futuristic pronouncements contributed by scientists a decade later to the thirtieth anniversary issue of *Amazing Stories*.

This optimism (and a little bit of sex) was repeated in the pitches for Margaret Mead's *Coming of Age in Samoa*, a 1949 Mentor Book (the successor to Pelican, once NAL spun off from Penguin), where it was touted on the back cover as "an extraordinary accomplishment in practical psychology in the domain of erotics" and "earnestly recommend[ed] . . . to everyone interested in education or the psychology of sex." Mead's study followed from another by her mentor, Ruth Benedict, whose 1934 study, *Patterns of Culture*, appeared in a Pelican edition in 1946, offering a vision of cultural understanding that was being fostered in the aftermath of World War II. *Patterns of Culture* was the second Mentor Book issued in 1948 (M2) with a stunning cover by Robert Jonas in which four profiles in various shades of grey, brown, orange, and beige are linked together in a Venn diagram. Mead's book also featured a Jonas cover—a stylized nod to Paul Gauguin's Tahitian idylls (figure 8.4). By 1950, the Mentor edition had become "the leading best-seller in the Mentor series . . . widely adapted [*sic*] by colleges and schools . . . [with] phenomenal newsstand sale[s]" touts the back-cover blurb.[13] It appeared annually throughout the 1950s.

Mead wanted her study to contribute to what she called in her 1949 preface, "the morals I drew for our society . . . our education,

Figure 8.4 Margaret Mead, *Coming of Age in Samoa* (Signet/Mentor, 1949). Cover by Robert Jonas.

[and] remain . . . pertinent to our world today."[14] Her story and analysis of "adolescence and sex" among "primitive" girls might be thought of as a precursor to the reform school/juvenile delinquent literature that flowered in the postwar years as fear of "Teen-Age Tyranny" took hold.[15] One chapter, on "the girl in conflict," details the moral and epistemological, even ontological, "distinctions"

between acts that might be considered asocial and the responses to them that might cast her as delinquent.[16] Mead's book, and her subsequent role as cultural interpreter of America's youth, served as a primer for a freer postwar child-rearing practice associated with Dr. Benjamin Spock.[17] Not only was a more open sense about sexuality being promoted by popular anthropology, but changing racial attitudes were being propelled by anthropologists as well. NAL explained in its biography of Benedict that her 1943 pamphlet, *Races of Man*, which sold more than 250,000 copies, had its sale "increased when Representative Andrew J. May, then chairman of the House Military Affairs Committee, banned its distribution in Army recreation centers and orientation courses, because the pamphlet stated that the Negro and white races were equal, if given equal economic and educational conditions." As with fiction, exposing how forms of government-sponsored censorship were limiting access to popular books became part of the story and used as marketing tools. With so much propaganda during the war about Nazi suppression of books and ideas, it was something of a coup to get an endorsement from Congress in the form of an order to ban a book for promoting racial equality, especially as the subtext of Representative May's concern was also sexual.

With its endorsement of a less restrictive view of adolescent sexuality, on the one hand, and growing fears of young people's newly visible presence as consumers, on the other, Mead's book, and even Benedict's, actually helped spread the image of teenage tyranny. By 1964, the Hechingers reported on a college instructor who no longer assigned "the new classic" *The Catcher in the Rye* because everyone had already read it.[18] A year after Leonard Bernstein's Broadway musical *West Side Story* became a smash hit—bringing the issue of youth gangs to the forefront of popular culture, Harrison E. Salisbury's 1958 "headline-making book" on "Teen-Age Terror in slum and suburb," *The Shook-Up Generation*, about gangs in New York, appeared (plate 19, *top*). A year later, the Crest Book paperback from Fawcett was published. With its back-cover photograph of a gang about to start a fistfight and a series of weapons from a long-shoreman's hook, like the one Brando flings over his shoulder in *On the Waterfront* (1954), to pistols, switchblades, and chains, it presents a cascade of violence. Its front-cover photograph of tough boys and girls in dungarees sprawled along an alley, laundry hanging between the tenements, recalled a series of images from earlier covers by James Avati and Stanley Zuckerberg, particularly Zuckerberg's cover for Vasco Pratolini's *Naked Streets* (NAL No. 1061, 1953) and may have served as a model for sets in the 1961 movie version of Bernstein's opera.[19]

Tracing the history of New York gangs by hanging out with members, Salisbury notes that his informants believed him to be a reporter from the *News*, as "this tabloid picture paper is about the only publication which is 'read'" in Red Hook.[20] Later, Salisbury notes the poor literacy of even suburban gang members; many, however, are fans of *Confidential* magazine because, as he comments, "reading about the scandalous conduct of persons who are well known or important makes the Chimp feel that he has done nothing very bad"; unlike him, they get away with murder.[21] As early as 1940, Caroline Slade, who, as her biography on the back cover of the Signet edition of *The Triumph of Willie Pond* notes, "is particularly interested in the problem of the so-called delinquent girl," had dissected the causes of "such terrible delinquency" as that of Mary Pond, who turns to prostitution to help support her family but mainly to be able to buy a few items of finery for herself. One of the social workers describes the situation as "an old, old story, the story of an unfit home—it really might be classed as a broken home, with such shiftless, weak parents. Out of such miserable homes came a whole regiment of criminals and prostitutes and delinquents. Statistics, which could not lie, proved that."[22]

James Avati's cover for the 1951 edition, abridged for a fee of seventy-five dollars by the go-to abridgement editor, Alice Ten Eyck, zeroes in on this sentiment. It portrays a sneering young woman, hand on her protruded hip, standing by a sink full of dirty dishes, who dominates two older people, a man seated and women standing behind her fading into the background.[23] This cover at least located the woman in her torn red sweater within the family; Avati's cover from the year before of Slade's novel about teenage pregnancy, *Lilly Crackell*, by contrast, displays a barefoot girl, her legs open, with dress unbuttoned and disheveled, sitting on a bed. The walls of the room are papered with torn newspapers, and a shoddy table with a steaming tea kettle partially hides her from view; she is alone within this sordid space. The tagline quotes from a review by Harry Hansen of the *New York World-Telegram*: "Lilly is unlike any other unwed mother in fiction." Even though these "terrifying" tales of "a wayward girl and her abandoned family," as the tagline for *Triumph* declared, were written during the 1940s and were concerned with the 1930s, they, like Torrès's *Women's Barracks* (1950), pointed to the perception that with the new decade—following the Chinese Revolution and the explosion of the hydrogen bomb—women's sexuality also had become uncontrollable.[24]

Slade sought to have her other titles reprinted by NAL, and during the early 1950s wrote often to Victor Weybright to nudge him to consider *Job's House, Mrs. Party's House,* and her controversial first novel, *Sterile Sun.* She discussed how important the issue of child rape was in contemporary America and deemed its portrayal in *Lilly Crackell* significant in one letter, and in another mentioned that a friend in Vienna had seen the Signet book "prominently displayed."[25] But, as an office memo on another of her books, *Lost: A Young Woman,* indicates, Slade's work—not just its covers—tended toward the sensational and risked appearing to cater to readers below those usually sought by NAL. "If this were not by Caroline Slade, I'd think it a straight pulp story, maybe out of *True Confessions*" and thus beneath the standards of NAL.[26] But this was precisely what interested some readers, as Willis Stevens indicated in a fan letter sent to Slade at NAL about *Margaret*: "After rehearsing my choir in the Bronx, I crossed the street and found your book on the Signet shelf in the corner drugstore; found also that I could not put it down having once begun to read." [27] This book clearly grabbed him; it packed a "wallop."

An undated, unattributed, handwritten memo that I found in the archives from the mid 1940s, after NAL had established itself as a reprint house providing "Good Reading for the Millions," explains some of the thinking behind the kinds of books, especially nonfiction titles, the editors were looking for. It first lists what they "Don't want": "no crusading books—unless controversial + sensational and good" (under "crusading" is the further explanation in small lettering, "punishment without crime"), "no historical romances—unless lusty, or top literary, or Forever Amber, Gone with the Wind, etc." (underneath "historical" are examples, "i.e. Bell Timson Salem Frigate" [two 1946 page-turners]), "no best sellers of pure lending library type" with further elaboration:

slickness not enough
no non-fiction on subjects we've just covered
only the best humor + biggest names only top, bestselling,
    prestige English books
≠ Do want:
realistic books that pack a wallop
books on contemporary themes that communicate feeling
books containing characters with whom readers can identify
    in feeling if not experience
the best of the younger writers
prestige books of literary value—but not those just for "the
    few"[28]

This list suggests that NAL had formulated an identity based on presenting itself as committed to controversial, realistic depictions of emotionally and sociologically significant materials, fictional and nonfictional, seen as responding to, even creating, the feelings of its readers. This self-conscious elision of differences between fiction and factual subject matter was part of Caroline Slade's mode of novel writing, which she gleaned from the case study,[29] but it was also understood as a marketing tool—though perhaps not so much by NAL, which tended to distinguish its early "scientific" works (in the Mentor series) with the stylized cover art of Robert Jonas from the steamy images for fiction portrayed by James Avati.

But other publishers clearly sought to blur genres, making little distinction between fiction, sci-fi, and nonfiction. Bantam brought out a paperback edition of Aldous Huxley's *Brave New World* in December 1952 as its first Bantam Giant for thirty-five cents, just as the House Committee was holding its hearings on "Current Pornographic Materials," and weeks after the United States detonated the first hydrogen bomb. Its cover features a picture, resonating with the first American paperback of John Hersey's *Hiroshima*, of a man and woman running from a fiery explosion in what seems a futuristic city; he is naked, his genitals covered by the flowing slip she wears. They seem to have burst through a cave opening, as if returning to or escaping from the Stone Age (figure 8.5). The cover by the same artist who did the 1954 Bantam title *Man Alone*, which also featured a naked man, might be, as Richard Lupoff notes of it, under "The signature on this unusual painting [that] is hard to make out (paperback covers rarely feature nude males). Is it Binger? Bingham? Or maybe Barye Phillips?"[30] So the image is erotic and suggestive of the Ballantine PBO (paperback original) of Arthur C. Clarke's *Childhood's End*, published in 1953, "breath-taking novel about the future evolution of man," as its tagline claims, where a naked man crouches before another futuristic city and a dazzling sky full of stars and giant eyeballs.

By 1960, when Bantam brought out Huxley's nonfiction update to his dystopian novel, *Brave New World Revisited*, excerpts of which had appeared in *Newsday*, *Medical Economics*, and the *Magazine of*

Figure 8.5 Aldous Huxley, *Brave New World* (Bantam, 1952). Cover by Baryè Phillips.

Fantasy and Science Fiction, showing clearly the generic slippage among legitimate newspapers, scientific journals, and popular pulp magazines so crucial to the demotics of reading promoted by paperbacks, Huxley's foreword begins "The soul of wit may become the very body of untruth."[31] He concludes by setting his meditations on the present "against the background of thoughts on the Hungarian uprising and its repression, about H-bombs, about the cost of what every nation refers to as 'defense,' and about those endless columns of uniformed boys, white, black, brown, yellow, marching obediently toward the common grave."[32] After all, "public interest increased each time the Nevada sky was illuminated by atomic detonations. During the Tumbler-Snapper series, in 1952, the entire nation witnessed an atomic blast from the comfort of their homes as the media provided television coverage to the American public."[33] At the moment of television's massive entry into the home, bringing scenes of blasts to millions, these smaller, more personal and private emblems of mass culture were offering atomic images that could be carried in one's pocket.

Just as futuristic images blurred distinctions among literature, science, and science fiction in the face of war and nuclear annihilation, the mid- to late 1950s crime books were in some ways also connected to Holocaust and war pulp; they presented the aftermath of the previous decades' horrors through more homegrown threats of lawlessness and anarchic violence and hinted that even with the destruction of German Nazism, Italian fascism, and Japanese imperialism, the residues of war's devastation lingered in disaffected and alienated youth, especially those living in American cities. The Federal Bureau of Investigation reported that more than two million major crimes were committed in 1952, an increase of 8.2 percent over the previous year, with trends continuing, as urban crime had increased 32.9 percent from the prewar average. Rape and aggravated assault accounted for the largest increases between 1937 and 1952, almost 100 percent. Moreover, while the ratio of arrests of men to women was eight to one, "more women than men [were] charged with murder, aggravated assault and liquor law violations while the criminal male leans more toward robbery, burglary, auto theft, and driving while intoxicated."[34] The Margarets and Lilly Crackells, who Caroline Slade had described as anomalous threats in the 1940s, were now figuring as a part of America's violent landscape, and the covers of paperbacks recorded this scene. The concern with women's aberrant behavior may have been part of the spur to NAL's interest in psychiatrist Marie N. Robinson's work, *The Power of Sexual Surrender*, which was described in the 1959 "dope sheet" memo—summaries of the potential books NAL might acquire, including plot summaries, sales information, and possible marketing ideas—as "this brilliantly titled book [that] deals with the problem of sexual frigidity.... [A]s a national phenomenon its sources are to be found in the double role woman plays in today's society, where emancipated from home and kitchen, she finds herself so often in competition with men."[35] Apparently this competition extended to crime too.

But criminality, as practiced by America's urban youth, had a longer history, perhaps epitomized by the "crime of the century," the murder of Bobby Franks by Nathan Leopold Jr. and Richard Loeb, who were spared the death penalty through Clarence Darrow's defense. The 1924 trial had riveted the nation, and when Meyer Levin's 1956 novel based on the crime and trial appeared in paperback a year later for seventy-five cents as the "contemporary historical novel or documentary novel" *Compulsion,* with a cover by Tom Dunn showing two disembodied men, one in a blue suit and the other in gray, holding hands framing a cartoon of a courtroom full of disapproving men (plate 19, *top right*), it spurred a national frenzy. In his *New York Times Book Review* column, "Detectives at Work," Anthony Boucher described *Compulsion* as "the finest novelization of a great true murder that I have ever read." He goes on to explain that novels come closest to "the truth of crime itself."[36] In effect, this review argued for noting the importance of the true crime genre of the nonfiction novel even before Truman Capote's 1966 nonfiction novel *In Cold Blood.* Thus even in its hardcover form, Levin's work was part of the phenomenon of sci-unfi, the pulping of social and physical sciences, again making possible a demotic reading practice that enabled, even encouraged, readers to cross into restricted areas not typical for them as readers or citizens.

Meyer Levin, husband and "translator" of Tereska Torrès, found himself—or rather entangled himself—in a number of civil suits over various works, which propelled his name into the news for both his work on the stage version of *The Diary of Anne Frank*, where he sued Otto Frank(!) claiming that Frank had interfered with his words, and for the suits and countersuits surrounding the stage version of *Compulsion*. Darryl F. Zanuck purchased screen rights, but Alfred Hitchcock had already used the story, based on the 1929 play by Patrick Hamilton, as the basis for his film *Rope* (1948), starring Jimmy Stewart. The money circulating because of these works (Meyer Levin had also written a play and screenplay based on his novel) caught the attention of Leopold, who sued both Zanuck and Levin.

The reemergence of this tale of murder came at the same time as Caryl Chessman's efforts to escape the death penalty at San Quentin had created another best seller—*Cell 2455, Death Row*—which appeared in 1954 as a hardcover, was condensed for various pulp magazines, and then issued by Perma Books in 1956 with the stunning cover by design studio Bollwin-Sommer of knuckles gripping prison cell bars. The *New York Times* called this work "a highly readable document liberally enriched with authentic lingo." Harrison Salisbury had also offered a glossary of teenage gang argot, in much the same way as Margaret Mead had included one in the appendix to *Coming of Age in Samoa*. In this sense, these books on adolescence were also primers on the study of foreign cultures and languages, anticipating Dell's *Look and Learn* series of paperback books from the 1960s that were designed for easy use as Americans began touring Europe and needed to know how to say "bonjour."

Meyer Levin's involvement with legal matters and law enforcement long predated World War II; his name surfaced in the FBI files after the publication of his 1940 novel, *Citizens*, about the massacre of striking workers at the so-called little steel company Republic Steel, which he had covered as a reporter in 1930s Chicago, and he continued to interact with the law throughout his life. This strike, and its bloody aftermath, was among the most important labor struggles mounted by left-wing, communist-affiliated unions, sealing Chicago's reputation as a tough, violent town for organizers, an image reinforced by novelist Clancy Sigal in his memoir about his socialist mother Jenny.[37] Levin, a graduate of the University of Chicago, had followed the notorious 1924 murder trial of the thrill-killers Leopold and Loeb, two UC alums and classmates of Levin's. Reporting from Europe during World War II, where he met his wife Torrès, the writer and member of the Free French Army, he was present at the opening of a number of concentration camps and traveled to Palestine to witness the inauguration of the state of Israel. Returning to the United States in the 1950s, he became a newspaper columnist (his column for the *Newark Star Ledger* was called "I Cover Culture"), writing about culture and politics through the lens of personal anecdotes, including illustrations by his son, on such topics as children's playgrounds, paperback books, comics, and public transportation.

He helped usher the writings of Torrès into print, translating her work from French and editing it for popular consumption. He is featured in her author's photograph with their four children on the dust jacket of her novel *Not Yet . . . .* The copy explains: "Tereska Torres writes in French. Her husband [earlier identified as Meyer Levin] translates her work into English, she translates his into French—an arrangement well suited to this versatile, gifted couple."[38] Because of his presence in liberated German concentration camps, he was asked to write the script for the dramatization of the *Diary of Anne Frank*. His work was never used, as the final version was scripted by Frances Goodrich and Albert Hackett, but he sued them for using parts of his work and for rights to use his version, even though he had signed his rights over to Otto Frank. The legal haggling ended with him suing Otto Frank, claiming that his original script was altered by Frank, Goodrich, and Hackett, and the producers and director of the show. He won damages of $50,000, which were never collected, because the judge tossed them out, and the writers countersued. At the time, he was also working on the novel *Compulsion*, a fictionalized account of the "crime of the century" that delved into the mind-set of Leopold and Loeb as they set about killing a young neighborhood boy.[39] Levin explores their anxieties as Jews, queers, and intellectuals in part 1 and recounts the extraordinary media frenzy that surrounded the sensational trial in which Clarence Darrow successfully defended the two against the death penalty after he urged them to plead guilty—by asserting they were mentally ill—and to forego a jury trial. Long portions of the novel consist of the interviews the fictional Dr. Allwin undertakes with "Judd," based on Leopold, to determine his mental state, as the narrative moves in and out of reporting and dialogue, so that narrator and characters seem to merge identities.

> The kids kept teasing him because he was such a shrimp, and a Jewboy. It was from those Irish kids at the public school that he first heard it as something dirty: Jewboy, sheenie. . . . And he tells how the boys teased him . . . they had hold of him, pulling him into an alley . . . "Hey, he got a pecker? Maybe he ain't even got a pecker! Hey! The sheenies they cut off a piece of the petzel, maybe they cut off too much! Hey, maybe he's a girl!"[40]

The novel is structured in many ways as an inverted mirror of another Chicago writer's account of a notorious trial—Richard Wright's *Native Son*, published the same year as *Citizens*, which fictionalized the Robert Nixon murder case. Like *Native Son*, *Compulsion* relies on newspaper reports and straddles the line between pulpy crime story and psychological narration; it too follows the mental journey of a youthful killer (or two) and ends with the almost verbatim summation by the defense lawyers working through sociological analysis, on the one hand (*Native Son*), and psychological explanation, on the other (*Compulsion*). The Leopold and Loeb case was considered to be among the first to bring expert testimony by psychologists to the courtroom as Darrow skillfully made the minds of the killers a key aspect of their case. Creating a sensation upon publication—almost immediately the rights were granted for numerous translations, *Compulsion* was reissued in paperback and adapted by Levin for Broadway and the movies. This notoriety, especially in the marketing of the book, play, and movie, incensed Nathan Leopold Jr. (Richard Loeb was dead by then, killed in prison by another convict), who, upon release of the film in 1959, sued Levin, Twentieth Century Fox, the book's publishers, and the play's producers, among others, for violation of his right to privacy. Eventually, in 1970, the Illinois Supreme Court affirmed the lower court's judgment in favor of the defendants, noting that "The court found no legally protected right of privacy when the topic was a matter of public interest . . . circumstances of the crime and the prosecution etched a deep public impression, which the passing of time did not extinguish. Furthermore, plaintiff himself did not seek retirement from public attention."[41] Leopold had already sold his story to various Chicago tabloids in a number of articles with titles such as "Leopold Tells Own Story—How It Felt To Be a Killer," and "Life Plus 99 Years."

In 1956, Zanuck paid close to $100,000 for the rights to Levin's adaptation of *Compulsion* for the stage, which would serve as the basis for a film.[42] The play, originally under consideration at Levin's request by director/producer José Quintero (who had Broadway hits with *The Iceman Cometh* and *Long Day's Journey into Night*), ultimately was produced by Michael Myerberg and Leonard Gruenberg. The ensuing saga of suits and countersuits, which were going on simultaneously with the suits Levin had filed over the production of the Anne Frank play, led his wife to leave him. He had just translated her novel based on their early years when they first met in Paris in 1939–40, which NAL was bringing out in paperback. She had endured the 1952 Gathings Committee hearings, which had investigated her book about her years in the Free French women's armed forces, *Women's Barracks*, as an example of the new pornography and sexual deviance available in the form of paperback books, as well as Levin's five-year legal tangles with Otto Frank, Cheryl Crawford, and many others, over his stage adaptation of Anne Frank's diary.

As a war refugee, who had been married before to a French Jew, this must have struck Torrès as unseemly (she says as much in a letter posted by their lawyer, Sam Friedman, found among Levin's papers) and with various legal imbroglios surrounding the stage production of *Compulsion*—Levin's "obsessional" suit against the producers, the actors' suit against him, mediation through the Dramatists' Union, and so on, she again felt abandoned by him as he increasingly appeared to be "crazy," a monomaniac convinced that there was a communist plot to foil his career as he repeated the ruinous fight he had carried on over the Anne Frank material.[43] She begged him to enjoy his success rather than devote unnecessary energy pursuing specious legal claims over the quality of the script, which had been deemed by many as "not dramatic." She saw him repeating almost verbatim his paranoid claims that he was being persecuted: "the rejection of your script was more important than love and life itself. You would have thought that the script was Dante [*sic*] Divine Comedy or the Bible and the world would collapse because Meyer Levin had a rejected script."[44] This was exactly the advice he was receiving from various counsel—why would a well-established and famous author expend time and money in legal battles with unknowns who had little evidence of any wealth? Instead of clearing his name, Levin risked looking like a bully and certainly would never recover any damages, assuming a judgment was found in his favor.

Nevertheless, Levin sent a telegram to every one of the play's backers—including a high school teacher from Teaneck, New Jersey—begging them to read both versions of the play. He had also solicited this request from the *New York Times* critic and other noted authors—all seem to have refused—save for the teacher who liked both versions and was intrigued by Levin's plan to have both versions staged on alternating weeks. Meanwhile, the play's two leads, Roddy McDowall and Dean Stockwell, sued Levin because they refused to perform his version, having rehearsed the version Levin called a "vulgarization." Citing insufficient public interest, the *New York Times* refused to publish Levin's long letter detailing the charges against the version in production that had been script-doctored by Robert Thom, although it did mention the dispute in an brief item describing the advertisement Levin took out when he could not get his letter published; it noted that Levin called the producers' version "vulgarized."[45] Levin then took out a paid advertisement in the paper on the eve of Yom Kippur (4 October 1957), two weeks before the show's scheduled opening, imploring producers Michael Myerberg and Leonard Gruenberg to perform both versions.[46] Myerberg had complained that Levin's version lacked "commercial appeal," which, as he had recently produced Samuel Beckett's *Waiting for Godot*, notoriously slammed on its first performances in the United States, seemed a specious claim to Levin. The day after the scheduled opening night, Tereska Torrès appeared on New York television in a *Nightbeat* interview about the play. She echoed Levin's call for the double performance. But it never happened. His *Compulsion* went unseen.

Only a month before, Levin had received an inquiry from Kinshiro Hayahi of Kyoto, Japan, requesting permission to translate *Compulsion*. Like many other letters Levin received from lawyers and psychologists (not to mention women readers, especially from Chicago), Hayahi noted how in postwar Japan, as "democracy" was permeating society, including the family, parents were losing control of their children, as the previously authoritarian family gave way to a greater laxity in rules governing the conduct of children. He saw Levin's novel as an astute analysis of the generational tensions leading Japanese youth to rebellion; Levin's novelization of this 1920s crime helped make sense of the growing fears about post–World War II delinquency. Levin notes in prefatory remarks to the book that the two boys' impenetrable stories stuck in his mind long after their imprisonment, so that *"once, in the war, I believed I understood . . . But at that moment in the war . . . these two, from their jail in my mind, and even though one of them had long been dead, rose up to influence an action of mine."*[47] Martha Gellhorn had written to Levin that the novel was "a whopping material success," praising him for the powerful vision he constructed; her husband, Ernest Hemingway, also extended laudatory remarks—even though the novel's heft was not at all akin to his style. Many women were attracted to the "Leopold" character, Judd Steiner, whose defiant yet self-effacing charisma and dangerously ambiguous sexuality appealed to them, not only as readers, because of Levin's ability to enter into the mind-set of his characters, but as women. A few wished they could meet him, asking Levin to convey their interest when he next visited Leopold to complete his *Coronet* magazine article, "Leopold Should Be Freed!," which pleaded for the Illinois governor to commute his life sentence and parole him.[48]

As Levin writes in the introductory paragraphs of the novel: *"I was, for a most personal reason, in the very center of the case. I partly identified myself with Judd, so that I sometimes felt I could see not only into the texture of events that had taken place without my presence but into his very thoughts. Because of this identification, it sometimes becomes difficult to tell exactly where my imagination fills in what were gaps in the documents and in the personal revelations. . . . and this is the reality through me."*[49] Levin's deep ties—through his politics, marriage, religion, and writing career to the subjects he covered as a reporter, novelist, and playwright—seemed to manifest themselves in his legal entanglements. The process of pulping crept into his being. His books courted controversy and his pugnacity found expression not only in the subject matter to which he was drawn but in his resort to convoluted legal battles over some of the most sensational events in the twentieth century. In this, his life story and the life stories he composed melded into a pulp plot of betrayal, appropriation, sex, death, and political intrigue. Torrès writes in the foreword to *Women's Barracks*, "My husband tells me I ought to write my memoirs of the women's army . . . My husband tells me laughingly that it will make a sensational book . . . the story will be interesting to Americans because we were a barracksful of Frenchwomen in exile, and it seems that Frenchwomen have a great deal of allure abroad."[50] He had a nose for news and for the kinds of tales that would grab public attention, connecting some of the key nonfiction pulp themes of the postwar years—delinquent youth, antiSemitism, wartime sexuality—in an uncanny series of writings and legal cases. Yet he could write a column about how his wife "rooted comics out of the house with broom and fire, not only because of the nightmarish content of some of this stuff, but because the pictures and colors were so ugly as to habituate the children to the acceptance of ugliness."[51]

By moving in and out of domestic and public disputes about taste, ugliness, and vulgarization, Levin strategically sought to mine the demotic tensions of pulp. Levin maintained, for instance, that Robert Thom's work on the play was misguided: "Because of the subject of my novel and play, the Loeb-Leopold case, one could, by over-emphasizing the sensational aspects of the crime and relationship between the criminals, reduce the work to a vulgar shocker . . . Thom had defiled and vulgarized the play . . . used dull, tasteless and jarring colloquialisms. . . ."[52] Levin wanted to convey, along with such popularizers of psychology as Robert J. Lindner's *Fifty-Minute Hour* but also Margaret Mead's *Coming of Age in Samoa*, a new worldview that understood a complex postwar psychology emerging out of the brutality of the holocaust and atomic weaponry, an awareness that included apprehension of multiple sexualities.[53] So his appeal against the actors Roddy McDowall and Dean Stockwell occurred because "McDowall was reported as having refused to proceed 'until the last remaining traces of Levin's work had been eliminated' from certain scenes, and as having described Levin's plays [sic]* as 'a dirty play about two dirty little boys!' "[54] Levin, like so many others involved in the pulping of crime, understood how to be outrageous and how to be outraged, and when to perform each affect for maximum publicity. He saw how the tag "sensational" (this is how he described *Women's Barracks* and how the paperback edition of *Compulsion* was described: "the sensational, best-selling novel based on a famous and brutal crime that horrified the nation!"), worked to connect private feelings to public issues and turn the law into a scandal. He knew how to pulp reality.

"A highly readable document" (*Cell 2455*); "A fascinating document" (*Brainwashing*); "a provocative social document" (*Compulsion*); "an authoritative document" (*Burn, Baby, Burn! The Watts Riot*): so the covers of each of these 1950s and 1960s accounts of true crime, war, torture, and rioting declare. In 1953, surveying the spectacular success of the paperback revolution, Freeman Lewis, executive vice president of Pocket Books, warned that "the total inventory of unsold paper-bound books today is at least 175,000,000 copies." He was especially concerned about the quality of the approximately nine hundred to one thousand titles appearing annually because of this flood of paperbacks; most were fiction and "the amount of fiction annually published by originating publishers has never been sufficient to provide that much high quality reprint material."[55] There just were not enough good books, specifically, good novels, or readers interested in the bad ones, to sustain the industry. In his overview of the state of the industry, Lewis points to a number of solutions to this dilemma, including a move into nonfiction, coming to terms with competition from television, and enduring the ongoing censorship battles in Congress, the courts, and from the Catholic Church. He argues that "the kind of fiction which represents an attempt to satisfy the needs of a pulp magazine audience had gone about as far as it can go."[56] Instead, paperback publishers should look to "biography, history, science, the liberal arts, philosophy, drama, poetry—the field has hardly been scratched"; these represent "opportunities for public service."[57] Pulp truth, sci-unfi, became one way to thwart the censoring urges of such organizations as the National Organization for Decent Literature, which published lists of books and magazines not approved by the Chicago Archdiocesan Council of Catholic Women (focusing on fiction).[58] Stressing facts or true stories or documents offered a way around censors' monitoring of "filth"; it also, as Freeman Lewis argued, opened up other realms of demotic reading and opportunities for public service that had become crucial as the industry faced threats to curb its widespread distribution.

CHAPTER 9

Demotic Ulysses: Policing Paperbacks
in the Courts and Congress

> Publishers of pocket-size books . . . have developed reproduc-
> tions of pornographic literature to such proportions that at 25
> to 35 cents a book, it comes within the price range of juveniles
> and is made accessible on the stands of more than 100,000 retail
> dealers throughout the Nation . . . Not only does this literature
> go to all parts of this Nation in the systems of distribution but
> to foreign countries and the cry of filth from such countries,
> among them Canada, Australia, England, the Philippines, and
> others, is now being raised against such literature coming to
> their shores. Whence is it coming? From the United States of
> America.
>
> —Report of Select Committee
> on Current Pornographic Materials

> We believe that every American community must jealously
> guard the freedom to publish and to circulate, in order to pre-
> serve its own freedom to read.
>
> —"The Freedom to Read," Joint Declaration of the
> American Book Publishers Council and the Council
> of the American Library Association

At the Corners, in All Directions

In his statement in the landmark 1868 obscenity case, *Regina v. Hicklin*, a case that set the precedent for subsequent legal considerations of pornography and obscenity in both Great Britain and the United States, Lord Chief Justice Alexander Cockburn indicated that the fear provoked by obscene materials was not so much of its content but of its accessibility: "This work, I am told, is sold at the corners of streets, and in all directions, and of course it falls into the hands of persons of all classes, young and old, and the minds of those hitherto pure are exposed to the danger of contamination and pollution from the impurity it contains."[1] His concern for the ubiquity of contaminants and pollutants, conveyed through works sold at every junction—but not those he has traversed, apparently, as he is only aware of the enormous spread of obscene materials by word of mouth, hearsay, you might say—gets repeated almost a century later in *Regina v. Penguin Books Limited.*

In 1960, another queen of England is prosecuting printed matter under the 1959 Obscene Publications Act; this time, the first unexpurgated edition, in paperback, of D. H. Lawrence's *Lady Chatterley's Lover*. The corners of streets where these books might be found were the sites of local shops, not necessarily booksellers, which prompted Mervyn Griffith-Jones, who prosecuted the case, to ask of the jury, "How freely is this book about to be distributed? Who is it that is going to read it? Is it a book that is published at £5 a time as, perhaps, a historical document, being part of the works of a great writer, or is it, on the other hand, a book which is widely distributed at a price that the merest infant can afford?"[2] So the very idea that had prompted Allen Lane to develop Penguin Books—a desire to bring literature to a wide audience through cheaply produced books sold at railway stations and newsstands—was the cause of the furor about this book's publication. As soon as railways appeared in Britain, W. H. Smith seized on the opportunity of the induced boredom from long train rides to sell reading matter to travelers; Lane expanded sales by putting books in stations without bookshops.³

The Chatterley trial, during which testimony from Rebecca West, Richard Hoggart, E. M. Forster, Raymond Williams, and scores of other writers and scholars was heard on behalf of Penguin, like many others in the United States during the mid-twentieth century, turned on twin points—the contents of the book, to be sure, but actually this was secondary to the ways in which it would be delivered. Much like the recent tobacco trials, which successfully targeted cigarettes as "nicotine delivery devices," the congressional hearings and local, state, and federal prosecutions of books deemed pornographic or obscene made their cases on the mode of delivery—the paperback book. What had been the greatest asset of the paperback revolution, begun in 1935 by Allen Lane—that a good book could be had for the same cost as a pack of cigarettes and bought in the same shops—became its greatest danger both here and abroad. Anne Enright explains about postwar Ireland's efforts, "Censorship was a measure to protect the ordinary public from foreign, corrupting material. As it turned out," she continues, "particular ire would be saved for Irish writers: when you are trying to keep 'indecent' and 'obscene' material from entering the country, it is a great betrayal to discover it bubbling up from within."⁴

The situation in the United States was clearly different. Without an official Catholic Truth Society, as in Ireland, to monitor "evil publications,"⁵ but with the First Amendment to ensure freedom of the press, which was lacking in the United Kingdom, the spread of "filth,"⁶ as censoring Americans could not stop calling the outpouring of paperback forms—books, comics, magazines—filling shelves and racks across the nation and leaking across borders, could not be controlled in the same ways. Hence the panic. Mr. Samuel Black, vice president of Atlantic Coast Independent Distributors

Association, submitted his brief to the House Select Committee on Current Pornographic Materials, convened by Representative E. C. Gathings (D-AR) in December 1952, arguing that "The scene is anytown in the Atlantic Coast District. Parents and teachers noticing the display racks of sex-exciting books and obscenely provocative magazines on sale at newsstands and in drug stores began to talk about it."[7] This vivid portrayal, worthy of a pulp fiction and film noir opening gambit, explains that book distributors are unfairly trapped between the Scylla and Charybdis of unscrupulous publishers—who compete for visual shock—and greedy shopkeepers looking to make a fast buck off the sensational titillations offered by cheap reading matter. This pervasive spectacle, found not only in urban America but in Anytown, USA, would seem a testament to a successful business model, but reading had become a dangerous act. As Roger Chartier notes, "reading, by definition, is rebellious and vagabond."[8]

Again, the problem was one of access and availability, as the prolific Minnesota novelist, Margaret Culkin Banning, explained in her essay "Filth on the Newsstands" (originally published in *Reader's Digest* and reprinted in the committee's report), which was concerned primarily with "cheesecake" and "girlie magazines" but also "pocket books."[9] "It is sometimes argued that sexy magazines have always been available in this country . . . they could be found in barber-shops, saloons, and Army posts. They were not in competition with family magazines and serious-minded periodicals and useful books. Today the sex magazines are competing right down at the corner drug store, with all other forms of reading" (115–19).[10] Competition for space on the corners—teeming with splashy covers featuring partially clothed women—was the primary issue for these two witnesses; but what excited the committee members was the content inside the covers, or at least certain passages from them. As Banning correctly observed:

The publishers of such materials will stop at nothing to catch the eye . . . The publishers of many lines of pocket books attempt to meet the competition by putting lurid, misleading pictures on the cover of serious and intelligent novels. In a pocket edition Tess of the D'Urbervilles is promoted in a red satin evening dress, on some sort of broken bridge, with a man bending over her bosom. The promotion says: "The gal: Tess Durbeyfield *** we are off for another round of cruel passion." Thomas Hardy would be stirring in his grave (*HSC*, 146) (plate 19, *bottom right*). [11]

These testimonies understood contemporary American culture—more readers than ever as literacy reached near universal proportions, propelled in part by the cheap books and magazines on sale everywhere—as inundated by what Banning called "pictorial prostitution." Moreover, in a reversal of the panic of widespread infiltration of the nation by the foreign and alien ideology of Communism, America was serving as the source for international contamination. Thus, it made sense that International Publishers, the press of the CPUSA, would endorse a call against censorship from the American Council of Book Publishers and the American Library Association (ALA) only a week after the execution of Ethel and Julius Rosenberg. Books and how they were sold had become part of the communist conspiracy, too. Banning saw a nation overrun with print and picture magazines—confession magazines, detective magazines, and sporting magazines (64). "I have been told by the heads of various homes for delinquent girls that the girls come in with their suitcases practically full of them, and little else, but I have heard the same thing from others of girls who come home from eastern boarding schools" (66), explained Banning.

Capitalism, in this view, was jeopardizing the nation's future. "Americans are now reading hundreds of millions of pocket-sized books and even more billions of magazines," observed Samuel Black, proudly noting that "Reading is now enjoyed by the entire Nation, and not just the privileged few."[12] It is precisely this demotic reading, which had occurred because of these new objects, the venues where they could be found—"noose-stands," as Ezra Pound called them in 1950[13]—and the pressures of competition that have fueled publishing that Black sought to maintain. He advocated for self-regulation—along the lines of motion pictures and television—to keep Congress from encroachment on the industry.[14] The books might be readily available; however, only 21 percent of Americans answered yes to the question, "Do you happen to be reading any book or books at the present time?"[15] So, while billions of magazines and millions of books were being sold, few were actually reading them. Still, their content and presentation provoked this congressional hearing, which was charged "to determine, by investigation and study, the extent to which books, magazines, and comic books containing immoral, obscene, or otherwise offensive matter, or placing improper advertising emphasis on crime, violence, and corruption, are being made available to the people of the United States . . . and . . . to determine the adequacy of existing law to prevent the publication and distribution of books containing immoral, offensive, and other undesirable matter."[16] This blanket determination zeroed in on "school children reading these publications at the newsstands" (*HSC*, 256).[17]

Fearing various legislative remedies and anticipating Griffith-Jones's concern about who is reading, "the objectionable, so-called salacious literature," which "those men are accused of placing within the reach of any child or teen-ager with the money to pay for it," Black was willing to control his industry, even while arguing that such control did not amount to censorship: "I am not a censor," he declared, but nevertheless decried how "our frenzy has reached a boiling point about filthy stories we are putting out as pocket-size books, covers that cry for improvement, and girly books that have no justification for their existence other than for the few tainted dollars that can be made catering to the moronic literati of our society."[18] Controlling reading matter for sale poses inherent contradictions. Even those disagreeing with the committee report that endorsed suppressing these "pornographic materials" were careful to state both that they abhorred pornography and obscenity and that the committee's project had not been censorship. Its process of investigation was in express violation of legal standards precluding excerpting select passages from a literary work—or even judging a book by its cover (RSC, 125)—because case law dictated that the entire work needed to be considered. This dispute over how to deal with the "filth" found in a book was also essential to the *Lady Chatterley* trial a decade later in London. However, despite the fact that even the Irish Censorship Board (containing a lone Protestant, until 1949, when he resigned in protest) had "a merit clause" to distinguish "rubbish" from legitimate literature, banned writer John McGahern remembered, "You often found that people were attacking people like Lawrence, and they hadn't read him at all."[19]

The Gathings Committee majority report was "replete with literary criticism," in the words of the minority report authors Emanuel Celler (D-NY) and Francis Walter (D-PA), who saw the other committee members as overstepping their mandate to investigate an industry by instead focusing on the isolated words of authors.[20] The report begins by looking into "books" now seen "as a serious menace to the social structure of the Nation" in part because of the "serious economic problem" caused by the "terrific overcrowding of the newsstands with books containing salacious material," in the words of the "general business manager of one of the leading magazines."[21] Thus, pornography is at once an economic threat to an industry, and so to the entire structure of society, and the foundation of the book publishing industry—and perhaps, given the First Amendment, the nation. The committee was careful to deny it was looking to instate censorship—advocating boycotts as an effective means of control—and was aware of the precedent set by Judge

John Woolsey and affirmed on appeal by Judge Augustus N. Hand in *United States v. One Book Called "Ulysses,"* that what counts as obscene must "stir the sex impulses or . . . lead to sexually impure and lustful thoughts" (RSC, 6). But if an obscene passage exists to delineate character, the book might not be considered obscene, a category it noted derisively "as elastic as rubber in its interpretative susceptibility and supplies the purveyors of obscenity with an excuse regardless of what is the degree of obscenity involved and requires each and every book to be judged separately, an impossible task" (RSC, ibid.). The *Ulysses* case can thus be seen as an impediment to controlling the flow of these materials, especially after the decision was upheld in *Commonwealth v. Gordon et al.* (1949), which included allegations against nine books, among them James T. Farrell's *Young Lonigan* (figure 9.1) and Erskine Caldwell's *God's Little Acre* (plate 20), both in paperback, "referred to in the committee hearings, December 5" (RSC, ibid.).

Testimony during the hearings often verged on political theater and parody, to the point that Congresswoman Katharine St. George (R-NY) remarked on the absurdity of the industry's zeal to attract passing readers when she referred to a scene in George Axelrod's hit Broadway play, *The Seven Year Itch*. In it, Tom Ewell's character, Robert, an editor at a paperback reprint house, explains why the paperback version of a book by Dr. Brubaker, a noted psychologist, features a cover depicting the criminal sex fiend Gustav Meyerheim attacking Jayne Mansfield:

> Cheer up, Doctor. If you think you have troubles, Mr. Brady wants to change "The Scarlet Letter" to "I am an Adultress." I know it all seems a little off to you—but Mr. Brady understands the 25-cent book field. Both Mr. Brady and I want to publish worthwhile books—like yours. Like "The Scarlet Letter." But you must remember that you and Nathaniel Hawthorne are competing in every drugstore with the basic writings of Mickey Spillane.[22]

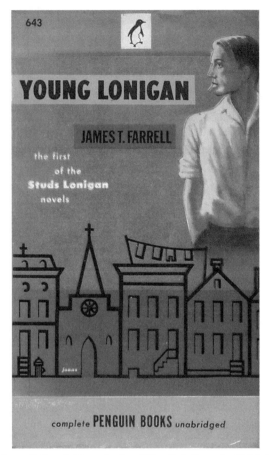

Figure 9.1 James T. Farrell, *Young Lonigan* (New York: Penguin, 1947). Cover by Robert Jonas.

If Broadway was already aware of the competition between "worthwhile" books and bodice rippers for the attention of America's readers, the Gathings Committee hearings could not help but lapse into rampant "literary criticism" as it sought to distinguish which books needed to be controlled among this slew of pocket-size items. After all, as one testifier explained, reading the Avon paperback version of

The Amboy Dukes "precipitated the delinquent act of the child . . . The child even knew what page it was on" (RSC, 110). But satire entered into the theater of the hearings too. John O'Connor, publisher of Bantam Books, noted that it was difficult to keep adolescent boys from reading:

> They will get it even if you don't put it out on the newsstands. I remember when the Kinsey reports were published. A very distinguished and respectable medical publisher in Philadelphia did not realize what he had until they started taking these books away from him, and it was common knowledge in the publishing business that around high schools the youngsters would get together and gather the $6 to buy the Kinsey report.

> *Mr. Rees:* Would you approve of youngsters getting together and buying this stuff?
> *Mr. O'Connor:* Well, they don't have to because this is only a quarter. (RSC, 101–2)

By 1955, when Wilder's film version of *The Seven Year Itch* appeared, another film, Ernest Borgnine's *Marty* (directed by Delbert Mann from the Paddy Chayefsky screenplay), included a scene of him hanging around with his friends, all Bronx working-class Italian guys, recounting the plots of Mickey Spillane novels and declaring him "a great writer"; a similar session is recounted in Richard Wright's novel *Lawd Today*, as a group of young black men read the tabloids together. Collective reading—enabled by cheap books and magazines—contributed to gangs and delinquency, according to a Brooklyn judge, but for Chayefsky and Wright, not to mention any number of authors or readers, talking about reading and analyzing texts was a social act that consolidated identity. During World War II, men stationed in the Pacific connected by reading Armed Service Editions of Herman Melville's *Typee* and *Omoo*. Publishers were proud of the ways paperbacks enabled book clubs and group reading: "Pocket Books, Inc., was the founder of and still serves as an adviser to the Teen-age Book Club which brings some 1,500,000 carefully selected paper-bound books to pupils in more than 8,000 junior and senior high-school classrooms," noted the written statement of Freeman Lewis, executive vice president of Pocket Books (RSC, 114).

Distinguishing obscenity and being driven to censor it, as Morris Ernst noted in the preface to H. Montgomery Hyde's 1964 *A History of Pornography*, was "not unrelated to the spread of literacy" in the late nineteenth century in both Britain and the United States, and, he goes on, "both cultures had trouble when paperback books came into existence." What is clear throughout discussions of the "*obscene, lewd, lascivious, dirty*, etc. . . . *pornography, prurient*, and, more recently, *hard-core*" is that as long as books were expensive, they would be limited to those wealthy few who might either be "incorruptible or had already been corrupted."[23] Since the Hicklin decision, censorship practices in both the United Kingdom and the United States focused on the single sentence, even a word, deemed obscene. As the magistrate in the 1929 British case against Radclyffe Hall's *Well of Loneliness* observed, "The whole book as to ninety-nine hundredths of it may be beyond criticism, yet one passage may make it a work which ought to be destroyed as obscene."[24]

That same year, when Anthony Comstock was secretary of the New York Society for the Suppression of Vice, the US case against bookseller Donald S. Friede was prompted because Hall's book, which had run into six editions, was sold at Macy's, making it available to a wide array of shoppers.[25] That paperbacks were sold for twenty-five cents in "Book Stores, Department Stores, Chain Stores, and all magazine outlets suitable . . . [and] require a first run of at least 250,000 copies" was part of the marketing plan Signet NAL cofounder Kurt Enoch used to convince Doubleday, Doran and Company to contract with the newly formed reprint house.[26] In 1933, the Woolsey decision in the *Ulysses* case had vacated the idea that a single fragment could be construed as obscene and that the entire work needed to be considered—dooming the Hicklin rule the same year Prohibition was ended—but the "trafficking" of books deemed "pornographic" continued to be prosecuted and investigated as the Gathings and Granahan hearings attest.

If book censorship appeared to correspond to mass literacy in the nineteenth century, twentieth-century censorship followed (at least in the United States) the Red Scare and fears of immigrants during the 1920s; it subsided, along with Prohibition, after Roosevelt's election and returned again during the Cold War. It was tied to efforts to control the masses. Arguments for censorship from the 1929 New York case against *The Well of Loneliness* through the 1952 Gathings hearings centered on questions of access also, though not because of the newly literate—as mass literacy was accepted due to widespread public education—but through concerns about where sales of these cheap books occurred. A book on sale at a department store, or "at the corners of streets and in all directions" meant anyone with a quarter—that is, "any infant," according to the prosecutor of *Lady Chatterley's Lover* in 1960—might purchase it to bring home, as Samuel Pepys had three centuries before with the erotic French novel *L'Escole des Filles*, reading it in secret (he was "ashamed" to be seen reading it in public at his bookseller), masturbating, and then burning it over his "shame."[27] Book buying and selling, because it was a robust market, needed restriction and control to maintain a rigid demarcation between the likes of Samuel Pepys, who at least knew to burn his "lewd book," and the infants and the juvenile delinquents hanging out on street corners who might possess enough spare change to bring them home and pass them on to their younger brothers and sisters. What is consistent across the centuries is a fear of mass literacy, of books being read by inappropriate readers, but the twentieth-century censorship cases concerned more than demotic reading; they centered on the marketplace and how a book might be seen in public and then transported into the private space of home.

The Gathings hearings focused on all manner of "current pornographic materials"—comics, magazines, even radio and television programs—but the key focus was "paper-bound books." (A later committee hearing, that of the House Interstate and Foreign Commerce Committee, headed by Kathryn Granahan [D-PA], looked into "Immoral or Otherwise Offensive Matter" [*HSC*, 3]). This form of book publication, which the committee noted had been around since the eighteenth century, appeared to be especially unsettling to contemporaries because publishers of such works "must make their appeal to the public almost solely by their covers and they must make that appeal against the competition of magazine covers and magazine-selling copy. As a result," remarked one such publisher in an address at the New York Public Library in November 1952 cited in the hearings, "many paper-bound publishers are using art work and copy designed for 'shock' effect, something to stop the transient potential customer in his tracks" (*HSC*, 4).

Only months before, Victor Weybright, publisher of the NAL, had been contacted by J. D. Salinger, who requested that the paperback cover of *The Catcher in the Rye* not be flamboyant (figure 9.2). He did not want Holden's face to appear, as he was meant to be a stand-in; rather, he saw the park bench and the carousel as significant settings.[28] This scene was deemed "a charming one" by cover illustrator James Avati in a memo to Weybright responding to Salinger's idea. In recounting this to Salinger, Weybright explained that it "would look like a cross between the New Yorker covers and a juvenile book rather than like a substantial modern novel."[29] Avati's memo praised the subtlety of Salinger's vision for a cover that hides Holden's face because he is not physically described in the novel, but explained that Salinger's concept "appeals strongly to those of us who have read the story . . . Perhaps it might sell." However, Avati explicated what a paperback cover is supposed to do—sell books—

and described his idea: "Let us show him [Holden] coming down Broadway or Forty-Second Street expressing his pained reaction to people who LIKE movies, etc. He is very much a definable personality, a foil to the crowd. And the crowd in its varied normality and the theatre background, exciting, suggestive, provide lures which will attract a very broad audience of readers."[30] This notorious cover ultimately led Salinger to insist on his own design, plain geometric shapes, for the cover of *Nine Stories* and the uniform color field of his future books. James Avati knew what his job was: to attract "a very broad audience of readers" and "lure" them to buy books.

Moreover, just as Hollywood films and Broadway plays were mocking the ubiquitous spread of sexy paperback covers, the paperback industry, at least in this case (and by 1954 *The Catcher in the Rye* had sold 1,250,000 copies in paperback) was picking up on Holden's sneering dismissal of "dumb stories in a magazine" and especially people "who *wanted* to go to the movies."[31] This was business, after all, and competition for audience attention acute. This was what concerned Congress, as Herbert Case of the Detroit Police Department explained: "A few years back you had your average hard-cover book which sold at anywhere from $2 on up . . . Now, it is out in the 25-cent book. It is placed out, easily obtainable by the youth . . . It is in the confectionery stores across from the schools, across from the playgrounds, the drug stores . . . in Detroit . . . definitely in every city and hamlet in the country" (RSC, 55).[32] Moreover, as a book expressly about "youth," the category of citizen most susceptible, according to this committee and many of those testifying, it represented what Leerom Medovoi called "a privileged cold war trope for American democratic character," one that to Cold War liberal critics, mostly not on the Gathings Committee, "seemed to confirm that postwar American capitalism's mass cultural forms, such as the paperback, could fulfill (for better or worse) America's cultural democratic potential by delivering the nation's youthful character to the next generation of citizens."[33]

D1667

J. D. SALINGER

THE
Catcher
IN THE Rye

This unusual
book may shock
you, will make
you laugh, and
may break your
heart— but you
will never forget it

A SIGNET BOOK   Complete and Unabridged

Figure 9.2 J. D. Salinger, *The Catcher in the Rye* (Signet/NAL, 1953). Cover by James Avati.

If Congresswoman St. George could refer to Broadway's spoofing of the paperback industry to point to its "absurd" excesses (RSC, 103), Hollywood was gleefully vamping not only the industry but mocking the congressional hearings as well. Fred Astaire's 1953 musical, *The Band Wagon*, features a long number that satirizes both the cheap paperbacks of Mickey Spillane and the black-and-white film noirs made from 1930s hard-boiled detective stories. Vincente

Minnelli's movie restaging of the 1930s Broadway play, in which Astaire had starred with his sister, revolves around resurrecting the stalled theatrical career of a song-and-dance man (as Astaire's was). The long number, "Girl Hunt: A Murder Mystery in Jazz," begins with a series of enlarged pulp covers of "Mickey Starr" novels, with titles like *Dames Kill Me* and *Stab Me Sugar* and Astaire's mock hard-boiled voice-over, as the splashy covers give way to a black-and-white streetscape—a wall covered with signs and posters and Astaire in a Fedora lighting a cigarette: "The city was asleep. The joints were closed. The rats and hoods and killers were in their holes . . . My name is Rod Riley, I'm a detective . . . and somewhere in a furnished room, some guy was practicing on a horn. It was a lonely sound." This number was added by screenwriters Betty Comden and Adolph Green for the film version and seems especially sardonic because among the books "named" by distributor Samuel Black to the Gathings Committee in 1952 as eliciting enough complaints to have it "withdrawn from sale" was "and this might start a controversy," *I, the Jury* by Spillane (RSC, 42).

Two years later, Jerry Lewis and Dean Martin had resurrected another 1930s movie, *Artists and Models*, and also updated it. This film, set among Greenwich Village artists, manages to mock the Gathings hearings, McCarthyism and national security, and psychoanalysis, and the interconnected worlds of advertising, comic book and pulp publishing, and television, as Lewis's obsession with a female superhero leads him to furiously imagine plots in his feverish dreams, which are recorded and deciphered by Martin, who turns them into comics. One side-plot includes using comics to divulge the mathematical formula for a top-secret rocket being developed by the military and under surveillance by the Soviets, causing both the Soviets and US military to wonder whether this is CIA/KGB disinformation or a serious security leak. These films, like the later film noirs *Pickup on South Street* and *Kiss Me Deadly* (based on an actual Mickey Spillane novel pulped by NAL in 1953), made at the height of Cold War hysteria over atom bomb spies (the Rosenbergs would be executed in June 1953) and popular concerns over juvenile delinquency (the Gathings hearings, Frederic Wertham's *Seduction of the Innocents*, and Marlon Brando as *The Wild One*), are manifestations of the baroque modes of film noir and hard-boiled prose, when at the very moment of intensifying paranoia about communist threats and sexual deviance, under investigation by law enforcement, Congress, and local citizens' groups, popular culture media was at once being policed and satirizing its surveillance.[34]

Writers and critics were constantly aware of what it meant to be published—or reprinted—by a paperback house. Farrell, who was negotiating with NAL in 1946 to publish *Bernard Clare*, commented to Arabel Porter, assistant editor, in 1946, on the sorry state of "books, movies, etc.," a subject he had explored in a series of essays for the *New Republic* in relation to questions about art and politics. Having had an earlier run-in with the Detroit police for his 1936 novel, *A World I Never Made*, which was withheld by a Michigan court "back around 1939," he would find himself again defending the 1952 NAL paperback version (with a James Avati cover) in another Michigan case brought against the book mentioned in the Gathings hearings. So when he argued that including introductions in reprints "would suggest to readers that it isn't so easy to write" and thus counteract the deleterious effects of the "reprint development [which] results in the fact that a mass of all kinds of books are thrown at the public, at, for books, a mass market in 1946," he had a prescient sense of what was to come. At the same time, "the critics, so-called, are res-dending [*sic*; descending] into a new low in literary debasement."[35]

Editors continually had their eyes out for new titles. More than a decade later, in an interoffice memo, Victor Weybright noted the "brilliantly titled book" (Marie N. Bonaparte's *The Power of Sexual Surrender*), which "takes issue with the Simone de Beauvoirs of our time who champion feminism and deny biology. Thus, you see, the book steps right into the middle of women's clubs' leading discussion subject." While this seems a surefire best seller, he also cautioned that the book might compete with another of NAL's titles, Eustace Chesser's *Love Without Fear*, but concluded that "books of this nature are like cookbooks—there's always room for one more." So he challenged his staff "to keep our eyes on Doubleday's results. Particularly important is how many they sell without the plain wrapper."[36] What might be "thrown at the public" might also be hidden under plain wraps, and the dance between what was widely visible and what must be hidden from view was a central element of the business of pulps—clearly one that Hollywood at least recognized. Plain wrapper-clad books sold through the mail were the subject of the 1959 Kathryn Granahan Committee hearings, a follow-up to the Gathings Committee and concerned with the use of the federal postal system to spread obscenity and pornography, and clearly on Weybright's mind.

While all the Hollywood dazzle and congressional performances focused attention on the pervasive publicity of the paperback book cover and how it was sold "without the plain wrapper," another aspect of the anxiety these objects produced could be found in Astaire's monologue on the late-night city street—that paperbacks created an intimate bond with readers. This connection was expressed in Astaire's noting the loneliness of the solo horn player in his furnished room as he walks the empty street. The files of NAL and the Council on Books in Wartime revealed more evidence of this private and personal attachment to these books. For instance, Farrell wrote to the assistant editor of NAL asking that she send two copies of *Martin Eden* along with the one he wanted for himself: "one for my brother-in-law, and one for my brother: they are both workers, and classify as the types for this mass market."[37] This Jack London classic, with a bold cover by Robert Jonas, was an appropriate choice for them. Farrell also goes on to list a number of suggestions for future editions: Ibsen, Tolstoy, the poetry of Carl Sandberg, *Man's Fate*; "short stories of William March."

Fualkner's [*sic*] PYLON. It is perhaps simpler than some of his others. I like best his LIGHT IN AUGUST, personally," he noted in an aside. *The Charterhouse of Parma,* some literary criticism, *The Rise of David Levinsky,* and "GINATS [*sic*] IN THE EARTH" round out his list. Many of these titles did appear as NAL titles; a year later NAL brought out *Pylon,* with a daring Avati cover, and in 1949 NAL editors discussed the contents of a selection of Faulkner stories including plot synopses of them. For instance, "HAIR The story of a barber who marries the small-town bad girl."[38] Mass reading is, as Farrell and various censors knew, classed reading. In another letter, he suggested Goncharov's *Oblomov* would be a suitable title.

"And Shakespeare Sells for a Quarter in Some Editions, Too"

That the covers—and not merely the contents—so exercised most of the Gathings Committee members suggests, despite their lapses into "literary criticism," that they understood the import of the *Ulysses* case: the book needed to be seen as a whole. Thus, the cover, enclosing the whole book, became crucial. In recounting (inaccurately) the scene from "a New York play" in which "Hester Prynne . . . will have to have a plunging neckline, and the scarlet letter below that," Congresswoman St. George injected a bit of theater into the hearings, eliciting this repartee from Bantam Books' John O'Connor: "there is a considerable problem of fraud here on the public . . . It had been carried to absurd lengths in some cases, even in one case, in my recollection, of taking a Sherlock Holmes book—and surely nobody has less sex in him than Sherlock Holmes—and I think it was The Hound of the Baskervilles [*sic*] and how in the world they were able to develop a sexy cover on The Hound of the Baskervilles [*sic*] is beyond me" (*HSC*, 103). The covers—as Hollywood, Broadway, publishing houses, and Congress knew—sparked the public's interest. They sent the public spectacle home for private consumption, opening readers to "dangers far worse than communism . . . this high road of Godless lust," as a writer stationed with the American Red Cross in the combat zone, Korea, wrote to the Committee on Obscene Literature on the anniversary of Pearl Harbor Day (RSC, 29). Of course, the Select Committee was not actually named the "Committee on Obscene Literature" but was rather charged with investigating "current pornographic materials." And the first adjective, as much as the second key one, also mattered. The committee was not interested in examining the long history of pornography and its varied definitions over time. Its job was ferreting out its contemporary manifestations. But with most paperbacks actually being reprints, often of the classics—Shakespeare, Hardy, Ovid—the updated material was not to be found within the text but on the covers, which encased the potentially offensive language in a new form, with images and taglines designed for the mid-twentieth-century marketplace. For instance, Émile Zola's *Nana* became an early Pocket Book, with a cover linking it to late Victorian iconography of the *Woman in White* and, with its declaration of being a complete, unexpurgated translation, it also signaled transgression. Moreover, it came from France. Less than a decade later, shortly before the congressional hearings, in a typical pulp remediation, we learn from the Avon edition that Nana had a mother, which might not have been clear from its original (and debased) title, *L'assommoir* (plate 22, *top*).

The 1949 decision by Judge Curtis Bok in *Commonwealth v. Gordon et al.*, which exonerated Caldwell's and Farrell's (and others') novels, gathered intense approbation from the majority for its "far reaching" impact on "all elements of our social structure, sanctioning by negative action the flow of salacious, scatological, and suggestive literature, reaching the degree of mass media" (RSC, 6). Through a process of guilt by association worthy of Senator Joseph McCarthy and noted as such by the minority, Bok's decision was put down to greed. Others appearing before the committee echoed the discourse of the House Un-American Activities Committee; for example, distributor Samuel Black responded to H. Ralph Burton's questions by asking, "Do you want me to name a few names, is that what you want of me?"[39] Later, questioning Victor Otterstein, a local distributor, about which books sell well in the nation's capital, Burton listed books that "describe the pleasures of narcotics, how to use them, how to use the needle; they expand upon homosexuality, and one books advises or supports polygamy, and any number of books deal with lesbianism and nymphomania[;] I have the names of them here" (RSC, 45). The committee asked John O'Connor to "give us the names of the stockholders" of Bantam Books, as well as their respective holdings, including the holdings of Grosset and Dunlap and Curtis Publishing (RSC, 97).

Smearing by naming names implied that as grandson of Cyrus H. K. Curtis, founder of one of the primary mass-magazine publishers, Curtis Publishing Company, and son of Mrs. Efrem Zimbalist, a board member of the company, Bok might have an economic interest in the case. This case, the committee report noted, was cited by "publishers of pocket-size books," while others, such as *Attorney General v. "God's Little Acre"* (Massachusetts), as well as *Attorney General v. "Forever Amber,"* which deemed these books obscene, as had other cases, were ignored. Even though the entire book might not be understood so, because, as *Commonwealth v. Isenstadt* (318 Mass. 543, 556, 557), from which the committee quoted were selectively found, the books "would tend to promote lascivious thoughts and to arouse lustful desire in the minds of substantial numbers of that public," because they were "obviously intended for general sale" (RSC, 11).

The committee recognized the paradox that it and any court found itself confronting: the *Ulysses* case precluded excerpting passages and insisted that literary context meant the entire work. But they asked, "How is it possible . . . for a tribunal to properly determine the question [of obscenity] without fully considering the particular parts of the book?" As parts of the book, covers became a focal point because of a national clamor to "clean up the newsstands" (RSC, 29), and the committee noted that since 1909 it had been illegal in the state of Indiana to sell "any paper novels with covers bearing dangerous or incendiary or obscene pictures in any show case or window, along any street or in any store" (quoted in RSC, 33). Visibility—on any corner, along any street (as opposed to "under the counter . . . or in behind closed doors"[40])—was responsible for the hundreds of millions of pocket-size books sold annually. The committee entered into the record hundreds of volumes, though "no effort has been made to record how extensive has been the reading of literature during the course [many months] of the committee's inquiry." Still this "research" yielded "obscenity, violence, lust, use of narcotics, blasphemy, vulgarity, pornography, juvenile delinquency, sadism, masochism, perversion, homosexuality, lesbianism, murder, rape, and nymphomania" (HSC, 12), introducing "as evidence" the following books, which "extol by their approbatory language accounts of homosexuality, lesbianism, and other sexual aberrations":

The Tormented
Women's Barracks
Spring Fire
Unmoral
Forbidden
Artist's Model
The Wayward Bus (HSC, 15–16)

It was necessary to see the front covers and read the back covers and flyleaves to fully grasp the contents—which, as the committee admitted, it may not have been read with due care—because these come-ons were "innovations to stimulate sales," deployed by publishers (HSC, 16). In fact, as Gathings said "right on the back of one of those books . . . there is a little synopsis to give you an idea what you are buying" (RSC, 46). Covers, as sales tools for this new commodity, were at once visible everywhere yet masked what was lurking, hidden deep within, which might be even more shocking than what could be seen.

Later in the hearings, Bantam publisher John O'Connor was bullied by Congressman Gathings in this testy exchange:

> *The Chairman:* What do you think, Mr. O'Connor, the committee was formed for? Had there been such a congressional committee prior to this time?
>
> *Mr. O'Conner:* Happily not.
>
> *The Chairman:* To ferret out this kind of trash?
>
> *Mr. [Edward] Rees:* Did you say "happily not"?
>
> *Mr. O'Connor:* Yes . . . (HSC, 99)

The contents of *Women's Barracks* were dissected thoroughly by the committee through questions concerning the nature of truth and fiction and their relation to literary history. As the vice president of Fawcett, Ralph Foster Daigh, explained, the book was, "a fact story," an adaptation and translation of the author's wartime diary by noted writer Meyer Levin: "it was a sincere, sincerely written, sincerely translated book rewritten by an admitted literary authority and expert, done sincerely" (HSC, 38). Judge Augustus Hand's decision in the *Ulysses* case had turned, according to O'Connor, on whether a "realistic scene which involved sexual episodes . . . was there with sincerity—in other words, if it was not just dirt for dirt's sake" (HSC, 100), so "a realistic novel which includes the sexual episode honestly and sincerely" is a suitable one for reprint (HSC, 103).

"Sincerity" became an important word for understanding whether a book was deemed obscene in a number of censorship cases in both state and federal courts; it functioned as one of the factors necessary to determine "the extent to which the book as a whole would have a demoralizing effect on its readers." Others included "the themes of the book, the degree of sincerity of purpose evident in it, its literary worth, the channels used in distribution, contemporary attitudes toward the literary treatment of sexual behavior and the types of readers (particularly with respect to age and intellectual development)."[41] So the dispute about fact and fiction, "sordid situations," and sincerity helped determine whether *Women's Barracks* was a "good book"; sincerity could trump sordid situations and so was crucial for deflecting the stigma of obscenity. The book's suspect or rather confusing nature was furthered by a letter read into the minutes by Daigh from "a literary expert named John Bakeless," who compared "Women's Barracks with Plato, Homer, Sappho, Shakespeare, and Marlowe," which outraged committee members who could not see this "publication in any sense of the word in the same category" with *Hamlet* or *Macbeth* (*HSC*, 37). But comparisons to Shakespeare, Flaubert, Boccaccio, the Bible—even Benjamin Franklin's 1745 "Advice to a Young Man on the Choice of a Mistress"—show up throughout court censorship cases, because, as the attorneys for Doubleday noted: "The censors generally apply their condemnation to recently published work . . . There is a strange feeling that public morals are harmfully affected only by books and by recently published books."[42] So to deflect this, publishers needed to link their wares to these durable authors and their works.

The comparative "literary criticism" in which the committee members engaged was reminiscent of how court cases dealt with the censorship of books, because since the *Ulysses* case, plaintiffs and/or defendants relied on textual references—either of the whole book, as was determined to be the standard in the 1934 case—or by pointing to explicit passages, as was the case in *Doubleday and Company, Inc. v. People of New York*, where both sides relied on book reviews and literary analysis to make their claim about whether or not Edmund Wilson's 1946 novel, *Memoirs of Hecate County*, could be considered to have violated the New York statute prohibiting distribution in any manner of "any obscene, lewd, lascivious, filthy, indecent or disgusting book."[43] This case, brought fairly recently against a publisher that also ran a bookstore in New York, served as a touchstone for the hearings, because the court's split vote left standing the New York appellate court's decision to uphold the guilty verdict and thus fine Doubleday for violation of the misdemeanor charges. But the idea of considering the whole book also sent the committee members beyond literary criticism into the realm of art history.

The cover of *Women's Barracks* elicited further questioning by committee counsel Burton: "Are the outside covers and front matter of your publications always a true indication of what the purchaser will find within?" Daigh (of Fawcett) replied, "In illustrating anything, there is a certain license permitted, a certain job that I, as an editor, wish to call attention to a thing, and I use a picture to do it, and the thing that I am selling is behind the picture. There is always a correlation. I couldn't say that it is always a true correlation nor would that be a desirable state."[44] "This business of souping up covers," as Congresswoman St. George noted, was clearly intended to boost sales. Of course, she demurred, pornographic matter usually came in the form of "booklets with blue covers" sold via truckers at New Jersey truck stops (RSC, 105). "Youths are also being baited into becoming salesmen of this slime among their young companions."[45]

The pocket-size books that were being published by Pocket Books, Avon, Dell, and many other publishers consisted of reprints, but by the time of the Gathings hearings, Fawcett had introduced their paperback originals (PBOs) in a 1949 press release to *Publishers' Weekly* announcing its first four titles to be published in 1950. Within months, more than nine million copies had been sold, prompting other houses to develop PBO lines.[46] Even NAL, which steadfastly adhered to its mission to bring "Good Reading for the

Millions" through reprints of hardcover fare seemed open to PBOs. One of its authors, William Gardner Smith, who had had two of his novels published already, noted in a letter to editor Arabel Porter that he was writing "murder stories, from the viewpoint of the criminal (along the lines—in all modesty!—of 'Crime and Punishment,') under the pseudonym, 'Mark Gardner'—not because I am ashamed of them (I'm proud of them), but because certain narrow critics assume, because one writes mysteries, one should not be taken seriously as a novelist." He offered her "a mystery involving a murder by a child. Is that taboo?" There is no record of a response; however, Porter's handwritten note on the letter indicates that NAL "turned down 3rd book—needed work/relationship friendly."[47]

The pressure on reprint houses from PBOs in the early 1950s contributed, according to Bantam's John O'Connor, to the proliferation of sensational covers (RSC, 103). The PBO was unseemly, causing Harold Arno of Lion Books, a well-known publisher of lesbian fiction, to declare that "[t]he original publishing program of Lion Books is a supplement, and only a supplement, to our reprint program."[48] As early as 1945, paperback publishers stressed that the books would be widely available and modeled on Penguin books, but the difference was in the covers: where Penguin insisted on its muted two-toned standard, a journalist at the *London Sunday Press* proclaimed: "In the United States pornography is triumphant . . . What Boston spews out of her mouth, New York devours."[49] The inspector in charge of licensing and censure in the Detroit Police Department, Herbert Case, explained that he tried to suppress sales of pocket-size books without going to court because he found that once a trial occurs, "the title is exploited, and it is given impetus toward sales in a great many parts of the country . . . sales have mounted up terrifically because of action that we have taken." In fact, he noted that "people have come in and tried to get us to prosecute to get front-page publicity" (RSC, 53).

The cover, as I have stressed, was part of a total package, was *itself* a package; editors routinely exacted changes to the designs in the interest of clarity. Shortly before terminating his "long-range" contract, Marc Jaffe wrote to longtime NAL cover artist Robert Jonas that his sketch for the 1955 Mentor book, *The Creative Process,* needed to be redone.[50] Titles as well as images were modified for effect too. NAL decided to rename a book by Fletcher Flora, originally titled *A Handful of Quietness* to *Whispers of the Flesh*, clearly a sexier title. NAL urged Flora, with his masculine/feminine name (like James Joyce) and known for his lesbian pulps but described as a "young school teacher from Oklahoma" (though his address was Leavenworth, Kansas) in the dope sheet for the novel, to break his contract with the less savory Lion Books so NAL could bring the book out. The editors argued to his agent that "we believe that this is a selling title."[51] *Whispers of the Flesh*, about a "girl dress designer better at business than men," appeared with a cover by Clark Hulings in 1958.[52] Apparently, NAL had been trying to use this title for a while: "The title WHISPERS OF THE FLESH . . . was proposed about two years ago for a Weldon book and was turned down by the author. I think it is ideally suited to Flora's book and will ask author's permission to change . . ." wrote an editor.[53]

The negotiations between editors and authors over the look of the book—as is clear from the response of "touchy author" Salinger—went to the heart of understanding the paperback as an object open to scorn and ridicule, or censure.[54] After his startling debut in paperback with *Other Voices, Other Rooms*, featuring one of Robert Jonas's signature designs—the broken window or shattered door opening onto a steamy scene far in the background—for the front cover (plate 22, *bottom*), and the louche full-length photograph of him reclining on the back (figure 9.3), Truman Capote felt it necessary to pressure Weybright to tone down the look of his next book, *A Tree of Night*. "As for the book," he wrote, "I hope the jacket will be plain—That is, not so gaudy as the one used on

OTHER VOICES. I would prefer, too, that you did not have a photograph of me . . . the biography, I think, should be simply that I was born in New Orleans and have published 3 books."[55]

With its gaudy cover, *Women's Barracks* caused a sensation and counselor Burton returned to it often, indicating that its publisher had testified "from that chair where you sit . . . that it was good reading matter for his daughter." It may not have been an example of "a serious book . . . [that] put on a very flashy cover so the book will be read," as Margaret Culkin Banning claimed resulted in pocket books and magazines "crowd[ing] out" "better" ones, but it shared subject matter with those slated for indictment. It was on the list of books worth mentioning by name. But titles of books could be tricky, because "if you get those [flashy covered books] out of existence, they come back with new titles, very often" (RSC, 69). This was certainly the case for a number of lesbian-authored reprints: Gale Wilhelm's second novel, *No Letters for the Dead*, was reprinted three times with three titles, including in 1956, *Paula* (a code name

Figure 9.3 Back cover of Truman Capote, *Other Voices, Other Rooms* (Signet/NAL, 1949). Photograph by Halma.

in lesbian fiction), and her third novel from 1938, an intimate pro-lesbian love story, *Torchlight to Valhalla*, reappeared from Lion Books as *The Strange Path* ("strange" being an even greater signifier than "Paula" of lesbianism and "path" indicating some form of queer identity) in 1953. Not only were the "perversion subjects, such as lesbianism" of *Women's Barracks* suspect (RSC, 48), so too was lesbianism's peculiar literary history—a case of remediation in print, not merely of the title but of its content. The long-standing interconnection of sex and media incurred the attention of the committee. Written in French (a surefire code for sex) as a diary kept by Tereska Torrès, it was refashioned into a "fact story" by her husband, journalist and novelist Meyer Levin,[56] whose legal tangles over his own works turned on some aspect of appropriating or translating another's words from court testimony or diary, one obviously available as a public record—and many pulps emerged from criminal court cases (such as Ira Wolfert's *Tucker's People*, pulped under the more provocative title *Underworld*)—or as a private account made public, in the case of Anne Frank.

One concern of the committee was how quickly the paperback explosion had swept the nation during the preceding decade, a point constantly referred to by various questioners and rebutted by those being interrogated that before then the industry did not exist because the books did not exist. "Since 1941 the paper-bound book industry has increased enormously," noted Burton in one of the numerous mentions of an obvious fact: mass-marketed pocket-size books first appeared in the United States in limited numbers only in 1939, and the postwar end to rationing paper had spawned this rapid growth (*HSC*, 75). To get a sense of how tremendous these sales were, one need only look at the NAL total figure for William Faulkner's six reprints in the four years between its first publication of *Sanctuary* in 1947 and its April 1951 release of *Pylon* (3,297,789).[57] "Now, how can you expect the parents of children to stop them from going in corner drug store and newsstands and buying this material and reading it?" Burton asked Arch Crawford of the Magazine Publishers (*HSC*, 75). This material, being the new fiction written "since Hemingway and that particular group came into vogue," as Crawford called it, or as Burton would have it, a "stream of filth" (*HSC*, 75), was enabled by, according to Carroll D. Kearns (R-PA), "these pocket-size books which have literature and reading material that are anything but good for youngsters are available to them" (*HSC*, 88). These congressional concerns about the mode of distribution for paperbacks, that is, the ways in which books were circulating through magazine and candy distributors and showing up on any corner, had been on the radar of publishers much earlier. In 1948, a year before Faulkner would win the Nobel Prize in Literature, Johiel Katsev of the Sunset News Company wrote to Allan Adams of Fawcett Publications to alert him about a contest held in May 1945 (while Adams was still in the service) by the Independent News Company's house organ to glean ideas about how the industry might sustain its "war-time prosperity." The winning entry "proposed a code of regulations for publishers and wholesalers engaged in newsstand sales . . . which . . . covered risqué publications." It called for allowing wholesalers to "refuse to distribute publications which are risqué and morally objectionable." But the real point of Katsev's letter was to alert Fawcett that he had been visited by an officer in the Morals Section of the Los Angeles Police Department and threatened with arrest for "placing on the newsstands of Los Angeles books which large segments of our population consider to be morally objectionable. . . . The specific book in question at this time is 'Wild Palms' by William Faulkner and we have given instructions to our promotion men to immediately pick up all copies of this book which are available on the newsstands."

Katsev continued that the "moral issues" aside, the

publicity . . . will do immeasurable harm to the dealer relationships . . . the conclusion is simple, Allan, we must impose self-censorship . . . the nation is getting back to an even keel after the hectic war time period. The home itself which was frequently torn up under the war conditions is again being reestablished and becoming the backbone of our nation economically as well as morally. It is possible that border line publications served some sort of purpose during the war . . . however, they have certainly outlived any usefulness today.

He concluded by refusing to distribute "books such as 'Wild Palms' in Los Angeles." Self-censorship in the form of refusal to distribute literary works deemed "morally objectionable" meant "dealers, in understandable fear, will remove from their stands many worthwhile books in order to insure that their skirts are absolutely clean." This three-page letter encapsulated and foresaw the entire thrust of what the Gathings Committee sought to achieve and how it proceeded, including the obligatory declaration that "free speech and freedom of the press have contributed much to the greatness of our nation," as it outlined how a new postwar morality required limiting access to books in the name of "a very deep and all inclusive obligation to our present and future citizens," the youth of America.[58]

Judge James Mulholland's congressional testimony explained that for a number of juvenile delinquency cases adjudicated before his Brooklyn court, Irving Shulman's 1947 novel, *The Amboy Dukes*, reprinted by Avon Publishing, was dissected by a series of psychiatrists, educators, clerics, and social workers whom he asked to comment on it. They found it to have been read "by a great number of them [delinquents]" (107) who modeled their "sex offenses" on actions found on "a particular page (p. 26) . . . Yet this book is available on the newsstands and could be purchased by any child" (*HSC*, 108, 110).[59] Again, the cover was of concern—not so much for its image, a boy and girl making out on the grass—as for the phrase at the bottom, "By special arrangement with Doubleday & Co.," as if this signified some secret code revealing information about how Avon maneuvered the book onto "newsstands" (*HSC*, 110).

And it might: Doubleday and Company was suspect; it had been the defendant in the 1946 New York case involving Edmund Wilson's *Memoirs of Hecate County*, which was found to violate a statute stipulating that anyone who

> offers for loan, gift, sale or distribution, any obscene, lewd, lascivious, filthy, indecent or disgusting book, magazine, pamphlet, newspaper, story paper, writing, paper, picture, drawing, photograph, figure or image, or any written or printed matter of an indecent character;***or who designs, copies, draws, photographs, prints, utters, publishes or in any manner manufactures, or prepares any such book, picture, drawing, magazine, pamphlet, newspaper, story paper, writing, paper, figure, image, matter, article or thing,***. Is guilty of a misdemeanor,***[60]

But, as the ACLU continued in its brief, "Literature is a form of art" and therefore subject to the "constitutional protection for a free press . . . [of] the most valuable as well as the least valuable literature."[61] In the trial and appeals, various literary critics were called upon—usually by having their reviews read into the record—to determine whether or not Wilson's book was a work of literature or pornography. Despite the detailed appeal to the Supreme Court made by Doubleday, the conviction was upheld. The People submitted a review outlining the six sections of the novel, calling into question its status as a novel, precisely for its fragmented form, use of French (one of the linked stories is written entirely in French), and varied generic signs, suggesting at once that it was a work of autobiography, social criticism, and satire—but not literature. The court split, with Justice Frankfurter taking no part. Thus, a marketing device was born with the 1961 NAL edition front cover, composed entirely of text without any image, stating simply, "Not for sale in New York State" above the author's name and title. The front and back covers quote from the same reviews entered into evidence that this was "one of the twentieth century's outstanding books by American's foremost living critic."

By this time NAL was charging seventy-five cents for its mass-market paperbacks, so the assumption behind the quarter price—that it was aimed at youth—was a bit mitigated; moreover, splashy covers were giving way to those featuring only text. NAL knew the trial could be a sales gimmick. In the editorial dope sheet for *Memoirs*, the marketing comment focuses on "The Princess with the Golden Hair," the longest story in the book; its "unusual depth and perception . . . merciless in cutting into these people to see what makes them tick . . . insures a reader acceptance in all circles such as colleges, book stores, and the newsstands." But the clincher notes that because the court case in New York "brought considerable notoriety as a result of the graphic description of love . . . every newspaper in the U.S. carried the story that should still be clear in the minds of the public."[62] So while *The Amboy Dukes* did not raise concerns when it first appeared in cloth cover, it was considered a danger in paper, while Wilson's work was immediately deemed obscene. But Shulman's novel held its young readers' attention in ways that *Memoirs of Hecate County* might not. "There is not basis whatsoever for assuming that the book [*Hecate*] would find wide circulation among the young, who are not notable for avid interest in fiction written by distinguished literary critics," wrote the attorneys appealing its publisher's guilty verdict.[63]

Censorship was not only a legal process concerning obscenity. The Coca-Cola Company wrote to complain that "On Page 12 of your book, SERENADE, by James M. Cain, there is a mention of Coca-Cola. However, the name was used without capitalization. And strange as it may appear, this seemingly trivial point might jeopardize the rights we hold in it as a registered trade-mark for our product."[64] A memo went out almost immediately reminding editors "to inform all your proofreaders to watch for things like this in our books. (I understand Kleenex fights the same battle—though we've never heard from them.)"[65] Copyright infringements also affected cover design, especially when works were tied to movies, as was the case for another Cain novel, *Double Indemnity*, in which the 1950 NAL cover (already a reprint of an earlier Avon paperback first published in 1943 and then reissued by Avon in 1947 with a cover by Tony Varaday [plate 24, *top*]) resembled a still from Paramount studios, and the men clearly looked like the film's actors, Fred Mac-Murray and Edward G. Robinson. Marc Jaffe, assistant editor, consulted attorney Rudolf Littauer. Paramount had no objection to the use of the image, but suggested that the actors "(since they are now independent) might have some feelings in the matter."[66] NAL went ahead with the cover. The Varaday cover features the leg of a man lying across railroad tracks, a man gazing at it, but dominated by a blonde in a yellow blouse with plunging neckline and fierce gaze. A later NAL cover anticipated the 1958 Hollywood film *Attack of the Fifty Foot Woman* as a campy image of female rampage.[67] But by the NAL second edition in 1957, these suggestive references to the film had been completely erased. Instead, Clark Hulings's expressive cover displayed a drawing of a woman's face over an all red background, returning to the image of female horror used for the cover of Olga Lengyel's *I Survived Hitler's Ovens* (plate 24, *bottom*).

Throughout the various congressional hearings and court cases charging "obscenity" or "pornography," prosecutors repeatedly proclaimed, as had Samuel Black, that they were not "censors" but, as many advocates for First Amendment cases note, the very threat of encountering a legal action often has a chilling effect on expression. For instance, despite its proud record of breaking many publishing taboos—such as delivering mass-market paperbacks by African American and gay authors throughout the nation, including the South—NAL's publisher, Victor Weybright, declined to bring one of the books of social-worker-turned-novelist Caroline Slade into print. As his staff indicated in response to *Lost: A Young Woman* on its dope sheet, if one did not know the status of the author, one would assume the works were "straight pulp."[68] This was precisely how Ruth Blodgett, in the "Book-of-the-Month Club News" had described Slade's novel *Margaret* (which had already been issued by NAL) as recorded on the back cover of the Vanguard cloth edition: "Some doubtless will read this story out of the same morbid curiosity with which they read of sex crimes in tabloids. They may not see behind the lurid facts." In rejecting her new book, Weybright urged Slade and her publisher, Jim Henle, to remember what happened in New Jersey, though he doesn't elaborate further on this ominous occurrence to explain his decision.[69] Slade's controversial books on child prostitution and sexual abuse came with strictures controlling their hardcover distribution. Yet in 1950 and 1951, NAL had brought out three of her novels—*Margaret*, about an abused girl who turns to procuring girls for older men, *Lilly Crackell*, about an unwed mother (these two marketed as the increasingly popular juvenile delinquent/reform school genre), and her Depression classic, *The Triumph of Willie Pond*, a savage critique of child welfare provisions that inadvertently led to child prostitution—in paperbacks, all with steamy James Avati covers; but, perhaps with the Gathings hearings in mind (Weybright's last letter to her is dated 8 December 1952), a week after the hearings, they declined to commit further.

Weybright was a shrewd businessman who knew how to gauge the limits of propriety and the law, and with whom to curry favor. Weeks after his extended testimony before the Gathings Committee, Samuel Black was on Weybright's radar. In a memo, he presented "a wild idea" to his editorial staff—"an advance presentation of Avati's INVISIBLE MAN cover to Sam Black, who 'covets it,' and says he would replace an original Saturday Evening Post cover with it in his office." Weybright's musing conveys how distribution, marketing, and censorship shaped the editorial processes at every step. He further explained:

Since some of the content of this remarkable novel which won
the National Book Award might frighten certain wholesalers, it
would seem to me worth a special effort to identify Sam Black
with the book . . . I would very much like to see a man of Black's
strong feelings, vigorously and frequently expressed, identified
with some old high-quality literature which by no stretch of the
imagination can be described as trash . . . I think the price of
admission is exploitation of INVISIBLE MAN as a book attached to Black's name.

His plot entailed setting up a photoshoot of Ellison and his
wife, along with Avati and a representative from Fawcett (the distributor), and NAL presenting "the framed cover" to "publicize the
book to wholesalers" (plate 21).[70]

Obviously, threats of legal actions or religious crusades against a
work scared publishers. Weybright indicated as much to Caroline
Slade when he mentioned the 1950 State of New Jersey case brought
against her novel *Margaret* after it appeared in paperback. He was
"terribly tempted to reconsider [her first novel] *Sterile Sun* for ulti-
mate reprint," but worried about Catholic censors' responses. Moreover, he sought "our lawyers to advise me on the hazard, censorwise,
created by the legend in the book in its original Vanguard edition,
commending it to a professional audience." She, too, was concerned
about legal and church censorship but also feared that "like *Forever
Amber*, it will be read not for social consciousness but for sex."[71]
Vanguard had skirted censorship problems for this novel, culled directly from Slade's case studies among girls in reform school after
their arrests for prostitution and narrated in their voices, by including a disclaimer that stated, "*Sterile Sun* is issued in a special edition,
the sale of which is limited to physicians, psychiatrists, sociologists,
social workers, educators and other persons having a professional
interest in the psychology of adolescence."[72] How this control over
who could possess the book operated remains unclear, though my

copy is signed by the author, which suggests that it came out in a limited edition, as was typical in the midst of the Depression, and perhaps was available only through special order. Because NAL was committed to bringing out the whole book (though many abridged editions also got published, especially in the early years when strict adherence to the 192-page maximum was necessary to rein in costs), this disclaimer posed a problem; as a paperback, the book would be mass marketed.

However, threats of censorship might also spur sales, or at least interest in the books; why else add the precautionary touch of reminding readers to keep a high-minded tone while indulging in the "lurid facts of sex crimes"? This was clearly the case for *Women's Barracks*, which sold more than a million copies during the year following its notoriety in Congress, and *Memoirs of Hecate County*, which, when it finally appeared in paperback, boldly proclaimed its status as banned in New York; this, in effect, marked the end of the line for book censorship. Important cases, *Roth v. United States* case in particular, continued into the 1960s, but paperbacks had already retooled for different markets—college courses focused on less racy mass-market and trade editions, for example—and the sensation these objects presented receded as their cost increased. Between the post–Korean War recession, causing the pulping of millions of unsold paperbacks in 1953; the rise of trade paperbacks, such as the Vintage editions Peter Eisenman's brother was sending him to pass the time while he was stationed along the Korean DMZ, aimed at university students, whose numbers were swelling; and the effects of the trials and hearings investigating pulp, the era of the "great American paperback," as Richard Lupoff referred to it, was over—at least visually. By 1961, *Ulysses* had literally become demotic; it came out in a Vintage paperback edition, its cover mimicking the Ernst Reichl hardcover, relying solely on typography with its elongated U and L signaling that paperbacks had moved beyond pulp.

Coda: The Afterlife of Pulp

Still the residue of pulp haunts us in myriad ways. The many reminders of its place in our cultural history—but, more important,
in our individual lives, at least those of us of a certain age—cannot
be fully accounted for by any of the sources or ideas I have amassed.
The Gathings Committee hearings lasted only a week in the midst
of the Korean War. It was shrouded, you might say, by the Great
London Smog that began on December 5, the final day of the hearings, continuing to December 9, when tens of thousands died from
air pollution; a month before it convened, on November 1, the
United States exploded its first hydrogen bomb on Eniwetok atoll
in the Marshall Islands, obliterating the fragile Pacific Ocean land-
mass. Stalin would be dead three months later on 1 March 1953. So
the committee's obsessive questioning about paperbacks was at best
a side show, no matter how important youth would become during
the rest of the decade after Brando sped through small-town America, sparking a vision of wildness on wheels. Moreover, the financial
crisis of 1953, erupting as the Korean War ended, sent the publishing industry into a tailspin. Of course, as the many delicious covers
from the mid- to late 1950s attest, pulp continued; but in 1953,
Anchor Books began publishing trade paperbacks, and a year later
Vintage appeared from Alfred Knopf, stressing quality and refined

taste for their literary and philosophical lists, which would appear on university syllabuses. In America, sleaze was coming to an end.[1]

The aftereffects reside in the private and weird mementos—the books themselves—and in the memories they induce. Gwendolyn Brooks's evocative novel from 1953 follows the inner life of a young, bookish housewife living in a Chicago kitchenette during World War II. *Maud Martha* includes a bedroom scene, sometime in the early 1940s, where the heroine and her husband are both lying in bed reading. This work by a Pulitzer Prize–winning poet moves across a strange, almost mythic, temporality, at once quite precise (we know Maud Martha was born in 1917) and vaguely dreamy (time shrinks and expands, especially after the birth of her daughter). In this chapter, "The Young Couple at Home," Maud Martha is reading Somerset Maugham's *Of Human Bondage*. She is the sort who regularly visits her public library, so, while the novel doesn't explicitly say so, it seems to be a hardcover book, especially because the paperback edition did not appear until 1950 from Pocket Books. This fact is made clear because her husband "settled down to his. His was a paper-backed copy of *Sex in the Married Life*."[2]

That the narrator calls attention to the book's cover material and title reveals something about the moment of *Maud Martha*'s publication and the place of reading in it. Maud Martha is reading the novel that had been made into the wildly popular Bette Davis film in 1934—when Maud Martha was seventeen and all her friends talked of "Joe Lewis . . . of Duke Ellington, of Bette Davis."[3] Its title suggests something about Brooks's gesture toward racial consciousness, even if the novel's content does not—Maugham's theme is cross-class desire. Maud is an intellectual—but her husband's thinking about sex—though he falls asleep within minutes of opening his book. In 1951, one of the first popular sex manuals, a paperback book entitled *Sex Lives of Married Couples*, was published by an outfit called Sex Guidance Publications; it had been preceded by a 1940 paperback translation of a German sexology work, "intended for circulation among mature persons only," published by Cadillac Publishing: *How to Attain and Practice the Ideal Sex Life*. With the exception of some religious or eugenics texts, this was the only paperback sex manual available in the United States in the 1940s. However, by 1953, others began to appear. So Brooks is indicating something about the changing sexual landscape of the period in which she is writing and which she is remembering, and she knows this is being facilitated by the paperback.

Darryl Pinckney offers his memory of this midcentury shift, connecting a scene of family car-trip nostalgia with one of coming to grips with his sexual identity, all courtesy of a cheap paperback, held close one hot midsummer day in 1967.

> I had no idea why I was so absorbed in James Baldwin's novel, *Giovanni's Room*, but everyone else in the car knew . . . We were actually on Route 66 and I didn't care. I was thirteen years old and I wasn't causing trouble, sitting between my two sisters with Baldwin's novel about a man's love for another man in my face . . . "Until I die there will be those moments, moments seeming to rise up out of the ground like Macbeth's witches . . . I will see Giovanni again, as he was that night, so vivid, so winning, all of the light of that gloomy tunnel trapped around his head." Soon enough I had *Another Country*, Baldwin's best seller, stashed away with what I considered porn.[4]

For Anne Enright, the family saga of paperbacks extends from before her birth yet seems fundamental to her self-awareness as an Irish writer.

> In September 1954, my parents went to Edinburgh on their honeymoon . . . and after that they went to Lourdes. My mother prayed at the grotto where the Virgin Mary appeared to Bernadette, and her prayers must have been answered, because two Enrights went out there, but three Enrights came back. In

fact, my mother carried more than this, as yet undeclared, baby through Irish customs . . . In among the clothes and the souvenir bottles of holy water were a couple of paperback books . . . "Aha!" said the customs man . . . [who] slapped the case shut and waved them through. She had been used, on her own honeymoon, as a books mule . . . One of my father's honeymoon books was a Penguin paperback copy of *The Golden Ass* by Apuleius.

Of her father's library, bought by this provincial farmer's son between the late 1940s and mid-1950s while working as a civil servant in Dublin, she explains "the books he bought there—just a couple every year—are still on the shelf. They are all paperbacks. Wilde's *Salome*, Shaw's *Man and Superman* were bought in 1949. These were followed by Dante, *The Greeks* by Kitto, *Spinoza* by Stuart Hampshire, *Barabbas* by Pär Lagerkvist, all the way to Sophocles and Rousseau in 1953. A very European selection. Also on the shelf is *Three to Get Married*, by Bishop Sheen. I thought this was about a ménage à trois, but the third turned out to be God."[5]

In addition to the books themselves, I collect these fragments, memories of objects one has lived among, lived with and through, hoping to unlock some private space—held within the book and its reader. Everywhere I look, I find these telltale traces of what Charles Simic called, writing of Joseph Cornell's boxes made of rummaged junk found in used bookstores and junk shops around New York, "Dime-Store Alchemy."[6] With the 2013 release of Baz Luhrmann's 3-D film of *The Great Gatsby*, we learn that the novel has once again been reissued in paperback by Simon & Schuster with two covers, one resurrecting the original hardcover dust jacket of two eyes and a mouth floating in a midnight blue sky above an art deco cityscape, the other featuring Leonardo DiCaprio splayed out in lavish decadence. It became the top-selling book on Amazon.com.[7] The upsurge of interest in all things Gatsby led Jeff Oloizia to the Matthew J.

and Arlyn Bruccoli Collection of F. Scott Fitzgerald at the University of South Carolina Libraries Special Collections. Spanning its eighty-three-year publishing history, the collection tracks changing tastes in book design and marketing strategies across time and national borders. Matthew Bruccoli, Fitzgerald scholar and biographer, collected these books "not as an investment. You buy them because it gives you pleasure to read them . . . to see them on the shelves."[8]

Memoirist Charlotte Nekola remembers her own private self-recognition through a paperback:

> My parents were proud of their hardbound books and they had a place of honor in the living room bookshelves. It was my wild, beautiful older Kim Novak sister who had the Dell paperbacks in her room—in a very orderly distinguished spot. She had my grandfather's former office desk, the one who was a dentist in the 20's and 30's . . . it was a big mission oak desk that had a drawer that pulled out revealing an inner writing desk like a school desk with an inkwell. AND on each side of the desk were bookshelves big enough for small books, certainly they did not have Dell in mind when the mission desk was conceived, but she had the entire shelf full of pulps. *East of Eden*, *The Life of Marie Curie* by Eve Curie. My sister was nine years older and . . . I cannot say we were close; she was always just out of reach for me, the kid sister with braids and glasses and blackberry stains, the tag-along pest. But I knew we were bonded, were sisters. She sealed that knowledge one day as we looked at ourselves in the mirror together; I am 7 and she is 16; and she said, see, we have the same color of eyes, green, like no one else in the family. That was a great moment for me—a fully acknowledged sister at last, perhaps just a bit as glamorous as she. But the best moment was a random desultory St. Louis hot summer afternoon, sitting on her bed with nothing to do.

She had something to do of course. She kind of flew by me but paused in front of the shelf of paperbacks. *Jane Eyre* by Charlotte Bronte was shelved obediently next to *Wuthering Heights.* "Look," she said, "There we are. Jane and Charlotte. On one book." It seemed like destiny itself was rolling out a long road in front of us, Jane and Charlotte on the very same book. If it wasn't a little pulp book, it wouldn't have been in her bedroom, so intimate, and I am sure she bought them herself at the Rexall drugstore with her allowance, a sort of rebellion from the distinguished classics and encyclopedia downstairs. It was like *Jane Eyre* by Charlotte Bronte was our private secret, and for that moment her whirlwind stopped. She had a way of making things seem magical, and certainly that paperback was a bit of magic created just for us. We were already on a book, maybe we would write books ourselves, or be a book. I was shocked when I saw that they were reading *Jane Eyre* in high school and even graduate school because of course like you I read it when I was 8 or so before I could really understand it, but I DID understand all that was needed . . . another feature of the pulps—you got what you needed when you needed it. Accessible.[9]

This long personal remembrance of the intimacy an "accessible" book provided Nekola places the paperback within a complex moment: a middle-class, midcentury, midwestern girlhood. But this passionate attachment with the object began as soon as they appeared: "A book is really like a lover," remarks Maurice Sendak. "It arranges itself in your life in a way that is so beautiful. Even as a kid, my sister, who was the eldest, brought books home for me, and I think I spent more time sniffing and touching them than reading. I just remember the joy of the book, the beauty of the binding. The smelling of the interior. Happy."[10] Of course, it is impossible to know what kinds of books Sendak's sister was bringing home to him, probably clothbound books—at least until 1939—but after that, who knows? His family was poor, and perhaps he was sniffing and fingering her newly acquired paperback editions found at the corner candy store.

The annals of modernism are strewn with apocryphal stories of those stranded during wartime with only a few books out of which to make art, make history: Erich Auerbach's ten books carted to Istanbul (a tale now disputed, as its libraries were full of works in many European languages); William Styron carried a paperback copy of Morris Edmund Speare's 1940 *Pocket Book of Verse* with him during his long stay in the syphilis ward of an army hospital, the very book that Ezra Pound retrieved from the latrine (and enshrined in his *Pisan Cantos*), and one of the few books—along with the volume of Confucius, the Chinese dictionary, and the army-issued Bible—Pound had while imprisoned in the Disciplinary Training Camp in 1945.

> That from the gates of death,
> > that from the gates of death: Whitman or Lovelace
> > > found on the jo-house seat at that
> in a cheap edition! [and thanks to Professor Speare]
> hast'ou swum in a sea of air-strip
> > through an aeon of nothingness
> when the raft broke and the waters went over me [11]

For the millions of servicemen, these cheap (or in the case of the Armed Services Editions, free) editions created a literary field connecting them, in ways reminiscent of Pound's pillaging of the past, in their isolation and confinement—on ships, in hospitals, brigs, or battle stations—to a history of reading. The emblem and object of the "cheap edition," ecstatically exclaimed by the exclamation point, a mark of punctuation associated with modernism—Joseph Conrad's "The Horror! The Horror!"—but also with advertisements and the taglines of pulpy novels: "She knew all about love!" proclaims the back cover of the twenty-five-cent Popular Library edition of George Orwell's *Burmese Days* (1952), (plate 11, *left*).

A decade and a half later, Frank O'Hara walked the hot city streets, "The Day Lady Died," on his lunch break "to have a hamburger and malted and buy / an ugly NEW WORLD WRITING to see what the poets / in Ghana are doing these days."[12] After lunch, he continued on the "muggy streets beginning to sun," stopping at the bank and then into the Golden Griffin to buy a present— Verlaine? the Richmond Lattimore translation of Hesiod? new plays by Brendan Behan or Genet?—for his weekend host, Patsy.[13] He picked the Verlaine with illustrations by Pierre Bonnard and, as we all know, when stopping for cigarettes he saw "her face" on the *New York Post*; and with Billie Holiday's death, time stops. These perambulations around Manhattan, a modern American's reenactment of Walter Benjamin's Baudelairean flaneur, chart the varying locations of mid-twentieth-century print: the tobacconist where one can get a carton of Gauloises, the small bookstore where one can find European classics, and the drugstore where one can not only get a quick burger and malt at the lunch counter but pick up the NAL paperback anthology, *New World Writing*, from a rack for something to read as well.

The first edition of this "ugly" annual from 1952 actually contains a poem by O'Hara entitled simply "Poem." It begins, "The eager note on my door said 'Call Me,'." O'Hara's adjective, "eager," and the casualness of the note's demand, "call me," mark one of the signal lines of queer desire and its dangers from the 1950s; the poem was eventually collected in the 1957 *Meditations in an Emergency*. His short biography describes him as a 1950 Harvard graduate who, in 1951, received both an MA and an Avery Hopwood Award in Poetry from the University of Michigan, noting that "Poem" had originally appeared in the *Harvard Advocate*.[14] The volume touts itself as "an important cross section of current literature and criticism," with new work by William Gaddis, Tennessee

Williams, Gore Vidal, James Schuyler, Alain Locke, Christopher Isherwood, Flannery O'Connor, and many others, a veritable who's who of modernist, even postmodern American writing. It concludes with "Literary Hospitality," an essay by Anabel Porter, editor at NAL since its inception in 1945, listing the little magazines and small presses developing the new writing from which this selection is culled. The back cover assures that

> Now, at last, The New American Library realizes another long-felt ambition: to bring to readers of Signet and Mentor Books an important and representative cross section of current literature and criticism . . . To the new—and particularly to the hitherto unpublished—writer of genuine talent, *New World Writing* offers an immediate, appreciative and influential audience.

With a list of the authors reprinted by Signet at the end of its three-hundred-plus pages, it helps situate those included within a larger pantheon, ranging from James Cain to Ann Petry to Sherwood Anderson to William Faulkner—the entire panoply of pulp modernism. O'Hara's dismissal of this ugly book—and his purchasing of a finer edition of poems for his friend—gestures that by 1959 he has moved on, both financially and professionally. Even so, he still buys the book, laying down the fifty cents to occupy his solitary lunchtime. It feels, perhaps, like home. This cycle of publication and reading repeats, to some extent, that recorded by Guy Pène du Bois's painting *Portia in a Pink Blouse*, a generation before *Lunch Poems*, in which the artist knows himself encased within the covers of an NAL book and, looking away, still holds on to the book.

There are other stories that chart the origins of twentieth-century American literature in pulp. In the archive, I discovered notes by E. L. Doctorow, a reader for NAL, signed "E.D." Later he expounded:

> When at the age of eight I was hospitalized with a burst appendix, I was given a new kind of book just then coming out, a

book that could fit into your pocket, a pocket book or paperback that cost only twenty-five cents. Not knowing myself to be
on the verge of death, I read in the interstices of my deliriums
Bring 'Em Back Alive by Frank Buck, a scurrilous self-promoting
white supremacist zoo supplier; *Bambi* by a bloodless Austrian
writer named Felix Salten, as only someone bloodless could
have written that insipid tale of a deer; then a not entirely reputable novel of Eastern mysticism by James Hilton, *Lost Horizon*,
my introduction to the idea of a nonmaterialistic and therefore
quite boring heaven on earth; and finally *Wuthering Heights*,
a novel about adult matters which did not interest me. These
were among the first ten titles released by Pocket Books, a new
idea in American publishing stolen from the Europeans, and I
still have them and remember their being placed on my bedside
table by my pale wan worried mother and father as amulets to
see me through it. . . .

How understandable it is that in my early twenties, when
out of the army, married with a child of my own, I hungrily
sought and found employment as an editor with another publisher of mass paperback books, New American Library—the
Signet line, the Mentor line—in what turned out to be the heyday of the mass market paperback, by then seventy-five cents
or as much as a dollar and a quarter for the thick ones. I was
cool enough not to reveal my larcenous excitement in having all
these books to hand, and in getting paid to find and read good
books and buy the rights and print up a hundred thousand,
say, of a good obscure first novel, give it a jazzy cover, and ship
it out to all the airports in the country, all the drugstores and
railroad stations, for people to buy for pocket change in those
days when you could find a consequential mass market book,
not a genre romance, not an assembly-line techno-thrill, but
a book—Pasternak's *Doctor Zhivago*, Ralph Ellison's *Invisible
Man*—"Good Reading for the Masses" as the publisher prom-

ised, of the kind my parents intended me to have when I was in the hospital in danger of dying.[15]

Childhood is suffused with the sense that these books held not only the possibility of survival, pulling one through the dreariness of a prolonged recuperation, but of danger as well. But the danger always seems to return home, or to the comfort of a bedroom and bookshelf rummaged. My friend Beth Spencer recalls:

My boyfriend and I, ages 16 and 15, were prowling around downtown Decatur, Illinois, in 1963. He was a risk taker by nature and dragged me into scary, uncharted territory occasionally. This time we were exploring alleys behind apartment buildings and climbed up a fire escape. Partway up, there was an open window into an apartment. Without hesitation he climbed in. With great hesitation I followed. Fortunately, the inhabitants were not home. We stole a battered copy of *Tropic of Cancer*. I can't remember what cover it was but I do remember how shocking the content was to me and of course I couldn't put it down. I didn't dare take it home so we kept it at his house. The next year I discovered that my grandfather had all kinds of lurid paperbacks in his library, hidden behind the more respectable books; I stayed up late reading at their house; fortunately I slept in the room with the books.[16]

Teenagers in love are central to many of the pulp plots and the plots of pulps' discovery, as a colleague, a scholar of eighteenth-century literary and scientific writings, Marcia Nichols, recounts in her story to me of "How I found a copy of *The Mask of Lesbos*."

It was when I, a Masters student in 2001 or 2002, and my boyfriend at the time were moving in together into a house at the corner of High Street and Kansas Expressway in Springfield, Missouri. We had rented one of those about-town U-Haul trucks and on our way back from dropping off a load, we saw a sign for an estate sale and decided to check it out. The people running the sale were really excited to see us pull up in a U-Haul—apparently they were selling their deceased dad's things and wanted it over with. They told us we could have whatever we wanted to haul away for, I think, 20 bucks. So we rifled through the remaining items, carting off a set of cheap china, several prints, including a framed one of this awesome modernist cityscape that I still have hanging in my living room, a large cabinet with sliding doors in the front, and various other odds and ends. When we got the items back to our new place and unloaded, I wiped down the cabinet inside and out, where I found, tucked on the bottom shelf in the back, a well-thumbed paperback copy of *The Mask of Lesbos*. We laughed about this and wondered if the man's kids knew their dad liked old-fashioned lesbian erotica, and I tucked the book onto my bookshelf, where it remains (though many bookshelves, houses, towns, and boyfriends later).[17]

The paperback, indeed, literature tout court, is suffused with desire and love, of and for sisters and parents, imagined lovers, real boyfriends.[18] It is a token and expression of what cannot be contained, a tangible object that, in its totality, offers entrance into the infinitude of time and memory and all one might want collapsed into the hours spent alone with it.

This collection of anecdotes pays homage to the strangeness incorporated within the book, the book one owns, that finds its way into one's hands in whichever way. As a young writer from Germany named Heinz wrote to Ann Petry after reading the paperback abridged version of her novel *The Street*, which within six weeks of its reprint by New American Library in 1949 already had 425,000 copies in print, "the other day I bought some Signet-Book and red [*sic*] it in bed. When the morning dawn of the following day crept over my window sill I reached the last page of your exciting, admirable novel 'The Street.' Small wonder when I fetched 'Country Place' soon after and enjoyed it even more, because here you used characters and a background which could have been taken out of this very country."[19] Petry's second novel, about the marital disarray caused by a returning veteran to a small Connecticut town, resonated with this young man; its lily-white characters and setting "could have been taken out of this very country," he confides. But his identification began with her dissection of a single mother living in a Harlem tenement. Moreover, it is not only the content that moves Heinz to write but also an act that responds to the conditions of reading itself. Reading in bed the night through brings an intimacy to the act that the dimensions (size, flexibility, affordability) of the paperback allow, even encouraging a connection to the book and its author. In this case a black woman in postwar America whose novels propelled this probably financially strapped twenty-one-year-old German reporter for a provincial newspaper (readership around 150,000, he tells her), who had been arrested at age fifteen and spent three years in "Soviet concentration-camps," to write asking for her thoughts on how to get a book published.

These tales, remembered from three decades in the middle of the last century, drip with nostalgia, each in its own way, but always told with a tinge of irony. Essentially sincere, they are felt recollections culled from the objects' presence in memory. But the cheesy covers and excessive prose of the cheapest pulps inhabit another landscape of memory—that of pastiche, which Fredric Jameson named "postmodernism." Artists Richard Prince, Long-Bin Chen, Joseph Kosuth, and writers Charles Bukowski and Robert Coover assume another kind of nostalgic allegiance to pulp in their work from the end of the twentieth and beginning of the twenty-first centuries—our time. Like Quentin Tarantino's *Pulp Fiction*—or even the Beatles' song "Paperback Writer"—these artists and their works tell us that the time of pulp is irrevocably over, precisely because it was so pervasive, even as this book, their work, and the many fans and websites cling to its continuing presence.

In a project begun in 1966, at the moment when paperback publishing had been resuscitated, after the mid-1950s industry-wide bust, thanks to the explosion of college enrollment and innovations in design, conceptual artist Joseph Kosuth began his work, *Purloined: A Novel*, finishing it in 2000. Consisting of 120 pages cut from dozens of paperbacks by many authors, it recounts a crime story, set in Minneapolis. Culled from excising a page from each author's novel, the work is a riff on Brion Gysin's and William Burroughs's cut-up method, demonstrating how form, content, and language—despite all the variations—converge around fixed narratives. It is a marvel of humor and patience, as sentences glide from page to page and author to author, beginning with the shift from first to second page: "He arranges the body to his satisfaction and traces two intersecting Xs over the upper left chest. With a sense of ceremony, he pours the accelerant. Anointing the dead. Symbolism of evil. His/pigs. Under other circumstances a tragic scene. But not now."[20] With an epigraph from Borges, the novel closes with a page from Kafka, but interspersed appear classic hard-boiled writers and their more contemporary heirs—Tami Hoag, Walter Mosley, Janet Evanovich, Jonathan Kellerman—who all pay homage to the past through their appropriative prose. As the scene from Kellerman that concludes chapter 3 acknowledges, "In the abstract it was X-rated comedy. Frederick's of Hollywood, a lampoon. But she was anything but abstract and I stood there, transfixed."[21] As we do, in awe of the tour de force effort spanning the decades spent constructing this novel.

The book, a beautiful hardcover edition with limited print run, features a picture of the artist in his studio surrounded by books; behind him shelves are full, spilling over to fill the gap remaining when one had been removed. On the floor, stacks of varying height are piled on a rug with the words "modus Operandi" legible between them. These are the sources, all paperbacks, each with a sheet of white paper marking its contribution. The artist, paperback in hand, sits between these two zones of books: shelf and floor. But unlike my study, also with its messy complement of books on shelves and floor, Kosuth's floor in his Rome studio appears ordered, studied.

Kosuth's novel makes clear how limited pulp narratives (as opposed to pulp itself) are, how intertextual the plots, settings, and characters that make up the hard-boiled world of sex and crime associated with paperback culture. But decades before Kosuth began his project of deconstructing the detective novel, his title an homage to Edgar Allen Poe's "Purloined Letter" (Doctorow being named for him, of course), Gertrude Stein, the mother of linguistic invention, had already stripped crime down to its constitutive parts in a series of texts written on the detective story during the 1920s and 1930s that culminated with her murder mystery, *Blood on the Dining-Room Floor*. Here and in "Forensics," she lays out the contours of the crime narrative—its reliance on objects and locations and a beautiful young woman: "Why should blood on the floor make anyone mad against automobiles and telephones and desks."[22] Her formula in this trance-inducing tale is to repeat the essential points that make up contemporary detective stories. But crimes often do not get solved; instead, they become public scandals that occur out of sight, in the privacy of home, late at night. They thrill, especially when they happen away from the seeming chaos of urban spaces.

> They said nothing happens in the country but there are more changes in a family in the country in five years than in a family in a city and this is natural. If nothing changed in the country there could not be butter and eggs. There have to be changes in the country, there had to be breaking up of families and killing of dogs and spoiling of sons and losing of daughters and killing of mothers and banishing of fathers . . . And so this makes

in the country everything happening in the country. Nothing happens in the city. Everything happens in the country. The city just tells what has happened in the country . . . Lizzie do you understand.[23]

Stein's crucial insight into the terror of French rural life in modern times echoes James Agee's fascination with the actual detective magazines that captivated him with tales of uncanny crimes committed in out-of-the-way American places. These two postmodern writers before their time saw in pulp a method and theory for understanding Americans' private longings. They understood, as Ben Hecht, Richard Wright, and Meyer Levin had, that incredulity was essential to modern affect.

More typical visions of crime narration locate them in the midsize cities and sprawling metropolises growing up as wars reshaped the American landscape, launching millions of people out of the rural South and Midwest toward new lives in sprawling cities, like Chester Himes's Los Angeles, where the virulence of racial violence in Chicago, Cleveland, or Detroit also played out. An early "true crimes . . . and real detectives" pulp, *Chicago Murders*, edited by Sewell Peaslee Wright, collects "a rogue's gallery of almost incredible crime and detection stories from America's most notorious city," declares the cover of the 1947 Bantam Book with art by Hy Rubin (plate 7, *bottom*). On the flyleaf, the cover art is described as "sum[ming] up as nearly as possible all the breathless tenseness and realism of these true crime stories." Tenseness and realism inspired two other novels from the late twentieth and early twenty-first centuries: *Pulp* by Charles Bukowski and Robert Coover's *Noir*, both of them explicit parodies of crime's "bad writing," as Bukowski's dedication to *Pulp* declares.

Bukowski's paean to pulp begins with a classic Philip Marlowe/ Sam Spade first-person encounter between the detective (sitting at his desk in his hot office awaiting eviction for failing to pay his rent) and a woman, who calls, asking in "such a sexy voice," "Do you read Celine?" She shows up walking on "heels so high they looked like stilts." Lady Death wants Celine, "real bad, buster." Set in Los Angeles, it proceeds from there as Nick Belane tracks Celine through bookstores, bars, and bus stations following leads—those various characters who might be reading Thomas Mann or the *New Yorker* or *National Enquirer*—at the same time as he pursues the elusive Red Sparrow for another client.[24] Eventually the plots entwine and Belane, as happens so often to Marlowe after he's knocked out, swoons, "enveloped" by "the blaze and blare of yellow [that] swept over" him.[25]

More recently, Robert Coover's *Noir* deadpans by combining a parody of second-person pulp ("You lean against a rough wall, light up a fag...") with movie references.[26] His detective, Mr. Philip M. Noir (with a secretary named Blanche), and an antagonistic cop named Captain Blue inhabit the rain-stained night streets of a grungy city. In the course of his/your investigation, he finds himself in Big Mame's ice-cream parlor, where he/you see(s) "a couple of kids sucking at a milkshake with two straws . . . They were blowing bubbles at each other . . . It was like they lived in a different world. They *did* live in a different world. It was called daytime." Left behind at the counter is a newspaper with "the usual miseries. Wars and threats of wars. Murders, robberies, crimes by the column. . . . rain . . . baseball . . . horoscope . . . the obits," where he discovers Fingers is dead (112). By the end, deflated and ready to quit, he/ you meet Blanche, who explains that "you still don't know who did what, but . . . that's not the point. Integrity is. Style" (191). Like Bukowski's Belane swooning in a pool of yellow, "you are moving through pools of wet yellow light, surrounded by a velvety darkness as soft as black silk" only to end up at an office building where stenciled on your office door are the words "BLANCHE ET NOIR... PRIVATE INVESTIGATIONS" (192). The world of pulp is black and white—but with that touch of French that signifies sex.

Both these novels owe much to David Thomson's 1985 mash-up novel *Suspects*, which begins with the birth of Roman Polanski's detective in *Chinatown*, Jake Gittes, in a Stockton whorehouse in 1901 and concludes with Frank Capra's George Bailey of Bedford Falls thinking about his ill-fated wonderful life and remembering a time, just before Christmas in 1946, when he'd gone "to see Laura, who had been in New York for several years. She was successful, it seemed, and I had a notion she might loan me some money. I had never met her husband, Mark, before, and I was taken aback by the animosity between them. They had a daughter, Paula . . ."[27] And so we are back to Laura and Paula and the pulpy postwar intrigues these doomed and dangerous women begat.

These are the literary homages paid to pulp. Richard Prince also unravels the strange history of American postwar modernism, particularly the relationship between abstract expressionism and paperback book covers, in his R'ville Books. Housing his collection built around the twin years of George Orwell's *1984* and its publication date 1949 (also the year of his birth), its titles formed the basis for his two series from 2002–3 and 2006–7, *Nurses* and *de Kooning*. Each set appropriates the visual style of other artists—pulp illustrators, abstract expressionist painters—and recasts them through various reproductive means, culminating with paint. As John McWhinnie explains, "*Nurses* began as nurse paperbacks . . . he did maybe twelve nurse paperbacks right in a row. Then the next thing you know, he's detached the cover and he's blowing them up and inkjetting and painting over them." He emphasizes that "Richard collects" (plate 8).[28] These series make clear the links between pulp and other forms of modernism. As series, they also foreground replication and reuse.

So too do the uncanny sculptures of Long-Bin Chen, whose carved telephone book Buddhas and installations posed within de-accessioned library books retrieve old dusty paper—the cheap pulp of the phone book, the fraying pages of unread volumes—found

Figure 10.1 Long-Bin Chen, *Ming Buddha* (White Pages) (2006). (White Pages phone books, 17½ × 10 × 11 inches). Author's collection. Photograph courtesy of the artist and Frederieke Taylor Gallery, New York City.

strewn in the trash and recycling bins, for his medium (figure 10.1). Chen's works literalize the "soft" core of pulp, asking its viewers to experience the tactile essence of the page, even as they also play on the trompe d'oeil that masks the material, as paper appears to be stone.[29]

More than likely, Richard Prince knew that NAL cover artist Robert Jonas (who did not produce any nurse covers, though one of his NAL successors, Rudy Nappi, made dozens of them) had shared a friendship with Willem de Kooning (and Arshile Gorky) during the 1930s, when roommates Jonas and de Kooning worked as window dressers for A. S. Beck's and Gorky relied on Jonas to pick up women. NAL's other primary cover artist, James Avati, moved to New York in 1939, also finding work making window displays for James McCreery and Company on Fifth Avenue.[30] Like these earlier pulp artists, Prince worked in the realm of New York merchandizing; his appropriations of advertisement photographs, found while working in the tear sheet department of Time Life, are, he "recorded" in his 1983 book, *Why I Go to the Movies Alone*. "He works for a magazine in a department called 'Tear Sheets.' He rips up magazines and tears out pages."[31] So, to some extent, the story of postwar art in America—from abstract expressionism to postmodern appropriation—like the story of literature, cannot be told apart from that of paperbacks: avant-garde and kitsch, as Clement Greenberg knew, go hand in hand for all these men, and, Robert Lesser, pulp art collector, contends, pulp was by and for "men—all men."[32]

But for all the men who collect and catalog and critique "the paperbacking of America," pulp's demotic tale is haunted by the presence of women, too. Lizzie and Laura and Paula and Vera and Liana, even Margaret: the many who read, wrote, and populated its pages and covers, studying and analyzing them now, as Blanche so deftly showed Noir—private investigators displayed in public.

Acknowledgments

....

With any project spanning a decade, one's debts are huge. This book has been written across four continents and has improved immeasurably from my encounters in each place with friends, scholars, and students who have listened to or read its sundry parts. My greatest debt is to the many used bookstores around the globe where I have found, stashed behind more reputable books, the ratty pages of moldy paperbacks. I am particularly thankful to Jay Platt, owner of Ann Arbor's Westside Books, for his basement full of them, but there are countless unknown others who have helped me do the research for this book. There are few collections of paperbacks in libraries; however, since 2004, I conducted research in various archives, aided by diligent and knowledgeable archivists: the Council on Books in Wartime at Princeton University's twentieth-century American Public Policy Collection at the Seeley G. Mudd Library (Adriane Hanson); the papers of James Agee at the Hoskins Library of the University of Tennessee and Richard Wright at the Yale Collection of American Literature at the Beinecke Rare Book and Manuscript Library of Yale University; the papers of Meyer Levin and Ann Petry at the Howard Gotlieb Archival Research Center at Boston University (Charles Niles); New American Library Papers at the Fales Library and Special Collections at New York University (Lisa Darms); congressional and court records (Illinois, New York); the George Kelley Paperback

Collection at the University of Buffalo (Judith Adams-Volpe); the Paley Center on Radio and Television in New York (Mark Ekman); the Joseph A. Labadie Collection at the University of Michigan Library (Julie Herrera); the Donald and Katharine Foley Collection of Penguin Books at the Bancroft Library, UC Berkeley (David Kessler and Peter Hanff); the Churchill archives (Cambridge, UK); and the Penguin archives (Bristol, UK). I thank the archivists at these libraries who have been gracious in helping me locate materials. At Minnesota, Jean-Nickolaus Tretter and Lisa Vecoli of the Jean-Nickolaus Tretter Collection in Gay, Lesbian, Bisexual and Transgender Studies; Mary Rumsey of the Law Library; Cecily Marcus of the Archie Givens Sr. Collection of African American Literature; and Vincente Garces, Jason Roy, and Nancy Sims of the Wilson Library were always available to pull material and answer my queries.

I've received funding from various sources to travel to archives and conferences: the Imagine Fund, the College of Liberal Arts Samuel Russell Chair in the Humanities, the Associate Dean for Graduate Programs, and the English Department of the University of Minnesota. I have been invited to present material from this project by colleagues at the American University in Paris, University of Sydney (Australia), Goldsmiths College (London), Hitotsubashi University in Tokyo, Johns Hopkins/Nanjing University Center for Chinese and American Studies (Nanjing), East China Normal University (Shanghai), Terza Università degli Studi di Roma (Italy), University of Michigan, Rutgers University in Newark, University of Vermont, Minnesota University at Mankato, Kennesaw State University, Washington University (St. Louis), La Sorbonne (Paris), and University of California, Irvine, as well as at the Modernist Studies Association meetings in Las Vegas, Tulsa, and Birmingham (UK); the Society for the Study of Authorship, Reading and Publishing meetings at Minneapolis and Copenhagen, Denmark; the Cultural Studies Association meeting in Chicago; the Walker Arts Center in Minneapolis; and the Reynolds Gallery of the University of the Pacific in Stockton, California, where Molly Toberer and I cocurated the exhibit *UNCOVER! Secret Places of Pulp* in 2005.

Permission to use materials by Ann Petry has been granted to me by Liz Petry and Russell & Volkening as agents for the author. Copyright © Ann Petry. Lines from "Forties Flick," copyright © 1974 by John Ashbery, from *Self-Portrait in a Convex Mirror* by John Ashbery. Used by permission of Viking Penguin, a division of Penguin Group (USA) Inc. Lines from Frank O'Hara, "The Day Lady Died," *Lunch Poems* © 1964 by Frank O'Hara. Reprinted by permission of City Lights Books. Materials from the Meyer Levin and Tereska Torrès papers used by permission of their estate and Jabberwocky Literary Agency Inc. The Truman Capote Literary Trust gave permission to quote from a letter by the author. Lines from Canto 80 by Ezra Pound, from *The Cantos of Ezra Pound* © 1948 by Ezra Pound. Reprinted by permission of New Directions Publishing Corp. and Faber and Faber Ltd. Sections of *Reporting the Universe*: Reprinted by permission of the publisher from *Reporting the Universe* by E. L. Doctorow, pp. 10–12 (Cambridge, MA: Harvard University Press) © 2003 by E. L. Doctorow. Permission to quote from the New American Library Archives, copyright © 2013 by Penguin Group (USA) Inc. Used by permission of Dutton Signet, a division of Penguin Group (USA) Inc. Permission to quote from a memo from Scott Meredith provided by Scott Meredith Literary Agency.

Permission to reproduce the following covers has been granted as follows: book cover (1950 Avon edition) from *Double Indemnity* by James M. Cain, copyright 1943 and 1947 by Avon Book Company, reprinted by permission of HarperCollins Publishers; book cover (1947 Avon edition) from *I Survived Hitler's Ovens* by Olga Lengyel, copyright, 1947 by the Ziff-Davis Publishing Company, reprinted by permission of HarperCollins Publishers; many thanks to Bruce, Leslie, and Clark Kinnaird II for permission to use the underlying image from Clark Kinnaird's 1945 *This Must Not Happen Again! The Black Book of Fascist Horror*; book cover (1958 Avon edition, front and back) from *Leave Her To Hell!* by Fletcher Flora, copyright 1958 by Avon Publishing Co. Inc., reprinted by permission of HarperCollins Publishers; book cover (1950 Avon edition) from *Nana's Mother* by Emile Zola, translated from the French by John Stirling, copyright 1950 by Avon Publishing Co. Inc., reprinted by permission of HarperCollins Publishers; book cover (1948 Avon edition) from *The Amboy Dukes* by Irving Shulman, 1946 and 1947 by Irving Shulman, Avon reprint edition, copyright 1948 by Avon Publishing Co. Inc., reprinted by permission of HarperCollins Publishers; lines from Kenneth Fearing's poems, "Longshot Blues" and "Aphrodite Metropolis II" reprinted by the permission of Russell & Volkening as agents for the author, copyright © 1994 by Jubal and Phoebe Fearing.

My students in a number of senior seminars at Minnesota—Red Pulp, Political Pulp, Fifty Years After: Cold War Culture during the Long 1953—have been keen observers of all things pulp; Sarah Engelmann and Amanda Brown were especially helpful. Friends, family, and colleagues have generously shared their books and insights into and memories of pulp with me; first among them: Charlotte Nekola, as well as Simon Frost, Caroline Blinders, Will Straw, Sandra Heard, Anca Parvulescu, Karl Baker, Brynnar Swenson, Alan Wald, Zhang Fenghui, Beth Spencer, Aaron Lecklider, Ben Friedlander, David Earle, Jack Zipes, Alexander Keefe, Jacob Bernstein, Raphael Rabinowitz, Sam Rabinowitz, Mark Rabinowitz, Laurie Ossman, Len and Elizabeth Rabinowitz, Kathleen Newman, Long-Bin Chen, E. L. Doctorow, Patricia Crain, Nicole Moore, Rita Copeland, Sara Blair, Stephanie Rothman, Merrill Schleier, Ivy Marvel, Nancy Reistenberg, David Jenemann, David Davies, Sarah Ehlers, Hiromi Ochi, Cristina Giorcelli, Melissa Hardie, Kate Lilley, Alice Craven, William Dow, Alex Lubin, Stefan Herbrechter, and Ivan Callus. My Minnesota colleagues, students, and friends—Hisham Bizri, Siobhan Craig, Maria Damon, Michael Hancher, Marcia Nichols, Charles Sugnet, Lisa Trochmann, John Wright, and Maria Zavialova—were willing to listen to my pulp sagas and offer contributions from their libraries. I owe special thanks to David Bernstein and Robert Cowgill, and the anonymous readers, who read the entire manuscript; and to Thomas Pepper, Josephine Lee, Charlotte Nekola, Cecily Marcus, Nuruddin Farah, Jani Scandura, and the anonymous reviewers who read early versions and portions of it. All have helped make it better in countless ways. Hanne Winarsky helped me craft its initial outlines and Alison MacKeen was a careful and encouraging editor as it was fleshed out;

she and production editor Ellen Foos were crucial to its final state, which was copyedited by Cathy Slovensky and finally overseen by editor Anne Savarese with assistance from Juliana Fidler.

Some parts of the book previously appeared in different versions: chapter 3 was published as "Savage Holiday: Documentary, True Crime and *12 Million Black Voices*," in Alice Craven and William Dow, *Richard Wright: New Readings in the 21st Century* (Palgrave/MacMillan, 2011); parts of chapter 4 first appeared in a special issue of *Angles on the English Speaking World* (2010), edited by Simon Frost as "Isak Dinesen Enlists: Pulp, the Armed Services Editions and GI Reading during WWII," and in *Theater Survey* (2011); a version of chapter 5 appeared in Alex Lubin, ed., *Revising the Blueprint: Ann Petry and the Literary Left* (University of Mississippi Press, 2007); chapter 6 first appeared in different form as "The Abysmal Problem of Time: Pulp Fiction by and about Borges," in Stefan Herbrechter and Ivan Callus, eds., *Cy-Borges: Memories of the Posthuman in the Work of Jorge Luis Borges* (Bucknell University Press, 2009); and much of chapter 7 was first published in Cristina Giorcelli, ed., *Abito e Identità*, vol. 7 (Ila Palma Editore, 2007), then reprinted in Cristina Giorcelli and Paula Rabinowitz, eds., *Exchanging Clothes: Habits of Being 2* (University of Minnesota Press, 2012). I am grateful to all these editors and publishers for allowing me to use this material in a new form.

My deepest debt is to the one who will now never know it—my mother Shirley Wolf Rabinowitz (1925–2012)—who first sent me on this strange path of demotic reading. This book is dedicated to her memory.

Notes

....

PREFACE

1. Rob Walker, "Shelf Expression," *New York Times Magazine*, 8 August 2010, 12.

2. Peter Campbell, "In a Bookshop," *London Review of Books*, 10 September 2009, 27. See also, Roberta Smith, review of Richard Hollis at Artists Space: Books & Talks, *New York Times*, 1 November 2013, C30.

3. Barnes and Noble's Nook reader and its management of more than seven hundred university bookstores seem to ensure its survival even in the face of Amazon's enormous footprint digitally, with Kindle, and as a point of sales of print books. See Lydia De Pillis, "Barnes & Noble's troubles don't show why bookstores are doomed. They show how they'll survive," Wonkblog, http://www.washingtonpost.com, 10 July 2013.

4. Scott Turow, "The Slow Death of the American Author," *New York Times*, 8 April 2013, A19.

5. Carol Vogel, "Words and More Words," *New York Times*, 28 February 2014, C26.

6. Robert Smithson, "A Tour of the Monuments of Passaic, New Jersey (1967)," in *Ruins*, ed. Brian Dillon (Cambridge, MA: MIT Press, 2011), 46–47.

7. Richard J. Crohn, "Good Reading for the Millions," in *The Wonderful World of Books*, ed. Alfred Stefferud (New York: New American Library, 1953), 202. This Mentor Book, sold for thirty-five cents, advertises itself as "your guide to the rewards of reading." It is typical of the self-referentiality so crucial to the processes of pulp. Indeed, as James W. Hall argues in his trade

paperback original, to the mechanics of all best sellers. The celebration of the act of private reading and of book ownership lets the reader/purchaser know she is part of a larger social world beyond mundane daily life. Hall describes the importance of scenes of reading (such as Allison MacKenzie's preference for reading rather than buying clothes, and her mother's annoyance with her for this, in *Peyton Place*) in his list of twelve features that contribute to the making of a best seller. *Hit Lit: Cracking the Code of the Twentieth Century's Biggest Bestsellers* (New York: Random House, 2012), 170.

8. James Wood, "Why? Life, Death, and the Novel," *New Yorker*, 9 December 2013, 35.

9. Information on the Kelley Collection comes from conversations with Judith Adams-Volpe. See Patricia Donovan, "Pulp Fiction," *UB Today* (Winter 2000): 26–29.

Chapter 1
Pulp: Biography of an American Object

The chapter opening epigraph is from the Ann Petry Collection, Box 9, Folder 22, Howard Gotlieb Archival Research Center at Boston University. This quotation from Lindeman, described as president of the National Conference of Social Welfare, also appears in Richard J. Crohn's essay, "Good Reading for the Millions," in the Mentor Book *The Wonderful World of Books* (1953), 207. The second epigraph is quoted from *Publisher's Weekly*, 27 June 1953, 2667

1. "Diaries of Fedor Minorsky (Alias Theodor Harris)," HARS (12 May 1941–9 October 1942). Churchill Archives Centre, Churchill College, Cambridge University.

2. James Thurber's story, about a reader of a pulp publisher's slush pile living as a nebbish in Perth Amboy, New Jersey, whose fantasy life takes on aspects of the plots he reads for work, was among the first sophisticated spoofs of the pulps (which had been making fun of themselves from the beginning); it was made into the 1947 musical starring Danny Kaye and revived as a comedy adventure film with Ben Stiller in 2013. Both original story and film served as the basis for the George Axelrod play *The Seven Year Itch* (which also became a movie).

3. Back cover of a small lined notebook with Penguin cover, 2008, Penguin Books Limited. This story is based in part on the opening statements by the defense in the 1960 trial of *Lady Chatterley's Lover* in which Gerald Gardiner explained that in 1936 Lane "formed this company, Penguin Books Limited, to publish good books at the price of ten cigarettes . . . 6c. He started off with novels and detective stories . . . Whether he was right or wrong in thinking the average person [the working classes] would buy good books if they had the chance is perhaps shown by the fact that since then this company has made and sold . . . 250 million books." In C. H. Rolph, *The Trial of Lady Chatterley: Regina v. Penguin Books Limited* (Baltimore: Penguin Books, 1961), 25.

4. Thanks to E. L. Doctorow for this tidbit—Signet being a secret code for another bird, a baby swan, cygnet.

5. Grace Glueck, in "Art in Review: Guy Pène du Bois," notes his "satirical edge," but she had not seen this commissioned portrait in a show dedicated to his work. *New York Times* online, 23 June 2006, http://query.nytimes.com/gst/fullpage.html?res=9906E3DF1630F930A15755C0A96 09C8B63.

6. Information on Guy Pène du Bois and his portraiture comes from the Indianapolis Museum of Art, as well as his autobiography, *Artists Say the Silliest Things* (New York: American Artists Group, 1940); Betsy Fahlman, *Guy Pène du Bois: Painter of Modern Life* (New York: Quantuck Lane Press, 2004), and *Guy Pène du Bois: Artist About Town* (Washington, DC: Corcoran Gallery of Art, 1980). Pène du Bois's art criticism offers further insight into his own methods and intentions. Writing about William Glackens, he might be describing his own color system: Glackens moved from his dark to his light period and "in the American the rhythm is extraordinarily quick . . . [He] avidly seeks to interpret reality, to get at the root of it by objective study." Guy Pène du Bois, *William J. Glackens* (New York: Whitney Museum of American Art, 1931), 11.

7. Erin A. Smith, *Hard-Boiled: Working-Class Readers and Pulp Magazines* (Philadelphia: Temple University Press, 2000).

8. Pritham K. Chakravarthy, "Translator's Note," in *The Blaft Anthology of Tamil Pulp Fiction*, ed. Rakesh Khanna, selected and trans. Pritham K. Chakravarthy (Chennai: Blaft Publications Pvt. Ltd., 2008), x.

9. Ibid., xi.

10. Ibid., xii, quoting from A. R. Venkatachalapathy, *Novallum Vasippum* [*The Novel & Readership*] (Chennai: Kalachuvadu Pathipagam, 2002), 22.

11. Quoted in Will Straw, *Cyanide and Sin: Visualizing Crime in 50s America* (New York: PPP Editions, 2006), 007.

12. Ibid.

13. Vanessa R. Schwartz, *Spectacular Realities: Early Mass Culture in Fin-de-Siècle Paris* (Berkeley: University of California Press, 1998), 6.

14. Edmund De Waal, *The Hare with Amber Eyes: A Family's Century of Art and Loss* (New York: Farrar, Straus and Giroux, 2010), 33.

15. Walter Benjamin, "Unpacking My Library: A Talk on Collecting," in *Selected Writings*, vol. 2 (1927–1934), trans. Rodney Livingstone et al., ed. Michael W. Jennings, Howard Eiland, and Gary Smith (Cambridge, MA: Belknap Press of Harvard University Press, 1999), 492.

16. In his history of book publishing in Japan, Edward Mack explains how the 1926 *Complete Works of Japanese Literature*, a series of one-yen books collecting a range of "literature," was designed to help restore Japan's publishing industry after the devastating 1923 Kantō earthquake and the fire in its aftermath, which had demolished most of Tokyo's bookstores, libraries, and publishers. These cheap, albeit hardcover, books also worked to consolidate a nationalist sensibility following the disaster, much as paperbacks did a generation later in the United States. See "The Stability of the Center: Tokyo Publishing and the Great Kantō Earthquake," in *Manufacturing Modern Japanese Literature: Publishing, Prizes, and the Ascription of Literary Value* (Durham, NC: Duke University Press, 2010), 51–90.

17. Jani Scandura defines the "problem with collecting" as one of "set[ting] limits . . . Collecting," she notes, "like writing, requires a sharp editorial hand. At each excision from the text, I feel simultaneously the pangs of loss and the euphoria that accompanies my extrication from the burden of words, from the burden of stuff." Jani Scandura, *Down in the Dumps: Place, Modernity, American Depression* (Durham, NC: Duke University Press, 2008), 162.

18. Thanks to Lisa Vecoli, archivist at the University of Minnesota Tretter Collection, for explaining this phenomenon to me.

19. Olivia Judson, "The Task: Home, Dismantled," *New York Times*, 16 February 2014, SR 8.

20. Ray Walters, "Paperback Talk," *New York Times* online, 9 May 1982, www.nytimes.com.

21. Michel Foucault, preface to *The Order of Things: An Archaeology of the Human Sciences* (1970; New York: Vintage, 1994), xv.

22. Ibid., xvii.

23. Robert Scholes and Clifford Wulfman, "The Hole in the Archive and the Study of Modernist Magazines," in *Modernism in the Magazines: An Introduction* (New Haven: Yale University Press, 2010), 196–222. See Richard J. Crohn, "Good Reading for the Millions," in *The Wonderful World of Books*, ed. Alfred Stefferud (New York: New American Library, 1953), 206.

24. William Styron, *Havana in Camelot* (New York: Random House, 2008), 22; Ezra Pound, canto 80, in *The Cantos of Ezra Pound* (New York: New Directions, 1993).

25. Pierson R. Davis, letter to the editor, *New York Times*, 19 September 2009, A17.

26. "An Interview with Peter Eisenman," in Jo Steffens, ed., *Unpacking My Library: Architects and Their Books* (New Haven: Yale University Press, 2009), 64.

27. John Updike, "Deceptively Conceptual: Books and Their Covers," *New Yorker* online, 17 October 2005, http://www.newyorker.com.

28. Benjamin, "Unpacking My Library," 486.

29. Since Quentin Tarantino's 1994 film *Pulp Fiction*, the word "pulp" has become a triggering term that conveys the sleazy underside of American culture and life. Obviously, I expand the term considerably from its more narrow reference to B-genre fiction. Large collections, such as *The Mammoth Book of Pulp Fiction*, edited by Maxim Jakubowski (New York: Carroll and Graf, 1996) or *The Black Lizard Big Book of Pulps*, edited by Otto Penzler (New York: Vintage, 2007), and the addition of hard-boiled and pulp novels to the Library of America collection, immediately jumped on the bandwagon as publishers resuscitated the hard-boiled writings of Dashiell Hammett, Mickey Spillane, Jim Thompson, and many more. In the bibliography of writings about pulp, the usual definitions confine it to genre writing—crime, mystery, romance, sci-fi—first written for the dozens of pulp magazines, such as *Black Mask*, of Bernarr Macfadden, Curtis, and other publishers. The study of pulp paperbacks occurs in waves, starting almost immediately after they disappeared in the 1960s, but really took off in the 1980s. See David Madden, ed., *Tough Guy Writers of the Thirties*

(Carbondale: Southern Illinois University Press, 1968); Kenneth C. Davis, *Two-Bit Culture: The Paperbacking of America* (Boston: Houghton Mifflin, 1984); Thomas Bonn, *Heavy Traffic and High Culture* (Carbondale: Southern Illinois University Press, 1989); Clive Bloom, *Popular Reading and Pulp Theory* (New York: Palgrave Macmillan, 1998); Christopher Breu, *Hard-Boiled Masculinities* (Minneapolis: University of Minnesota Press, 2005); David M. Earle, *Re-Covering Modernism: Pulps, Paperbacks, and the Prejudice of Form* (Farnham, UK: Ashgate, 2009); Scott McCracken, *Pulp: Reading Popular Fiction* (Manchester: Manchester University Press, 1998). On British pulp, see Steve Holland, *The Mushroom Jungle: A History of Postwar Paperback Publishing* (Wiltshire, England: Zeon Books, 1993). On hardboiled crime fiction and true crime, see Stephen Duncombe and Andrew Mattson, *The Bobbed Haired Bandit: A True Story of Crime and Celebrity in 1920s New York* (New York: New York University Press, 2006); Greg Foster, *Murdering Masculinities: Fantasies of Gender and Violence in the American Crime Novel* (New York: New York University Press, 2000); Sean McCann, *Gumshoe America: Hard-Boiled Crime Fiction and the Rise and Fall of New Deal Liberalism* (Durham, NC: Duke University Press, 2000); William Marling, *The American Roman Noir: Hammett, Cain, Chandler* (Athens: University of Georgia Press, 1995); William F. Nolan, *The Black Mask Boys: Masters in the Hard-Boiled School of Detective Fiction* (New York: William Morrow, 1985); Geoffrey O'Brien, *Hard-Boiled America: Lurid Paperbacks and the Masters of Noir* (New York: Da Capo Press, 1997); and Erin Smith, *Hard-Boiled: Working-Class Readers and Pulp Magazines* (Philadelphia: Temple University Press, 2000). On pulp modernism, see V. Penelope Pelizzon and Nancy M. West, *Tabloid, Inc.: Crimes, Newspapers, Narratives* (Columbus: Ohio State University Press, 2010) and Paula Rabinowitz, *Black & White & Noir: America's Pulp Modernism* (New York: Columbia University Press, 2002). Regarding cover art, one needs to also look at the coffee table books, such as Peter Haining, *The Classic Era of Crime Fiction* (Chicago: Chicago Review Press, 2002); Richard A. Lupoff, *The Great American Paperback* (Portland, OR: Collector's Press, 2001); Thomas L. Bonn, *Under-Cover: An Illustrated History of American Mass Market Paperbacks* (New York: Penguin, 1982); and on pulp magazine covers, Frank M. Robinson and Lawrence Davidson, *Pulp Culture: The Art of Fiction Magazines* (Portland, OR: Collector's Press, 2007); Robert Lesser, *Pulp Art: Original Cover*

Paintings for the Great American Pulp Magazines (New York: Gramercy Books, 1997), and Will Straw, *Cyanide and Sin: Visualizing Crime in 50s America* (New York: PPP Editions, 2006).

30. On remediation, see Jay David Bolter and Richard Grusin, *Remediation: Understanding New Media* (Cambridge, MA: MIT Press, 1999), which deals with visual and electronic media from film to television to computer screens. I follow Marshall McLuhan in *Understanding Media: The Extensions of Man* (1964; Cambridge, MA: MIT Press, 1994) and argue that paperback books present a case for seeing remediation in this much older medium—print and paper. McLuhan implicitly understood the power of the paperback when his book *The Medium is the Massage* cleverly refashioned his famous statement, "the medium is the message," to allude to soft-core pornography in the edition boldly designed by Quentin Fiore as a paperback original by Bantam Books (to come out in simultaneous hardcover from Random House) in 1967. It sold half a million paperback copies (according to Clarence Petersen, *The Bantam Story: Twenty-Five Years* [New York: Bantam Books, 1970], 39).

31. Moreover, archives collect writers' manuscripts and letters, not their computers or personal libraries, which might include a world of pulp along with high-quality hardcover editions. The libraries of Herman Melville were scrapped for paper; Stephen Crane's books were auctioned off to pay his widow's debts; David Markson's turned up in the Strand, a New York used bookstore. We are missing a history of writers' reading materials. See Craig Fehrman, "Lost Libraries: The Strange Afterlife of Author's Book Collections," *Boston Globe* online, 19 September 2010, www.boston.com /bostonglobe/ideas/articles/2010/09/19/lost_libraries.

32. For examples of New Modernist studies, see Jeff Allred, *American Modernism and Depression Documentary* (Oxford: Oxford University Press, 2009); Alfred Appel, *Jazz Modernism: From Ellington and Armstrong to Matisse and Joyce* (New Haven: Yale University Press, 2004); Rita Barnard, *The Great Depression and the Culture of Abundance* (Cambridge: Cambridge University Press, 1995); Michael Denning, *The Cultural Front: The Laboring of American Culture* (New York: Verso, 1998); David M. Earle, *Re-Covering Modernism: Pulps, Paperbacks, and the Prejudice of Form* (Farnham, UK: Ashgate, 2009); Susan Edmunds, *Grotesque Relations: Modernist Domestic Fiction and the U.S. Welfare State* (Oxford: Oxford University Press, 2008);

Joseph Entin, *Sensational Modernism: Experimental Fiction and Photography in Thirties America* (Chapel Hill: University of North Carolina Press, 2007); Saverio Giovacchino, *Hollywood Modernism: Film and Politics in the Age of the New Deal* (Philadelphia: Temple University Press, 2000); Walter Kalaidjian, ed., *The Cambridge Companion to American Modernism* (Cambridge: Cambridge University Press, 2005); Douglas Mao and Rebecca Walkowitz, eds., *Bad Modernisms* (Durham, NC: Duke University Press, 2006); Justus Nieland, *Feeling Modern: The Eccentricities of Public Life* (Urbana: University of Illinois Press, 2007); Michael North, *Reading 1922: A Return to the Scene of the Modern* (Oxford: Oxford University Press, 2002); Paula Rabinowitz, *Black & White & Noir: America's Pulp Modernism* (New York: Columbia University Press, 2002); Jani Scandura, *Down in the Dumps: Place, Modernity, American Depression* (Durham, NC: Duke University Press, 2008); Jani Scandura and Michael Thurston, eds., *Modernism, Inc.: Body, Memory, Capital* (New York: New York University Press, 2001); Terry Smith, *Making the Modern: Industry, Art and Design in America* (Chicago: University of Chicago Press, 1994); Juan Suarez, *Pop Modernism: Noise and the Reinvention of the Everyday* (Bloomington: Indiana University Press, 2007); Michael Szalay, *New Deal Modernism: American Literature and the Invention of the Welfare State* (Durham, NC: Duke University Press, 2000); Michael Trask, *Cruising Modernism: Class and Sexuality in American Literature and Social Thought* (Ithaca: Cornell University Press, 2003), and many more.

The phrase "vernacular modernism" is Paul Buhle's and Miriam Bratu Hansen's, among others; Cary Nelson discusses the modernism "we have wanted to forget" in *Revolutionary Memory: Recovering the Poetry of the American Left* (New York: Routledge, 2001). Marshall Berman speaks of "low" and "street" modernism in *All That Is Solid Melts into Air: The Experience of Modernity* (New York: Penguin, 1988). Suzanne Clark offers the seeming oxymoron, *Sentimental Modernism: Women Writers and the Revolution of the Word* (Bloomington: Indiana University Press, 1991). In *Modernism and the Harlem Renaissance* (Chicago: University of Chicago Press, 1987), Houston A. Baker Jr. outlines an "Afro-American modernism." One might go back to 1938, Simon Bessie, *Jazz Journalism: The Story of the Tabloid Newspapers* (New York: E. P. Dutton), for an early recognition of the multiplying vernacular forms of modernist writing. In his address to the

2001 Modernist Studies convention, Ramón Saldívar identified a "transnational modernism" in the poetry of Américo Paredes.

In addition, critical interest in pulp fiction and true crime is evidenced in the Feminist Press reprint series Women Write Pulp, the voluminous bibliography on film noir and hard-boiled detective fiction, including the Library of America's reprints of works by Raymond Chandler and Dashiell Hammett, reprinting of Gore Vidal's third novel, the gay pulp classic *The City and the Pillar*, and Patricia Highsmith's pseudonymous lesbian pulp, *The Price of Salt*, and so on. James Ellroy's work pushed "true crime" from its tabloid origins to the best-seller list.

33. For examples of sociologies of American reading, see Thomas August, *The Clerk's Tale: Young Men and Moral Life in Nineteenth-Century America* (Chicago: University of Chicago Press, 2003); Patricia Crain, *The Story of A: The Alphabetization of American Literature from "The New England Primer" to "The Scarlett Letter"* (Stanford, CA: Stanford University Press, 2002); Cathy N. Davidson, *Revolution and the Word: The Rise of the Novel in America* (Oxford: Oxford University Press, 1988); Karla F. C. Holloway, *BookMarks: Reading in Black and White* (New Brunswick, NJ: Rutgers University Press, 2006); Gordon Hutner, *What America Read: Taste, Class, and the Novel, 1920–1960* (Chapel Hill: University of North Carolina Press, 2009); Michael Warner, *The Letters of the Republic: Publication and the Public Sphere in Eighteenth-Century America* (Cambridge, MA: Harvard University Press, 1992). In addition, see also the ongoing *A History of the Book in America*, edited by David Hall et al., a five-volume compendium published by the University of North Carolina Press.

34. Walter Benjamin, "One-Way Street" (vol. 1), "The Newspaper" (vol. 2), and "A Short History of Photography" (vol. 4), in *Selected Writings*, Michael W. Jennings, general editor (Cambridge, MA: Belknap Press of Harvard University Press, 1996, 1999, 2002).

35. Editorial dope sheet from TMT, 17 January 1951, Box 20, Folder 307; New American Library (hereafter NAL) Archives, MS 070, Fales Library and Special Collections, New York University (hereafter NYU).

36. Memo, AJP [Arabel Porter] to VW [Victor Weybright], 14 August 1946, Box 89A, Folder 2842; NAL Archives, MS 070, Fales Library and Special Collections, NYU.

37. Gertrude Stein, "Lecture 1," *Narration* (1935; Chicago: University of Chicago Press, 2010), 10.

38. "America's Top Negro Authors," *Color* (June 1949): 28–31. The article recounts the history of a new generation of black writers replacing those of an earlier generation of Harlem Renaissance artists who "Find Money Can Be Made in Hollywood" (31): "There are a number of Negro authors whose early works contain promise. Chester Grimes [*sic*] who wrote 'If He Hollers Let Him Go,' Zora Neale Thurston [*sic*] who has yet to write the book of which she seems capable are two that immediately come to mind. Miss Thurston's [*sic*] latest book, 'Seraph On The Suwanee' is out at the booksellers. Recently another voice was heard from with the publication of 'Last of The Conquerors' by young Philadelphian William G. Smith" (30).

39. Stein, "Lecture 1," *Narration,* 7.

40. Ibid., 9.

Chapter 2
Pulp as Interface

The chapter opening epigraph is from p. 59 in *The Pleasure of the Text*, trans. Richard Miller (New York: Hill and Wang, 1975); the quote in the second epigraph appears on p. 26 in *The Medium is the Massage: An Inventory of Effects* (New York: Bantam Books, 1967).

1. On 1 May 2013, the six major publishers—Hachette, HarperCollins, Macmillan, Penguin Group, Random House, and Simon & Schuster—announced that they "will make e-books available to public libraries," according to the president of the New York Public Library, Anthony W. Marx, "E-Books and Democracy," *New York Times*, 1 May 2013, A23.

2. Richard Howard, "A Note on the Text," in Barthes, *The Pleasure of the Text*, viii; emphasis in the original.

3. See "interface, n.," *Oxford English Dictionary* online, http://www.oed .com.

4. Marshall McLuhan and Quentin Fiore, *The Medium is the Massage: An Inventory of Effects*, 88.

5. Geoffrey O'Brien, *Hardboiled America: Lurid Paperbacks and the Masters of Noir*, expanded ed. (New York: Da Capo Press, 1997), 9.

6. For early references to "transmediation" as a mode of reading in a multimedia environment, see Charles Suhor, "Towards a Semiotics Based Curriculum," *Journal of Curriculum Studies* 16 (1984): 247–57. His call to

incorporate a transmedial approach—visual, aural, aesthetic—into the language arts classroom was advanced by Ladislau M. Semali and Judith Fueyo, "Transmediation as a Metaphor for New Literacies in the Multimedia Classroom," *Reading Online* 5:5 (December/January 2001), http://www.readingonline.org/newliteracies/semali2/.

7. For instance, "Border-line cases" of books straddling some imagined line between propriety and pornography are mentioned three times by Roy C. Frank of the Post Office Administration (see the Report of the House Select Committee on Current Pornographic Materials, 93–95). For a brief discussion of her concept, see Mary Louise Pratt, "Arts of the Contact Zone," *Profession* (1991): 33–40.

8. Joan Schenkar, *The Talented Miss Highsmith: The Secret Life and Serious Art of Patricia Highsmith* (New York: St. Martin's Press, 2009), 131.

9. David Madden, ed., *Tough Guy Writers of the Thirties* (Carbondale: Southern Illinois University Press, 1968), xxi; subsequent references in text.

10. William Rollins Jr., "Chicago Confetti" (1932), in Otto Penzler, ed., *The Black Lizard Big Book of Pulps* (New York: Vintage Crime, 2007), 221–36.

11. For the complete history of how this story of Celia Cooney of Brooklyn took hold in the popular imagination, see Stephen Duncombe and Andrew Mattson, *The Bobbed Haired Bandit: A True Story of Crime and Celebrity in 1920s New York*. The authors stress how interconnected the actions of the criminals and their literary depictions were. Celia staged "a little hold-up . . . Just like I'd read in a magazine. . . . I had been reading magazines and books about girl crooks and bandits and it began to seem like a game or play acting after Ed [her accomplice] really came home with the guns." They explain: "Celia loved reading. And the scene, the gun, the language—it all seemed like something out of the detective magazines and cheap pulp novels she voraciously consumed. A story come to life" (28–29).

12. J. G. [Thurber], "More Authors Cover the Snyder Trial," *New Yorker*, 7 May 1927, 69; emphasis in the original. The rest of the page is taken up with an advertisement for a shampoo, Taroleum, declaring "bobbed hair is *easy to dress* after this new CRUDE-OIL SHAMPOO . . . Get some Taroleum today, at any drug-store. You'll find that a shampoo can be joyful!"

13. Kenneth Fearing, *The Big Clock*, in *Crime Novels: American Noir of the 1930s and 40s*, ed. Robert Polito (New York: Library of America, 1997), 444 and 461.

14. Vera Caspary, *Laura* (New York: Popular Library, 1950), 8; subsequent references in text.

15. Or so wrote critic Ken Johnson in "Eugene Speicher: An Artist Reconsidered," a review of his work in 2003. "Speicher liked to paint portraits of beautiful women, and some have the hazy idealism of the old Breck shampoo ads. His expert drawings—portraits and nudes, mostly—look like ads for correspondence school art courses." *New York Times* online, 7 November 2003, http://www.nytimes.com/.

16. Caspary's first novel from 1929 was entitled *The White Girl*, about a light-skinned black woman passing as white; it is thus a contemporary of Nella Larsen's novel *Passing*.

17. Aaron Lecklider notes that 1930s and 1940s left culture was full of a gay campiness more or less tolerated by straights but fully accepted and invoked by the myriad gay party members. "Dreaming of Franco: William Aalto, the Dolly Sisters and the Emergence of Queer Antifascism," paper delivered at the October 2011 American Studies Association Annual Meeting, Baltimore.

18. Famously, Caspary and Preminger had a dispute over Laura's character but also disagreed about Waldo—not for this scene but for altering the murder weapon from the clever walking stick pistol shooting BBs to the shotgun Waldo hid in the grandfather clock in Laura's apartment, which Caspary noted would hardly go unnoticed as he walked along the streets of New York. As Caspary described it, "this was not merely a murder story device, a shock to the reader, menace to the heroine, but a symbol (Freudian) of Waldo's impotence and destructiveness," in "My 'Laura' and Otto's," *Saturday Review*, 26 June 1971, 36.

19. Ruth Snyder's trial was one of several "crimes of the century" occurring between the 1920s and 1950s. She had conspired with her lover to kill her husband, and the story was the basis for the James M. Cain novels, *The Postman Always Rings Twice* and *Double Indemnity*. This case is dissected by Pelizzon and West as an example of the multiple remediations of sensational stories occurring during the era of what they call "Tabloid, Inc."

20. Sarah Engelmann makes a convincing argument for seeing Caspary's unmasking of heteronormativity and the sexism within detective and noir genres as being channeled in part through Waldo's campy gay persona in "'Dames Are Always Putting a Switch on You': The Disruption of the

Femme Fatale in *Laura*," magna cum laude thesis, University of Minnesota, 2012, University of Minnesota Digital Conservancy, http://conservancy. umn.edu/handle/143934.

21. The 1950 Avon paperback No. 634 declares *Miss Lonelyhearts* to be "A Savage Novel of Woman's Brutality to Man." This novel, which John Dos Passos declares on the cover "certainly packs a wallop," influenced Caspary in many ways. Waldo being a gossip columnist, which was where Miss Lonelyhearts hopes his job as an advice man "might lead to a gossip column and anyway he's tired of being a leg man" (53). Miss Lonelyhearts walks New York, commenting "Ah Humanity" (with Melville) and his coworkers call him Dostoevsky. In the section entitled "Miss Lonelyhearts and the Clean Old Man," a group of the advice columnist's friends are drinking at Delehanty's speakeasy "complaining about the number of female authors. 'And they've all got three names,' he said. 'Mary Roberts Wilcox, Ella Wheeler Catheter, Ford Mary Rinehart . . .'" (25). This modernist repetition of that other Nathaniel's dismissal of that "damn'd mob of scribbling women" merely confirms my point about interfaces—in this case, between the nineteenth century and the twentieth.

22. See Alan Wald, *Trinity of Passion: The Literary Left and the Antifascist Crusade* (Chapel Hill: University of North Carolina Press, 2007), 186–94, who sees this as part of a trend during the mid-twentieth century of American Jewish leftist writers assuming the mask of African Americans in various literary and musical works as a means to resist a cultural nationalism aligned with Judaism (as most were secular) while seeing Jewish history in Europe (especially as Nazism was unfolding and in its aftermath) as paralleled by black oppression in the United States due to white supremacy and racism. See, for instance, Elie Seigmeister's music. In 1992, Michael Rogin (*Blackface, White Noise: Jewish Immigrants in the Hollywood Melting Pot* [Berkeley and Los Angeles: University of California Press, 1996]) made the astute point, picked up by Eric Lott (*Love & Theft: Blackface Minstrelsy and the American Working Class* [Oxford: Oxford University Press, 1993]), that Jews needed to masquerade as black in order to become white. Karen Brodkin argues that after World War II this process was reversed—Jews needed to divorce themselves from identification with blacks in order to solidify their whiteness; *How Jews Became White Folks and What that Says about Race in America* (New Brunswick, NJ: Rutgers University Press, 1998).

23. Chester Himes, *If He Hollers Let Him Go* (New York: New American Library, 1949); subsequent references in text.

24. Himes received a one-thousand-dollar advance from NAL for his novel *The End of a Primitive*, bowdlerized in 1955 (and published in paperback under the title *The Primitive*) in a Signet edition in 1956. He began this satirical work on the theme of sexual frustration in black writers and white women in 1948, when the French edition of *If He Hollers* appeared to wide acclaim. See Grégory Pierrot, "Chester Himes, Boris Vian, and the Transatlantic Politics of Racial Representation," *African American Review* 43 (Summer/Fall 2009): 247–62. For information on Himes's biography, including his NAL advance, see James Sallis, *Chester Himes: A Life* (New York: Walker, 2000), 206.

25. A few years later, *Amazing Stories* would ask Robert Lindner, "the author of the recent best-seller: 'The Fifty-Minute Hour'" to offer his prediction for the future of neurosis in 2001. *Amazing Stories*, "Thirtieth Anniversary Issue, Productions for 2001 A.D." (April 1956): 248; subsequent references in text.

26. Martha Gellhorn, afterword to *Liana* (London: Virago Press Limited, 1987), 254.

27. Ibid., 255. See Carl Rollyson's biography, *Nothing Ever Happens to the Brave: The Story of Martha Gellhorn* (New York: St. Martin's Press, 1990), 180. Winston Guest, a submarine-hunting buddy of Hemingway, thought the novel "was really about how Ernest was keeping Martha incarcerated in Cuba" when he read it in draft (182).

28. In fact, in the 1930s, bibliotherapy was a widely recognized method of treatment for those recovering from psychological problems, especially World War I shell shock. See, for instance, Fairfax Downey, "Dose: Books as Needed," *American Legion Monthly* 12:3 (1932): 6–7; Salomon Gagnon, "Is Reading Therapy?" *Diseases of the Nervous System* 3 (1942): 206–12; Sadie Peterson Delaney, "The Place of Bibliotherapy in a Hospital," *Library Journal* (1938): 305–8. Thanks to Monique Dufour's Virginia Polytechnic and State University, PhD dissertation, "Reading for Health: Books as Medicine in the 20th Century United States," for alerting me to this trend.

29. See David M. Earle, "Conrad Under Wraps: Reputation, Pulp Indeterminacy, and the 1950s Signet Edition of *Heart of Darkness*," *Studia Neophilologica* (iFirst, 2012), which situates the novel and any number of

others within this complex social and political moment. "Pulp Conrad" dates to the turn of the twentieth century, as his work was published in various reprint magazines that, in Earle's words, serve as "a training ground for literacy," because "Conrad became a gateway for class mobility" for many—including Richard Wright and John Fante (6). Earle describes the relationship between surface and depth—or cover and interior (the heart of darkness, so to speak)—of these books as a "contact zone" in which the form of the paperback makes concrete the themes of Conrad's works (12). David M. Earle's 2009 *Re-Covering Modernism: Pulps, Paperbacks and the Prejudice of Form* looks at the pulp covering, both literally and in its musical sense, of works by William Faulkner and other literary writers in magazines and paperbacks.

30. For more on this saga, see Jeremiah Rickert, "The Faulkner Incident," *Oregon Literary Review* 2:2, http://orelitrev.startlogic.com/v2n2/OLR-rickert.htm.

31. See his two 1968 edited collections—*Tough Guy Writers of the 1930s* and *Proletarian Writers of the 1930s* (Carbondale: Southern Illinois University Press, 1968)—for some of the overlap among them. "Indeed, the tough and proletarian novels had common social and political origins and causes, and depicted similar elements: violence, poverty, lawlessness, disenchantment, and a certain sentimentality" (xxxii), Madden says in *Tough Guy* as he survey's Alfred Kazin's take on the overlap in 1930s writing noted already in his 1942 book, *On Native Grounds*.

32. Alfred Kazin, *On Native Grounds: A Study of American Prose Literature from 1890 to the Present*, abridged with a new postscript (1942; Garden City, NY: Doubleday Anchor Books, 1956), 301; subsequent references in text.

33. Quoted in Madden, ed., *Tough Guy Writers of the Thirties*, 233.

34. Josephine Herbst, "The Year of Disgrace," in *The Starched Blue Sky of Spain and Other Memoirs* (Boston: Northeastern University Press, 1991), 77–78. Elinor Langer, *Josephine Herbst: The Story She Could Never Tell* (Boston: Atlantic-Little, Brown, 1984), 95, indicates the "pulp mill" is Dell.

35. Hope Hale Davis, *Great Day Coming: A Memoir of the 1930s* (South Royalton, VT: Steerforth Press, 1994), 3; subsequent references in text.

36. Herbst, "The Year of Disgrace," 66.

37. As the title of Tom Dardis's book called it.

38. Roland Barthes, *Camera Lucida: Reflections on Photography*, trans. Richard Howard (New York: Hill and Wang, 1981), 98; subsequent references in text.

39. Clarence Petersen, *The Bantam Story: Twenty-Five Years of Paperback Publishing* (New York: Bantam Books, 1970), 17.

40. Raymond Chandler, *The Big Sleep* (New York: Avon, 1943), 16.

41. Ibid., 17.

42. William Emrys Williams, *Allen Lane: A Personal Portrait* (London: Bodley Head, 1973), 80.

43. See BBC, *On This Day*, 10 November 1960, http://news.bbc.co.uk /onthisday/hi/dates/stories/november/10/newsid_2965000/2965194 .stm, as well as the Penguin Archives in the University of Bristol Library Special Collections. Details of the testimony appear in C. H. Rolph, *The Trial of Lady Chatterley: Regina v. Penguin Books Limited* (Baltimore: Penguin, 1961). That Penguin brought this book out a year after the trial is typical of a self-referential aspect of paperback book publishing and its ability to produce instant books.

44. C. H. Rolph, *The Trial*, 63, 64.

45. In 2013, three "newly discovered" unpublished stories by J. D. Salinger appeared for sale on eBay. One entitled "Paula" was apparently written in the early 1940s, presumably for submission to the *New Yorker* but it instead found its way to *Stag*, a magazine for men that borders on pulp, though it was never published there either. A horror story about a middle-class housewife who declares to her husband that she must remain in bed throughout her (false) pregnancy, it ends with a macabre scene when the husband finds his wife curled in a fetal position in the baby's crib. Perhaps "Paula" had already been associated with "strange" sexuality. See Andrew Romano, "What Salinger's New Stories Reveal about the Author," *Daily Beast*, 30 November 2013, http://www.thedailybeast.com/. But there might be another explanation for choosing the name Paula as a signifier of alternative sexualities midcentury: Margaret Mead's 1928 *Coming of Age in Samoa* first appeared in a Mentor Book from New American Library in 1949 (and every year throughout the 1950s). Three of her seventeen informants, the young sexually liberated Samoan teens she interviewed, were named Pola, Pala, and Pula. And so mothers seeking to free their daughters, or authors seeking to

signal their protagonists' (or their own) sexual fluidity, may have seized on this most Christian name.

46. Gale Wilhelm, *Paula* (New York: Lions Books, 1956), 1; subsequent references in text.

47. Chris Vials, in *Realism for the Masses: Aesthetics, Popular Front Pluralism, and U.S. Culture, 1935–1947* (Jackson: University of Mississippi Press, 2009), discusses this novel (and others) by Caldwell as presenting Popular Front "challenges" to Margaret Mitchell's *Gone with the Wind*, claiming that "with scenes of bawdy flirtation, passionate kissing, and direct and indirect references to sexual intercourse" (91), it shows how "a proletarian novel could become mass culture" (84). He mentions its paperback cover by "Jonas" without mentioning his first name.

48. The 1949 Bantam edition of Hemingway's *The Sun Also Rises* sports a cover with a man sitting at a table with clenched fist posed between a framed picture of a beautiful woman and an oversized open beer bottle. The tagline reads, " 'You gave more than your life,' the Colonel had said. It was a rotten way to be wounded." On the back, a small drawing of a naked man looking at himself in a full-length mirror, though only his torso is visible, next to the single word "Undressing . . ." Part of the total package of the paperback from its early years often included a description of the cover artwork. Many publishers sought imagery that came directly out of scenes in the book—an attempt to forestall claims of false advertising as well as potential legal battles. Impotence cannot be spoken so the blurbs must hint at how it might suppress desire: "They were desperate—For Pleasure" reads the first page, even before the title page. On the next page is a note, "About THE COVER," which excerpts a few sentences from within in italics: "*It was Brett I thought about . . . It was awfully easy to be hard-boiled about everything in the daytime, but at night it is another thing.*" Underneath is an explanation: "Brawny Jake Barnes wanted only one thing—Brett Ashley. But neither she—nor *any* woman—could ever be his. It was truly a rotten way to be wounded . . . *Illustrated by Ken Riley.*" All these typefaces and prefatory come-ons are designed to entice readers deeper into the book.

The image in the mirror became a staple of pulp covers. Robert Jonas expanded on this with his signature "keyhole" covers in which a scene is revealed in the deep background through a hole in a broken window or a wall (for example, the covers of *Other Voices, Other Rooms* and *God's Little*

Acre, respectively). The cover itself serves as a kind of mirror or window so that in George Gross's cover for the NAL 1950 edition of *Lady Chatterley's Lover*, the couple embrace in close-up—her face and his hair dominate a background of green leaves and tiny purple flowers, which surround them between the upper and lower borders that were standard for NAL books.

49. Don Kingery, *Paula* (New York: Dell, 1959), 74; subsequent references in text.

50. D. H. Lawrence, *Lady Chatterley's Lover* (New York: New American Library, 1946), 121–22.

51. Rachel M. Brownstein, *Becoming a Heroine: Reading about Women in Novels* (Harmondsworth, UK: Penguin, 1984), 5.

52. Ibid., 8.

53. David K. Johnson, "Buying Gay: Consumer Culture and Community before Stonewall," lecture, University of Minnesota, 19 April 2013. He notes, for example, a feature in a 1954 issue of Chicago's *VIM* magazine about Dick Lee showing him engaged in various activities, including reading *Twenty-One Variations on a Theme*, a 1953 collection of stories by and about gay men edited by Donald Webster Cory (Edward Sagarin), known for his 1951 book, *The Homosexual in America: A Subjective Approach*, and his Cory Books Service list of gay books and magazines. Again, the reading matter featured lessons in reading this matter.

54. Lizabeth Cohen, *A Consumers' Republic: The Politics of Mass Consumption in Postwar America* (New York: Vintage, 2004), 293.

55. Ben Hecht, *A Child of the Century* (New York: Signet, 1955), 142; subsequent references in text.

56. Lyle H. Lanier, "A Critique of the Philosophy of Progress," in Twelve Southerners, *I'll Take My Stand: The South and the Agrarian Tradition* (1930; New York: Harper & Row, 1962), 145; Donald Davidson, "A Mirror for Artists," in Twelve Southerners, *I'll Take My Stand*, 33. Subsequent references to both essays from this landmark book inaugurating what would become New Criticism are given in the text, respectively.

57. This is the scene Avati depicts:

> That night she had come to his room, for the first time.
> Later, moving from the bed toward the door to return to her room, she had hesitated with her face in the direction of the window. "Look," she had

whispered, pointing. He had slipped out of the bed and gone to the window. The night had been unusually dark, the dark mass of the earth scarcely darker than the sky. But a patch of flame had been on the horizon, a single center of rich, cherry-colored glow fading outward and upward into the enormous hollow of darkness. A dog had barked very faintly, very far off.

Lucille Christian had come to stand beside him. "What is it?" she had whispered.

He had told her that he did not know, and had drawn her to him. She had shivered as she stood there against him, watching the distant point of light in the darkness.

He had told her he did not know what the patch of flame on the horizon was; but he did know. He knew it was a burning tobacco barn. It was a barn belonging to some man who after receiving warnings, had not listed his crop with the Association. He knew that a band of men from some other locality, Band Number Six, he remembered, Mr. Burden's band from over Hunter County, had picked up its guide, a mounted man waiting in the shadows by the roadside at an appointed place, and had been led to that spot where the flames now made that little center of rosy light against the black sky. And he knew that some other night, soon, he himself would stand and watch men apply the match and then would mount and ride away, the hoofs of the horses drumming the frosty earth and the flames climbing the sky behind him. He knew, because that was the way it had already been.

Robert Penn Warren, *Night Rider* (1939; repr., introduction and abridged by George Mayberry [New York: Signet Books, 1950]), 127–28 (plate 10).

58. Edith Wharton, "Expiation," *Cosmopolitan* 34 (December 1908): 209–22, reprinted in *The New York Stories of Edith Wharton* (New York: New York Review of Books Original, 2007), 197.

59. Henry James, "The Future of the Novel," in *Theory of Fiction: Henry James*, ed. James E. Miller Jr. (Lincoln: University of Nebraska Press), 363–44; subsequent references in text.

60. Leslie Fiedler, "Up from Adolescence," *Partisan Review* 29 (1962): 127.

61. In addition to the two 1950s novels I discuss, I also include the main character of March Hastings's [Sally Singer] novel, *Three Women* (New York: Beacon Books, 1958).

CHAPTER 3
Richard Wright's Savage Holiday

The chapter opening epigraphs are from, respectively, Richard Wright, holograph note, Box 63, Folder 734, Richard Wright Papers (hereafter RWP), Yale Collection of American Literature (hereafter YCAL), Beinecke Rare Book and Manuscript Library, Yale University; Richard Wright, *Native Son* (New York: Harper and Brothers, 1940), 331 (subsequent references given in text); and Kenneth Fearing, "Reading, Writing, and the Rackets," in *New and Selected Poems* (Bloomington: Indiana University Press, 1956), ix.

1. Frank Rich, "McCain's McClellan Nightmare," *New York Times*, national ed., 1 June 2008, section 4, 12; my emphasis.

2. D. H. Lawrence, *Studies in Classic American Literature* (1922; Garden City, NJ: Doubleday, 1951), 60.

3. Mark Seltzer, *True Crime: Observations on Violence and Modernity* (New York: Routledge, 2007), 2.

4. Theodor W. Adorno, *The Stars Down to Earth and Other Essays on the Irrational Culture*, ed. Stephen Crook (New York: Routledge, 2001), 44.

5. Sandra Rena Heard, "Washington, DC's 'Negro' Press: The Unmaking of a Cooperative Black Society," American Studies Association Annual Meeting, Albuquerque, New Mexico, October 2008.

6. One could read almost any of Kenneth Fearing's poems as spoofs of/ homages to what he called the "True Confession Story" (xii). See, for instance, this excerpt from "Longshot Blues":

> Whose whole life falls between roto-press wheels moving quicker than
>   light, to reappear, gorgeous and calm, on page eighteen,
> Who reads all about it: *Prize-winning beauty trapped, accused*,
> Who rides, and rides, and rides the big bright limited south, or is found,
>   instead, on the bedroom floor with a stranger's bullet through the
>   middle of his heart,
> Clutching at a railroad table to the south wile the curtains blow wild and
>   the radio plays the sun shines on, and on, and on, and on, (87)

Or from "Aphrodite Metropolis (2)":

> On Sunday, when they picnic in emerald meadows they look at the
>   Sunday paper:

GIRL SLAYS BANKER-BETRAYER
They spread it around on the grass
BATH-TUB STIRS JERSEY ROW
And then they sit down on it, nice. (14)

Both excerpts are from *Collected Poems* (New York: AMS Press, 1977). See also Nelson Algren's *Chicago: City on the Make* (1951; repr., Chicago: University of Chicago Press, 2001) or Horace McCoy's *I Should Have Stayed Home* (1938; repr., London: Serpent's Tail Press, 1996).

7. Nicolas Abraham and Maria Torok, *The Wolf Man's Magic Word*, trans. Nicholas Rand, foreword by Jacques Derrida (Minneapolis: University of Minnesota Press, 1986). They define the process as "a precocious traumatic scene, removed, sent to a crypt, encrypted" (lxxi).

8. So, by arguing that Wright was creating crime fiction, even in his nonfiction accounts of black life, I disagree with Justin Gifford, who claims Chester Himes was "the first of many black novelists to employ the crime fiction form to critique the dominant cultural and racial ideologies of twentieth-century American society." *Pimping Fiction: African American Crime Literature and the Untold Story of Black Pulp Publishing* (Philadelphia: Temple University Press, 2013), 17.

9. Richard Wright, *Black Boy (American Hunger): A Record of Childhood and Youth* (New York: HarperPerennial, 1993), 156.

10. Margie Weinstein, "Reframing Law and Lens: Jacob Riis's Documentary Photography and Legal Discourse during the Progressive Era," PhD dissertation, University of Minneapolis, 2008.

11. Jeffrey Allred, "From Eye to We: Richard Wright's *12 Million Black Voices*, Documentary, and Pedagogy," *American Literature* 78 (2006): 550.

12. See Susan Rubin Suleiman, *Authoritarian Fictions: The Ideological Novel as a Literary Genre* (New York: Columbia University Press, 1983).

13. Journals in James Agee Papers, University of Tennessee, Box 1, Folder 17, MS 1500, Series 1. This journal is reprinted in Hugh Davis and Michael Lofaro, eds., *James Agee Rediscovered: The Journals of "Let Us Now Praise Famous Men" and Other New Manuscripts* (Knoxville: University of Tennessee Press, 2005), 158, though I decipher Agee's handwriting a bit differently in some places. Thanks to Jeff Allred, "Boring from Within: Luce, *Life*

and the Avant-Garde (1941)," Seventh International Conference on Word and Image, Philadelphia, September 2005, for bringing this volume to my attention.

14. Davis and Lofaro, eds., *James Agee Rediscovered*, 158–59.

15. Again, thanks to Allred, "Boring from Within," for alerting me to the Evans scrapbooks. For more on Evans's immersion in vernacular imagery and other "folk documents," see Jess L. Rosenheim, *Walker Evans and the Picture Postcard* (New York: Steidl Publishers and the Metropolitan Museum of Art, 2009), 13.

16. Not necessarily in the overt way, I argue one finds magazine culture in *12 Million Black Voices*, but there nevertheless—in Evans's photographs of the decoration they provided on the tenants' walls, in Agee's careful rendering of the texts found in the newspaper doilies saved in their trunks, or, most spectacularly, his mocking inclusion of the *New York Post* fluff piece on Margaret Bourke-White's career. See James Agee and Walker Evans, *Let Us Now Praise Famous Men* (Boston: Houghton Mifflin, 1941), 450–54. For more on this, see Paula Rabinowitz, *They Must Be Represented: The Politics of Documentary* (London: Verso, 1994). John T. Frederick in his conversation with Arna Bontemps broadcast from Northwestern University on the Air radio show *Of Men and Books*, Evanston, Illinois, 18 November 1941, and more definitively in a corollary text also mentioned in the show (on black poetry), *12 Million Black Voices*. RWP, YCAL, Beinecke Rare Book and Manuscript Library, Box 63, Folder 741.

17. *Let Us Now Praise Famous Men* sold only about six hundred copies after its first publication in April 1941; however, as a royalty statement from Viking shows, *12 Million Black Voices* was considerably more popular despite its appearance just weeks before Pearl Harbor was attacked. For instance, it was assigned in Dartmouth sociology classes and was widely available, thanks to a campaign by Viking and the FSA to distribute it to leading New Deal jurists and politicians (Edwin Rosskam, letter to Robert Hatch, RWP, YCAL, Box 105, Folder 1585, 1941). Royalty statement April 1943 for *12 Million Black Voices*: "Regular 4,705; Export and Special 429; Preview 504. Royalties to Richard Wright $42.91."

18. See the radio interview by John T. Frederick with Arna Bontemps on Negro writers broadcast from Northwestern University on the Air radio show *Of Men and Books*, 18 November 1941, in RWP, Box 63, Folder 742.

19. See *Letters of James Agee to Father Flye* (New York: George Braziller, 1962).

20. James Agee Papers, University of Tennessee, Box 1, Folder 17, MS 1500, Series 1. Since this excerpt from Agee's journal was transposed from handwritten notes, parts of it are difficult to decipher, and it is possible that the original editors may have substituted terms for what Agee actually wrote on the page. For instance, where the editors have used "FEELING" in one part of the quotation, I read it as "FUCKING." Whether this was a purposeful expurgation of Agee's writing that arose from a desire to be sensitive to the climate of the times or just an honest deciphering of the handwritten notes is difficult to know. In any regard, it may affect how we interpret Agee's thought process at the time he was writing.

21. RWP, holograph, 1938, Box 63, Folder 734.

22. See *Revistas y Guerra, 1936–39* (Madrid, Spain: Museo Nacional Centro de Arte Reina Sofía, 2007); the University of Illinois website of Spanish Civil War posters and magazine covers; and Jordana Mendelson, *Documenting Spain: Artists, Exhibition Culture, and the Modern Nation, 1929–1939* (University Park: Pennsylvania State University Press, 2005).

23. Wright, *Black Boy*, 288.

24. James Agee Papers, University of Tennessee, Box 1, Folder 17, MS 1500, Series 1, Notebook 20, Monday (10 January 1938).

25. In *Hud*, the seventeen-year-old boy, Lon, leafs through pulp paperbacks in the local drugstore of his Texas town as he waits for his uncle to finish drinking at the bar. When the druggist starts talking to him about the racy parts, Lon replaces the book and moves on.

26. Richard Wright, *12 Million Black Voices*, ed. Edwin Rosskam (New York: Viking Press, 1941), 10; subsequent references in text are to this edition. The later edition, Richard Wright, *12 Million Black Voices*, ed. Edwin Rosskam (New York: Basic Books, 2002), and subsequent editions do not include Wright's single photograph that appeared in the first edition. It is replaced by an Esther Bubley photograph. (Further references to this volume in text.)

27. Joseph Entin's reading of the first two images—the headless white man holding a hoe and "bodyless" black face haloed by white hair—remarks on them as a "bizarre biracial Frankenstein," cobbling together two parts of the racial makeup of Southern rural sharecropper culture (*Sensational Modernism*, 222).

28. Walter Benjamin, "Post No Bills," in *Selected Writings*, vol. 1, ed. Marcus Bullock and Michael Jennings (Cambridge, MA: Belknap Press, 1996), 459.

29. Walter Benjamin, "Critique of the New Objectivity," in *Selected Writings*, vol. 2, ed. Michael Jennings and Howard Eiland (Cambridge, MA: Belknap Press, 1998), 417.

30. Walter Benjamin, "Left-Wing Melancholy," in *Selected Writings*, 2:424.

31. Walter Benjamin, "The Author as Producer," in *Selected Writings*, 2:774; subsequent references in text.

32. See Sara Blair's *Harlem Crossroads: Black Writers and Photography in the Twentieth Century* (Princeton: Princeton University Press, 2007), which offers the most comprehensive reading of Wright's photographic interests to date; she sees his photography as intimately linked to his writing practice.

33. See Weinstein, "Reframing Law and Lens."

34. Walter Benjamin, "The Newspaper," in *Selected Writings*, 2:741.

35. Carla Cappetti, *Writing Chicago: Modernism, Ethnography and the Novel* (New York: Columbia University Press, 1993) has argued persuasively for reading Wright's autobiography as "the conjunction between literary autobiography and sociological life history," a methodology Wright borrowed from the Chicago school sociologists with whom he worked closely and to whom he owed his "story," as he noted in the introduction to St. Clair Drake and Horace R. Cayton, *Black Metropolis: A Study of Negro Life in a Northern City* (New York: Harcourt, Brace, Jovanovich, 1945). Chicago school sociology—with its interest in caste and class, and the movement of rural folk to urban proletariat as marginal men, which, as Carla Cappetti argues, dovetailed with the CPUSA's interpretation of Stalin's ideas (dimly acknowledged in early drafts of *12 Million Black Voices*) about the national question—offered an overview for a story of self (198). Actually, all his fiction and nonfiction owes the same rendering of life-course case study through journalistic anecdote, ethnography, and personal reminiscence, as John M. Reilly notes in "Richard Wright Preaches the Nation: *12 Million Black Voices*," *Black American Literature Forum* 16:3 (Autumn 1982): 116–19.

36. RWP, holograph notes, 1938, Box 63, Folder 734 (handwriting unclear).

37. RWP, typescript, 1940, Box 62, Folder 728. "To paint the picture [of how] we live on the tobacco, cane, rice and cotton plantations is to compete against mighty artists: the movies, the radio, the newspaper, the magazines, and even the Church. They have painted one picture: charming, idyllic, romantic; but we live another; full of fear . . ." is how it reads on p. 35.

38. Richard Wright, *Lawd Today* (1963, repr., Boston: Northeastern University Press, 1986); 117–19; subsequent references in text as *LT* followed by page number.

39. See June 1942. This and all other reviews come from Richard Wright's scrapbook, with clippings and other ephemera related to *12 Million Black Voices*. RWP, YCAL, Box 63, Folder 741.

40. Ann Petry, "The Novel as Social Criticism," in Helen Hull, *The Writer's Book* (New York: Barnes and Noble, 1956), 37–38.

41. See 20 December 1941, vol. 1, no. 41. This and all the quotations come from RWP Clippings file on *12 Million Black Voices*, Box 63, Folder 741.

42. For instance, pages 152–53 in *Lawd Today* are rendered as choral dialogue in what became repeated almost word for word as a prose poem in *12 Million Black Voices* on page 32–33.

43. Reilly, "Richard Wright Preaches the Nation," 117.

44. Maren Stange, "'Not What We Seem': Image and Text in *12 Million Black Voices*," in *Iconographies of Power: The Politics and Poetics of Visual Representation*, ed. Ulla Haselstein, Berndt Ostendorf, and Peter Sneck (Heidelberg: C. Winter Press, 2003), 184 and 183.

45. Interview with Edwin and Louise Rosskam, conducted by Richard Doud at their home in Roosevelt, New Jersey, 3 August 1965, Smithsonian Archives of American Art, n.p., http://www.aaa.si.edu/collections/oralhistories/transcripts/rosska65.htm#top.

46. Ibid.

47. Karla F. C. Holloway, *BookMarks: Reading in Black and White* (New Brunswick, NJ: Rutgers University Press, 2006), 44–45, 49.

48. For more on America's irrational culture, see Theodor W. Adorno, *The Stars Down to Earth and Other Essays on the Irrational Culture*. I am arguing that it is precisely this irrationality—in the form of the haunted American landscape full of ghosts unacknowledged—that comprises American pulp

literary history and politics. See Avery F. Gordon, *Ghostly Matters: Haunting and the Sociological Imagination* (Minneapolis: University of Minnesota Press, 1997), who sees the ghostly as "a paradigmatic way in which life is more complicated than those of us who study it have usually granted," 7.

49. Quoted in Drake and Cayton, *Black Metropolis*, xvii.

50. The quotations come from Mikhail Bakhtin, *Problems of Dostoevsky's Poetics*, ed. and trans. Caryl Emerson (Minneapolis: University of Minnesota Press, 1984), 70–73, and "Discourse in the Novel," in *The Dialogic Imagination: Four Essays*, trans. Michael Holquist and Caryl Emerson (Austin: University of Texas Press, 1981), 73.

CHAPTER 4
Isak Dinesen Gets Drafted: Pulp, the Armed Services Editions, and GI Reading

1. According to Jean Tretter, founder of the Jean-Nickolaus Tretter Collection of Gay, Lesbian, Bisexual and Transgender Studies, Special Collections and Rare Books at the University of Minnesota Library, this advertising campaign became a source of underground gay beefcake and helped forge a gay male identity within the military during and after the war. Personal interview, February 2005.

2. The definitive history of this project is John B. Hench, *Books as Weapons: Propaganda, Publishing and the Battle for Global Markets in the Era of WWII* (Ithaca: Cornell University Press, 2010).

3. Weldon B. Durham, *Liberty Theatres of the United States Army, 1917–1919* (Jefferson, NC: McFarland, 2006), 41.

4. *A History of the Council of Books in Wartime: 1942–1946* (New York: 1946), 85. The book was written by Robert O. Ballou from a working draft prepared by staff member Irene Rakosky and printed by Country Life Press in an edition of two thousand copies (2).

5. Davis, *Two-Bit Culture*, 70.

6. This was attested to by the many letters written from the front, for instance, Charles Rawlings, a correspondent in the South Pacific, who wrote his friend, publisher Stanley Rinehart, on 5 June 1944 lauding the program. This and all other letters come from the Council on Books in Wartime Records (hereafter CBWR), Public Policy Papers, Department of Rare Books and Special Collections, Princeton University Library, Box 32, Folder 3.

The Seeley G. Mudd Manuscript Library of the Princeton University Library houses the council's papers, including the myriad missives, V-letters— short handwritten postcards sent from the theaters of war—telegraphs, and notes, even whole manuscripts inspired by the selections, which contain criticism of the works, acclaim for the project, and constant appeals for individual copies of an edition. I thank the archivists who assisted my research there.

7. CBWR, Box 31/32, Folder 2.

8. "Revised Specifications—Armed Services Editions," 11 January 1945. CBWR, Box 31, Folder 7.

9. There were two page sizes: "one 5½ × 3⅞, which is one half of *Reader's Digest*, larger size 6½ × 4½, which is one-half the height of a pulp magazine. The books were bound on the short edge and set two columns to the page. The exact sizes were worked out to enable the Council to take advantage of some of the biggest production equipment in the country." *A History of the Council on Books in Wartime: 1942–1946*, 75. Fortuitously, they were also exactly the size of pockets. A long handwritten letter from T/S Elmer Peace to the council dated 6 July 1944 summed it up as follows: "The practical way the books are constructed cannot go unmentioned either. Our modern 'bloomer-pocket' uniforms makes [*sic*] it possible for us to conceal one of them perfectly from the watchful eyes of a superior officer. Also they are easy to hide when you should be doing something else. Just think we don't need the geography as we did in school days," he added (CBWR Box 32, Folder 4).

10. *A History of the Council on Books in Wartime*, 8.

11. J. D. Salinger, *The Catcher in the Rye* (1951; New York: Signet, 1953), 20. "I thought it was going to stink," muses Holden, "but it didn't. It was a very good book." Salinger began *Catcher* in 1941. Much of his fiction features characters debating the merits of literary works.

12. Such was the intensity of immersion in this book that almost sixty-five years later Pierson R. Davis recalled that "On V-J Day, I was sitting on the deck of the troopship, U.S.S. *Maui*, leaning against the stack reading *The Robe*. We were moving up from New Guinea to Okinawa to stage the invasion of Japan. We sailed through the Philippine Islands to avoid the Japanese submarines. The bosun's whistle over the loudspeaker was followed by 'Now hear this.' The captain announced that official word had just been received

334 • Notes to Chapter 4

that Japan had surrendered." Letter to the editor, *New York Times*, 19 September 2009, A17.

13. Unfortunately, the pages pertaining to the lists in which her books appeared are missing from the Council on Books in Wartime Records.

14. CBWR, Box 32, Folder 3.

15. Letter, Ray Trautman to Philip Van Doren Stern, 11 April 1944, CBWR, Box 18, Folder 6.

16. Letter, 20 July 1945 and V-mail, 9 July 1945, CBWR, Box 32, Folder 30.

17. Letter, 6 November 1944, CBWR, Box 31/32, Folder 1.

18. V-Letter, 21 July 1944, CBWR, Box 32, Folder 5.

19. CBWR, Box 31/32, Folder 1.

20. 27 December 1944, CBWR, Box 26, Folder 3.

21. CBWR, Box 26, Folder 3.

22. *A History of the Council on Books in Wartime*, 83. See also the letter from Corporal Robert Friedlander to Mrs. Simonson, 28 February 1945, about *Our Hearts*, CBWR, Box 31/32, Folder 2.

23. CBWR, Box 26, Folder 3.

24. CBWR, Box 32, Folder 3.

25. William Styron, who served out the Second World War stateside, where ASE books were unavailable, begins his chronicle of his convalescence from misdiagnosed syphilis by describing his habits: "I was wearing a blue hospital robe, in the pocket of which I had thrust a copy of one of the first paperback anthologies ever published, a volume that had kept me company for at least two years—*The Pocket Book of Verse*, compiled by an academic named M. Edmund Speare." "A Case of the Great Pox," in *Havanas in Camelot: Personal Essays* (New York: Random House, 2008), 22.

26. Sadly, both the "sales" figures for the "U" (May 1945) and "X" (August 1945) series, which included Dinesen's books *Seven Gothic Tales*, No. 687, and *Winter's Tales*, No. 802, are missing from—but most lists remain consistent—each run (monthly) of thirty to forty books of close to a million copies in editions of about 25,000 to 50,000 each. Other information on the ASEs is from *Editions for the Armed Services, Inc.: A History Together with the Complete List of the 1324 Books Published for American Armed Forces Overseas* (New York, n.d.). A handwritten note indicates it was accessioned by the University of Minnesota Library through a gift from the Department

of the Army, 1948. NB: Various figures for the number of books published differ due to republications and collapsing different programs together at war's end.

27. In a letter dated 11 April 1944, during the Soldiers' Vote Act controversy, Ray Trautman, lieutenant colonel in charge of the Army Library Section, wrote Philip Van Doren Stern with a copy of a memorandum from his office (the Special Services Division) for the director of Control Division A.S.F. It details the "plan for preparation of [a] list [of] periodicals and books for distribution in accordance with Section 501 of Public Law 277" Inclosure [sic] #1:

2. Selection of books for military personnel outside the continental limits of the United States includes books for recreational readings, for information and for education. The criteria for book selection includes the following definite aims:

a. Stress readability and masculine viewpoint.

b. Avoid the mediocre, subversive and trash.

c. Provide the representative, important books in all subject fields.

d. Provide authentic military books of interest to any soldiers and the military books pertinent to his special branch of the service.

e. Provide non-military informative books, stressing accuracy, clear presentations and modernity.

f. Provide recreational reading which men of various backgrounds would read in civilian life: humor, biography, stories, poetry and travel.

g. Provide recent fiction, avoiding only the mediocre, trashy, mawkish and books with a decided feminine interest.

h. Provide fiction of enduring value in a format of good print.

i. Provide books with simple vocabulary and adult interest for the near-illiterates.

j. Provide supplementary reading for classes and correspondence courses.

k. Exclude political argument or political propaganda of any kind designed or calculated to affect the result of any election for President, Vice-Presidential elector, Member of the Senate, or Member of the House of Representatives. Inclosure [sic] #2 (CBWR, Box 18, Folder 6)

28. Ibid.

29. For instance, the interview with Lillian Smith included her denunciation of the segregated army that was fighting Nazi anti-Semitism.

30. See William Leary, "Books, Soldiers and Censorship during the Second World War," *American Quarterly* 20, no. 2, part 1 (Summer 1968): 237–43.

31. Letter, 1 June 1944, CBWR, Box 18, Folder 6.

32. Hench, *Books as Weapons*, 8.

33. This case was summarized in *A History of the Council on Books in Wartime*, 20–26. The minutes of meetings and synopses of various strategies and drafts of press releases and letters to legislators are in CBWR, Box 18.

34. CBWR, Box 31/32, Folder 2.

35. For some reason this book sparked a number of letters from those stationed in New Guinea. See CBWR, Box 31/32, Folder 1.

36. CBWR, Box 32, Folder 3.

37. Ibid.

38. Letter from Robert Sherwood, 20 February 1946, "now being in jail is in many ways not far different from being in the army. There is much boredom, little recreation, and lots of time on one's hands," he wrote from Bellingham, Washington, for "extra books" for the Whatcom County jail. CBWR, Box 26, Folder 5. See also Holloway, *BookMarks*, chapter 4, "A Prison Library," for a discussion of the significance of reading matter available to black prisoners, in particular, Angela Davis and Eldridge Cleaver, 75–90.

39. Nicholas Hengen, "Texts as Tactics: How People Practice Politics with Books," PhD dissertation, University of Minnesota, 2011, sees the ASE book program as part of a longer history of public reading in which communities—or the government—promote collective acts of reading to strengthen a sense of belonging and citizenship among readers. This can be in the cause of either resisting or upholding the state.

40. Personal communication, Hiromi Ochi.

CHAPTER 5

Pulping Ann Petry: The Case of *Country Place*

1. José Yglesias, "A Classy-Type People," *New Masses* (9 December 1947):18

2. Richard Sullivan, "Injustice, Out of Focus," *New York Times Book Review*, 28 September 1947, 12.

3. This *Ebony* spread, "First Novel," from April 1946, was in Clippings, Ann Petry Papers, Box 14, Folder 10, Howard Gotlieb Archival Research Center at Boston University.

4. David Littlejohn, *Black on White: A Critical Survey of Writing by American Negroes* (New York: Grossman Publishers, 1966), 154–56.

5. Lee Server, *Over My Dead Body: The Sensational Age of American Paperbacks, 1945–1955* (San Francisco: Chronicle Books, 1994), 67.

6. While there are many references to *Country Place* in interviews and reviews, few scholarly works deal with it directly. More typical is Lindon Barrett, *Blackness and Value: Seeing Double* (Cambridge: Cambridge University Press, 1999), which despite two significant chapters on Petry's novels doesn't mention it at all. But perhaps this is changing. See Cherene Sherrad-Johnson, "City Place/Country Place: Negotiating Class Geographies in Ann Petry's Writing," in Catherine Rottenberg, ed., *Black Harlem and the Jewish Lower East Side: Narratives Out of Time* (Albany: SUNY Press, 2013), 65–86, and John C. Charles, *Abandoning the Black Hero: Sympathy and Privacy in the Postwar African American White-Life Novel* (New Brunswick, NJ: Rutgers University Press, 2013), both of which have included extensive discussions of the novel.

7. John O'Brien, *Interviews with Black Writers* (New York: Liveright, 1973), vii.

8. Littlejohn, *Black on White, 154.*

9. Feminist film critics have theorized the relationship among scandal and melodrama, especially as it pertains to racialized female subjects, and national identity. See Jackie Byars, *All that Hollywood Allows: Re-Reading Gender in 1950s Melodrama* (Chapel Hill: University of North Carolina Press, 1991), especially chapter 5, 210–58; and Linda Williams, *Playing the Race Card: Melodramas in Black and White from Uncle Tom to O. J. Simpson* (Princeton: Princeton University Press, 2002). See also Lauren Berlant, *The Queen of America Goes to Washington: Essays on Sex and Citizenship* (Durham, NC: Duke University Press, 1997).

10. Rochelle Girson, review of *The Narrows, Hartford Times*, 15 August 1953.

11. Ann Petry, "The Great Secret," *Writer,* July 1948, 217.

12. McKee to Weybright, 11 May 1948, NAL Collection, MS 070, Series 2, Box 62, Folder 1438, Fales Library and Special Collections, Elmer Holmes Bobst Library, NYU.

13. Ann Petry, *Country Place* (1947; New York: New American Library, 1950), 5. All further references appear in the text. Petry's other novels, *The Street* and *The Narrows*, were each originally published by Houghton Mifflin (1946 and 1953, respectively). They appeared in paperback editions from NAL in 1949, 1954, 1961 [Pyramid](*Street*), and 1955 (*Narrows*). She also published two children's biographies: *Harriet Tubman, Conductor on the Underground Railroad* (1955) and *Tituba of Salem Village* (1964) with Thomas Crowell Company.

14. See Paula Rabinowitz, *Black & White & Noir*, chapter 6, especially 160–62.

15. William Kanyusik analyzes the portrayal of disabled veterans in film and novels in "The Wound at the Heart of Vision: Fraught Masculinities, Marked Bodies, and the 'Subject' of Disability," PhD dissertation, University of Minnesota, 2013.

16. Holding's 1947 novel was also set in coastal Connecticut; it, too, registers a changed racial and gender dynamic as white middle-class mother Lucia Holley maintains her household while her husband is stationed in the Pacific by conspiring with her black maid and a blackmailer to protect her daughter's reputation. For the Max Ophüls film, *The Reckless Moment*, its location was changed to Balboa Island, and its postwar reason for absenting Tom was his work as an engineer in Germany repairing bridges under the Marshall Plan. Despite the patriotic reasons for the father's absence, both versions hint at the failure of heterosexual married men as the more engaged criminal offers a deeper intimacy to Lucia. Holding also registers how "queer" this wartime family arrangement had become (see Elisabeth Sanxay Holding, *The Blank Wall* [1947; Chicago: Academy Chicago Publishers, 1991], 206). Lisa Fluet argues that middle-class housewives actually have more in common with gangsters than with their absent husbands, as each must "negotiate" multiple invisible tasks. "Housewife Noir: Accidental Death, Time-Binds, and Negotiation," MLA Convention, Washington, DC, 29 December 2006.

17. Josephine Herbst, "The Year of Disgrace," in *The Starched Blue Sky of Spain and Other Memoirs* (New York: HarperCollins, 1991), 104.

18. See Alan Wald, *American Night* (Chapel Hill: University of North Carolina Press, 2012), 179–94. Wald also reads *The Narrows* as a complex narrative compressing various aspects of postwar politics and culture, espe-

cially cross-class alliances and interracial sex. He, too, sees its debt to pulp. For example, in his reconstruction of the chronology of the plot, he notes that Camilo gives a diamond-studded cigarette case to Link for Christmas, which goes missing from his room in January. The cigarette case, Wald remarks, was "a popular World War II gift of women to servicemen, to protect their hearts." Moreover, it "resembles the one in Vera Caspary's *Laura*, ... [which] turn[s] up to identify clandestine lovers on the eve of a marriage thwarted by murder" (194).

19. "First Novel," *Ebony,* April 1946, 36.

20. Notebook, Ann Petry Papers, Box 19, Howard Gotlieb Archival Research Center at Boston University.

21. Mixed in with this notebook in Box 4 are manuscript pages for both *The Narrows* and *Country Place*.

22. Gwendolyn Brooks, *Maud Martha* (Chicago: Third World Press, 1993), 179. The book's back cover includes an endorsement from Petry, expressed as "delight in the beautiful structure of the book, delight in the way Maud Martha comes alive as a person caught up in timeless elemental situations." Rita Dove's "Not Welcome Here," a long section from *American Smooth* (New York: W.W. Norton, 2004) touches on a similar experience for black GIs returning from World War I.

23. Ann Petry, "The Novel as Social Criticism," in *The Writer's Book*, ed. Helen Hull (New York: Harper and Brothers, 1950), 31–39.

24. Quoted in Thomas Bonn, *Heavy Traffic and High Culture: New American Library as Literary Gatekeeper in the Paperback Revolution* (Carbondale: Southern Illinois University Press, 1989), 31. Weybright had long had an interest in publishing works by African American authors and signed up Richard Wright as an early NAL author.

25. Victor Weybright, *The Making of a Publisher: A Life in the 20th Century Book Revolution* (New York: Reynal, 1967), 211.

26. Quoted in Herbert Ruhm, "Raymond Chandler: From Bloomsbury to the Jungle—and Beyond," in Madden, *Tough Guy Writers of the Thirties* (Carbondale: Southern Illinois University Press, 1968), 172.

27. Review of *The Narrows*, in *New Statesman and Nation*, 14 August 1954, Clippings, Box 14, Folder 10, Petry Papers, Howard Gotlieb Archival Research Center at Boston University.

28. Weegee [Arthur Fellig] worked for the same newspapers as Petry; their tenure at *PM* overlapped. His two books, *Naked City* and *Weegee's People*, featuring his photos of crime scenes and automobile accidents, were reviewed on the verso of the same *Saturday Review of Literature* in which Martha Foley's *Best Stories of 1946*, featuring Petry's story "Like a Winding Sheet," got a favorable notice.

29. James Ivey, "Mrs. Petry's Harlem," *Crisis* 53 (May 1946): 154.

30. Concerning George Petry, with the exception of a mention by Jerre Mangione in *The Dream and the Deal: The Federal Writers Project, 1935–1943* (Philadelphia: University of Pennsylvania Press, 1983), 248, of him being a "left-wing" member of the writer's union and a WPA employee and repeated tales about him as a mystery writer, I cannot actually ascertain that he published anything, though Ann Petry notes his work on *People's Voice* in her journals and in an interview says he used to write copy for an advertising agency—which she did, too. This was clearly a touchy subject for her; the dedication page mock-up for New American Library's *Country Place* needed to be revised from George W. Petry to George D, possibly suggesting that there were two George Petrys or else hinting at some unconscious wish to alter his identity, or most likely, just a mistake (see NAL Collection, Fales Library and Special Collections, Elmer Holmes Bobst Libraries, NYU).

In an interview, Petry was asked, "Is your husband a writer also?" and Petry replied, "Well, yes, in a way. He used to write copy for an advertising agency . . . One of the first questions that people used to ask me was, 'What does your husband do?' and I would look them right in the eye and say, 'If I were a man, would you ask me what my *wife* did?' " "A Visit with Ann Petry," interview, College of Pharmacy, University of Illinois, Chicago, 16 May 1984, in *The Critical Response to Ann Petry*, ed. Hazel Arnett Ervin (New York: Praeger, 2005), 88. Moreover, in 1947, Petry had published a proto-feminist essay: "What's Wrong with Negro Men?" the same year she published *Country Place*. On the story by Arnold Petri and the "pulp" facsimile and text of "Marie of the Cabin Club," see Gene Jarrett, "Introduction: African American Noms de Plume," *PMLA* 121 (January 2006): 245–54.

31. "Visit with Ann Petry," 79. Marjorie Green, "Ann Petry Planned to Write," *Opportunity* 24 (April–June 1946): 79.

32. Petry, "The Great Secret," 216. Information for much of this comes from her Notebooks.

33. Littlejohn, *Black on White*, 154.

34. Graham Greene, screenplay of *The Third Man* (London: Faber and Faber, 1988), 71–73.

35. Frank Gruber, *The Pulp Jungle* (Los Angeles: Sherbourne Press, 1967), 136–37.

36. The sense that reading pulp fiction led to social depravities of its readers, of course, had a much longer history. In Lois Weber's 1916 film *Shoes*, for instance, the daughter Emmy resorts to prostitution to pay for a new pair of shoes in order to keep her job as a shopgirl at a five-and-dime store. She must turn all her earnings over to her mother for housekeeping because her father spends his time and carfare buying and reading cheap paperbacks instead of holding down a job. In this morality tale by a former crusader for the Salvation Army, it's not liquor but literature that dooms the working class.

37. In "Time, Transmission, Autonomy: What Praxis Means in the Novels of Kenneth Fearing," David Jenemann and Andrew Knighton argue that all Fearing's novels dissect Taylorism and the forces of capitalism pushing to reduce the time of transmission—of information, money, labor, and capital. As such, they also describe the limits of autonomy, even for authors and especially for popular authors, working within industrial enterprises, which, by the 1940s, included all pulp magazine publishing and, because it relied on magazine distribution, all paperback publishing. In *The Novel and the American Left: Critical Essays on Depression-Era Fiction*, ed. Janet Galligani Casey (Iowa City: University of Iowa Press, 2004), 172–94.

38. Kenneth Fearing, *The Big Clock* (New York: Harcourt, Brace, 1946), 114. "I am a fiction factory," Erle Stanley Gardner wrote to the new editor of *Black Mask*, Joseph Thompson Shaw, in 1926, quoted in Erin A. Smith, *Hard-Boiled: Working-Class Readers and Pulp Magazines* (Philadelphia: Temple University Press, 2000), 21.

39. Lula Jones Garret, *Afro-American* (Baltimore), 13 September 1958, 13, in Ervin, *Ann Petry*, 32.

40. Petry, "Great Secret," 217.

41. Notebooks, Box 14, Folder 12, Ann Petry Papers, Howard Gotlieb Archival Research Center, Boston University.

42. For more on Petry's children's biographies and their connection to midcentury left-wing women's publishing history, see Julia Mickenberg, *Learning from the Left: Children's Literature, the Cold War, and Radical Politics in the United States* (Oxford: Oxford University Press, 2006), 259–71.

43. Her feminist anger at social constraints on motherhood and men's desire for feminine demureness seems to have later developed into crankiness when, for instance, she ends up writing complaint letters to newspapers such as the *New York Times* about Bonwit Teller advertisements and fashion articles displaying women in short skirts in the 1970s, which I found among her papers in the folder marked "Notebooks" at the Howard Gotlieb Archival Research Center at Boston University.

44. Stephanie Rothman, lecture, Working Girls Film Series, Walker Art Center, Minneapolis, 21 May 2005, and personal interview the same day.

45. Ervin, *Ann Petry*, 102.

46. Gertrude Stein, *The Geographical History of America: or The Relations of Human Nature to the Human Mind* (1936; Baltimore: Johns Hopkins University Press, 1973), 79, 95.

47. Ervin, *Ann Petry*, 102.

CHAPTER 6
Señor Borges Wins! Ellery Queen's Garden

The chapter opening epigraph is by Jorge Luis Borges from Norman Thomas di Giovanni, ed., *In Memory of Borges* (London: Constable, 1988), 39.

1. Joan Schenkar, *The Talented Miss Highsmith: The Secret Life and Serious Art of Patricia Highsmith* (New York: St. Martin's Press, 2009), 131. Highsmith published a story in *EQMM* in 1957 (132).

2. However, two years before, Manly Wade Wellman beat William Faulkner for the prize. A few years later, another mystery-writing duo, Wade Miller (Bob Wade and Bill Miller), won. Their Signet No. 1013 edition, *Shoot to Kill*, has a cover alerting readers to their *EQMM* prize. For a history of EQMM, see "Ellery Queen Restores Order," in David Welky, *Everything was Better in America: Print Culture in the Great Depression* (Urbana: University of Illinois Press, 2008), 177–92.

3. "Let us imagine what might have happened to a book, at a time when books were not printed in editions but were written out individually. We will suppose that a book of this kind contained statements which in later times were regarded as undesirable. . . . At the present day, the only defensive mechanism to which the official censorship could resort would be to confiscate and destroy every copy of the whole edition. At that time, however, various methods were used for making the book innocuous. One way would

be for the offending passages to be thickly crossed through so they were illegible. In that case they could not be transcribed, and the next copyist of the book would produce a text which was unexceptionable but which had gaps in certain passages, and so might be unintelligible to them. Another way, however, if the authorities were not satisfied with this, but wanted also to conceal any indication that the text had been mutilated, would be for them to proceed to distort the text. Single words would be left out or replaced by others, and new sentences interpolated. Best of all, the whole passage would be erased and a new one which said exactly the opposite put in its place. The next transcriber could then produce a text that aroused no suspicion but which was falsified. . . . [w]e may say that repression has the same relation to the other methods of defence as omission has to distortion of the text . . ." Sigmund Freud, "Analysis Terminable and Interminable," in *Standard Edition of the Works of Sigmund Freud*, ed. and trans. James Strachey (London: Hogarth Press, 1964), 23:236; hereafter ATI.

4. Jorge Luis Borges, "Flow of Memory," in *Selected Poems*, ed. Alexander Coleman (New York: Viking 1999), 57; hereafter *SP*.

5. Freud, ATI, 219.

6. Jorge Luis Borges, "The Garden of Forking Paths," trans. Anthony Boucher, in *Ellery Queen's Mystery Magazine*, August 1948, 109; hereafter *EQMM* (this is the version I quote from throughout the chapter).

7. Borges, "The Mythical Founding of Buenos Aires," in *SP*, 55.

8. Quoted in Edgardo Cozarinsky, *Borges in/and/on Film*, trans. Gloria Waldman and Ronald Christ (New York: Lumen Books, 1988), 60; hereafter *Cine*.

9. Di Giovanni, ed., *In Memory of Borges*, 48.

10. Jorges Luis Borges, "The Aleph," in *A Personal Anthology*, ed. Anthony Kerrigan (New York: Grove Press, 1967), 147; hereafter *PA*.

11. Sigmund Freud, *Moses and Monotheism: Three Essays*, in *Standard Edition*, trans. and ed. James Strachey (London: Hogarth Press, 1964), 23:103; hereafter *M&M*.

12. "It was apparently during the summer of 1934 that Freud completed his first draft of this book, with the title: *The Man Moses: a Historical Novel.* . . . What is perhaps likely to strike a reader first about *Moses and Monotheism* is a certain unorthodoxy, or even eccentricity, in its construction: three essays of greatly differing length, two prefaces, both situated at the beginning of the third essay, and a third preface situated half-way

through that same essay, constant recapitulations and repetitions." Editor's note to Freud, *M&M*, 23:3–4.

13. Richard Burgin, ed., *Jorge Luis Borges: Conversations* (Jackson: University Press of Mississippi, 1998), 21; hereafter *Conv.*

14. On dubbing, see Adrienne L. McLean, *Being Rita Hayworth: Labor, Identity, and Hollywood Stardom* (New Brunswick, NJ: Rutgers University Press, 2004), 234. The film *The Atomic Café* uses stills from an official air force photo (1946) that shows Hayworth as the bombshell pinup.

15. Jorge Luis Borges, *Selected Non-Fictions*, ed. Eliot Weinberger, trans. Esther Allen, Suzanne Jill Levine, Eliot Weinberger (New York: Viking, 1999), 529; subsequent references given as *SNF* followed by page numbers in the text.

16. "Pseudonyms are endemic to the detective genre. . . . Dannay and Lee's pseudonym was the name of the main character of their fiction, Ellery Queen; between 1932 and 1933, this same Queen also 'wrote,' under the name of Barnaby Ross, for novels featuring a retired Shakespearian actor named Drury Lane. In this case, the readers were not even stirred by the fact that a character was writing under yet another name about another detective. . . . One reader, as Borges reports, said: 'Those writers do not exist; there is a name but there isn't a writer.' It is a fact that a reader accustomed to Borges's or Bioy Casares's literary style would not have recognized either writer under the guise of Bustos Domecq, who truly was a *third man*," Jorge Hernández Martín, *Readers and Labyrinths: Detective Fiction in Borges, Bustos Domecq, and Eco* (New York: Garland, 1995), 139; hereafter *RL*. Graham Greene delivered the second Jorge Luis Borges lecture and his novella, *The Third Man* (New York: Penguin, 1999), features a pulp Western author named Rollo Martins who writes under the name Buck—and delivers a lecture to a Viennese audience on the contemporary British novel—but in the Carol Reed film his name is changed to Holly Martins. Daniel Nathan and Emanuel Lepofsky were Dannay and Lee, respectively.

17. Freud, *M&M*, 70–71.

18. Jorge Luis Borges (with Margarita Guerrero), *The Book of Imaginary Beings*, trans. Norman Thomas di Giovanni (New York: E. P. Dutton, 1969), 159; subsequent references given as *BIB* followed by page numbers in the text.

19. Theodor Adorno, *Minima Moralia: Reflections from Damaged Life*, trans. E.F.N. Jephcott (New York: Verso, 1974), 235–38.

20. Charles Baudelaire, "Une Martyre"/"A Martyr," in *The Flowers of Evil*, ed. Marthiel and Jackson Mathews (New York: New Directions, 1955), 108–13.

21. Adorno, *Minima Moralia*, 235–38.

22. Jorge Luis Borges, "The Garden of Forking Paths," in *Collected Fictions*, trans. Andrew Hurley (New York: Viking, 1998), 127–28; hereafter *CF*.

23. Jonathan Eburne, *Surrealism and the Art of Crime* (Ithaca: Cornell University Press, 2008) reveals surrealism's debt to criminality. Surrealist "discussions and arguments about collective action . . . invoked dime novel villains and other fictional criminals." Moreover, "pulp criminal figures were central to surrealist political thought . . . such figures embodied rebellion." This discourse about criminality and its literary expressions provided "a means of exploring urban modernity," and more significant, "French colonialism, intellectual responsibility, and political agency" (98). Gothic and other debased artistic modes open psychic mechanisms to popular scrutiny, making it clear how mundane yet extraordinary criminality is within modern culture—popular literature, newspaper scandal sheets, and so on. This grim but salacious worldview, tapped into by fascism, found on every street-corner kiosk, did more than simply offer an aesthetic mode through which to express the inner world of dream states, desires, and paranoid terrors, this *habitude noir* provided a political practice that guided the surrealists into an uneasy, and ultimately futile, alliance with the French Communist Party.

24. In his poem "The Golem," Borges makes clear the connections, so central to American modernism's afterthoughts found in William Carlos Williams's "No ideas but in things": "the name is archetype to the thing" (*PA*, 77).

25. See "1941," *Sur* 87 (December 1941). Andrew Hurley's notes to this piece provide this information: "Maurice Leblanc: French writer (1864–1941), creator of the Arsène Lupin mystery series. [E.] Phillips Oppenheim: British writer (1866–1946) and author of immensely popular espionage novels in the 1910s and 1920s. Baldur von Schirach: German head of the Hitler Youth (1907–1974), who was later tried and convicted at Nuremburg" (*SNF*, 536).

26. Quotation from "A Brief History of Ellery Queen Mystery Magazine," http://www.themysteryplace.com/. Editor notes to the United Nations

issue explains: "This united effort on the part of detective-story writers proved that while we still have long way to go politically, the planet Earth is truly One World detective-storywise. Detective-story writers can work together in a common cause; while others are still fighting for life and liberty in some parts of the world, detective-story writers are demonstrating the essential oneness of the world by striving, all for one, one for all, to recapture the most peaceful of peacetime pursuits—the pursuit of happiness. This is a step in the right detection—toward international harmony and cooperation, toward goodwill on earth" (*EQMM*, August 1948).

27. Jorge Luis Borges, *An Introduction to American Literature*, in collaboration with Esther Zemborain de Torres (Lexington: University of Kentucky Press, 1971), 82; hereafter *AL*.

28. Cozarinsky, *Cine*, 1. Translators Gloria Waldman and Ronald Crist note that Madame Delly was the "[p]en-name of Marie (1875–1947) and Frédèric (1876–1949) Petitjean di la Rosière, sister and brother whose romantic fiction was immensely popular with female readers in the first half of this century."

29. In 1945, Vanevar Bush, elaborating on the complex postwar world of science, coined the term "hypertext" to describe the new kinds of libraries, media, and narratives necessary to capture the multiplying effects of technology on human consciousness. "As We May Think," *Atlantic Monthly*, July 1945. Of course, Borges was imagining all this already.

30. Robert Frost, "The Road Not Taken," in *The Poetry of Robert Frost* (New York: Holt, Rinehart, Winston, 1969), 105.

31. Erin A. Smith, "'The ragtag and bobtail of the fiction parade': Pulp Magazines and the Literary Marketplace," in *Scorned Literature: Essays on the History and Criticism of Popular Mass-Produced Fiction in America*, ed. Lydia Cushman Schurman and Deirdre Johnson (Westport, CT: Greenwood Press, 2002), 123–45.

32. James M. Cain, *Double Indemnity* (New York: Avon Books, 1943), 128.

33. McLean, *Being Rita Hayworth*, 47.

34. Cain, *Double Indemnity*, 129.

CHAPTER 7
Slips of the Tongue: Uncovering Lesbian Pulp

1. This chapter is dedicated to the memory of my mother-in-law, Rae Bernstein, née Rivka Masler, immigrant and Communist Party and ILGWU labor organizer, who as Rae Miller, during the winter of 1937–38, successfully led a strike of young Italian, Jewish, and Puerto Rican women brassiere makers in Bridgeport, Connecticut.

2. As Leisa D. Meyer notes, "The sexual stereotypes of servicewomen as 'camp followers' or 'mannish women,' prostitutes or lesbians, had a long history both in the construction of notions of femaleness in general and in the relationship of 'woman' and 'soldier' in particular." "Creating G.I. Jane: The Regulation of Sexuality and Sexual Behavior in the Women's Army Corps during World War II," in *Lesbian Subjects: A Feminist Studies Reader*, ed. Martha Vicinus (Bloomington: Indiana University Press, 1996), 66. However, uniforms provided an easy way for lesbians to avoid the problem of how to dress. In her study, Rosa Ainley quotes one woman describing her career choice in terms of wardrobe: "I didn't realize at the time, when I went into nursing, how much I would hide behind the uniform and how comfortable I felt in a traditional female role, where I could be totally hidden . . . I was in a dress with a little cap perched on my head. It wasn't really until I left the health service for another job that I realized I did not know how to dress, I did not know how I wanted to look. Or I did know how I wanted to look, but might well be accused of being lesbian." *What Is She Like: Lesbian Identities from the 1950s to the 1990s* (London: Cassell, 1995), 137. The nurse is a staple of pulp novels—both pornographic and romantic—and the icon of the white cap and white dress served as the basis for the *Nurses* series by artist Richard Prince (plate 8).

3. Joan Schenkar, *The Talented Miss Highsmith: The Secret Life and Serious Art of Patricia Highsmith* (New York: St. Martin's Press, 2009), 135.

4. See Joan Nestle, "Desire So Big It Had to Be Brave," *Ms.* (January 1983): 2; Kate Millett, *Flying* (New York: Ballantine, 1975); and many others. Lillian Faderman sums up the sentiment: "The pulps, with their lurid covers featuring two women exchanging erotic gazes or locked in an em-

brace, could be picked up at newsstands and corner drugstores, even in small towns, and they helped spread the word about lesbian lifestyles to women [who] might have been too sheltered otherwise . . . ," *The Well of Loneliness*, especially "providing an example of how to be a lesbian among the young who had no other guide." *Odd Girls and Twilight Lovers: A History of Lesbian Life in 20th-Century America* (New York: Columbia University Press, 1991), 147, 173. For a comprehensive analysis of the place of lesbian pulp fiction in developing a lesbian identity in postwar America, see Yvonne Keller, " 'Was It Right to Love Her Brother's Wife So Passionately?': Lesbian Pulp Novels and U.S. Lesbian Identity, 1950–1965," *American Quarterly* 57 (June 2005): 385–410. My point is to stress a small aspect of the "nourishment" that Lee Lynch argues in "Cruising the Libraries," in *Lesbian Texts and Contexts*, ed. Karla Jay and Joanne Glasgow (New York: New York University Press, 1989), 40–41, which was so crucial to reading about lesbians in pulp fiction—the pedagogy these books offered on how to accessorize one's lesbian body. Pulp collector Linnea A. Stenson makes the point that "the pulp novels themselves make explicit references to their own importance in the formation of identity and community." She cites one Toronto woman claiming to have traveled to Greenwich Village with her girlfriend "because they had learned from the pulps that that was where lesbians were." *Tretter Letter*, University of Minnesota Library (June 2006): 5.

5. Katherine V. Forrest, ed., introduction to *Lesbian Pulp Fiction: The Sexually Intrepid World of Lesbian Paperback Novels, 1950–1965* (San Francisco: Cleis Press, 2005), ix. Forrest concludes, "the writers of these books laid bare an intimate, hidden part of themselves and they did it under siege, in the dark depths of a more than metaphorical wartime, because there was desperate urgency inside them to reach out, to put words on the page for women like themselves to read" (xix).

6. Quoted in Anne MacKay, ed., *Wolf Girls at Vassar: Lesbian and Gay Experiences, 1930–1990* (New York: St. Martin's Press, 1992), 52.

7. Joan Nestle, "My Mother Liked to Fuck," in *A Restricted Country* (Ithaca, NY: Firebrand Books, 1987), 120–22.

8. John Rechy, *City of Night* (New York: Grove Press, 1963) maps the contours of gay sex in the 1950s as the protagonist drifts around the perimeter of America, moving from El Paso to Chicago to New York and across

the country to San Francisco and Los Angeles, landing in New Orleans for Mardi Gras before heading home to chart the journey.

9. Faderman, *Odd Girls and Twilight Lovers*, 161.

10. Quoted by Jaye Zimet, introduction to *Strange Sisters: The Art of Lesbian Pulp Fiction, 1949–69* (New York: Viking Studio, 1999), 21.

11. Susan Stryker, *Queer Pulp: Perverted Passion from the Golden Age of the Paperback* (San Francisco: Chronicle Books, 2001), 8.

12. Christopher Nealon, "Invert-History: The Ambivalence of Lesbian Pulp," *New Literary History* 31:4 (Autumn 2000): 745–64, notes that "the ambivalence about the novels extends to its latter-day readers: as lesbian pulp gets claimed as US queer 'heritage,' it turns out to be hard to say what exactly is being claimed—is it the novels' production, or their consumption? Is it the courage it took to have written such novels in the McCarthy era, or the camp pleasure we feel, reading them now, that we can recycle earlier forms of pain at an ironic distance?" (745).

13. Susan Rubin Suleiman, *Authoritarian Fictions: The Ideological Novel as a Literary Genre* (New York: Columbia University Press, 1983), 2.

14. This is the substance of David K. Johnson's argument for gay men in "Physique Pioneers: The Politics of 1960's Gay Consumer Culture," *Journal of Social History* (Summer 2010): 867–93.

> District attorneys around the nation argued that despite physique publishers' claims to be serving a market of artists, sculptors and photographers, they were knowingly pandering to homosexuals and promoting homosexuality in American society. Federal and local judges acknowledged that these publishers were reaching a gay market, even as those judges defended their right to serve it. Magazine publishers who were losing business wrote scathing editorials against the new "homo" magazines. Bodybuilders and physique models complained that their fan mail came from gay men. Most importantly, gay men themselves—particularly young, isolated gay men like Bill Kelley, living beyond major cities—saw them as a lifeline to a larger world. Countless men who came of age in cold war America vividly remember their first encounter with physique magazines as part of their journey to self-identification as homosexual. As A.R. from Los Angeles wrote in 1967, "I have [physique model] Glenn Bishop to thank more than any other individual for my becoming homosexual." (870)

15. Elizabeth Lapovsky Kennedy and Madeline D. Davis, *Boots of Leather, Slippers of Gold: The History of a Lesbian Community* (New York: Penguin Books, 1994), 157.

16. Ibid., 160–61.

17. Quoted in Faderman, *Odd Girls and Twilight Lovers*, 185.

18. Donna Penn, "The Meanings of Lesbianism in Post-War America," *Gender and History* 3 (Summer 1991): 190.

19. Regina Kunzel, "Pulp Fictions and Problem Girls: Reading and Rewriting Single Pregnancy in the Postwar United States," *American Historical Review* 100 (December 1995): 1470.

20. Ann Bannon [Ann Weldy], foreword to *Strange Sisters*, by Zimet, 11–12.

21. Stephen J. Meyer notes that the draft jacket copy for Gertrude Stein's *Geography and Plays* (1922) says of the book: "She continues to experiment and renew her realizations of people and objects, ways of revealment." "Gertrude Stein," in *The Cambridge History of Literary Criticism*, vol. 7, *Modernism and the New Criticism*, ed. A. Walton Litz, Louis Menand, and Lawrence Rainey (Cambridge: Cambridge University Press, 2006), 100. While no one would have seen this usage, he suggests that the phrase "ways of revealment" may have been part of a code publishers used to suggest lesbian content.

22. In the apocryphal story, after reading a magazine account, the editor asked his assistant Marijane Meaker if she knew of any lesbianism at her boarding school. Her notorious response, "why yes and even more of it in college," led to a career shift as she became Vin Packer and Ann Aldrich (among many other "authors") not to mention their agent too. Terry Gross, *Fresh Air*, National Public Radio, 18 June 2003.

23. Farid Chenoune, *Beneath It All: A Century of French Lingerie* (New York: Rizzoli, 1999), 13.

24. I am drawing on Nancy Armstrong's provocative claim in *Desire and Domestic Fiction: A Political History of the Novel* (New York: Oxford University Press, 1987) for the priority of literature in the fashioning of bourgeois class consciousness to describe how lesbian fiction's domain of the body—sketched visually on the cover of pulps and limned as narrative in the text—helped create a recognizable lesbian sensibility and thus forge

a subjectivity, and a collective knowledge of how to be a lesbian, or at least how to dress as one.

25. March Hastings [Sally Singer], *Three Women* (New York: Beacon, 1958), 39.

26. Luce Irigaray, "When Our Lips Speak Together," in *This Sex Which Is Not One*, trans. Catherine Porter (Ithaca: Cornell University Press, 1985), 205.

27. Hastings, *Three Women*, 61 and 63.

28. Mary McCarthy, *The Company She Keeps* (San Diego: Harcourt, 1942), 84, 88; subsequent references in text.

29. Luce Irigaray, "Commodities among Themselves," in *This Sex Which Is Not One*, 196–97; subsequent references are in the text. This essay originally appeared in English as "When the Goods Get Together."

30. Katalin Medvedev compares oral histories and memoirs of 1950s dress in "Pointy Bras and Loose House Dresses: Female Dress in Hungary and the United States in the 1950s," *AHEA: E-Journal of the American Hungarian Educators Association* 3 (2010), http://ahea.net/e-journal/volume-3–2010/3.

31. Katharine Brush, *Red-Headed Woman* (New York: Farrar & Rinehart, 1931), 23. On the periodic return of the slip, see Ruth La Ferla, "What's Sexy Now? The Slip," *New York Times*, 12 January 2006, E1–2.

32. Theodore Dreiser, *Sister Carrie* (Signet/New York: New American Library, 2000), 67.

33. Louis-Ferdinand Céline, *Journey to the End of Night*, trans. Ralph Mannheim (1932; New York: New Directions, 2006), 63. Quoted in Chenoune, *Beneath It All*, 49.

34. Valerie Taylor [Velma Young], *The Girls in 3-B* (1958; New York: Feminist Press, 2003), 98.

35. Ibid., 163.

36. "Pro-lesbian" is Yvonne Keller's term; Taylor is quoted in an interview with Kate Brandt. Both are quoted in Lisa Walker, afterword to Taylor, *The Girls in 3-B*, 194.

37. Patricia Highsmith, writing as Claire Morgan, *The Price of Salt* (1952; Tallahassee, FL: Naiad Press, 2001), 331–32; subsequent references in text.

38. Dreiser, *Sister Carrie*, 58.

39. Highsmith [Claire Morgan], *The Price of Salt* (reprinted in England in 1990 under her own name as *Carol*) is an intensely autobiographical novel; its genesis was a chance encounter Highsmith had when she worked the Christmas rush at Bloomingdale's toy counter (to make money to pay for her psychoanalysis, which was to "cure" her homosexuality), that was followed by Highsmith's stalking the blond woman customer buying gifts for her daughter. Andrew Wilson, *Beautiful Shadow: A Life of Patricia Highsmith* (London: Bloomsbury, 2003), 1–2 and passim. But Schenkar notes that the novel also comes out of Highsmith's love affair with Ginnie Catherwood, as well as her 1948 Christmas rush sales job in Bloomingdale's toy department (266–86).

40. Sardonically critical of psychoanalysis, and an anti-Semite as well, according to her biographer and lover, Marijane Meaker, Highsmith, who, according to Andrew Wilson, her biographer, was seen by a Jewish woman psychoanalyst in the 1940s, may very well be quoting from one of the most widely read (in America) of Freud's texts. See Marijane Meaker, *Highsmith: A Romance of the 1950s; A Memoir* (San Francisco: Cleis Press, 2003). In *The Psychopathology of Everyday Life*, Freud cites a number of instances where undergarments—chemise, drawers, and slips—figure in parapraxes. In "Slips of the Tongue," Freud recounts, verbatim, this citation from Dr. Alfred Robitsek of Vienna, of two examples of slips of the tongue recounted by an old French writer: "Brantôme (1527–1614), *Vies des Dames galantes,* Discours second: 'Si ay-je cogneu une très-belle et honneste dame de par le monde, qui, devisant avec un honneste gentilhomme de la cour des affaires de la guerre durant ces civiles, elle luy dit': 'J'ay ouy dire que le roy a faict rompre tous les c . . . de ce pays là.' Elle vouloit dire *les ponts.* Pensez que, venant de coucher d'avec son mary, ou songeant à son amant, elle avoit encor ce nom frais en la bouche; et le gentilhomme s'en eschauffa en amours d'elle pour ce mot.'" Freud, *The Psychopathology of Everyday Life*, in *Standard Edition*, trans. James Strachey, vol. 6 (London: Hogarth Press, 1953), 79. This was also among the most popular of Freud's works to appear in paperback.

41. Edmund Wilson, *Memoirs of Hecate County* (1946; New York: Signet/New American Library, 1961), 199.

42. Edmund Wilson, "The Stieglitz Exhibit," *New Republic*, 18 March 1925, 97. In Barbara Buhler Lynes, *O'Keeffe, Stieglitz and the Critics, 1916–1929* (Ann Arbor: UMI Research Press, 1989), 227–29.

43. Though I cannot find any direct mention that Wilson had seen this painting, by this time, Kahlo was widely recognized by modernist art critics, collectors, and curators, especially in New York following her shows at Julian Levy's gallery and Peggy Guggenheim's exhibitions. Her story of bodily pain, revolutionary politics, and bisexuality were widely known.

44. Quoted in Erika Billeter, ed., *The Blue House: The World of Frida Kahlo* (Seattle: University of Washington Press, 1993), 142.

45. Quoted in Hayden Herrera, *Frida: A Biography of Frida Kahlo* (New York: Harper and Row, 1983), 345.

46. Leane Zugsmith, *A Time to Remember* (New York: Random House, 1936). I believe this novel, like Freud's "slips of the tongue," may be another source for *The Price of Salt*. Set in a department store, it, too, features cross-class allegiances among women, including a scene where the young female clerk forgets to fill out the sales *slip* for a female customer and is chastised by her supervisor.

47. Freud, *The Psychopathology of Everyday Life*, in *Standard Edition*, 6:59.

CHAPTER 8
Sci-Unfi: Bombs, Ovens, Delinquents, and More

1. George Lipsitz, *Rainbow at Midnight: Labor and Culture in the 1940s* (Urbana: University of Illinois Press, 1994), 40. Lipsitz's tale of labor militancy during and after the war surveys novels, movies, and music of the period that contributed to this new culture, but he does not address the means and technologies through which these art forms were disseminated to workers—paperbacks, neighborhood rerun houses, radio, and records.

2. Lupoff, *The Great American Paperback*, 118.

3. This is not a unique result of the postwar American paperback. In his history of reading and writing books in the ancien régime, Roger Chartier remarks on how "the same texts were appropriated by 'popular' readers and other readers ... Either readers of more humble social condition were put in possession of books that were not specifically designed for them ... or else

inventive and canny bookseller-printers made available to a very large clientele texts that formerly had circulated only in the narrow world of wealth and letters (which was the case with the *pliegos sueltos* of Castile and the Catalan *plecs*, English chapbooks or the publishing formula known in France under the generic title of the Bibliothèque bleue)." *The Order of Books: Readers, Authors, and Libraries in Europe between the Fourteenth and Eighteenth Centuries*, trans. Lydia G. Cochrane (Stanford, CA: Stanford University Press, 1994), 8.

4. Eugen Kogon, *The Theory and Practice of Hell* (New York: Berkley Books, 1955), 9–10, publishers' introduction to the American edition. Berkley was founded in 1955 and this was among its first books, though it was known as a publisher of science fiction during its first decade. See http://www.us.penguingroup.com/ static/pages/publishers/adult/berkley .html.

5. Thanks to Benjamin Friedlander for reminding me of these and other mass-marketed Holocaust pulps published very soon after the war, which he said sat on the bookshelves of his father, Henry Friedlander, a historian and Holocaust survivor, and which I remember seeing on my parents' as well, though only my personal paperback copy of Anne Frank's diary remained in my possession. The others were reacquired recently. Conversation with author, 17 February 2013, Minneapolis, Minnesota.

6. Eve Curie, *Madame Curie: A Biography*, trans. Vincent Sheean (New York: Pocket Books, 1946), 190.

7. Julia Mickenberg, *Learning from the Left: Children's Literature, the Cold War, and Radical Politics in the United States* (New York: Oxford University Press, 2006), 191.

8. Ibid., 177, 179.

9. Ibid., 266.

10. Kogon, *The Theory and Practice of Hell*, 85.

11. George Gamow, *The Birth and Death of the Sun* (New York: Penguin Books, 1945), 211.

12. [Saul?] Bellow, report on *Death of a Hero*, 16 January or June 1946, Box 89A, Folder 2842; NAL Archives, MS 070, Box 63, Folder 1507, Fales Library and Special Collections, NYU Libraries.

13. Ruth Benedict, *Patterns of Culture* (New York: New American Library), 1950.

14. Margaret Mead, *Coming of Age in Samoa: A Psychological Study of Primitive Youth for Western Civilization* (New York: New American Library, 1955), 10. Perhaps this book's popularity may offer one explanation for the rise in popularity of the girl's name "Paula" in the 1950s, when it reached number forty-six. Three of her informants had variations of the name: Pula, Pala, and Pola.

15. Grace Hechinger and Fred M. Hechinger, *Teen-Age Tyranny* (New York: Crest Books, 1964), who cite Margaret Mead as advocating that "it should be up to each boy and girl to grow from one stage to another," in their discussion of sex and lipstick (49). This book considers how the teenager has become the dominant force in all aspects of American commodity (but also political) culture.

16. Ibid., 116.

17. Kenneth C. Davis rightly quips, "In the Beginning, There Was Spock," explaining that "Since its appearance in June 1946 as *The Pocket Book of Baby and Child Care*, Dr. Spock's book has become the second-bestselling book in American history, trailing only the Bible. In fact," he continues, "for two generations [now three] of American parents, it has been the bible for coping with their newborns" (*Two-Bit Culture*, 3).

18. G. Hechinger and F. Hechinger, *Teen-Age Tyranny*, 114.

19. Geoffrey O'Brien, *Hard-Boiled America: Lurid Paperbacks and the Masters of Noir*, expanded ed. (New York: Da Capo Press, 1997), 56.

20. Harrison E. Salisbury, *The Shook-Up Generation* (New York: Crest Books of Fawcett World Library, 1959), 13.

21. Ibid., 55.

22. Caroline Slade, *The Triumph of Willie Pond*, authorized abridgement (1940) (New York: Signet/New American Library, 1951), 98.

23. Lilly Crackell, n.d., Box 66, Folder 1662; NAL Archives, MS 070, Box 63, Folder 1507, Fales Library and Special Collections, NYU Libraries. A sales record from 8 December 1953 noted that No. 769, *Margaret*, had sold 531,730 copies; No. 829, *Lilly Crackell*, 577,845; and No. 895, *Triumph*, 337,662. But troubles with her work predated the declining sales: the 1950 case, *State of New Jersey v. Margaret* (records of which I cannot locate) and the sense expressed in a dope sheet memo on *Job's House* that her novel "seems out of place these days . . . the depression of the thirties is a long way off and remote psychologically from the present," indicated as early as 1951

that NAL was reluctant to take up other books by Slade, even though those published were enormously successful titles. Moreover, both Weybright and Slade were aware of the pressure the Catholic Church was putting on publishers through its National Organization for Decent Literature. WF to VW [Victor Weybright], KE [Kurt Enoch], AJP [Arabel Porter], RJG, Interoffice memo, 13 December 1951, and various letters back and forth between Weybright and Slade, Box 67, Folder 1661; NAL Archives, MS 070, Box 63, Folder 1507, Fales Library and Special Collections, NYU Libraries.

24. In *The Woman and the Body: A Cultural Analysis of Reproduction* (Boston: Beacon Press, 1987), Emily Martin notes the tendency of modern medical discourse regarding menstruation to figure the body as a production site, one that during menstruation is often construed as a body out of control because it is "a productive system that has failed to produce . . . making products of no use . . . waste, scrap" (46). A mid-twentieth-century medical textbook explained that "menstruation is the uterus crying for lack of a baby" (45). But this loss is only significant for legitimate reproduction; clearly wayward girls—especially those on pulp covers—all express defiance, even pleasure, in their nonproductivity.

25. Caroline Slade, letter to Victor Weybright, 3 March 1953, Box 67, Folder 1661; NAL Archives, MS 070, Box 63, Folder 1507, Fales Library and Special Collections, NYU Libraries.

26. Memo, 1 December 1952, Box 67, Folder 1661; NAL Archives, MS 070, Box 63, Folder 1507, Fales Library and Special Collections, NYU Libraries.

27. Willis Stevens, letter to Caroline Slade, 2 February 1950, Box 66, Folder 1663; NAL Archives, MS 070, Box 63, Folder 1507, Fales Library and Special Collections, NYU Libraries. Granted that Mr. Stevens, who lived in Morningside Heights, was probably not a typical reader—as he lived in the shadow of Columbia University—he seems to have bought the book elsewhere, in the Bronx, still he is emblematic of the sort of reader I am constructing, someone who would know the "Signet shelf" at his local corner drugstore, recognize it at another, and take a risk for a quarter on an unknown book and then be moved to write its author. Cover art and brand were crucial to this process of aleatory book buying, as Clarence Petersen notes, "The average man may never set foot inside the Guggenheim, but he

can't stay out of Walgreen's." *The Bantam Story: Twenty-Five Years of Paper-back Publishing* (New York: Bantam, 1970), 46.

28. "Marked copy of list," undated but seems to be sometime around 1946, holograph, Box 99A, Folder 2842; NAL Archives, MS 070, Box 63, Folder 1507, Fales Library and Special Collections, NYU Libraries.

29. See my discussion of this in *Black & White & Noir.*

30. Lupoff, *The Great American Paperback*, 150.

31. Aldous Huxley, *Brave New World Revisited* (New York: Bantam Books, 1960), vii.

32. Ibid., viii.

33. Nevada National Security Site History pamphlet on "Atomic Culture," DOE/NV 1042, January 2011. In addition to television and movies, between 1951 and 1964, twenty-three songs made up the "Atomic Hit Parade," including 1954's "Atomic Kiss" by Earney Vandagriff and "Atomic Bomb Baby" by the Five Stars, among other titles. The covers of various paperbacks continue this suggestion of atomic bombing, through the images of fiery skies, and in the case of *Brave New World Revisited*'s cover, suggestions of Jackson Pollock juxtaposed to Massacio's *Expulsion of Adam and Eve*, to convey a sense of modern art as an expression of the bomb's disastrous effect and to point to the image of the heterosexual couple fleeing into an unknown future that can be seen in both the original *Hiroshima* and *Brave New World* pulp covers.

34. "Crime," Federal Bureau of Investigations, in *The 1954 Pocket Almanac* (New York: Pocket Books, 1954), 291–92. This paperback, full of facts, was "especially designed to give you quick answers to the questions you are most likely to ask," revealed the cover's blurb.

35. Interoffice memo ED [Edgar Doctorow] to VW [Victor Weybright], 23 July 1959, NAL Archives, MS 070, Box 63, Folder 1507, Fales Library and Special Collections, NYU Libraries.

36. A[nthony] Boucher, "Detectives at Work," *New York Times Book Review*, 2 December 1956, 30.

37. Clancy Sigal, *A Woman of Uncertain Character: The Amorous and Radical Adventures of My Mother Jennie (Who Always Wanted to Be a Respectable Jewish Mom) by Her Bastard Son* (New York: Carroll and Graf, 2006).

38. Tereska Torrès, *Not Yet* ... (New York: Crown, 1957).

39. Gilbert Geis and Leigh B. Bienen dissect the "ingredients" of such crimes, which include "locations," "something sensational," " 'suitable' protagonists," "the times," "the politically ambitious," and "their mystery." *Crimes of the Century: From Leopold and Loeb to O. J. Simpson* (Boston: Northeastern University Press, 1998), 5–8.

40. Meyer Levin, *Compulsion* (New York: Pocket Books, 1958), 333.

41. *Nathan F. Leopold, Jr., Appellant, v. Meyer Levin et al., Appellees,* No. 41498, Supreme Court of Illinois 45 Ill. 2d 434; 259 N.E.2d 250; 1970 Ill Lexis 601, 27 May 1970, filed.

42. Sam Zolotow, "Zanuck Acquires Levin Stage Play," *New York Times,* 30 November 1956, 19. The $100,000 figure appears in a number of letters between Levin, his lawyers, and agents. Meyer Levin Collection, Howard Gotlieb Archival Research Center, Boston University.

43. Lawrence Graver "found that Levin's preoccupation was by far the most complex and resonant" of the American Jewish writers "gripped by the Anne Frank story." *An Obsession with Anne Frank: Meyer Levin and the Diary* (Berkeley: University of California Press, 1995), xvi. His is an exhaustive study of the controversy covering its thirty years.

44. Letter, Tereska Torrès to Meyer Levin, 22 September 1957, Box 17, Folder 5, Meyer Levin Collection, Howard Gotlieb Archival Research Center, Boston University. All references to letters and briefs from this collection's box are used with permission of the estate of Meyer Levin and the estate of Tereska Torrès in conjunction with Jabberwocky Literary Agency.

45. "Plan for 'Compulsion,' " *New York Times,* 4 October 1957, 26.

46. See the paid advertisement in the *New York Times,* 4 October 1957, 28, that reads:

> At sundown begins our Day of Atonement, whose peace-making meaning is known to all.
> In this spirit, I appeal to producers Michael Myerberg and Leonard Gruenberg to settle our differences about "Compulsion." The dispute revolves about which of two texts is to be presented. As the author, I suggest that the producers' version and my version be performed on alternate weeks. The play could open as scheduled on October 21; I would wait my turn. There is not variation in the play's action, but only in style, motivation, and characterization as reflected in the text. I have discussed all practical prob-

lems that might ensue from this proposal; they can be solved. Paying the actors for learning the extra set of lines would be preferable to continued strife. The theatrical public could find stimulation in the values posed by the differing texts. I trust that all people of good will may urge this solution.

Faithfully,
Meyer Levin

(Address: c/o Monica McCall Literary Agcy., 667 Madison Avenue, N.Y.C.)

47. Levin, *Compulsion*, 1; emphasis in original.

48. Meyer Levin, "Leopold Should Be Freed!" *Coronet* (May 1957): 36–42. This article begins by setting the scene in the Stateville Penitentiary, near Joliet, Illinois, by noting that after a while the conversation seemed so natural that "suddenly I realized that I had completely forgotten I was in the presence of a 'notorious' murderer. We might have been talking in a library or an office" (36).

49. Levin, *Compulsion*, 2–3; emphasis in original.

50. Tereska Torrès, *Women's Barracks* (New York: Fawcett, 1950), 4.

51. Meyer Levin, "Comic Books Find Champion," *Newark Star-Ledger*, 16 May [year and page unknown]. In Box 2, Articles, Meyer Levin Collection, Howard Gotlieb Archival Research Center, Boston University.

52. Appellant's Brief, Robert Thom, Plaintiff-Respondent against Meyer Levin, Defendant-Appellant and Michael Myerberg and Leonard Gruenberg, Defendants, Supreme Court, Appellate Division—First Department, To be Argued by Ephraim London, 4–5. Box 17, Business 1954–57, Meyer Levin Collection, Howard Gotlieb Archival Research Center, Boston University.

53. Even anticommunist works, such as Edward Hunter's *Brainwashing* (1956; New York: Pyramid Books, 1961) about Korean War victims of torture, which investigated North Korean appeals to black soldiers' racial oppression and discussed how soldiers "cracked up and died" or "mustered their last remnants of courage to defy and best the evil twisting of their minds" by "their diabolical Communist captors" sought to place psychology at the center of understanding actions. These passages come from the back cover. Cover by Mel Crair.

54. Appellant's Brief, 2. This quotation came from a *Herald Tribune* article in which McDowall claimed to have been misquoted, but Levin's appeal

claims this was erroneous; at any rate, it's what was quoted in the article apparently.

55. Freeman Lewis, "The Future of the Paper-Bound Book," *Publisher's Weekly*, 27 June 1953, 2665.

56. The range of pulp magazine readers was always far more diverse than imagined. Research by Eric Drown and Sandra Heard indicates that while targeting certain readers—say working-class boys (science fiction and popular mechanics magazines), or white working-class girls (true confessions or romance magazines)—readership exceeded these boundaries. Gender may have prevailed in the generic divisions, but classed and racial audiences were more diverse. Drown found that scientists and engineers regularly read, wrote letters to the editor, and even penned stories for Hugo Gernsback's publications. Sandra Heard's careful inspection of E. Franklin Frazier's 1930s interviews of Washington, DC, black girls analyzes their obsession with the "marked" women of *True Confessions* and other pulp romance periodicals that did not feature African American characters. See Eric Drown, "Usable Futures, Disposable Paper: Popular Science, Pulp Science Fiction and Modernization in America, 1908–1937," PhD dissertation, University of Minnesota, 2001, and Sandra Heard, "The 'Bad' Black Consumer: A Study of African-American Consumer Culture in Washington, DC, 1910s–1930s," PhD dissertation, George Washington University, 2009.

57. Lewis, "The Future of the Paper-Bound Book," 2668.

58. For instance, *The Censorship Bulletin* of the American Council of Book Publishers noted in its March 1956 issue that "Books added to the list in January include *Bhowani Junction* by John Masters, *Mademoiselle de Maupin* by Theophile Gautier, and *The Cold of Their Bodies* by Charles Gorham. Among paper bound books listed as 'objectionable' in February are *The First Lady Chatterley* by D. H. Lawrence, *Hotel Tallyrand* by Paul Hyde Bonner, *Act of Love* by Ira Wolfert, *The World in the Evening* by Christopher Isherwood, and *The Narrows* by Ann Petry" (3). This last name is circled, as I found this pamphlet among Ann Petry's papers at the Howard Gotlieb Archival Research Center at Boston University.

Chapter 9
Demotic Ulysses: Policing Paperbacks in the Courts and Congress

The first chapter opening epigraph is from the appendix to the Report of the Select Committee on Current Pornographic Materials, House Reports, 82nd Congress, 2nd Session, No. 2510, 116; the second is from "The Freedom to Read," Joint Declaration of the American Book Publishers Council and the Council of the American Library Association, 26 June 1953, and is cited as the epigraph to *Looking Forward* (New York: International, 1954), 2.

1. See Cockburn decision, *Regina v. Hicklin*, http://en.wikisource.org /wiki/Regina_v._Hicklin#Decision.

2. C. H. Rolph, ed., *The Trial of "Lady Chatterley's Lover": Regina v. Penguin Books Limited* (Harmondsworth, UK: Penguin Books, 1961), 13.

3. Paul Fyfe, "Boz on the Bus: Dickens and the Traffic in Victorian Accidents," lecture at University of Minnesota, 4 February 2013.

4. Anne Enright, "Diary," *London Review of Books*, 21 March 2013, 42.

5. Ibid.

6. It is interesting to remember that in a review of Émile Zola's *Nana*, appearing in 1880, no less than Henry James himself "lamented its 'filth' and 'foulness,'" while noting that "the English novel labors under too much of a burden of self-censorship;—'a good thing for virgins and boys, and a bad thing for the novel itself,'" and thus for realism. The history of condemning books for their inherent dirtiness, even while castigating the effects of censorship, seems to have extended even to this sophisticate. Henry James, *Literary Criticism*, ed. Leon Edel, vol. 2 of *French Writers, Other European Writers: The Prefaces to the New York Edition* (New York: Library of America, 1984), 869, quoted in Peter Brooks, *Henry James Goes to Paris* (Princeton: Princeton University Press, 2007), 161. *Nana* was an early Pocket Books paperback, No. 104, from 1941. My copy from 1945 declares on the front cover that it is the "complete unexpurgated translation," on the back a reminder to "Share this book with someone in uniform." Five years later, Avon Books No. 271 (1950) brought out *Nana's Mother*, with a tagline, "The Passions that Spawned the Immortal NANA." So again, replication and reproduction—the hallmark of the reprint—were literalized and

the very aspects that had disturbed James became its selling point as Pocket Books insisted that "No one should miss reading this masterpiece of the greatest French realist of modern times." With both the signifier "French" and "realist," which Anne Enright notes was also a signifier for sex within Irish censorship discourse, the book could not but succeed (plate 22, *top left* and *right*).

7. Samuel Black, "This Literature We Distribute," appendix to the Report of the Select Committee on Current Pornographic Materials, House Reports, 82nd Congress, 2nd Session, No. 2510, 130. (He is not to be confused with Douglas M. Black, president of the American Council of Book Publishers, who also testified before the committee.) Subsequent references to the Report of the Select Committee on Current Pornographic Materials, House Reports, 82nd Congress, 2nd Session, No. 2510 will be given parenthetically in the main text as RSC followed by the page number

8. Chartier, *The Order of Books*, viii. He goes on to explain: "Readers use infinite numbers of subterfuges to procure prohibited books, to read between the lines, and to subvert the lessons imposed on them."

9. Margaret Culkin Banning, "Filth on the Newsstands," *Reader's Digest*, October 1952, 65; reprinted in the appendix to RSC, 135–36. Subsequent references to this article are given parenthetically by page number in the text.

10. It is perhaps important to note that a case in the 1930s, *People v. Fellerman*, which concerned the distribution of a specialty nudist magazine containing photographs from nudist colonies, contended that because "the magazine was placed on sale to the general public where it could have been purchased by the young as well as the old, and a charge of twenty-five cents was made for it[, w]e are naturally constrained, therefore, to adopt the view that there was a mercenary motive underlying its publication and sale" (quoted in Amicus Curiae appellant, *Doubleday v. People*, 40). (In 1936, the conviction was overturned.) Thus, the issue of public, visible, and affordable availability, which had seemed settled, reappeared.

11. My copy of the 1952 Pocket Books Cardinal edition does indeed feature the cover image by Baryè Phillips, the sort of illustrator whose work resembled the artist who painted Laura's portrait, she describes; but the tagline is far tamer. It reads, "The classic novel of a woman's unwilling fall from virtue." The flyleaf blurb reads, "When Thomas Hardy's greatest novels were originally published, they were immediately branded 'immoral and obscene.' One passionately disturbed woman sent Hardy the ashes to which she had

reduced his 'filthy book!' Today we are not so easily shocked by realism in fiction." As the congressional hearings' questioners made clear, publishers often relied on a reference to past prudery by appealing to contemporary ideas of a more progressive nature, seeing "the problem of dealing with obscene or objectionable matter was too often treated as something of a joke. . . . Many regarded the problem, and still do, as nothing more threatening than the legendary French post card vendor who occasionally attempted to peddle his wares in an unobtrusive alley or bookstall in a large metropolitan area" (RSC, 35). Marketing these modern consumer objects relied on a nod to a quaint past and a benign titillation provided by a knowing complicity between publisher, bookseller, and buyer about what was contained within. Moreover, it was an American success story, as Margaret Culkin Banning explained when she noted that no other country she had visited had the excess of newsstands teeming with "disgraceful" materials. "In France you can always go out and buy a book of nudes, you can buy what they call their filthy postcards, but they are not displayed for public sale on any of the bookstands along the larger streets." Continuing her global roundup, she found a "great protest against the fact that we send this material over there . . . in Canada, anyway, they feel that they send us their pulp, and—here it is" (RSC, 68).

12. Black, "This Literature We Distribute," in RSC, 134.

13. Quoted in Robert Scholes and Clifford Wulfman, *Modernism in the Magazines: An Introduction* (New Haven: Yale University Press, 2010), 1.

14. A friend relates that she first picked up a paperback copy of *Lady Chatterley's Lover* she found at her grandmother's house because it was a book she'd heard of—due to its scandalous content. Thus, sensation spurred her reading. Jani Scandura, conversation with author, 2 February 2013. This story is a reboot of the one told by Francine Prose in her review of the John Worthen biography of D. H. Lawrence, which begins, "Raised in the 1950's, I belong to a generation that first met D. H. Lawrence between the covers of a paperback copy of 'Lady Chatterley's Lover' from the bottom of Dad's sock drawer. Its lurid cover and hiding place marked it as a book to skim, a little feverishly, for sexual information. That was how I began reading Lawrence, if you can call that reading." "Slayer of Taboos," *New York Times Book Review*, 4 December 2005, 1.

The Report of the Gathings Committee hearings refers, without naming either author or title, to a comment by psychologist Joseph Collins, in his book, *The Doctor Looks at Literature* (New York: George Doran, 1923), which declares Lawrence's *Women in Love* to be "obscene, deliberately, studiously, incessantly obscene" (278). However, in the same chapter, Collins also recalled, "Ten years have gone since Henry James, walking up and down the charming garden of his picturesque villa in Rye, discussing the most promising successor of Hardy, Meredith, and Conrad, said to me 'The world is sure to hear from a young man, D. H. Lawrence'" (287). The committee focused, as it had for many of the paperbacks it considered, on a single line, without seeing it in context.

15. *The 1954 Pocket Almanac*, ed. American Institute of Public Opinion (New York: Pocket Books, 1954), 8.

16. "Investigation of Literature Allegedly Containing Objectionable Material," in *Hearings before the Select Committee on Current Pornographic Materials*, House of Representatives, 82nd Congress, 2nd Session, on House Resolution Nos. 596 and 597, 1–5 December 1952 (Washington, DC: United States Government Printing Office, 1953), 1. Subsequent references will be given as *HSC* followed by the page number.

17. This question was raised by Chairman Gathings and represents the core concerns of the hearings.

18. Black, "This Literature We Distribute," in RSC, 132–33.

19. Quoted in Enright, "Diary," 42.

20. "Minority Report," in RSC, 123.

21. "Pornographic Materials," in RSC, 4.

22. George Axelrod and Robert A. Arthur, *The Seven Year Itch* (New York: Dramatists Play Service, 1952), 37.

23. Morris L. Ernst, introduction to H. Montgomery Hyde, *A History of Pornography* (New York: Farrar, Straus and Giroux, 1964), vii–viii; italics in the original. As an aside, Hyde had written a number of books on the Oscar Wilde case and had been stripped of his seat in Parliament in part for his fervent championing of the rights of homosexuals and prostitutes. He wrote his history by chance in Lamb House, Rye, the home of his distant cousin, Henry James, who had noted that widespread literacy and the spread of novels sold cheaply would lead to new forms of writing as books became available to women and children.

24. Ibid., 5.

25. The department store, where women of many classes mingled, served as a scene of potential lesbian encounters in many postwar lesbian novels; see chapter 7.

26. Letter, Kurt Enoch to Clara Claasen, 22 October 1945, NAL Archives, MS 070, Box 89A, Folder 2842, Fales Library and Special Collections, NYU Libraries.

27. This episode from Pepys's diary on 15 January 1668 (and a few subsequent days, as it took him a while to finish the novel) is recounted in Hyde, *A History of Pornography*, 19–20.

28. See Letter, J. D. Salinger to Victor Weybright, 26 March 1952, NAL Archives, MS 070, Box 65, Folder 1566, Fales Library and Special Collections, NYU Libraries.

29. Letter, Weybright to Arthur Thornhill (Little Brown), 23 April 1952, NAL Archives, Box 65, Folder 1566, MS 070, Fales Library and Special Collections, NYU Libraries.

30. Memo Re: Cover treatment on *Catcher in the Rye*, by J. D. Salinger, James Avati to Victor Weybright, 3 April 1952, NAL Collections, NYU Libraries.

31. J. D. Salinger, *The Catcher in the Rye* (New York: Signet, 1953), 51 and 106.

32. Case went on to explain that he and his staff reviewed 1,039 books in 1951 and "withheld from circulation or banned, 54." "We are probably one of the only ones [police departments] wading through this filth to the tune of about 750 hours overtime" (RSC, 62). Again, the scene of reading paperbacks becomes crucial; here it enters into the budget of a city—indeed, into the budget of the federal government as well because postal inspectors "have to wade through this filth to where you get to what they say their objective is in good literature . . . have to read every book . . . read every bit of material that comes in to our office, and determine for ourselves whether it is good or bad" (Exchange between Congressman Kearns and Mr. Frank, counsel to the Post Office, in RSC, 96).

33. Leerom Medevoi, "Democracy, Capitalism, and American Literature: The Cold War Construction of J. D. Salinger's Paperback Hero," in Joel Foreman, ed., *The Other Fifties: Interrogating Mid-Century American Icons* (Chicago: University of Illinois Press, 1997), 257, 281. "*Catcher*, then, was

not read as mere psychological narrative by cold war literary critics, but as national allegory" (259), one that, if one believes the range of letters voicing disgust at the NAL paperback, was sparked by a sense of its "filth." See Mark T. Greene to NAL, 24 June 1953, and Gordon W. Mattice to NAL, 8 September 1953. "A Heartsick and Nauseated Reader" went further, calling it "the filthiest literature it has been my unpleasant task to read"; 22 March 1955, Box 65, Folder 1566, NAL Archives, MS 070, Fales Library and Special Collections, NYU Libraries.

34. See Jonathan Auerbach's *Dark Borders: Film Noir and American Citizenship* (Durham, NC: Duke University Press, 2011) and Robert Corber's *Cold War Femme: Lesbianism, National Identity, and Hollywood Cinema* (Durham, NC: Duke University Press, 2011). It is interesting to note that while "homosexuality" exists as a category, on a par with the "pleasures" of drug use, for the Gathings Committee (RSC, 45), "lesbianism and nymphomania" are linked to polygamy and "all the various types of perversion" (RSC, 75). "I have the names of them here" (RSC, 45), declared Burton of the various titles brimming with "pornographic content" (RSC, 75). It should be understood that naming names and identifying titles by name—and many titles were named in the course of the hearings, including those distributed by Cadillac Publishing (*Pulpit Digest, Pastoral Psychology*, and *Movie Life* [RSC, 49]), not to mention the prose poem of those Mr. Black did not distribute (*Good Humor, Picture Follies, Candid Whirl, Buddies, Fun Parade, Whisper, Beauty Parade, Eyeful, Wink, Jones' Laugh Book, Photo Arts, Paris Models, Keyhole, Man's Life, Zowie, Show, Foo, Frolic, Gala, Jest, Joker, Peeko Show, Mirth, Nighty, Pack O' Fun, Pepper, Sexology, Smiles, Stare, Wham, Zip, Sex Guidance, Paris Life*, and "one book that I did not distribute and wouldn't handle . . . the *Revolt of Mamie Stover*" [HSC, 40])—was the method of coercion used by congressional investigations into communist association. The listed names imply exactly what Corber argues: that the figure and image of the lesbian—especially as femme—was akin to the hysteria about communism lurking within the State Department. These were hidden, secret threats undetectable to the eye and so far more dangerous, far more alluring to the unknowing innocents.

35. Letter, Farrell to Porter, 24 May 1946, Box 37, Folder 579, NAL Archives, MS 070, Fales Library and Special Collections, NYU Libraries.

36. Memo, VW [Victor Weybright] to KE [Kurt Enoch], TMT, Editors, 23 July 1959, Box 63, Folder 1507, NAL Archives, MS 070, Fales Library and Special Collections, NYU Libraries.

37. Farrell to Porter, 24 May 1946, Box 37, Folder 579, NAL Archives, MS 070, Fales Library and Special Collections, NYU Libraries.

38. Interoffice Memo: Suggested selection of Faulkner Stories, 19 April 1949, Box 38, Folder 628, NAL Archives, MS 070, Fales Library and Special Collections, NYU Libraries.

39. Victor Navasky details how the entire process of naming names infected daily life during the McCarthy period. See *Naming Names*, especially the chapter entitled "The Community as Victim." "Guilt was in the air," or, as he quotes blacklisted writer Clancy Sigal's comment, "Guilt was like a bed companion," as one could never trust what had been said by whom to whom (New York: Viking Press, 1980), 351, 355.

40. This was how Roy E. Blick of the Washington Metropolitan Police Department in charge of "vice, sex perversion, and pornographic literature" described the kinds of books his department went after to the Gathings Committee (RSC, 44).

41. Amicus Curiae appellant brief, SC 335, US 848, citing *People v. Berg* (241 App Div 543), 27.

42. Ibid., 40. This was a typical response of censors worldwide. For example, Nicole Moore explains how "[b]anned bestsellers such as Kathleen Winsor's *Forever Amber* (1945) show that the class-based tastes of the censors dictated definitions of obscenity aimed specifically at banning cheap and popular books." *The Censor's Library: Uncovering the Lost History of Australia's Banned Books* (St. Lucia: University of Queensland Press, 2012), 15.

43. Text of Section 1141, subdivision (1), New York Penal Law recounted in the Amicus Curiae to Supreme Court filed by the American Civil Liberties Union (ACLU), October 1948, 335 US 848, 3.

44. This exchange about visual representations and their linguistic referentiality was followed by Utah congresswoman Reva Bosone's nonsequitor inquiry: "are you married . . . any children . . . belong to a church?" (RSC, 39).

45. So declared the "Report of Legislative Committee Submitted by Commissioner Donald S. Leonard, Chairman, to Conference of International

Association of Police, Miami, Fla., November 1, 1951" and read into the Gathings record (RSC, 114).

46. Ralph Foster Daigh, editorial director and vice president of Fawcett, reported to the Gathings Committee that by January 1951, a year after launching its Gold Medal imprint of PBOs, sales had reached 43,149,063 copies (RSC, 36) and that some titles sold in excess of a million copies, including *Women's Barracks*, which prompted extensive interrogation:

> *Mr. Rees:* You think it compares favorably with Shakespeare's books?
> *Mr. Daigh:* I don't think that is the question. I think both are eminently entitled to publication, exposure to the public.
> *The Chairman:* And the book sells for a quarter?
> *Mr. Daigh:* Yes, sir; and Shakespeare sells for a quarter in some editions, too.
> *Mr. Burton:* Can you find anything in Shakespeare in equal number of pages, with as much obscene material as you find in Women's Barracks in the same number of pages? (RSC, 38).

47. Letter, William Gardner Smith to Arabel Porter, undated, Box 68, Folder 1682, NAL Archives, MS 070, Fales Library and Special Collections, NYU Libraries.

48. Arnold Hano, quoted in "Plan for Simultaneous Publication of Both Hard and Paper Originals Stirs Discussion," *Publishers' Weekly*, 17 May 1952, 1995. This information, and much more on the history of paperbacks, come from *Paperback Quarterly* 1:1 (Spring 1978); see especially "Paperback Originals" by Bill Crider, 3–8.

49. James Douglas, quoted in RSC, 32.

50. The changes that he wanted were as follows:

1. Gold band at the top since this is a 50¢ book
2. Light background, yellow or some other bright color, so that type will be prominent in black.
3. Hand should be subordinated to head in the design.
4. Design should be dropped down sufficiently to make room for copy.

Marc Jaffe, memo to Robert Jonas, 7 July 1954, Box 51, Folder 1031, NAL Archives, MS 070, Fales Library and Special Collections, NYU Libraries. Contract cover artists were expected to have read the titles they were illustrating, extract a key image, and produce between two and four books a month.

51. Letter to Scott Meredith, 26 November 1956, Box 38, Folder 665, NAL Archives, MS 070, Fales Library and Special Collections, NYU Libraries.

52. On 25 November 1957, James Bohan, Flora's agent, enclosed a list of ten alternative titles dreamed up by Flora, and another agent, Scott Meredith, proposed eight more on 25 October 1957, to which Weybright noted in the margin, "*no* Let's try again." Box 38, Folder 665, NAL Archives, MS 070, Fales Library and Special Collections, NYU Libraries. The original list reads like a catalog of pulp:

1. The Catalyst
2. The Gold Ring "Like a gold ring in a swine's snout is a beautiful woman with no discretion." Proverbs
3. This Side of Ruin
4. Give Odds on Trouble
5. Uncle Aubrey
6. Endure the Night "Weeping may endure for a night . . .": Psalms, XXX, 5
7. The Last Hand's Pat
8. Satan also Came Job I, 6
9. For Every Evil "For every evil under the sun there is a cure, or there is none. If there be one, try and find it; If there be none, never mind it." Nursery Rhyme
10. Midsummer Night's Dame

The second list is just as good—demonstrating again the admixture of canonical and crass that is pulp's demotic form:

1. Whom the Devil Drives "They needs must go whom the Devil drives" Cervantes
2. The Devil for All "Every man for himself, his own ends the Devil for All" Robert Burton
3. Under the Devil's Belly "What is got over the Devil's back is spent under the belly" Rabelais
4. A Place to Die
5. Death before Dying
6. Salvage
7. To Beat the Devil
8. Crucible of Evil

53. Walter Freeman, Memo, 25 November 1957, Box 38, Folder 665, NAL Archives, MS 070, Fales Library and Special Collections, NYU Libraries.

54. "Arthur" at Little Brown, letter to Victor Weybright, 1 June 1951, Box 65, Folder 1560, NAL Archives, MS 070, Fales Library and Special Collections, NYU Libraries. "Mr. Salinger is rather a touchy author about jackets so I hope you will agree to submit to us for approval the cover design." Of course, Holden is "touchy" too. This letter elicited a reply from Weybright to Salinger dated 31 March 1952: "James Avati, our best man on covers, is now working on it."

55. Truman Capote, letter to "Arabel [Porter]," 17 January 1951, Box 20, Folder 307, NAL Archives, MS 070, Fales Library and Special Collections, NYU Libraries. Used by permission of the Truman Capote Literary Trust. This request may have been because numerous men were writing NAL requesting Capote's address (and one woman asked for cover artist Tom Dunn's). Despite this request, NAL intended to use a quotation from a 2 October 1951 *New York Times* review by Orville Prescott of *The Grass Harp* on its cover: "a few unnecessarily vulgar passages and references to degeneracy, but it's practically wholesome compared with the reeking decadence of its predecessor."

56. However, the report mentions that a judge in Ottawa, who found the book obscene, and fined its distributor, referred in his statement to "this book, which is fiction" (RSC, 40).

57. Interoffice Memo, DRD to VW [Victor Weybright], 11 May 1951. Within a few years (no date) but the handwritten list "Faulkner in print" includes twelve titles and the total sales reached 5,941,837. Box 38, Folder 628, NAL Archives, MS 070, Fales Library and Special Collections, NYU Libraries. David M. Earle, *Re-Covering Modernism: Pulps, Paperbacks and the Prejudice of Form* (Farnham, UK: Ashgate, 2009), 204–6, explains how this perception of Faulkner as a pulpy novelist was thematized in *The Wild Palms*, casting it, as so much of pulp, as another meditation on the place of fiction, either when read or when written (in this case pulp magazine stories) in pulp fiction itself. He concludes "what Faulkner's pulp reliance—symbolic, formulaic, or economic—illustrates is an unavoidable gravitational pull of (at least in critical academia) an unseen presence, huge

and submerged, within modernism," which he names "a popular, sensational form" (206).

58. Johiel Katsev, copy of letter to Allan Adams, 3 March 1948, Box 38, Folder 68, NAL Archives, MS 070, Fales Library and Special Collections, NYU Libraries.

59. Testimony of Hon. James V. Mulholland, Justice, Domestic Relations Court, City of New York (*HSC* 325–39).

60. Amicus curiae, ACLU, *Doubleday and Co., appellant v. State of New York*, 335 U.S. 848, Supreme Court, October 1948.

61. Ibid., 7.

62. WF, editorial dope sheet, 19 July 1961, Box 84, Folder 2779, NAL Archives, MS 070, Fales Library and Special Collections, NYU Libraries.

63. Amicus curiae, ACLU, *Doubleday and Co., Appellant v. State of New York*, 335 U.S. 848, 50, Supreme Court, October 1948.

64. Letter from Edgar S. Bayol, 22 September 1949, Box 16, Folder 269, NAL Archives, MS 070, Fales Library and Special Collections, NYU Libraries.

65. Memo Re: Capitalization of trademark names, DRD to JN, 6 October 1949, NAL Archives, MS 070, Fales Library and Special Collections, NYU Libraries.

66. Marc Jaffe, letter to Rudolf Littauer, 19 January 1950, Box 16, Folder 269, NAL Archives, MS 070, Fales Library and Special Collections, NYU Libraries.

67. Usually the hardcover editions—often published between a few months and many decades before the paperbacks—featured covers with designs that abstracted an image from the title or content and used bold, simple type; however, many paperbacks appeared almost simultaneously with film versions of the novels. Visuals from the films and the pulps infected each other; the revolution in cinematography made possible by wartime developments in 16-mm Eyemo and Bolex cameras coincided with the pulp revolution, each giving America a chiaroscuro vision of itself as vernacular forms of pulp modernism. For more on the books (and dust jacket covers) that first inspired some films noirs, see Kevin Johnson, *The Dark Page: Books that Inspired American Film Noir (1940–1941)* (New Castle, DE: Oak Knoll Press, 2008).

68. See the various memos and correspondence between Weybright and his staff, and between them and Caroline Slade, that stretches for two years between 1950 and 1952. Box 66, Folders 1661, 1662, and 1663, MS 070, NAL Collection, Fales Library and Special Collections, NYU Libraries.

69. *State of New Jersey v. Margaret* (3 May 1950). I cannot find this case.

70. Interoffice Memo, VW [Victor Weybright] to JA, HL cc: KE [Kurt Enoch], RJC, PA, TMT RE: Sam Black and INVISIBLE MAN cover, 13 April 1953, Box 36, Folder 537; NAL Archives, MS 070, Box 63, Folder 1507, Fales Library and Special Collections, NYU Libraries. The cover of *Invisible Man* is typical of 1950s covers of African American literature. During the 1940s, covers by Robert Jonas of the abridged edition of Ann Petry's novel *The Street* or Richard Wright's story cycle, *Uncle Tom's Children*, featured bold designs foregrounding a solitary and imposing figure—a sort of visual analog to the cool jazz of early bebop (even James Avati's cover of the first paperback edition of Chester Himes's *If He Hollers Let Him Go*, full as it is of narrative energy, still featured decisively individual characters). However, by the 1950s, Avati's covers suggest a teeming and anonymously populated ghetto scene with bodies bursting out of the book's frame. Granted the eponymous character, whose back is to the reader, is meant to remain unnamed, the image of chaotic streets offers a view of potential violence poised to erupt as, of course, white Southerners would in response to the 1954 *Brown v. Board of Education* decision.

71. Letters between Victor Weybright and Caroline Slade, 2 February 1952 to 3 March 1953, Box 67, Folder 1661, NAL Archives, MS 070, Box 63, Folder 1507, Fales Library and Special Collections, NYU Libraries.

72. Caroline Slade, *Sterile Sun* (New York: Vanguard Press, 1936), 9 (unnumbered). For more detail on the controversies surrounding the novels of Slade, see chapter 6, "Not 'Just the Facts, Ma'am': Social Workers and Private Eyes," in Rabinowitz, *Black & White & Noir*, 142–67.

CODA
The Afterlife of Pulp

1. The opposite trajectory was happening in Britain, as Penguin began to deconstruct and reconstruct its covers, moving away from "a northern (German, Dutch and English) European influence," according to John Miles, which dominated its first three decades after Germano Facetti was hired in

1961 to redesign the Penguin package. See Penguin Collectors' Society, *Penguin by Designers* (London: Victoria and Albert Museum, 2007), 24.

2. Gwendolyn Brooks, *Maud Martha* (1953; Chicago: Third World Press, 1993), 67.

3. Ibid., 5.

4. Darryl Pinckney, "On James Baldwin," *New York Review of Books*, 4 April 2013, 78.

5. Anne Enright, "Diary," *London Review of Books*, 21 March 2013, 42.

6. "Rimbaud should have gone to America instead of Lake Chad. He'd be a hundred years old and rummaging through a discount store. Didn't he say he liked stupid paintings, signs, popular engravings, erotic books with bad spelling, novels of our grandmothers?" Charles Simic, *Dime-Store Alchemy* (New York: New York Review of Books, 1992), 23.

7. Julie Bosman, "Judging 'Gatsby' by Its Cover(s)," *News York Times*, 26 April 2013, A1, 3. In this article we learn that while Barnes & Noble is stocking both versions, Walmart is only carrying the movie tie-in cover (although both are available online through Walmart.com).

8. Quoted in Jeff Oloizia, "A Book by Its Covers," *T–New York Times Style Magazine,* 9 April 2013, 134.

9. Personal e-mail message to the author, 24 July 2012. See also Jeanette Winterson's memoir, *Why Be Happy When You Could Be Normal?* (New York: Grove Press, 2012), 35–45, for a description of the freedom cheap reading afforded her during her awful 1950s British girlhood.

10. Maurice Sendak, interview by Emma Brockes, published in the November/December 2012 issue of *The Believer*, six months after his death at eighty-three, excerpted in *Harper's*, March 2013, 25.

11. Canto 80.661–67, in *The Cantos of Ezra Pound* (New York: New Directions, 1993), 533. Thanks to Benjamin Friedlander for alerting me to this.

12. Frank O'Hara, *Lunch Poems* (San Francisco: City Lights Books, 1964), 25–26.

13. The year before, according to Anne Enright, Brendan Behan would sing: "My name is Brendan Behan, I'm the latest of the banned, / Although we're small in numbers we're the best banned in the land, / We're read at wakes and weddin's and in every parish hall, / And under library counters sure you'll have no trouble at all." Enright, "Diary," 42.

14. Frank O'Hara, "Poem," in *New World Writing* (New York: New American Library, 1952), 248.

15. E. L. Doctorow, "Childhood of a Writer," in *Reporting the Universe* (Cambridge, MA: Harvard University Press, 2003), 10–12. Doctorow explained to me that he held the "Jewish desk" at NAL when he worked there as an editor. Personal communication, 10 April 2007. He is misremembering the logo of NAL and putting a proletarian spin on it. It was "Good Reading for the Millions," not "the Masses."

16. E-mail message to author, 30 March 2013.

17. E-mail message to author, 19 February 2013.

18. "Fiction and poetry are doses, medicines. What they heal is the rupture reality makes on the imagination." This line from chapter 4 of Winterson is part of a meditation on the practice of reading at random, what comes to hand, in libraries and in parents' bookshelves; even with repressive parents like her mother, Mrs. Winterson, a young girl might pick up T. S. Eliot's *Murder in the Cathedral*, thinking it one of her mother's mystery books or latch onto the family copy of *Morte D'Arthur* and find tonic.

19. Information on sales contained in a letter from Julien D. McKee to Ann Petry, 4 May 1949 and letter from Heinz E. (last name indecipherable) to Petry, Bielefeld, Germany, 29 October 1950, Box 7, Ann Petry Collection, Howard Gotlieb Archival Research Center at Boston University.

20. Joseph Kosuth, *Purloined: A Novel* (Cologne: Salon Verlag, 2000), 1–2.

21. Ibid., 12.

22. Gertrude Stein, *Blood on the Dining-Room Floor*, ed. John Herbert Gill (Berkeley, CA: Creative Arts Book Company, 1982), 13. See also Gertrude Stein, "Forensics," in *How to Write* (1931; New York: Dover Publications, 1975), 381–95.

23. Stein, *Blood on the Dining-Room Floor*, 51.

24. Charles Bukowski, *Pulp* (Santa Rosa, CA: Black Sparrow Press, 1994), 9–13.

25. Ibid., 202.

26. Robert Coover, *Noir* (New York: Overlook Duckworth, 2010), 113; subsequent references in text.

27. David Thomson, *Suspects* (New York: Alfred Knopf, 1985), 266.

28. Glenn O'Brien interview with John McWhinnie, in Nancy Spector, *Richard Prince* (New York: Guggenheim Museum Publications, 2007), 316–17.

29. Information on Long-Bin Chen comes from the catalog for his exhibits at the Frederieke Taylor Gallery and other locations, *Reading Sculpture: 2003–2006* (Taiwan: 2006), and personal communication with the artist.

30. Information on Jonas and Avati comes from Piet Schreuders, "The Paperback Art of James Avati," *Illustration* 1:1 (October 2001): 16–33, and Gary Comenas "Abstract Expressionism," http://www.warholstars.org/abstractexpressionism/timeline/abstractexpressionism28.html. For connections between Arshile Gorky and Jonas, see Harry Rand, *Arshile Gorky: The Implications of Symbols* (Berkeley: University of California Press, 1999), 200, where Rand describes a conversation with Jonas in 1977 discussing Gorky's essay "Camouflage," purportedly written by Jonas, who in the 1920s was a communist and went on in the 1930s to help organize the Artists' Union. See also Hayden Herrera, *Arshile Gorky: His Life and Work* (New York: Farrar, Straus and Giroux, 2005), 229, on Jonas as a "lady's man."

31. Quoted in Spector, *Richard Prince*, 27.

32. O'Brien interview with Robert Lesser, in Spector, *Richard Prince*, 318. Lesser salvaged hundreds of pulp magazine and dime novel covers, kept since 1855, when Condé Nast tossed the paintings out on the street, and he managed to save about nine hundred of them.

Index

Boucher, Anthony, 159, 167, 168, 233
Bourke-White, Margaret, 100, 328n16
Bradley, Marion Zimmer, 188
Brecht, Bertolt, 93
Brodkin, Karen, 319n22
Brooks, Gwendolyn, 143, 282, 339n22
Brown v. Board of Education of Topeka,
    Kansas, 145, 372n70
Brownstein, Rachel, 74
Brush, Katharine, 198
Bubley, Esther, 4, 105
Buhle, Paul, 314n32
Bukowski, Charles, 27, 293, 296–97
Burton, H. Ralph, 264, 272, 273
Bush, Vanevar, 346n29

Caesar, Sid, 58
Cadillac Publishing, 283, 366n34
Cain, James, M., 43, 59, 73, 181–82,
    185, 276–77
Caldwell, Erskine, 37, 71, 100, 251,
    323n47
Cansino, Eduardo, 182
Capek, Karel, 160
Capote, Truman, 36, 145, 233, 270–
    71, 370n55
Cappetti, Carla, 107, 330n35
Casares, Adolfo Bioy, 168, 174
case study, 96, 107, 161, 230, 279,
    330n35
Caspary, Vera, 45–51, 58, 146, 185,
    318n20, 319n21. See also Laura
Cassill, R.V., 59
Catholic Truth Society, 246
Caulfield, Holden, 80, 114, 211, 256–
    57, 370n54
Cayton, Horace, 96
Celler, Emanuel, 250
censorship: See also obscenity;
    pornography
    —court cases: A Book Named John
    Cleland's Memoirs of a Woman

of Pleasure v. Massachusetts, 25;
    Attorney General v. "God's Little
    Acre," 264; Attorney General v.
    "Forever Amber," 264; Common-
    wealth v. Gordon et al., 251, 263;
    Commonwealth v. Isenstadt, 264;
    Doubleday and Company, Inc. v.
    People of New York, 267–68, 275–
    76, 362n10; People v. Fellerman,
    362n10; Regina v. Hicklin, 245,
    254–55; Regina v. Penguin Books
    Limited, 245, 309n3, 322n43;
    Roth v. United States, 280; United
    States v. One Book Called "Ulysses,"
    251, 254, 262, 264, 266–67;
    —by governments, 246, 283–84,
    365n32, 367n42
    —as marketing tools, 26, 237, 269,
    275–76, 278–80, 362n11
    —in publishing, 21, 249, 273–74,
    277; 355n23, 360n58
    —spoofs of, 373n13
    —during wartime, 122, 124–27,
    186, 226
    —in writing (self-censorship), 161,
    342n3, 361n6
Cerf, Bennett, 115, 122, 124, 146
Chakravarthy, Pritham K., 11
Chandler, Raymond, 139, 146; The Big
    Sleep, 65–66, 185
Chartier, Roger, 247, 353n3, 362n8
Chayefsky, Paddy, 253
Chekhov, Anton, 160
Chen, Long-Bin, 27, 293, 298–99
Chenoune, Farid, 199
Chesser, Eustace, 261
Chessman, Caryl, 234
Chicago, 141, 200, 235–37, 282, 296;
    Archdiocesan Council of Catholic
    Women, 243; Ben Hecht's memoir
    of, 75–77; Richard Wright and, 93,
    104, 106, 330n35

Popular Library, 57, 59, 212, 288
pornography, 192, 250, 254–55,
263, 265, 269, 3317n38, 366n34,
367n40. *See also* censorship;
obscenity
Porter, Arabel J., 36, 260, 269, 289
Pound, Ezra, 21, 249, 287
Pratt, Mary Louise, 42
Prince, Richard, 27, 293, 298–300,
347n2
productivity: of pulp writers, 341nn37,
38; and women's bodies, 356n24.
See also under publishing industry
promiscuous reading, 36, 67–68, 77,
129, 178 213, 286, 341n36. *See also
under* reading; scenes of reading
Prose, Francine, 363n14
Psychological Warfare Branch, 112
Publishers' Weekly, 124, 268
publishing industry, 42, 59–60, 77,
110, 129, 220, 276, 33n9; and
writers' labor, 114, 150–54, 175,
341nn37, 38, 368n48, 369n52;
spoofs of, 62, 78–79, 251, 258–59,
308n2
pulp modernism, 24, 27, 30, 147, 150,
160, 370n57, 371n67. *See also*
secondhand modernism, vernacular
modernism
pulp: as consumer object, 41, 57;
imagery of, 65; as interface, 41, 45,
50, 57, 81, 132, 188, 296, 319n21;
landscapes within, 66; as material,
35, 113; as medium, 34, 62; movies
in, 52, 156; 282, music in, 52, 282;
as slang, 32; self-referentiality of,
50, 370n57; and sex manuals, 261,
282–83; subgenres of, 33–34, 36–
37, 128, 165, 210–42, passim, 259;
and taboos, 157; titles of, 369n52.
See also cover art, paperback
Pyramid Books, 70, 192

Queen, Ellery, 167, 173–74, 183. *See
also* Dannay, Frederic; Lee, Manfred
B.
Quintero, José, 237

racism, 35, 99–100, 143, 226; and
book covers, 372n70; challenged by
African American writers in pulp,
37, 51–57 passim, 148–50
radio, 49, 51, 99, 124, 146; *Double
Furlough*, 130–40
Rand, Harry, 375n30
Random House, 70
Ray, Man, 164, 171
reading: as community practice,
116–17, 127, 356n27, 336n39;
demotics of 3, 20–22, 31, 41, 50,
75, 119, 145, 160, 176, 233, 249,
255; women and, 11, 363n14. *See
also* promiscuous reading; scenes of
reading
Rechy, John, 188, 348n8
Red-Headed Woman (d. Jack Conway,
1932), 199–200
Reichl, Ernst, 70, 280
Reilly, John, M., 102, 107
remediation, 23, 189, 272, 313n30; of
crime stories, 170, 296, 318n19; and
reprints, 70–71, 260, 268, 271–72,
277, 315n32, 361n6
Rich, Frank, 83, 85
Riis, Jacob, 86–87
Rivera, Diego, 164
Robert Nixon case, 96, 236
Robeson, Paul, 142
Robinson, Marie N., 233
Robitsek, Alfred, 352n40
Rogers, Ginger, 47, 50, 139
Rogin, Michael, 319n22
Rollins, Jr., William, 43
Rosenberg, Ethel and Julius, 248, 260
Rosskam, Edwin, 85–86